PROFESSIONAL
Android™ Sensor Programming

PROFESSIONAL

Android™ Sensor Programming

Limerick Institute of Technology
Institiúid Teicneolaíochta Luimnigh
Library and Information Resource Centre

ACC No: ....

PROFESSIONAL

Android™ Sensor Programming

Greg Milette
Adam Stroud

John Wiley & Sons, Inc.

Limerick Institute of Technology
Institiúid Teicneolaíochta Luimnigh
Library and Information Resource Centre

Class No.: _OOO· 7 6 MiL_

ACC. No.: _33828_

Date: _____

Professional Android™ Sensor Programming

Published by
John Wiley & Sons, Inc.
10475 Crosspoint Boulevard
Indianapolis, IN 46256
www.wiley.com

Copyright © 2012 by John Wiley & Sons, Inc., Indianapolis, Indiana

Published simultaneously in Canada

ISBN: 978-1-118-18348-9
ISBN: 978-1-118-22745-9 (ebk)
ISBN: 978-1-118-24045-8 (ebk)
ISBN: 978-1-118-26505-5 (ebk)

Manufactured in the United States of America

10 9 8 7 6 5 4 3 2 1

No part of this publication may be reproduced, stored in a retrieval system or transmitted in any form or by any means, electronic, mechanical, photocopying, recording, scanning or otherwise, except as permitted under Sections 107 or 108 of the 1976 United States Copyright Act, without either the prior written permission of the Publisher, or authorization through payment of the appropriate per-copy fee to the Copyright Clearance Center, 222 Rosewood Drive, Danvers, MA 01923, (978) 750-8400, fax (978) 646-8600. Requests to the Publisher for permission should be addressed to the Permissions Department, John Wiley & Sons, Inc., 111 River Street, Hoboken, NJ 07030, (201) 748-6011, fax (201) 748-6008, or online at http://www.wiley.com/go/permissions.

Limit of Liability/Disclaimer of Warranty: The publisher and the author make no representations or warranties with respect to the accuracy or completeness of the contents of this work and specifically disclaim all warranties, including without limitation warranties of fitness for a particular purpose. No warranty may be created or extended by sales or promotional materials. The advice and strategies contained herein may not be suitable for every situation. This work is sold with the understanding that the publisher is not engaged in rendering legal, accounting, or other professional services. If professional assistance is required, the services of a competent professional person should be sought. Neither the publisher nor the author shall be liable for damages arising herefrom. The fact that an organization or Web site is referred to in this work as a citation and/or a potential source of further information does not mean that the author or the publisher endorses the information the organization or Web site may provide or recommendations it may make. Further, readers should be aware that Internet Web sites listed in this work may have changed or disappeared between when this work was written and when it is read.

For general information on our other products and services please contact our Customer Care Department within the United States at (877) 762-2974, outside the United States at (317) 572-3993 or fax (317) 572-4002.

Wiley publishes in a variety of print and electronic formats and by print-on-demand. Some material included with standard print versions of this book may not be included in e-books or in print-on-demand. If this book refers to media such as a CD or DVD that is not included in the version you purchased, you may download this material at http://booksupport.wiley.com. For more information about Wiley products, visit www.wiley.com.

Library of Congress Control Number: 2012936847

Trademarks: Wiley, the Wiley logo, Wrox, the Wrox logo, Wrox Programmer to Programmer, and related trade dress are trademarks or registered trademarks of John Wiley & Sons, Inc. and/or its affiliates, in the United States and other countries, and may not be used without written permission. Android is a trademark of Google, Inc. All other trademarks are the property of their respective owners. John Wiley & Sons, Inc., is not associated with any product or vendor mentioned in this book.

For Tanya and Madison, my inspiration!!!

—G.M.

To Sabrina, Abigail and Elizabeth...I love you.

—A.S.

ABOUT THE AUTHORS

GREG MILETTE is a professional Android developer and founder of Gradison Technologies, an app development company. He enjoys building practical apps like Digital Recipe Sidekick and contributing to StackOverflow.

ADAM STROUD is the lead developer for the Android version of RunKeeper. He is a self-proclaimed "phandroid" and is an active participant in the Android virtual community on StackOverflow and Android Google groups.

ABOUT THE CONTRIBUTORS

DAVID N. HUTCHISON (http://davidnhutch.com) was born and raised in New Zealand, and is currently a PhD candidate in physics at Cornell University, where he is developing next-generation inertial sensors. He loves to hack up microcontroller-enabled gadgets in the machine shop, ride his motorcycle, and start companies. David wrote Chapters 5 and 6, and contributed to Chapters 7 and 10.

JON WEBB, the developer of Jon's Java Imaging Library, has been developing software professionally for over three decades. He enjoys programming image processing on Android as it brings back fond memories of his early days. Jon wrote Chapters 12 and 13.

PEARL CHEN takes a cross-disciplinary approach to her work, from HTML to LEDs, Android to Arduino. Both an educator and developer, Pearl teaches programming and electronics, while also acting as CTO of http://thehungryveg.com. To find out more about Pearl's upcoming workshops and Arduino kits, visit http://klab.ca/arduino. Pearl wrote Chapter 11 and contributed to Chapter 10.

CREDITS

EXECUTIVE EDITOR
Robert Elliot

PROJECT EDITOR
Brian Herrmann

TECHNICAL EDITOR
Jim Steele

PRODUCTION EDITOR
Christine Mugnolo

COPY EDITOR
Kimberly A. Cofer

EDITORIAL MANAGER
Mary Beth Wakefield

FREELANCER EDITORIAL MANAGER
Rosemarie Graham

ASSOCIATE DIRECTOR OF MARKETING
David Mayhew

MARKETING MANAGER
Ashley Zurcher

BUSINESS MANAGER
Amy Knies

PRODUCTION MANAGER
Tim Tate

VICE PRESIDENT AND EXECUTIVE GROUP PUBLISHER
Richard Swadley

VICE PRESIDENT AND EXECUTIVE PUBLISHER
Neil Edde

ASSOCIATE PUBLISHER
Jim Minatel

PROJECT COORDINATOR, COVER
Katie Crocker

PROOFREADER
Josh Chase, Word One New York

INDEXER
Robert Swanson

COVER DESIGNER
Ryan Sneed

COVER IMAGE
© Antonis Papantoniou / iStockPhoto

ACKNOWLEDGMENTS

WE WOULD LIKE TO THANK David Hutchinson, Pearl Chen, and Jon Webb for providing content and guidance throughout the process of authoring this book. Their expertise in physics, AOA, NFC, and image processing allowed us to describe some exciting ways to use Android in a level of detail we would have otherwise been unable to achieve.

We would like to thank our editors for inspiring us to write the book and their hard work in making us sound more human-like and less like little green robots.

Finally, we could not have written this book without the help of people in the Android developer community who share and help us all work towards a common goal. We hope this book and its code help to repay the favor.

ACKNOWLEDGMENTS

CONTENTS

INTRODUCTION

ANDROIDS ARE ALIVE. THEY CAN LOCATE THEMSELVES, see, listen, and understand speech. They can sense radio signals and detect orientation, movement, and environmental properties. Can your computer do all of that?

The availability of sensors is one feature Android devices have that makes them different from other computers. Without sensors, an Android device is just an underpowered, mobile web browser with a screen that is too small and has an awkward input mechanism.

Sensors also allow apps to do amazing things. For example, sensors can help save users from painfully slow manual input and manipulation, and sensors can help users do tasks that they could never do before. Because of this, it may be essential for an app to incorporate sensors to be successful.

Sensors will continue to be an important part of the Android platform. As the hardware specifications of Android devices improve, so do the number of available sensors and their quality. While this happens, users will continue to expect apps to use any existing and new sensors when possible. Therefore, using Android's sensors is a crucial skill for any Android programmer to master. This book gives you the knowledge and code you need to develop this skill and make great apps that use sensors.

PROGRAMMING WITH ANDROID SENSORS

Writing apps that use Android's sensors involves understanding the sensing capabilities of an Android device, selecting which sensors to use in an app, and implementing an app that can acquire sensor data and interpret it.

Android's Sensing Capabilities

An Android device can have a wide variety of sensors. This book uses a definition of sensor that incorporates many of an Android device's capabilities. In this book a sensor is:

> *A capability that can capture measurements about the device and its external environment.*

Sensing capabilities are derived from the available hardware on Android devices and from creative use of it. A capability may use values directly from hardware that can measure physical quantities, such as the magnetic field sensor. It may use hardware that the user typically interacts with, such as the camera and microphone. A capability may even use a combination of hardware and server-based processing, such as speech recognition. Whatever the source, the resulting data can inform an app about the device's state and the environment in which it resides.

This book describes how to program apps that process information from the following sensor types:

➤ **Location sensors:** Determine a device's location using a variety of sensors including GPS.

➤ **Physical sensors:** Detect device-specific properties such as orientation, acceleration, and rotation and environmental properties such as light, magnetic field, and barometric pressure.

➤ **NFC scanner:** Detects near field communication (NFC) tags and shares data with other NFC-enabled Android devices.

➤ **Camera:** Collects visual images.

➤ **Microphone:** Records audio.

➤ **Speech recognition:** Converts audio to text using a combination of recorded audio from the microphone and recognition algorithms.

➤ **External sensors:** Any sensor connected using the Android Open Accessory (AOA) mechanism.

Selecting Sensing Tasks

Understanding how the sensors work helps you know which of your app's tasks can benefit from sensor-related input. It also helps you interpret the sensors' performance under various conditions and know their limitations. For example:

➤ **Location:** Knowing how various location sensors work, as described in Chapter 1, may lead you expect poor accuracy while a device is indoors.

➤ **Physical sensors:** Knowing information about what the physical sensors measure, as discussed in Chapter 5, can help you understand what inferences an app can reasonably make with the sensor output.

Using API Boilerplate

In any app, acquiring sensor data requires similar code. Each kind of data requires different boilerplate. In many cases, is not trivial to initialize the API and acquire the data. This book provides code examples and libraries to help make it easier to implement. Some examples of the difficulties involved in using the APIs include:

➤ **Camera:** Before an app can analyze an image, it must acquire the image from the camera. However, using a device's camera requires handling device rotation, hardware constraints, and using the `Camera` and `View` objects properly. Chapters 12 and 13 describe abstract classes that handle these details.

➤ **NFC:** Using NFC involves understanding the various steps needed to read and write NFC tags and what data to put in them. Chapter 11 explains a complete code example that is easy to adapt.

Collecting Sensor Data

Once an app can initialize and acquire sensor data, it then needs utilize the APIs to collect the data while the app is running. Data can be collected in different ways depending on how an app uses it. This book describes different ways to collect data for various tasks. Some examples include:

➤ **Location:** Location tracking is a common use of location sensors. Some apps need to persistently track location while an app performs other tasks. Chapter 3 describes several approaches for implementing location tracking reliably.

➤ **Speech recognition:** To acquire speech recognition results an app needs to have other components besides actually running the speech recognizer. An app also needs to allow the user to activate speech and mediate turn taking between when the user can speak and when the app is listening. Part 4 describes all the necessary software components you need to implement complete voice commands.

Interpreting Sensor Data

After an app has collected some sensor data, it then needs to analyze the data to achieve a desired effect. Each sensor requires different analysis algorithms. Some examples include:

➤ **Physical sensors:** Interpreting data from physical sensors involves calculations to convert raw data into usable values and algorithms to help detect changes and ignore noise. Part 2 describes how.

➤ **Camera:** Processing images from the camera involves setting up an image-processing pipeline. An app must reduce the large image that the camera collects to a manageable size that would otherwise be too large to fit in memory or too slow to process. Then the app needs to transform the collected image in various ways to detect something within it.

➤ **Microphone:** Analyzing audio recordings involves signal-processing algorithms. Chapter 14 describes algorithms for volume detection and frequency estimation.

➤ **Speech recognition:** Executing voice commands involves matching what the user said with command words using text search methods. Chapter 17 describes methods to improve matching success.

Applications in This Book

This book presents applications that utilize sensors for specific purposes. The applications provide practical code components that solve common problems.

Some example applications in this book include:

➤ **Chapter 3:** Using a database and a `BroadcastReceiver` to implement persistent, reliable location tracking.

➤ **Chapter 4:** Using a service to implement an efficient proximity alert that conserves battery life.

➤ **Chapter 7:** Using various physical sensors to determine if the device is face up or face down.

➤ **Chapter 7:** Using the rotation vector sensor to implement features needed for an augmented reality app.

➤ **Chapter 8:** Using the acceleration sensors to detect movement.

➤ **Chapter 9:** Using the barometer to detect altitude.

➤ **Chapter 10:** Using AOA to collect data from an external temperature sensor.

➤ **Chapter 11:** Using NFC tags with custom data to track inventory.

➤ **Chapter 13:** Using the camera to detect the Android logo.

➤ **Chapter 14:** Using the microphone to implement a clapper by detecting loud noises and a singing tone.

➤ **Chapters 17 and 18:** Using speech recognition and Text-to-Speech to implement voice commands that query and manipulate data in a food database.

ADVANCED ANDROID PROGRAMMING

This book is for developers familiar with programming for Android. It assumes you understand basic Android concepts like `Activities` and `Intents` but may have not have used the sensor-related APIs. It also assumes you understand some math concepts and fully explains any physics concepts you need to know.

Additionally, this book focuses on programming sensors. This focus allows sufficient space to fully describe how to process each kind of data and go beyond explaining simple uses of the APIs.

Beyond sensor programming, this book describes techniques that are applicable in any app. For example, the chapters in this book show you how to use `BroadcastReceivers`, `Services`, `AsyncTasks`, and databases for various tasks.

START SENSING!

Apps can utilize sensors to create amazing features that are unique and save a user's time. Android's sensing capabilities will only improve over time and continue to be an important component in many apps. This book arms you with the knowledge and code you need to use these capabilities to create great apps.

ANDROID SENSING PLAYGROUND APP

This book comes with an app called Android Sensing Playground. The app enables you to execute most of the applications and example code from this book and also utilize "playgrounds" which allow you to observe the relevant APIs working under various parameter settings.

Download the app from Google Play here: `https://play.google.com/store/apps/details?id=root.gast.playground`.

GREAT ANDROID SENSING TOOLKIT (GAST)

The code in this book is part of an open source project called Great Android Sensing Toolkit (GAST). The latest updates and code are available on Github at the following link: `https://github.com/gast-lib`.

SOURCE CODE

As you work through the examples in this book, you may choose either to type in all the code manually, or to use the source code files that accompany the book. All the source code used in this book is available for download at www.wrox.com. When at the site, simply locate the book's title (use the Search box or one of the title lists) and click the Download Code link on the book's detail page to obtain all the source code for the book. Code that is included on the website is highlighted by the following icon:

Available for download on Wrox.com

Listings include the filename in the title. If it is just a code snippet, you'll find the filename in a code note such as this:

code snippet filename

 Because many books have similar titles, you may find it easiest to search by ISBN; this book's ISBN is 978-1-118-18348-9

Once you download the code, just decompress it with your favorite compression tool. Alternately, you can go to the main Wrox code download page at www.wrox.com/dynamic/books/download .aspx to see the code available for this book and all other Wrox books.

CONVENTIONS

To help you get the most from the text and keep track of what's happening, we've used a number of conventions throughout the book.

 Warnings hold important, not-to-be-forgotten information that is directly relevant to the surrounding text.

 Notes indicate notes, tips, hints, tricks, and asides to the current discussion.

TRY THIS

The Try This sections throughout the book highlight how you can use the book's app to learn about the concepts being discussed.

As for styles in the text:

➤ We *highlight* new terms and important words when we introduce them.

➤ We show keyboard strokes like this: Ctrl+A.

➤ We show file names, URLs, and code within the text like so: `persistence.properties`.

➤ We present code in two different ways:

```
We use a monofont type with no highlighting for most code examples.
We use bold to emphasize code that is particularly important in the present context
or to show changes from a previous code snippet.
```

ERRATA

We make every effort to ensure that there are no errors in the text or in the code. However, no one is perfect, and mistakes do occur. If you find an error in one of our books, like a spelling mistake or faulty piece of code, we would be very grateful for your feedback. By sending in errata you may save another reader hours of frustration, and at the same time you will be helping us provide even higher quality information.

To find the errata page for this book, go to `www.wrox.com` and locate the title using the Search box or one of the title lists. Then, on the Book Search Results page, click on the Errata link. On this page, you can view all errata that has been submitted for this book and posted by Wrox editors.

 A complete book list including links to errata is also available at `www.wrox.com/misc-pages/booklist.shtml`.

If you don't spot "your" error on the Errata page, click on the Errata Form link and complete the form to send us the error you have found. We'll check the information and, if appropriate, post a message to the book's errata page and fix the problem in subsequent editions of the book.

P2P.WROX.COM

For author and peer discussion, join the P2P forums at `p2p.wrox.com`. The forums are a web-based system for you to post messages relating to Wrox books and related technologies and interact with other readers and technology users. The forums offer a subscription feature to e-mail you topics of interest of your choosing when new posts are made to the forums. Wrox authors, editors, other industry experts, and your fellow readers are present on these forums.

At `p2p.wrox.com`, you will find a number of different forums that will help you, not only as you read this book, but also as you develop your own applications. To join the forums, just follow these steps:

1. Go to `p2p.wrox.com` and click the Register link.

2. Read the terms of use and click Agree.

3. Complete the required information to join, as well as any optional information you wish to provide, and click Submit.

4. You will receive an email with information describing how to verify your account and complete the joining process.

 You can read messages in the forums without joining P2P, but in order to post your own messages, you must join.

Once you join, you can post new messages and respond to messages other users post. You can read messages at any time on the web. If you would like to have new messages from a particular forum e-mailed to you, click the Subscribe to this Forum icon by the forum name in the forum listing.

For more information about how to use the Wrox P2P, be sure to read the P2P FAQs for answers to questions about how the forum software works, as well as many common questions specific to P2P and Wrox books. To read the FAQs, click the FAQ link on any P2P page.

PART I
Location Services

1

Introducing the Android Location Service

WHAT'S IN THIS CHAPTER?

➤ Providing overview of how location information is provided in Android

➤ Presenting an overview of GPS

➤ Discussing why A-GPS is used in Android

➤ Providing an overview of the network location provider

Location information is becoming increasingly important in the world of mobile development. Apps that were once location agnostic now make use of location information to provide a richer user experience. Being able to combine a simple web search engine with up-to-the-minute location information allows Android devices to provide a level of functionality that was previously not possible. The capability to easily retrieve and provide location data to apps is becoming a major feature of today's mobile platforms. Android provides this functionality with its location service.

Android's location service provides access to facilities that can be used to determine a device's current location. This information can be used for a wide variety of functions and can allow a device and the software that runs on it to have a better understanding of its surroundings.

METHODS USED TO DETERMINE LOCATION

Android makes use of different methods to provide location information to an app. In Android, these facilities are called *location providers*, and each has its own unique set of strengths and weaknesses. In addition, because location providers have such unique characteristics, they each lend themselves to be used differently in different situations.

The following sections give some high-level explanations as to how the different location acquisition methods work. Although an app has little control over how the providers work, it can decide which location provider to use. Understanding how each provider works goes a long way in understanding its limitations and characteristics.

GPS Provider

The Global Positioning System (GPS) uses a system of satellites orbiting the planet to help a receiver (an Android handset in this case) determine its current location. The term *GPS* refers to the entire GPS system, which consists of satellites, receivers, and the control stations that monitor and adjust it. The receiver that is located in the phone is useless without the rest of the system.

How It Works

In general, a GPS receiver uses information from the GPS satellites orbiting the earth to calculate its current location. The GPS system contains 27 satellites that continually orbit the earth, transmitting information to would-be receivers. Each satellite follows a defined path, ensuring that at least four satellites are "visible" from any point on earth at any given time. Being able to have a "line of sight" to at least four satellites is necessary to determine location using GPS. Figure 1-1 shows a depiction of the GPS satellite constellation.

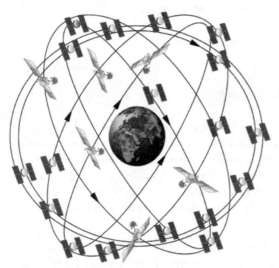

SOURCE: HTTP://GPS.GOV/MULTIMEDIA/IMAGES

FIGURE 1-1: GPS satellite constellation

Each GPS satellite in the constellation continuously transmits its current position (ephemeris data) and almanac data. The almanac data includes data about each satellite in the constellation, including orbiting data as well as information about the overall state of the system as a whole. To say it another way, ephemeris data is information about a single satellite, and almanac data is information about every satellite. Every satellite transmits both. Though both the ephemeris data and almanac data provide location data for a given satellite, the ephemeris data provides accuracy for location calculation.

To calculate its location, a GPS receiver must be able to determine its distance from multiple satellites. It does this using the ephemeris data. Included in the data that is transmitted from the satellite, along with the position data, is the time at which the transmission started. Each GPS satellite contains a highly accurate timekeeping mechanism that allows the satellite to keep its time in sync with the rest of the satellites. To produce an accurate location calculation, the GPS satellites and GPS receivers must have their clocks highly synchronized. Even the slightest difference in time can cause large errors when computing location.

Using the transmission start time, the GPS receiver can calculate the time it took for the transmission to be received (the receiver knows when the transmission ended). This calculation is made with the assumption that the radio waves that transmit the data travel at the speed of light in a vacuum (which is not always the case). Using the start time, end time, and a constant for the speed of light, a GPS receiver can calculate the distance of the satellite from the receiver.

Using the distance from multiple satellites, the GPS receiver can triangulate its current location. Essentially, the point at which all the spheres intersect is the location of the receiver. A minimum of three satellites is needed to determine a two-dimensional location (latitude and longitude). Communications from additional satellites allow a GPS receiver to determine additional positional information such as altitude. A GPS receiver will not limit itself to only four satellites. In general as the number of satellites from which the receiver can receive data increases, so does the accuracy of the location (there is an upper limit, however).

GPS is useful for determining current location, but it does have some drawbacks (especially for mobile platforms), one of which is the time it can take to calculate the current position. Before the location can be calculated, multiple satellites must be found. Many satellites are orbiting the earth, but only a handful can be "seen" at any given time because most will be below the horizon and blocked by the earth (remember, a line of sight is needed). The almanac used by the GPS system can provide assistance in determining which satellites should be used for a given location at a given time. However, if the GPS does not have a relatively current almanac, it will need to have the almanac data transmitted by a GPS satellite. This can be a slow process.

GPS Improvements

Although standard GPS can provide accurate location data, the limitations it imposes make it difficult for mobile devices to use it. To help circumvent some the limitations of standard GPS, modern mobile devices make use of assisted GPS (A-GPS) and possibly simultaneous GPS (S-GPS).

A-GPS

A-GPS uses the mobile network to transmit the GPS almanac along with other pieces of information to a mobile device. This use of the mobile network allows for faster transmission of the almanac, which may lead to faster determination of the device's current location. In addition, because the almanac contains information about all of the GPS satellites, the device will know the approximate location of the GPS satellites in its line of sight. This will also improve the time it takes to acquire a GPS location.

Examination of the GPS configuration file provides some insight into where the A-GPS data comes from. Listing 1-1 shows an example of a GPS configuration file that is used in Android for a device located in North America.

LISTING 1-1: An example of a GPS configuration file located in /system/etc/gps.conf

```
NTP_SERVER=north-america.pool.ntp.org
XTRA_SERVER_1=http://xtra1.gpsonextra.net/xtra.bin
XTRA_SERVER_2=http://xtra2.gpsonextra.net/xtra.bin
XTRA_SERVER_3=http://xtra3.gpsonextra.net/xtra.bin
```

Listing 1-1 shows that the GPS configuration file can specify the location of the A-GPS data to download (XTRA_SERVER_1, XTRA_SERVER_2, and XTRA_SERVER_3) as well as a Network Time Protocol (NTP) server that can be used to coordinate time (NTP_SERVER). NTP can be used to force coordination of time. This is important because GPS relies heavily on the clocks of a GPS receiver and the GPS satellites being in sync. Although the use of NTP does not guarantee true time synchronization down to the millisecond, it does help to prevent large time differences. Because of the numbers used in calculating times, like the speed of light, a small difference in time can lead to large inaccuracies in location calculations.

Though most users can read /system/etc/gps.conf, increased permissions are required to write to the file. Generally, users should not need to edit this file.

S-GPS

Devices that use standard GPS may use the same hardware to communicate with GPS satellites and make mobile phone calls. This means that only one of these actions can take place at a time. S-GPS addresses this issue by adding additional hardware that allows the GPS radio and the cellular network radio to be operational simultaneously. The ability to have two radios active can speed up GPS data transmission because it allows the data to be received while the cellular network radio is active.

Limitations

Although GPS can provide the most accurate location data, it does have limitations that may be difficult to work around. First is the fact that a GPS receiver needs a clear path to a GPS satellite. This means that GPS receivers are unlikely to work indoors, and may even have problems outside in areas where the sky is not visible (such as dense forests). Additionally, because multiple GPS satellites are needed to produce location information, it may take a substantial amount of time to acquire a location. This is exacerbated by that fact that devices may contain low-powered GPS radios. For these reasons, other sources of location information are sometimes needed.

Objects that obstruct a GPS signal may cause the signal to be reflected before it reaches the GPS receiver. As stated earlier, the time it takes a signal to reach the GPS receiver is used to calculate the distance between the GPS satellite and the GPS receiver. GPS signals that are reflected off of objects have a different path from the GPS satellite to the GPS receiver and cause the distance calculation to be erroneous. These types of errors are called *multipath errors* and can cause the location to appear to jump from one place to another. This is often seen in urban areas where GPS signals frequently bounce off of tall buildings.

Controlling GPS

For most cases, GPS should "just work" as far as app developers are concerned. Typically, there will be no reason to interfere with the source of the A-GPS data, or when the A-GPS data should be purged and reinitialized.

However, Android does provide an API for controlling certain aspects of GPS data. The `LocationManager` class (which is introduced in detail in the next chapter) contains a `sendExtra-Command()` method that can be used to manipulate device GPS state. The `LocationManager.send-ExtraCommand()` method takes three parameters: a string specifying the location provider, the extra command, and a `Bundle` that provides additional information for performing the command.

At the time of this writing, the GPS location provider supports only three extra commands:

- ➤ `delete_aiding_data`
- ➤ `force_time_injection`
- ➤ `force_extra_injection`

The `delete_aiding_data` command is used to remove the A-GPS data that has been previously downloaded. It is the only extra command that makes use of the `Bundle` parameter, which is used to control what A-GPS data should be removed. The `Bundle` can contain `Boolean` values with keys to indicate which data to remove. The keys can be any of the following strings:

- ➤ `ephemeris`
- ➤ `almanac`
- ➤ `position`
- ➤ `time`
- ➤ `iono`
- ➤ `utc`
- ➤ `health`
- ➤ `svdir`
- ➤ `scsteer`
- ➤ `sadata`
- ➤ `rti`
- ➤ `celldb-info`
- ➤ `all`

Passing a null for the `Bundle` causes all the A-GPS data to be removed.

The `force_time_injection` command causes the current time to be retrieved from the configured NTP server and updated for the purposes of GPS calculations.

The `force_extra_injection` command causes the A-GPS data to be downloaded from one of the configured servers and used by the GPS location provider.

Network Provider

In Android, network-based location can use different methods for determining the location of a device. As of this writing, the network location provider can provide location information using cell towers, or based on wireless network information.

Using Wireless Network Access Points

Providing location information based on wireless network access points is one of the ways that Android supports location resolution with the network provider. Although it does require that the Wi-Fi radio is active, the Wi-Fi radio often consumes less battery power than the GPS hardware.

How It Works

Wi-Fi-based location detection works by having a device track what Wi-Fi access points it can detect and the current signal strength of those access points. The device then makes a query to the Google location service (which is different from the Android location service), which provides location data based on the Wi-Fi information. The Wi-Fi information collected by the device includes the mandatory access control (MAC) addresses of the Wi-Fi access points that are in range and the strength of the signal being received from those access points.

To provide location information based on visible Wi-Fi access points, the Google location service must obtain information about Wi-Fi access points and their locations. This information is collected by Android devices when a user enables use of Google's location service in the Location Settings screen. Figure 1-2 shows the confirmation screen that is presented to a user when enabling the Google location service as a source of location data.

Pressing Agree on this screen allows the device to record Wi-Fi information as well as current location information (possibly provided by GPS) and transmit this information to Google. This essentially allows Google use each and every Android device as a way to update the Wi-Fi location information and constantly maintain up-to-date data.

One of the main benefits of the Wi-Fi location source is that it allows devices to acquire location information in areas where GPS cannot provide location data. As stated in the previous section, GPS is problematic when used indoors or even in an urban environment where tall buildings can cause signal problems. In contrast, an urban environment may increase the accuracy of Wi-Fi-based location because of the abundance of Wi-Fi networks available to determine a device's current location.

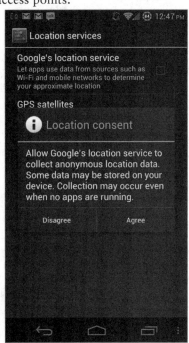

FIGURE 1-2: Confirmation screen displayed when enabling Google's location service

Limitations

As with GPS, using Wi-Fi networks as a source of location information does have its limitations. First, to determine the location, Wi-Fi networks must be in range. Additionally, the networks must have a publicly broadcasted service set identifier (SSID) that has not been configured to be ignored by Android. Access points that have an SSID that ends in _nomap will not have their information sent to the Google location service.

Additionally, changes to the location of Wi-Fi access points can cause inaccuracies in the location data that is produced. For example, many people now have wireless networks in their homes for daily use. Assuming an Android device has been configured to use the Google location service, Android would have sent the access point MAC address and location to the Google location service. If the user were to change the location of that access point (take it to a vacation home, for example), the location service might determine the device to be in the wrong location when the Wi-Fi location source is used.

Although the location service does allow for access point location to be updated via Android devices, Google does not allow users to explicitly set the location of an access point. An Android device will push the information to the location service, which may wait until other devices can confirm the change before the location service is updated.

Using Cell IDs

In addition to using Wi-Fi information to determine device location, Android can also use the cellular network. The cellular network is used in a similar way as Wi-Fi access points to determine device location.

How It Works

To function properly, a cellular device must be in contact with a cell tower. As a device moves, it may connect to a different cell tower as the signal strength of an approaching cell tower becomes stronger. Knowing the unique ID of the tower that a device is currently connected to, and possibly the towers that a device was previously connected to, can provide insight to where the device is located assuming the location of a given cell tower is known.

Android and the Google location service work together to map cell tower IDs to location data in a way that is similar to Wi-Fi data. Once a device has been configured to use the network provider, it collects data on the current cell tower ID in addition to the visible wireless networks. For cell towers, this data includes the cell tower the device is currently connected to and the device's current GPS location. With this information, the Google location service can develop a "map" of cell towers that includes their locations.

By again allowing Android devices to update cell ID information, the Google location service can maintain a constantly updated store of information that increases in accuracy as the number of entries increases.

When a device needs to find its current location, it sends the ID of the cell tower it is currently connected to, as well as historic information about past cell towers it has used, to the Google location service. With this information, the Google location service can provide information about the device's current location based on the data it has about the cell tower network. If the IDs of multiple cell towers are sent to the Google location service, it can use triangulation to provide increased location accuracy. The Google location service cannot do this if the device submits only a single cell tower ID.

Limitations

The limitations for using cell tower IDs are similar to the limitations that exist when using Wi-Fi networks to determine location. However, because the location of cell towers is less likely to change than the location of wireless access points, some of the complications that may exist when using Wi-Fi access points are removed.

However, just like Wi-Fi access point data, the Google location service must have data on the cell tower IDs that are sent by a device in order to provide location data.

SUMMARY

This chapter presented an overview of how the location providers available in Android work and discussed their limitations. The decision of which location provider to use in which situation can be a complex topic, and is discussed at length in the following chapters.

2

Determining a Device's Current Location

WHAT'S IN THIS CHAPTER?

➤ Introduction to the Android Location API components

➤ Introduction to the different sources of location information in Android

➤ Example usage of the Location API to determine a device's current location

Mobile app developers often have to determine the device's current location. Knowing a device's location enables app developers to add increased functionality to a wide range of apps. Location data is a key component to apps like Google Maps and Google Navigator, and is also used in Google search, Twitter, and Facebook to add another dimension to the data they are already collecting.

For developers who have made the decision to include location data, Android provides a fairly robust API to its location service. Although on the surface this API may seem trivial to use, plenty of details — such as battery life and accuracy of location data — need to be considered.

As an introduction to the topic of location services in Android, this chapter provides a guided tour of the location portions of the API. In addition, the chapter presents an app that answers the most basic Android question ("Where am I?") and presents location data on the screen. Figure 2-1 shows the app's screen.

FIGURE 2-1: Current location app

KNOW YOUR TOOLS

This chapter starts the discussion of the location service by first taking a bird's-eye view of some of the tools that Android has to offer. One of the first things I do when I need to solve a problem is to take a look at what tools I have to work with. For Android, the majority of the classes that you will need when working with location data are located in the `android.location` package. For the example app, you will need to use five members of the location package. These just happen to be the five members of that package that you will frequently use when dealing with location data in Android.

Classes:

➤   LocationManager

➤   LocationProvider

➤   Location

➤   Criteria

Interfaces:

➤   LocationListener

Figure 2-2 shows a high-level overview of how the location components fit together. Because these members are so important and used so frequently, the following sections discuss each one in a little more detail.

LocationManager

The main point of entry when using the location service in Android is the `LocationManager`. The `LocationManager` allows an app to tell Android when it is interested in receiving updated location information and when it no longer wants location updates. In addition, the LocationManager provides information about the current state of the location system such as available location providers, enabled location providers, and GPS status information. The LocationManager can also provide the last known (cached) location of the device.

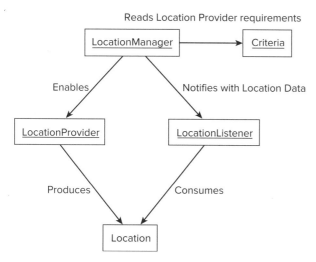

FIGURE 2-2: Android location components

LocationProvider

LocationProvider is an abstraction for the different sources of location information in Android. Android provides different sources of location data that have drastically different characteristics. Though each provider generates location data differently, they all communicate with an app the same way and provide similar data to an app in the same manner.

Location

The Location class is what encapsulates the actual location data provided to an app from a location provider. It contains the quantifiable data such as latitude, longitude, and altitude. Once an app has received a Location object, it can start the application-specific processing on that data.

One important point about the Location class is that, although it has properties for a wide range of location data, not all location providers will populate all the properties. For example, if an app uses a location provider that does not provide altitude, the Location instance will not contain altitude information. The Location class also provides methods that allow an app to check if an instance contains the information (hasAltitude() in this case).

Criteria

An app can use the Criteria class to query the LocationManager for location providers that contain certain characteristics. This is useful for times when an app is less concerned with which actual providers are used and more concerned that location providers have some common characteristics. The Criteria class prevents an app from worrying about the implementation details of working with individual location providers directly. Once instantiated, an app can set/unset attributes on a `Criteria` class to reflect the characteristics of the location providers that it is interested in. Table 2-1 provides the list of the attributes on the `Criteria` class that can be used to select a location provider.

TABLE 2-1: Location Criteria Attributes

ATTRIBUTE	EXPLANATION	POSSIBLE VALUES
`accuracy`	Indicates the overall level of accuracy for a location provider.	`Criteria.ACCURACY_FINE` or `Criteria.ACCURACY_COURSE`
`altitudeRequired`	Indicates whether a location provider needs to provide altitude information.	True or false
`bearingRequired`	Indicates whether a location provider needs to provide bearing (the direction being traveled) information.	True or false
`bearingAccuracy`	Required accuracy for bearing information.	`Criteria.ACCURACY_HIGH` or `Criteria.ACCURACY_LOW`
`costAllowed`	Indicates whether the location provider is allowed to cost the user money.	True or false
`horizontalAccuracy`	Required accuracy for latitude and longitude values.	`Criteria.ACCURACY_LOW`, `Criteria.ACCURACY_MEDIUM`, or `Criteria.ACCURACY_LOW`
`powerRequirement`	Amount of battery power required by the location provider.	`Criteria.POWER_LOW`, `Criteria.POWER_MEDIUM`, or `Criteria.POWER_LOW`
`speedRequired`	Indicates whether a location provider needs to provide speed information.	True or false
`speedAccuracy`	Required accuracy for speed information.	`Criteria.ACCURACY_HIGH` or `Criteria.ACCURACY_LOW`
`verticalAccuracy`	Required accuracy for altitude information.	`Criteria.ACCURACY_HIGH` or `Criteria.ACCURACY_LOW`

LocationListener

The `LocationListener` interface contains a group of callback methods that are called in reaction to changes in a device's current location or changes in location service state. The `LocationManager` enables an app to register/unregister a location listener implementation that can be used to process the changes in state.

There are two ways to receive location updates from the location service: a `LocationListener` and a `PendingIntent`. This chapter focuses on using a `LocationListener`; the use of a `PendingIntent` is deferred until the next chapter.

Now that the tools needed to implement the app have been introduced, the following sections dig into the mechanics of requesting and processing the location information.

SETTING UP THE ANDROID MANIFEST

As with many of the services that Android provides, the location service requires an app to declare its intentions to use it in the Android manifest. The Android manifest declaration must define the precision of the location data that will be requested. Like any other Android permission, the end user will be shown the list of requested permissions at install time and will be able to decline installation upon seeing that list. Some users are a little squeamish at the thought of allowing an app to determine their location if it is not clear why the app would need this information. Adding superfluous permissions is a good way to scare users away.

The two permissions that deal with live location data are `android.permission.ACCESS_FINE_LOCATION` and `android.permission.ACCESS_COARSE_LOCATION`. As the names might indicate, the permissions define the level of accuracy that will be provided to an app from the location service. Ultimately, these permissions define which location providers can be used in an app. Because the `android.permission.ACCESS_FINE_LOCATION` permission provides more accurate location data, it can be used without explicitly specifying `android.permission.ACCESS_COARSE_LOCATION` to grant permission for both fine-grained and coarse-grained location data. However, `android.permission.ACCESS_COARSE_LOCATION` only allows for coarse-grained location data to be provided to an app.

For the app in this chapter, highly accurate location data is desired. So, the following code snippet is added to `AndroidManifest.xml`:

```
<uses-permission android:name="android.permission.ACCESS_FINE_LOCATION" />
```

 Failure to request the correct permissions causes a `java.lang.` `SecurityException` *to be thrown at run time when requesting location updates.*

DETERMINING THE APPROPRIATE LOCATION PROVIDER

Multiple sources of location data in Android provide varying levels of accuracy and battery consumption. Determining when to use the different providers can have a big impact on the overall user experience of an app. The location providers available in Android are:

➤ GPS location provider

➤ Network location provider

➤ Passive location provider

An app can declare which location provider to use in one of two ways: by explicitly registering each desired location provider with the `LocationManager`, or by specifying attributes in a `Criteria` object and passing that object to the `LocationManager`. Using the `Criteria` object is useful for allowing the user to customize the source of location data at run time. This may be of importance to a user because use of some location providers can cost them money.

GPS Location Provider

The GPS location provider uses orbiting satellites and time to determine the current location of a device, and tends to produce the most accurate location data. However, because it relies on a separate radio, the GPS provider can also consume more battery power than other location providers. This can be a major issue depending on the length of time an app needs to actively be receiving and processing location data.

In addition to consuming more battery power, the GPS location provider can also take a long time to acquire a fix (location data). Time to first fix (TTFF) values of over a minute are common, and can vary drastically from device to device or between different versions of Android. In addition, obtaining a GPS fix indoors is unlikely because a direct line to the sky is usually required. TTFF is important to pay attention to because it is generally a bad idea to block the user from performing a task while an app is waiting for location data.

Network Location Provider

The network location provider uses two data sources to provide a location fix: Wi-Fi network location and cell-tower location. The TTFF for the network provider can be substantially less than the TTFF for the GPS provider. However, the network provider produces much less accurate location data. Depending on the needs of an app, it might be worth trading the location accuracy of the GPS provider for the low TTFF values of the network provider. The network provider may also consume less battery power than the GPS provider because it allows the user to leave the GPS radio and (possibly) the Wi-Fi radio off.

Passive Location Provider

The passive location provider allows an app to receive location information without having to explicitly request location update information from the `LocationManager`. The passive provider provides location updates when another app has explicitly requested location updates with either the GPS or network providers. This allows an app to piggy-back on the location information requested from another app and prevent Android from making a special request for location data.

At first glance, it may not be obvious how to use this provider. Essentially, the passive location provider allows an app to receive location updates in the background without consuming any additional battery power, because it receives updates only when something else is receiving updates.

This implies that an app does not have any control over which other providers are used to receive location updates, or the frequency at which the updates will arrive (the other apps have defined this when setting up the `LocationManager`). Because of this, use of the passive provider mandates the use of the `android.permission.ACCESS_FINE_LOCATION` permission so that data from both the GPS and network providers can be received. The `Location` object that is received will contain information about the source of the location data.

The passive provider is not guaranteed to receive any location updates. If no other apps are receiving location updates, the passive provider will not receive any either. Because of this, the passive provider is generally not appropriate to use when an app is in the foreground and actively interacting with the user. Use the passive location provider to keep application data up to date while running in the background and without explicitly requesting location data.

It is good form for apps to be a "good citizens" on an Android device and remove requests for location updates when they app exit. If an app makes the distinction of closing as opposed to backgrounding (user clicks "back" as opposed to user pressing "home"), then the app should unregister for updates even when using the passive provider.

Accuracy versus Battery Life

The common theme when choosing location providers is deciding between increased accuracy and increased battery consumption. Although most apps that need location data could benefit from more accurate data, many of them do not truly need the accuracy, especially at the expense of additional battery power.

Table 2-2 provides a summary of the location providers available in Android.

TABLE 2-2: Location Providers

LOCATION PROVIDER	REQUIRED PERMISSION	BATTERY CONSUMPTION	ACCURACY
GPS Provider	`android.permission.ACCESS_FINE_LOCATION` or `android.permission.ACCESS_COARSE_LOCATION`	Consumes more battery power than other location providers	Provides the most accurate location data
Network Provider	`android.permission.ACCESS_COARSE_LOCATION`	Consumes less battery power than the GPS provider	Provides less accuracy than the GPS provider
Passive Provider	`android.permission.ACCESS_FINE_LOCATION`	N/A	N/A

Determining which location providers are the appropriate the source of location data is an important decision when using location services. As with many other development decisions, trade-offs exist that need to be considered.

RECEIVING LOCATION UPDATES

Before getting knee-deep into Java code, one more topic warrants discussion: how an app actually gets notified about location updates. Recall from an earlier discussion that location data can be delivered to an app in two ways: a direct call to a `LocationListener`, or by a broadcasted `Intent`. The `LocationListener` approach is the simpler approach (and the one used for this chapter's example app), but the broadcast `Intent` approach can offer more flexibility, especially if location update information needs to be provided to more than one application component.

In either case, an app must tell the `LocationManager` when it is ready to start receiving updates as well as when it no longer wants location updates. How the location updates get sent to an app is defined by how an app registers for location updates with the `LocationManager`.

Receiving Location Updates with a LocationListener

Objects that implement `LocationListener` are notified of location updates by a call to their `onLocationChanged()` method. The specific `LocationListener` instances which will be notified about a location update are registered with `LocationManager`. When the `LocationManager` has a new location to offer, it makes a call to `onLocationChanged()` for each listener. Further discussion of `LocationListener` usage is deferred to when the Java code for the example app is introduced in the section "Implementing LocationListener."

Receiving Location Updates with a Broadcast Intent

Having an `Intent` broadcasted with location updates can offer increased flexibility in situations where an app needs the update to be received by multiple application components. To make use of the broadcasted `Intent`, an app needs to implement a `BroadcastReceiver` and register it to receive location update `Intent`(s). This can happen either in an Android manifest or at run time. The app created in Chapter 4 includes use of a broadcast `Intent`.

IMPLEMENTING THE EXAMPLE APP

This section provides the details of how to put all the pieces of the location API together and start getting location data.

The example app has an activity, `CurrentLocationActivity`, that displays the current location and contains a button that allows the user to enable/disable location providers. Once the app gets a single location, it displays some of the location details on the screen. This will enable the user to see with the location service in action on an actual device and enable the user to start getting a feel for how accurate the various location providers are as well as how their TTFF values differ. It is important to understand the details of accuracy/TTFF and how they correlate to different providers when making app development decisions.

Implementing LocationListener

To implement `LocationListener`, a class must contain a concrete implementation for the following methods:

➤   `abstract void onLocationChanged(Location location)`

➤   `abstract void onProviderDisabled(String provider)`

➤   `abstract void onProviderEnabled(String provider)`

➤   `abstract void onStatusChanged(String provider, int status, Bundle extras)`

These methods are discussed in the following sections.

onLocationChanged()

The method that an app is most likely to interact with is `onLocationChanged()`. This is the method that is called when a new location is ready for consumption by an app. The single parameter to this method is a `Location` object that contains the details of the location (latitude, longitude, altitude, and so on). At times, this will be the only method an app needs to implement from the `LocationListener`. However, the app will need to provide an implementation for the other methods to avoid compilation errors, the implementations can be left empty (I like to add a comment indicating that they were intentionally left blank for future developers). For this app, the `onLocationChanged()` method simply takes the `Location` object it was passed and uses its data to populate the UI views (see Listing 2-1).

LISTING 2-1: Receiving a location update

```
@Override
public void onLocationChanged(Location location) {

    latitudeValue.setText(String.valueOf(location.getLatitude()));
    longitudeValue.setText(String.valueOf(location.getLongitude()));
    providerValue.setText(String.valueOf(location.getProvider()));
    accuracyValue.setText(String.valueOf(location.getAccuracy()));

    long timeToFix = SystemClock.uptimeMillis() - uptimeAtResume;

    timeToFixValue.setText(String.valueOf(timeToFix / 1000));

    findViewById(R.id.timeToFixUnits).setVisibility(View.VISIBLE);
    findViewById(R.id.accuracyUnits).setVisibility(View.VISIBLE);
}
```

onProviderDisabled() and onProviderEnabled()

The `onProviderDisabled()` and `onProviderEnabled()` methods provide a way for an app to be notified when the user enables or disables a location provider from the location settings menu. Imagine, for example, that a user is currently running an app and decides to put the app in the background by pressing the home button and returning to the desktop. From there, the user can navigate to the device settings and enable or disable different location providers. These actions may be of interest to an app. If the user were to enable the GPS provider, the app would be able to get more accurate location information for the device.

The `onProviderDisabled()` and `onProviderEnabled()` methods are Android's way of letting an app know when the state of a provider changes. Each method provides a string parameter that specifies the name of the location provider that was either enabled or disabled. The `String` provider name can be matched to the static constants in `LocationManager` to determine which provider had its state changed. These methods work well with `LocationManager.getProviders()`, which can be used to initially register providers that are currently enabled and dynamically add or remove more providers as they are enabled or disabled when `onProviderEnabled()` or `onProviderDisabled()` is called.

onStatusChanged()

The `onStatusChanged()` method is called when a provider either goes offline or comes back online. This is a different scenario than in the previous section where the user enabled or disabled the provider. In this scenario, the user has not changed the location settings; instead, the status of the actual provider has changed.

The parameters to this method are a string that represents the provider, an `int` representing the current status, and a `Bundle` that has optional data. The provider name is the same string that is passed to both `onProviderEnabled()` and `onProviderDisabled()`. The status will be one of the three values listed in Table 2-3.

TABLE 2-3: onStatusChanged() Status Values

VALUE	STATUS
`LocationProvider.OUT_OF_SERVICE`	The `LocationProvider` is currently offline and probably will not come back online anytime soon.
`LocationProvider.` `TEMPORARILY_UNAVAILABLE`	The `LocationProvider` is currently offline and should come back online soon.
`LocationProvider.AVAILABLE`	The `LocationProvider` is currently online.

The `Bundle` parameter contains optional provider-specific information. For example, a bundle for the GPS provider will contain the number of satellites used to come up with the location update.

Obtaining a Handle to LocationManager

Because the `LocationManager` is the front door into the location service, the app needs to get a reference to it. This is done with a call to `Activity.getSystemService(LOCATION_SERVICE)`. This is generally done in the `onCreate()` method of an `Activity` because multiple calls to the `LocationManager` throughout the lifetime of an `Activity` are common. Because the `onCreate()` method is the first method to be called in an activity's life cycle, it is appropriate to acquire the location manager reference here. For the example app in this chapter, the remainder of the `onCreate()` method is spent retrieving references to the UI views that will hold and present the location data. Listing 2-2 shows the implementation for the `onCreate()` method.

LISTING 2-2: Obtaining a reference to the LocationManager

```
@Override
protected void onCreate(Bundle savedInstanceState) {
    super.onCreate(savedInstanceState);
    setContentView(R.layout.current_location);

    locationManager = (LocationManager) getSystemService(LOCATION_SERVICE);

    latitudeValue = (TextView) findViewById(R.id.latitudeValue);
    longitudeValue = (TextView) findViewById(R.id.longitudeValue);
    providerValue = (TextView) findViewById(R.id.providerValue);
    accuracyValue = (TextView) findViewById(R.id.accuracyValue);
    timeToFixValue = (TextView) findViewById(R.id.timeToFixValue);
    enabledProvidersValue = (TextView) findViewById(R.id.enabledProvidersValue);
}
```

Listing 2-3 shows the layout for the activity that will display the current location data:
`latitudeValue`, `longitudeValue`, `providerValue`, `accuracyValue`, `timeToFixValue`, and
`enabledProviderValue`.

Available for download on Wrox.com

LISTING 2-3: Layout for CurrentLocationActivity

```xml
<?xml version="1.0" encoding="utf-8"?>
<RelativeLayout xmlns:android="http://schemas.android.com/apk/res/android"
    android:orientation="vertical"
    android:layout_width="match_parent"
    android:layout_height="match_parent">

    <TextView android:id="@+id/latitudeLabel"
        android:layout_height="wrap_content"
        android:layout_width="wrap_content"
        android:text="@string/latitudeLabel"
        android:layout_alignParentTop="true"
        android:layout_marginRight="4dip" />

    <TextView android:id="@+id/latitudeValue"
        android:layout_height="wrap_content"
        android:layout_width="wrap_content"
        android:layout_alignTop="@id/latitudeLabel"
        android:layout_toRightOf="@id/latitudeLabel" />

    <TextView android:id="@+id/longitudeLabel"
        android:layout_height="wrap_content"
        android:layout_width="wrap_content"
        android:text="@string/longitudeLabel"
        android:layout_below="@id/latitudeLabel"
        android:layout_marginRight="4dip" />

    <TextView android:id="@+id/longitudeValue"
```

ACC·Nᵒ 33828

Limerick Institute of Technology
Institiúid Teicneolaíochta Luimnigh
Library and Information Resource Centre

CLASS No   006.76 MIL

LISTING 2-3 *(continued)*

```
        android:layout_height="wrap_content"
        android:layout_width="wrap_content"
        android:layout_alignTop="@id/longitudeLabel"
        android:layout_toRightOf="@id/longitudeLabel" />

    <TextView android:id="@+id/providerLabel"
        android:layout_height="wrap_content"
        android:layout_width="wrap_content"
        android:text="@string/providerLabel"
        android:layout_below="@id/longitudeLabel"
        android:layout_marginRight="4dip" />

    <TextView android:id="@+id/providerValue"
        android:layout_height="wrap_content"
        android:layout_width="wrap_content"
        android:layout_alignTop="@id/providerLabel"
        android:layout_toRightOf="@id/providerLabel" />

    <TextView android:id="@+id/accuracyLabel"
        android:layout_height="wrap_content"
        android:layout_width="wrap_content"
        android:text="@string/accuracyLabel"
        android:layout_below="@id/providerLabel"
        android:layout_marginRight="4dip" />

    <TextView android:id="@+id/accuracyValue"
        android:layout_height="wrap_content"
        android:layout_width="wrap_content"
        android:layout_alignTop="@id/accuracyLabel"
        android:layout_toRightOf="@id/accuracyLabel" />

    <TextView android:id="@+id/accuracyUnits"
        android:layout_height="wrap_content"
        android:layout_width="wrap_content"
        android:text="@string/metersUnit"
        android:layout_alignTop="@id/accuracyLabel"
        android:layout_toRightOf="@id/accuracyValue"
        android:layout_marginLeft="4dip" />

    <TextView android:id="@+id/timeToFixLabel"
        android:layout_height="wrap_content"
        android:layout_width="wrap_content"
        android:text="@string/timeToFixLabel"
        android:layout_below="@id/accuracyLabel"
        android:layout_marginRight="4dip" />

    <TextView android:id="@+id/timeToFixValue"
        android:layout_height="wrap_content"
        android:layout_width="wrap_content"
        android:layout_alignTop="@id/timeToFixLabel"
        android:layout_toRightOf="@id/timeToFixLabel" />

    <TextView android:id="@+id/timeToFixUnits"
```

```
        android:layout_height="wrap_content"
        android:layout_width="wrap_content"
        android:text="@string/secondsUnit"
        android:layout_alignTop="@id/timeToFixLabel"
        android:layout_toRightOf="@id/timeToFixValue"
        android:layout_marginLeft="4dip" />

    <TextView android:id="@+id/enabledProvidersLabel"
        android:layout_height="wrap_content"
        android:layout_width="wrap_content"
        android:text="@string/enabledProvidersLabel"
        android:layout_below="@id/timeToFixLabel"
        android:layout_marginRight="4dip" />

    <TextView android:id="@+id/enabledProvidersValue"
        android:layout_height="wrap_content"
        android:layout_width="wrap_content"
        android:layout_alignTop="@id/enabledProvidersLabel"
        android:layout_toRightOf="@id/enabledProvidersLabel" />

    <Button android:id="@+id/changeLocationProviderSettings"
        android:layout_height="wrap_content"
        android:layout_width="match_parent"
        android:text="@string/changeLocationProviderSettingsText"
        android:onClick="onChangeLocationProvidersSettingsClick"
        android:layout_alignParentBottom="true" />

</RelativeLayout>
```

Code snippet current_location.xml

Now that the app has a reference to the `LocationManager`, it is ready to request location information for the Location Service.

Requesting Location Updates

The app is now ready to ask Android to provide it with location information when it becomes available. It is important to understand that an app cannot ask Android to provide it with on-demand location information. Apps can only request to be notified when updated location information is available.

This app needs only a single location update, so a call to one of the `LocationManager.requestSingleLocation()` methods is needed. Examining the Android reference docs reveals two flavors of the `LocationManager.requestSingleLocation()` methods. One flavor passes a `PendingIntent` in order to broadcast an `Intent` with location data and the other passes a `LocationListener` in order to receive direct callbacks. Again, this app uses the `LocationListener` approach. The `CurrentLocationActivity` has been made a `LocationListener` by having it implement the `LocationListener` interface. This allows the app to keep all the location code in one class.

Before a `LocationListener` can be registered with the `LocationManager`, the app developer must decide which location provider(s) the app will use. For this app, the decision is left to the end user because the app will use only the location providers that the user has enabled. To get the list of enabled location providers, a `Criteria` object is created and the attributes are set to include both the network and GPS location providers. Both the network and GPS providers provide at least a coarse location fix, so passing `Criteria.ACCURACY_COARSE` to `Criteria.setAccuracy()` will include both providers for consideration. The initialized `Criteria` instance is then passed to the `getProviders()` method along with a `boolean` (hard-coded to `true`) to indicate that only enabled location providers should be returned. Each location provider in the returned list is then used to obtain location data.

Because the app needs a new location every time the `CurrentLocationActivity` is presented to the user (because the user is allowed to enable or disable location providers in-app), the `onResume()` method is where the `LocationManager` is formally asked to provide a location update as they become available, as shown in Listing 2-4.

Available for
download on
Wrox.com

LISTING 2-4: Registering with the LocationManager

```java
protected void onResume() {
    super.onResume();

    StringBuffer stringBuffer = new StringBuffer();

    Criteria criteria = new Criteria();
    criteria.setAccuracy(Criteria.ACCURACY_COARSE);

    enabledProviders = locationManager.getProviders(criteria, true);

    if (enabledProviders.isEmpty())
    {
        enabledProvidersValue.setText("");
    }
    else
    {
        for (String enabledProvider : enabledProviders)
        {
            stringBuffer.append(enabledProvider).append(" ");

            locationManager.requestSingleUpdate(enabledProvider,
                    this,
                    null);
        }
        enabledProvidersValue.setText(stringBuffer);
    }

    uptimeAtResume = SystemClock.uptimeMillis();

    latitudeValue.setText("");
    longitudeValue.setText("");
    providerValue.setText("");
    accuracyValue.setText("");
    timeToFixValue.setText("");

    findViewById(R.id.timeToFixUnits).setVisibility(View.GONE);
    findViewById(R.id.accuracyUnits).setVisibility(View.GONE);
}
```

code snippet CurrentLocation.java

Thus far, this chapter has discussed how to register a `LocationListener` to receive updates. The final step is unregistering for those location updates when they are no longer required by the app.

Cleaning up After Yourself

At this point, the app is ready to start receiving and processing location data in `CurrentLocationActivity`. The last part of the implementation is to have the app clean up after itself by unregistering the location listener when it no longer needs location updates. Forgetting to unregister a location listener could cause the providers and underlying hardware to remain active, thus wasting battery life. Not removing a location listener registration for the GPS provider causes (an enabled) GPS provider to actively retrieve and compute location data. This is visible to the user because the GPS provider has its own icon alerting the user to the issue. Leaving the GPS running when it is no longer needed is bad practice and can result in negative feedback in the Android Market.

The app doesn't need any location updates when the `CurrentLocationActivity` is not interacting with the user. As shown in Listing 2-5, it will unregister the `LocationListener` on the `onPause()` method.

LISTING 2-5: Removing a LocationListener

```
@Override
protected void onPause() {
    super.onPause();
    locationManager.removeUpdates(this);
}
```

Had the `BroadcastReceiver` approach been used, the app would have again called `locationManager.removeUpdates()`, and would have passed in the `PendingIntent` that was passed to `registerSingleUpdate()`.

Now that the app has code to initialize itself, process location updates, and clean up after itself, the next step in the example app implementation is responding to the user enabling/disabling location providers while the app is running.

Launching the Location Settings Activity

The final detail of the app worth discussing is the button on the screen that enables the user to change location provider settings. In order to receive location data from a specific location provider, an app should ensure that the location provider is enabled by the user. If the user does not currently have the provider enabled, the location settings activity can be for them and allow them to enable the provider without leaving the app. This occurs in the example app when the Change Location Provider Settings button is pressed. Accomplishing this is actually pretty trivial, as evidenced by Listing 2-6, and it happens in the handler for the button click.

LISTING 2-6: Launching the location settings activity

```
public void onChangeLocationProvidersSettingsClick(View view)
{
    startActivity(new Intent(Settings.ACTION_LOCATION_SOURCE_SETTINGS));
}
```

The location settings activity screen is displayed in Figure 2-3.

FIGURE 2-3: The location settings screen

Now that you have an app capable of determining your current location, try loading the app on an actual device and spending some time playing with the different location providers, paying special attention to TTFF and accuracy differences. Try running the app in different environments (indoors and outdoors, sunny and overcast, urban and rural) to see how they affect the various location providers. Spending some time getting a feel for how the providers work will give you an idea of their limitations.

SUMMARY

This chapter provided a tour around some of the basic SDK elements that are needed to work with Android location services. The chapter discussed some of the foundation classes, and examined the implementation of a simple app for determining the current location of a device. This app really is the "sunny day" scenario and does not handle some of the real-world problems an app will face when using location services. Although the information in this chapter is enough to get up and running, the next few chapters describe how to take full advantage of Android location services.

3

Tracking Device Movement

WHAT'S IN THIS CHAPTER?

➤ Using the Android location service to continuously track device location

➤ Using the Google Maps library to plot location data on a map

➤ Using broadcast receivers to track location in the background

➤ Considering effects on battery life

As an introduction to the Android location service, Chapter 2 discussed how to get the current location of a device. This chapter showcases additional functionality and presents an example app that tracks the location of a device as it moves. The app built in this chapter demonstrates how to receive the device's current location, persist that location in a database, and plot the path traveled — all the persisted locations — on a map using the Google Maps external library for Android.

With the additional functionality comes additional complexity. Continuously tracking device location data implies keeping more device hardware (such as Wi-Fi radio or GPS radio) active, which can adversely affect battery life. Also, the app needs to handle cases where it receives incorrect location data, as well as cases where one or all of the location providers are not available.

The example app for this chapter consists of three Android application components: an activity to display both the current location and previous locations, a broadcast receiver that receives location data in the background and stores the new locations in a database, and another broadcast receiver that receives location updates only when the app is in the foreground in order to update the display.

The main screen of the app looks like Figure 3-1.

FIGURE 3-1: Main screen for the example app showing the map and the start and stop buttons

COLLECTING LOCATION DATA

One of the tasks that the example app needs to perform is the collection and persistence of location data. Additionally, the app should continue to collect and save location data even when not in the foreground. The app should not stop tracking location data simply because the user receives a phone call or decides to respond to an e-mail.

Two of the Android application components that can be used to perform background tasks are services and broadcast receivers. Each one has a unique list of pros and cons for tracking location data. The decision of which one to use will be heavily based on the needs of the app.

This chapter's example app uses a broadcast receiver to receive location updates in the background. However, this chapter also provides the shell of a service for receiving the location updates in the background, and provides some guidance for determining when to use a broadcast receiver and when to use a service.

Receiving Location Updates with a Broadcast Receiver

Using a broadcast receiver to acquire location information is similar to using a broadcast receiver to receive notification of other Android events. A receiver is passed intents based on a filter, and those intents contain data for the broadcast receiver to read and process.

To receive location updates with a broadcast receiver, a developer must, in no particular order:

➤ Create a class that extends `BroadcastReceiver`.

➤ Register the child class as a `BroadcastReceiver` with Android.

➤ Register an intent to be broadcast when Android receives new location information with the `LocationManager`.

The following sections tackle these three musts.

Extending BroadcastReceiver

As stated earlier, the example app uses two broadcast receivers to track and display device location. Because these two classes will share some common functionality, both broadcast receivers extend `LocationBroadcastReceiver`. `LocationBroadcastReceiver` contains the functionality for retrieving location data from an intent and passing it along to its children.

The intent that is passed to `LocationBroadcastReceiver` can contain more than just the updated location information. Recall from Chapter 2 that the `LocationListener` interface provides methods that not only allow the Android location service to send location updates, but to also send messages to a `LocationListener` about the status of location providers as well as when location providers are enabled or disabled. The same information can be retrieved from the intent that is passed to a broadcast receiver. Table 3-1 lists the extras that can reside in an intent's extras bundle when the intent is sent from the Android location service.

TABLE 3-1: Intent Extra Constants

CONSTANT	DATA TYPE	PROVIDED DATA
`LocationManager.KEY_LOCATION_CHANGED`	`Location`	Updated location information
`LocationManager.KEY_PROVIDER_ENABLED`	`boolean`	Flag for broadcast event when a provider is enabled/disabled
`LocationManager.KEY_PROXIMITY_ENTERING`	`boolean`	Indicates when a proximity alert is entering or exiting
`LocationManager.KEY_STATUS_CHANGED`	`int`	The updated status of a location provider when the change in status is broadcast

Querying the intent extras for the values presented in Table 3-1 provides the reasons why the intent was broadcast. For example, if `LocationManager.KEY_LOCATION_CHANGED` exists in the extras, the intent was sent in response to a new device location becoming available.

To handle all of the possible location information, a broadcast receiver must look for all the possible location-based keys in the intent extras. The implementation for `LocationBroadcastReceiver.onReceive()` would look similar to Listing 3-1.

LISTING 3-1: Reading a location intent

```
@Override
public void onReceive(Context context, Intent intent)
{
    if (intent.hasExtra(LocationManager.KEY_LOCATION_CHANGED))
    {
        // ...
    }
    else if (intent.hasExtra(LocationManager.KEY_PROVIDER_ENABLED))
    {
        // ...
    }
    else if (intent.hasExtra(LocationManager.KEY_PROXIMITY_ENTERING))
    {
        // ...
    }
    else if (intent.hasExtra(LocationManager.KEY_STATUS_CHANGED))
    {
        // ...
    }
}
```

Registering the BroadcastReceiver with Android

To have a broadcast receiver receive intents that were broadcast, it needs to be registered with Android. There are two ways to perform the registration: in the manifest for your app or by calling `registerReceiver()` on a `Context`. Although each registration method will ultimately achieve the same result, they cause Android to interact differently with a broadcast receiver.

Manifest Registration

The manifest registration method allows a broadcast receiver to receive intents as they become available even if no other application components are currently running. With location intents, this means after the `LocationManager` has been made aware of the desire to receive location information via a call to `LocationManager.requestLocationUpdates()`. Manifest registration provides an easy method to have an app be notified of location updates in the background, which is one of the requirements of this chapter's example app.

The broadcast receiver that will receive location updates in the background for the example app is `TrackLocationBroadcastReceiver`. To register the broadcast receiver in the application manifest, a `<receiver>` element must be placed in the `<application>` section of the `AndroidManifest.xml`. Though only the name of the class that extends `BroadcastReceiver` needs to be specified, it makes sense to also specify the filter in the manifest as well so the broadcast receiver will only receive intents relevant to the app. The application manifest declaration for the broadcast receiver that tracks location updates is presented in Listing 3-2.

LISTING 3-2: Broadcast receiver manifest declaration

```
<receiver android:name=".location.TrackLocationBroadcastReceiver">
  <intent-filter >
    <action android:name="root.gast.playground.location.ACTION_LOCATION_CHANGED"/>
  </intent-filter>
</receiver>
```

In Listing 3-2, the `android:name` attribute for the receiver is used to declare which class is the broadcast receiver that should receive the location updates. The code also specifies that intents with the action `"root.gast.playground.location.ACTION_LOCATION_CHANGED"` should be sent to the receiver by declaring an action in the intent filter element.

The name of the action that is specified is unique to this app. The string declared as the name in the manifest will match a string that is used to set up the intent that will be broadcast for location updates.

Registering broadcast receivers in the manifest enables you to "hook in" your broadcast receiver to Android in order to receive intents without needing to do anything with the broadcast receiver in your code. If you scan the example app for references to `TrackLocationBroadcastReceiver`, you won't find any. The code does not even need to instantiate a `TrackLocationBroadcastReceiver` instance because Android will take care of creating the instance and managing its life cycle. `TrackLocationBroadcastReceiver` automatically starts receiving location updates when a pending intent is registered with the `LocationManager` (and location updates are provided from a location provider) and stops receiving updates when the pending intent is unregistered from the `LocationManager`. In the example app, the pending intent is registered when the user presses the Start Tracking button and is unregistered when the user presses the Stop Tracking button in the main activity.

One important point to keep in mind when using manifest-registered broadcast receivers is that the actual instance that receives the call to `onReceive()` is valid only for the duration of the `onReceive()` call. In fact, each call to `onReceive()` may be on a different instance of the broadcast receiver. This means that you should avoid making asynchronous calls to other classes, or storing class-level state that may be needed for subsequent calls to `onReceive()`.

Manual BroadcastReceiver Registration

To register a broadcast receiver outside the application manifest, an app needs to call `registerReceiver()` on a `Context` instance. This should be done in application components that have life cycle methods for both starting and stopping a component (such as services and activities) because the broadcast receiver also needs to be unregistered with a call to `unregisterReceiver()`. Failure to unregister a broadcast receiver in an activity results in an exception where Android warns about a memory leak. This is one of the differences between manifest-based registration and manual registration. When using manual registration, the app is responsible for the life cycle of the broadcast receiver, whereas in manifest-based registration, Android takes care of the life cycle.

The other, more significant difference between manifest-based registration and manual registration is that manual registration causes Android to use the same broadcast receiver instance. For manually registered broadcast receivers, this means an app can store class-level state to be used for subsequent calls to `onReceive()`.

The example app uses a manually registered broadcast receiver to update the display with new location data as it arrives. `TrackLocationActivity` is responsible for maintaining the state of the display and ensuring new locations are added to the map. Because `TrackLocationActivity` needs to be made aware of location updates, it contains an inner class broadcast receiver that will receive location updates.

Because the broadcast receiver is needed only while the activity is in the foreground, it makes sense to register a broadcast receiver in the `onResume()` method and unregister it in the `onPause()` method of the activity. Listing 3-3 shows the partial implementation of the `TrackLocationActivity` `.onPause()` and `TrackLocationActivity` `.onResume()` life cycle methods.

LISTING 3-3: Register/unregister broadcast receiver

Available for download on Wrox.com

```java
@Override
protected void onResume()
{
    super.onResume();
    registerReceiver(broadcastReceiver, new IntentFilter(ADD_LOCATION_ACTION));
    // perform additional onResume tasks
}
@Override
protected void onPause()
{
    super.onPause();
    unregisterReceiver(broadcastReceiver);
    // perform additional onPause tasks
}
```

code snippet TrackLocationActivity.java

The registering and unregistering of a broadcast receiver does not affect whether or not location updates in the form of intents are broadcast. It only affects the broadcast receiver's ability to receive those intents.

Requesting Location Updates with a PendingIntent

Once the broadcast receiver has been implemented and registered with Android, the app needs to request that an intent is broadcast when location data updates are available. Before this request is made, a `PendingIntent` needs to be created. The example app creates the pending intent in `createPendingIntent()`, as shown in Listing 3-4.

LISTING 3-4: PendingIntent creation

Available for download on Wrox.com

```java
private PendingIntent createPendingIntent()
{
    Intent intent = new Intent(ADD_LOCATION_ACTION);
    return PendingIntent.getBroadcast(getApplicationContext(),
                                      REQUEST_CODE,
                                      intent,
                                      PendingIntent.FLAG_UPDATE_CURRENT);
}
```

code snippet TrackLocationActivity.java

The parameters passed to `getBroadcast()` are the context which should perform the broadcast, a user-defined request code (which is not used), the intent to be broadcast, and a flag that controls which parts of the intent can be set when the intent is broadcast. The intent that will be broadcast is passed an action in its constructor when it is created. This string must match the action in any intent filter that is declared to receive this intent; whether it is in a manifest-registered broadcast receiver, or a manually registered broadcast receiver.

Once the pending intent is created, location updates are requested by calling `LocationManager.requestLocationUpdates()` in a similar way that was done in Chapter 2 to register a `LocationListener`. The code to register for location updates is displayed in Listing 3-5.

LISTING 3-5: Registering enabled location providers

```
Criteria criteria = new Criteria();
criteria.setAccuracy(Criteria.ACCURACY_COARSE);
for (String provider : locationManager.getProviders(criteria, true))
{
    Log.d(TAG, "Enabling provider " + provider);
    locationManager.requestLocationUpdates(provider, 0, 0, pendingIntent);
}
```

As in Chapter 2, the code uses a criteria object to specify the characteristics of the location providers to use and limits the list of possible location providers to those that are currently enabled by the user.

One Intent, Multiple Receivers

Upon close inspection of the example app, you will notice that it makes use of two broadcast receivers: one that is manifest-registered and will collect location updates in the background, and one that is manually registered/unregistered and will collect location data in the foreground in order to update the UI. Because both broadcast receivers should process incoming location data in a similar fashion, neither of the broadcast receivers extends `BroadcastReceiver` directly. Both `TrackLocationBroadcastReceiver` and `UpdateViewBroadcastReceiver` instead extend `LocationBroadcastReceiver`. `LocationBroadcastReceiver` provides code to receive the intent that was broadcast, extracts the relevant location data, and calls the correct callback methods on the two broadcast receivers (see Figure 3-2). This may seem a tad superfluous, but this allows the app to uniformly provide location filtering via `FilteringLocationBroadcastReceiver`, which is discussed later in the chapter.

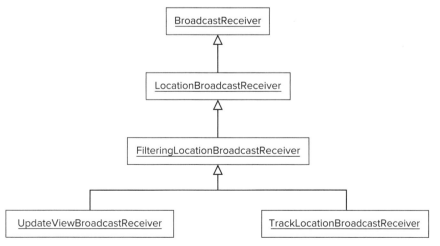

FIGURE 3-2: BroadcastReceiver class diagram

While it makes sense to use a broadcast receiver to obtain background location updates in this case, a service can also be used. The next section introduces how to implement a service to receive background location updates.

Why Not Use a Service?

Services are a commonly used application component for performing tasks in the background in Android. Allowing a service to receive location updates is as easy as implementing the `LocationListener` and registering or unregistering the service to receive location updates from the `LocationManager` in the service's `onStartCommand()` and `onDestroy()` lifecycle methods, respectively. A service that tracks location in the background would look similar to Listing 3-6.

LISTING 3-6: Skeleton service that implements LocationListener

```java
public class LocationTrackingService extends Service implements LocationListener
{
    private LocationManager locationManager;

    @Override
    public IBinder onBind(Intent intent)
    {
        // ...
    }

    @Override
    public void onLocationChanged(Location location)
    {
        // ...
    }

    @Override
    public void onProviderDisabled(String provider)
    {
        // ...
    }

    @Override
    public void onProviderEnabled(String provider)
    {
        locationManager.requestLocationUpdates(provider, 0, 0, this);
    }

    @Override
    public void onStatusChanged(String provider, int status, Bundle extras)
    {
        // ...
    }

    @Override
    public void onCreate()
    {
        super.onCreate();

        locationManager = (LocationManager) getSystemService(LOCATION_SERVICE);
```

```
    }

    @Override
    public int onStartCommand(Intent intent, int flags, int startId)
    {
        for (String provider : locationManager.getProviders(true))
        {
            locationManager.requestLocationUpdates(provider, 0, 0, this);
        }

        return super.onStartCommand(intent, flags, startId);
    }

    @Override
    public void onDestroy()
    {
        super.onDestroy();

        locationManager.removeUpdates(this);
    }
```

This is very similar to the example presented in Chapter 2 when registering an `Activity` to be notified of location updates. When an app starts the service, the service will begin receiving location data on its callback methods. When the service is destroyed, it will unregister itself from the `LocationManager` and no longer receive location updates.

If a broadcast receiver and a service can provide similar functionality for this use case, why choose one over the other? One reason to choose a broadcast receiver over a service for certain background tasks is that they can be a lighter weight application component for passively collecting location data compared to a service. A broadcast receiver that is manifest-registered does not need to exist outside of the call to `onReceive()`, and therefore, it is available for garbage collection immediately after the method returns. Additionally, because a broadcast receiver can be declared in the application manifest, a broadcast receiver can require less setup code. In the case of this app, the manifest-registered broadcast receiver is not referenced at all in the app outside of the manifest.

The major downside of using manifest-registered broadcast receivers is that they should not maintain state across invocations of `onReceive()`. Once the `onReceive()` method has returned, the actual instance is a candidate for garbage collection. This may prevent instance data from being kept for the next call to `onReceive()`. This can be a tough limitation to overcome. If an app needs to store state across multiple location updates, a service may be a better application component to use. Broadcast receivers can be more convenient for simple computation, but services are better suited to complex routines that require a lot of state.

Now that the app can receive the data, the next step is to present the location data to the user. This will be discussed in the next section.

VIEWING THE TRACKING DATA

In order to present the location data to the user, the `TrackLocationActivity` will display a Google map with the tracked points plotted on it. While the activity is in the foreground, the app will also update the screen as new points are received in order to present the user with the most up-to-date location information.

Google Map Library Components

To display the Google map with the point data, `TrackLocationActivity` uses the following classes from the Google Maps external library:

➤ `MapView`

➤ `OverlayItem`

➤ `ItemizedOverlay`

➤ `MapActivity`

To make use of the maps library, the application manifest needs to contain the following code: `<uses-library android:name="com.google.android.maps" />`. In addition to the manifest entry, the maps `.jar` file must be referenced. In Eclipse, this is done by setting the project build to a version of the Google APIs rather than a version of the standard Android platform. Figure 3-3 shows the target build selection screen in Eclipse.

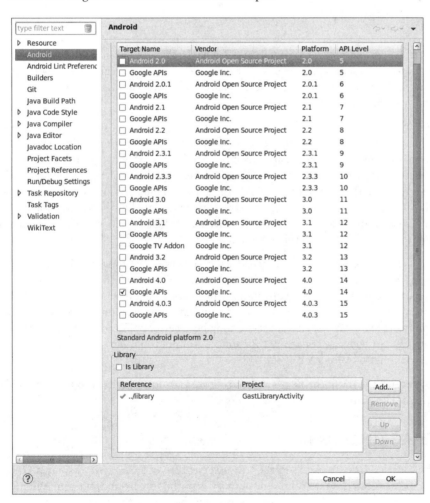

FIGURE 3-3: Selecting the Google API build target in Eclipse

MapView

The `MapView` is the view that displays the map in `TrackLocationActivity`. The layout for the activity includes a `<com.google.android.maps.MapView>` element with an `android:apiKey` attribute (see Listing 3-7). The API key attribute is necessary to use the map view. The key is generated from the certificate that is used to sign the APK for your app and can be obtained from the Google Maps external library homepage, which is located at `http://code.google.com/android/add-ons/google-apis/maps-overview.html` (see Listing 3-7).

LISTING 3-7: TrackingLocationActivity layout

```
<com.google.android.maps.MapView
        android:id="@+id/mapView"
        android:layout_width="fill_parent"
        android:layout_height="fill_parent"
        android:clickable="true"
        android:apiKey="<app_api_key>"
        android:layout_alignParentTop="true"
        android:layout_above="@id/buttonsLayout" />
```

OverlayItem

`OverlayItem` is an object that is drawn on the map. The overlay item is a container for the location data — latitude, longitude, and accuracy — that needs to be represented on the map.

The class `PointOverlayItem` extends `OverlayItem` and is used in the example app as a container for location information that is received from the Android location service. The implementation of `PointOverlayItem` is shown in Listing 3-8.

Available for download on Wrox.com

LISTING 3-8: PointOverlayItem

```
public class PointOverlayItem extends OverlayItem
{
    private float accuracy;

    public PointOverlayItem(double latitude, double longitude, float accuracy)
    {
        super(createGeoPoint(latitude, longitude),
                String.format("(%f, %f)", latitude, longitude),
                "");
        this.accuracy = accuracy;
    }

    private static GeoPoint createGeoPoint(double latitude, double longitude)
    {
        int e6Latitude = (int) (latitude * 1E6);
        int e6Longitude = (int) (longitude * 1E6);

        return new GeoPoint(e6Latitude, e6Longitude);
    }

    public float getAccuracy()
    {
```

continues

LISTING 3-8 *(continued)*

```
        return accuracy;
    }
}
```

code snippet PointOverlayItem.java

ItemizedOverlay

ItemizedOverlay holds the list of overlay items that need to be drawn on the overlay, and defines how to draw the items. Because ItemizedOverlay is abstract, the example app creates the class TrackLocationOverlay that extends ItemizedOverlay. TrackLocationOverlay maintains a list of PointOverlayItems that will be plotted in the map by the draw() method.

The draw() method defines how each overlay item will be drawn, and in this case will iterate over the list of PointOverlayItems and draw each one on the map. In addition, the method will also draw a line between each point to let the user easily determine the path that was tracked. In addition, a circle is drawn around each point, which indicates the accuracy of the location received from the location services. Listing 3-9 shows the implementation of the draw() method and the constructor that initializes the paint instances used to draw on the map.

LISTING 3-9: TrackLocationOverlay

Available for
download on
Wrox.com

```
public class TrackLocationOverlay extends ItemizedOverlay<OverlayItem>
{
    private List<PointOverlayItem> pointOverlayList =
            new ArrayList<PointOverlayItem>();
    private Paint trackingPaint;
    private Paint strokePaint;
    private Paint fillPaint;
    private MapView mapView;

    public TrackLocationOverlay(Drawable defaultMarker, MapView mapView)
    {
        super(boundCenterBottom(defaultMarker));

        trackingPaint = new Paint();
        trackingPaint.setColor(Color.RED);
        trackingPaint.setStrokeWidth(7);

        strokePaint = new Paint();
        strokePaint.setColor(Color.BLUE);
        strokePaint.setStrokeWidth(2);
        strokePaint.setStyle(Paint.Style.STROKE);

        fillPaint = new Paint();
        fillPaint.setColor(Color.BLUE);
        fillPaint.setStyle(Style.FILL);
        fillPaint.setAlpha(32);

        this.mapView = mapView;
    }

    @Override
```

```
protected OverlayItem createItem(int i)
{
    return pointOverlayList.get(i);
}

@Override
public int size()
{
    return pointOverlayList.size();
}

public void addPoint(double latitude, double longitude, float accuracy)
{
    pointOverlayList.add(new PointOverlayItem(latitude,
            longitude, accuracy));
    populate();

    mapView.invalidate();
}

@Override
public void draw(Canvas canvas, MapView mapView, boolean shadow)
{
    super.draw(canvas, mapView, shadow);

    // If list is empty, then there is nothing to draw
    if (!pointOverlayList.isEmpty())
    {
        PointOverlayItem previous = null;

        for (PointOverlayItem pointOverlayItem : pointOverlayList)
        {
            if (previous != null)
            {
                Projection projection = mapView.getProjection();

                android.graphics.Point previousPoint =
                        projection.toPixels(previous.getPoint(), null);

                android.graphics.Point currentPoint =
                        projection.toPixels(pointOverlayItem.getPoint(), null);

                canvas.drawLine(previousPoint.x,
                            previousPoint.y,
                            currentPoint.x,
                            currentPoint.y,
                            trackingPaint);
            }

            previous = pointOverlayItem;
        }

        PointOverlayItem last =
                pointOverlayList.get(pointOverlayList.size() - 1);
        android.graphics.Point lastPoint =
                mapView.getProjection().toPixels(last.getPoint(), null);
```

continues

LISTING 3-9 *(continued)*

```
        // Draw circle(s) for accuracy. The inner circle will be translucent
        // so it does not cover up the point marker.
        canvas.drawCircle(lastPoint.x,
                    lastPoint.y,
                    last.getAccuracy(),
                    strokePaint);

        canvas.drawCircle(lastPoint.x,
                    lastPoint.y,
                    last.getAccuracy(),
                    fillPaint);
    }
  }
}
```

code snippet: TrackLocationOverlay.java

MapActivity

To use the Google Maps external library, `TrackLocationActivity` will need to extend `MapActivity`. `MapActivity` adds two methods that deserve some special attention: `isRouteDisplayed()` and `isLocationDisplayed()`. These methods are used by the Google Maps library for accounting purposes and need to accurately reflect if the activity is currently displaying route and location information, respectively. The `isRouteDisplayed()` method should return a value of `true` if the `MapActivity` is being used to provide a route for directions. Because this app only displays the historical points received from the GPS, a value of `false` will be returned. Failure to accurately provide this information is against the terms of service (TOS) for the library.

The `MapView` is what displays the map and the points on the screen. `MapActivity`, and any class that extends it, will take care of the initialization and cleanup of the `MapView`.

Thus far, the book's companion app can receive and display location data. The next section discusses how and why location data needs to be filtered.

FILTERING LOCATION DATA

Often, it is necessary to filter the raw location data that is acquired from the Android location service. One of the motivations to provide location data filtering is that multiple location providers may be providing location data simultaneously. Though this does add robustness to an app, it also adds complexity in that the app must determine which location updates to accept, and which ones to ignore.

For example, if an app is receiving location updates from the GPS provider with high accuracy, and then receives a location update from the network provider with a low accuracy, the app will probably want to ignore the location update from the network provider. Alternatively, if the app has not received any location updates for a long period of time, it may want to accept a location update from any location provider with any accuracy because inaccurate data is often better than no data.

The example app provides the filtering algorithms in the `FilteringLocationBroadcastReceiver` class. This is the parent class for both location broadcast receivers that are directly used in the app, and as such provides common filtering for both receivers. This is essential for the app because the user would not want a location to be persisted to the database but not updated on the screen. This architecture allows both broadcast receivers to use the same filtering algorithm without having to directly communicate to one another.

The filtering code is located in FilteringLocationBroadcastReceiver .onLocationChanged() (see Listing 3-10) which is the callback method LocationBroadcastReceiver will call when a new location is received.

Available for download on Wrox.com

LISTING 3-10: FilteringLocationBroadcastReceiver

```java
public abstract class FilteringLocationBroadcastReceiver extends
LocationBroadcastReceiver
{
    private static final String TAG = "FilteringLocationBroadcastReceiver";
    private static final int TIME_THRESHOLD = 30000; // 30 sec.
    private static final int ACCURACY_PERCENT = 10;
    private static final int VELOCITY_THRESHOLD = 200; // m/s

    @Override
    public void onLocationChanged(Context context, Location location)
    {
        Point lastPoint =
                PointDatabaseManager.getInstance(context).retrieveLatestPoint();
        if (lastPoint == null)
        {
            Log.d(TAG, "Adding point");
            onFilteredLocationChanged(context, location);
        }
        else
        {
            float currentAccuracy = location.getAccuracy();
            float previousAccuracy = lastPoint.getAccuracy();

            Point point =
                    PointDatabaseManager.getInstance(context).retrieveLatestPoint();

            // True IFF accuracy is greater, but limited to 10% of the previous
            // accuracy and new point was generated by the same provider
            float accuracyDifference = Math.abs(previousAccuracy - currentAccuracy);
            boolean lowerAccuracyAcceptable = currentAccuracy > previousAccuracy
                    && lastPoint.getProvider().equals(location.getProvider())
                    && (accuracyDifference <= previousAccuracy / ACCURACY_PERCENT);

            float[] results = new float[1];

            Location.distanceBetween(point.getLatitude(),
                                    point.getLongitude(),
                                    location.getLatitude(),
                                    location.getLongitude(),
                                    results);

            float velocity =
                    results[0] / ((location.getTime() - point.getTime()) / 1000);

            // Accept the new point if:
```

continues

LISTING 3-10 *(continued)*

```
                    // * The velocity seems reasonable (point did not jump)and one of the
                    //   following:
                    //   * It has a better accuracy
                    //   * The app has not accepted a point in TIME_THRESHOLD
                    //   * It's worse accuracy is still acceptable
                    if (velocity <= VELOCITY_THRESHOLD
                            && (currentAccuracy < previousAccuracy
                                || (location.getTime() - lastPoint.getTime()) > TIME_THRESHOLD
                                || lowerAccuracyAcceptable))
                    {
                        Log.d(TAG, "Adding point");
                        onFilteredLocationChanged(context, location);
                    }
                    else
                    {
                        Log.d(TAG, "Ignoring point");
                    }
                }
            }

        protected abstract void onFilteredLocationChanged(Context context,
                Location location);
    }
```

code snippet: FilterintLocationBroadcastReceiver.java

Listing 3-10 provides the code that does the location filtering for the app. It compares the recently received location update with the last persisted location update, which needs to be retrieved from the internal app database because the manifest-registered broadcast receiver will not be able to store any instance state across a call to onLocationChanged(). A new location will be persisted only if:

➤ No other points have been persisted yet.

➤ The accuracy of the new point is better than the accuracy of the previous point.

➤ No point has been received in a defined time threshold (30 seconds in this example).

➤ The accuracy is slightly worse than the accuracy of the previous point, and the new point came from the same provider.

The justification for the first two bullet points is fairly obvious. These are the scenarios in which the app is receiving its first location and the app has received more accurate location data, respectively.

The third bullet point is the scenario in which the device may have been using location updates from the GPS provider and suddenly loses the ability to receive further updates. Because the app is receiving location updates from all enabled location providers, it should use less accurate data when more accurate data is not available.

The fourth bullet point handles the case where a given location provider continues to provide location updates. Location accuracy can fluctuate and the app should not ignore updates with less accuracy as long as the accuracy is bounded.

The other filter being applied in `FilteringLocationBroadcastReceiver` is a velocity filter. This filter will ignore location updates where the location seems to "jump" to a location in a very short amount of time by calculating the velocity and comparing that value to a threshold.

The velocity is determined by calculating the distance between the most recent persisted point and the current location, and the difference in time between the most recent persisted point and the current location. The distance between the two points is retrieved with a call to `Location.distanceBetween()`. This method takes the latitude and longitude coordinates of the two points and an array of floats, which will hold the results of the calculation. The result array must have a size of at least 1 and will return approximate distance in meters on the zero-ith position in the array. Distance calculations are defined using the WGS84 ellipsoid.

For the example app, the velocity threshold is set to 200 m/s and the time threshold is set to 30 seconds, meaning that any location that would have required a velocity greater than 200 m/sec to reach it will be ignored.

At this point, the example app for this chapter is fully functional. However, a discussion on how continuous location tracking affects battery is in order because the battery life is adversely affected by continuously keeping device hardware active.

CONTINUOUS LOCATION TRACKING AND BATTERY LIFE

Continuously tracking a device's location can have huge implications on battery life. This is mainly due to enabling hardware components like the GPS radio and the Wi-Fi radio. Chapter 2 briefly discussed location and battery life, but really downplayed the issues because the app collected only a single point. Because the example app in this chapter is collecting multiple points at the user's discretion, the issue of battery life can no longer be ignored.

Reducing Location Update Frequency

One of the simplest ways to reduce battery consumption while receiving location data is to reduce the frequency at which location updates need to be acquired from the location services. You do this by configuring the parameters passed to `LocationManager.requestLocationUpdates()`. Recall that when the user presses the Start Tracking button, the click handler made the following call to the `LocationManager`:

```
locationManager.requestLocationUpdates(provider, 0, 0, pendingIntent);.
```

The second and third parameters define minimum time and minimum distance at which location updates should be received. By passing zeros for parameters, the location service will provide location updates as frequently as possible. Although this approach might yield the most complete data set, it is also the least efficient from the perspective of battery life. Specifying values greater than zero may prevent the radios for the location providers from constantly remaining on, which can preserve battery life. Though some apps may absolutely require location updates as often as they can be provided, this is not always the case. Limiting the time between updates and allowing the radios to rest is a simple way to improve battery consumption of an app.

The minimum time and minimum distance values don't have to be applied to each location provider uniformly because the `requestLocationUpdates()` method allows the minimum time and minimum distance to be specified per location provider.

Limiting Location Providers

Another way to improve battery life is to limit the location providers that are used to acquire location updates. Although the user may have every location provider enabled, an app does not need to request updates from all of them. There may be times when an app can perform its desired task using low-power location providers and work around the reduced accuracy.

Remember from Chapter 2 that parameters to select location providers can be set in the `Criteria` class. `Criteria.setPowerRequirement()` will define which location providers may be used by passing `POWER_LOW`, `POWER_MEDIUM`, or `POWER_HIGH`.

SUMMARY

This chapter described a more complex use case for using location data and provided a runnable solution that demonstrates how Android can be used to track location data. Through the use of broadcast receivers and the Google Maps external library, the example app is able to both record and present location information to the user. This chapter also presented some solutions to common problems that can arise when tracking location data, such as dealing with erroneous location points and loss of connectivity with a location provider.

Proximity Alerts

WHAT'S IN THIS CHAPTER?

➤ Using the geocoding API to convert a location to latitude and longitude points

➤ Using Android proximity alerts

➤ Understanding the limitations of the proximity alert API

➤ Achieving better battery life with an alternative proximity alert implementation

Previous chapters discussed the basics of the Android location service: how to get a device's current location and how to track a device as it moves. This chapter discusses the proximity alert functionality of the location service. Proximity alerts present a slightly different paradigm in that they allow an app to be notified when a device enters or leaves a defined area as opposed to notifying an app when new location data is available. In addition to showcasing the proximity alert functionality, this chapter also presents some of the limitations associated with proximity alerts.

To demonstrate the Android proximity alert functionality, this chapter provides an app that allows a user to set a proximity alert for a target area. Once the device enters or leaves the target area, the app displays a notification to alert the user that the device has either entered or left the target area.

APP STRUCTURE

The example app must perform three main tasks to achieve the overall goal of notifying the user when the device enters or leaves a user-defined area. These tasks are:

➤ To allow the user to define the target location in terms that can be used by the LocationManager to set a proximity alert

➤ To make a call to the LocationManager to set the proximity alert

➤　To respond to the proximity alert in order to set the `Notification`

To accomplish the first task of allowing the user to define the target area for a proximity alert, the app must translate a location entered by the user into a form that can be used by the `LocationManager`. The complexity here is that the `LocationManager` needs latitude and longitude coordinates to set a proximity alert, whereas humans tend to refer to locations by name. To help bridge this gap, Android supports geocoding.

Geocoding

Geocoding is the act of converting a location name to its latitude and longitude coordinates. Android provides the ability to geocode and reverse geocode (convert from latitude and longitude coordinates to location information) natively without the need for a third-party library. To set a proximity alert for a location on the user's behalf, the app will allow the user to search for a location and then geocode that location to obtain the latitude and longitude coordinates for the proximity alert.

The example app contains the activity `GeocodeActivity` that is responsible for both collecting target location information from the user and geocoding the location for use by the `LocationManager`. Figure 4-1 depicts the `GeocodeActivity` class's layout used to collect the user's input.

The UI for `GeocodeActivity` allows the user to enter free-form text and perform a location query by pressing the Lookup Location button. The user will then be presented with a list of possible matches based on the user's entry. From here, the user will be able to select a target location for the proximity alert. Figure 4-1 shows the app running `GeocodeActivity` just after the user has entered a location string and pressed the Lookup Location button. Notice that the user does not need to be very specific when entering a location. In this case, the user has simply entered Springfield and the app has presented a list of Springfield locations as candidate target locations for the proximity alert. This list of possible location matches is generated by passing the location string provided by the user to the `Geocoder` class.

FIGURE 4-1: The GeocodeActivity screen

android.location.Geocoder

The `Geocoder` class is responsible for both geocoding and reverse geocoding in Android. In the example app, a call to `Geocoder` is made when the user clicks the Lookup Location button. The manifest for `GeocodeActivity` specifies that the method `onLookupLocationClick()` will be run when the button is clicked. The implementation for `onLookupLocationClick()` is shown in Listing 4-1.

Available for
download on
Wrox.com

LISTING 4-1: Use of Geocoder

```java
private static final int MAX_ADDRESSES = 30;
public void onLookupLocationClick(View view)
{
    if (Geocoder.isPresent())
    {
        EditText location =
                (EditText) findViewById(R.id.enterLocationValue);

        try
        {
            Geocoder geocoder = new Geocoder(this);
            List<Address> addressList =
                    geocoder.getFromLocationName(location.getText().toString(),
                            MAX_ADDRESSES);

            List<AddressWrapper> addressWrapperList =
                    new ArrayList<AddressWrapper>();

            for (Address address : addressList)
            {
                addressWrapperList.add(new AddressWrapper(address));
            }

            ArrayAdapter<AddressWrapper> arrayAdapter =
                    new ArrayAdapter<AddressWrapper>(this,
                            android.R.layout.simple_list_item_single_choice,
                            addressWrapperList);
            setListAdapter(arrayAdapter);
        }
        catch (IOException e)
        {
            Log.e(TAG, "Could not geocode address", e);

            new AlertDialog.Builder(this)
                .setMessage(R.string.geocodeErrorMessage)
                .setTitle(R.string.geocodeErrorTitle)
                .setPositiveButton(android.R.string.ok,
                        new DialogInterface.OnClickListener()
                {
                    @Override
                    public void onClick(DialogInterface dialog, int which)
                    {
                        dialog.dismiss();
                    }
                }).show();
        }
    }
}
```

code snippet GeocodeActivity.java

The method starts with a call to `Geocoder.isPresent()` to ensure that the methods needed to perform geocoding and reverse geocoding (`Geocoder.getFromLocationName()` and `Geocoder.getFromLocation()`) have concrete implementations in the version of Android that the device is running. The `isPresent()` method is available only in API level 9 and greater. One thing to note is that even when `Geocoder.isPresent()` returns `true`, the methods that perform the geocoding may still return empty lists. Though the `Geocoder.isPresent()` method provides some guidance as to whether geocoding can be performed, it does not offer any guarantees.

After checking the return value from `Geocoder.isPresent()`, the location string that the user has entered is read from the `EditText` view and passed to `Geocoder.getLocationFromName()` along with the maximum number of locations to return (`MAX_ADDRESSES`). The example app limits the `Geocoder.getLocationFromName()` to 30 addresses. This value should ensure that location that the user wants is included in the return value.

The string parameter that is passed to `Geocoder.getLocationFromName()` does not need to be a proper address in order to perform geocoding. As shown in Figure 4-1, the user can enter a loosely defined location such as the name of a city. In this case, `Geocoder.fromLocationName()` will return a list of possible matches. Naturally, the more specific the location string is, the fewer number of locations will be returned. For example, a regular street address complete with street number, street name, city, state, and country will produce a small number of matches (most likely one). On the other hand, a simple city name will produce a larger number of matches because multiple cities can exist with the same name.

The `Geocoder.fromLocationName()` method is pretty flexible when it comes to the query strings that it can resolve. In addition to locations, it can also resolve the coordinates of landmarks as shown in Figure 4-2.

`Geocoder.fromLocationName()` relies on a network lookup to resolve a location's coordinates for a query string. If the network lookup fails due to connectivity problems, an `IOException` will be thrown by `Geocode.fromLocationName()`. In the example app, An `AlertDialog` is then displayed to inform the user of the problem and suggest they resubmit the query. Displaying the `AlertDialog` will provide some insight for how often the call fails.

FIGURE 4-2: Geocoding the Statue of Liberty

Reading the Geocoded Response

The output of `Geocoder.fromLocationName()` is a list of `Address` objects that represent the possible locations for the string that was passed as a parameter. The `Address` class contains several pieces of information about a location including the locale-specific address representation and latitude and longitude coordinates for the location. The data contained in the `Address` is based on the xAL (eXtensible Address Language) specification (`http://www.oasis-open.org/committees/ciq/ciq.html#6`) for representing addresses.

Because the `Address` class, and the xAL spec, are meant to support addresses in multiple locales (which have different formats), there is a fair amount of member data in the `Address` class. For the example app, only the latitude and longitude coordinates and enough address information to construct a meaningful string to display to the user are needed.

The example app requires the textual address information (street number, state, and city) for the purpose of displaying a meaningful location address to the user. The simplest way to access the textual address information is through the address line list member of the `Address` class. The address line list contains the lines of the address that are suitable to be displayed for any locale. The xAL documentation states that the address list is a free-form list of text-based address lines that maintain order. This allows an app to simply iterate through the address line list and append each line in order to produce a string suitable to display to a user in any locale. Figures 4-3 and 4-4 show examples from locations that were geocoded in different locales. Pay attention to how the different addresses are represented in different areas of the world.

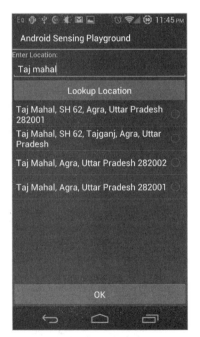

FIGURE 4-3: Geocoding the Taj Mahal

FIGURE 4-4: Geocoding Big Ben

Because the `Address` list that is returned is displayed in a `ListView`, the `GeocodeActivity` contains an inner class that wraps each returned `Address` object. This is necessary because the default `toString()` method provided by `Address` returns a full string representation of the object.

Although this is useful to developers in debugging, this is not acceptable data to display to a user. In the example app, the address lines need to be appended together in order to produce a string that is suitable to show the user. Thus, the `AddressWrapper.toString()` method has the following implementation:

```
@Override
public String toString()
{
    StringBuilder stringBuilder = new StringBuilder();
    for (int i = 0; i < address.getMaxAddressLineIndex(); i++)
    {
        stringBuilder.append(address.getAddressLine(i));

        if ((i + 1) < address.getMaxAddressLineIndex())
        {
            stringBuilder.append(", ");
        }
    }

    return stringBuilder.toString();
}
```

Now that the app has an `Address` instance, which also contains latitude and longitude for the location, it can set a proximity alert to notify the user when the device is close to the target location.

Setting a Proximity Alert

Like many other operations that use location data in Android, an app sets a proximity alert through the `LocationManager`. Obtaining a reference to the `LocationManager` has been discussed in previous chapters, so the details are left out of this chapter.

In the example app, the proximity alert is set in the `ProximityAlertActivity` class. The `ProximityAlertActivity` launches the `GeocodeActivity` in order to generate the latitude and longitude coordinates for a location. These latitude and longitude coordinates are returned to the `ProximityAlertActivity` through an `Intent` so the proximity alert can be set. Figure 4-5 shows the screen for `ProximityAlertActivity`.

Figure 4-5 depicts the `ProximityAlertActivity` after it has received the geocoded location information from `GeocodeActivity`. From here, `ProximityAlertActivity` is ready to set a proximity alert once the user presses the Set Proximity Alert button. The code then handles the button click and sets the proximity alert as displayed in Listing 4-2.

FIGURE 4-5: The ProximityAlertActivity screen

Available for
download on
Wrox.com

LISTING 4-2: Adding a proximity alert

```java
public void onSetProximityAlertClick(View view)
{
    EditText radiusView = (EditText)findViewById(R.id.radiusValue);
    int radius =
            Integer.parseInt(radiusView.getText().toString());

    if (androidProximityTypeRadioButton.isChecked())
    {
        locationManager.addProximityAlert(latitude,
                                          longitude,
                                          radius,
                                          -1,
                                          pendingIntent);
    }
    else
    {
        Criteria criteria = new Criteria();
        criteria.setAccuracy(Criteria.ACCURACY_COARSE);
        Intent intent = new Intent(this, ProximityAlertService.class);
        intent.putExtra(ProximityAlertService.LATITUDE_INTENT_KEY, latitude);
        intent.putExtra(ProximityAlertService.LONGITUDE_INTENT_KEY, longitude);
        intent.putExtra(ProximityAlertService.RADIUS_INTENT_KEY, (float)radius);
        startService(intent);
    }

    setProximityAlert.setEnabled(false);
    clearProximityAlert.setEnabled(true);
}
```

code snippet ProximityAlertActivity.java

The `else` clause in Listing 4-2 is used to set up the custom proximity alert service, which is discussed later in this chapter.

Before a proximity alert can be set, `onSetProximityAlertClick()` first must read the radius value that was entered by the user. This is necessary because to define a target region for a proximity alert, the `LocationManager` needs the latitude and longitude coordinates for a location and a value to define a radius (in meters) around that location. Once the radius is read, a call to `LocationManager.addProximityAlert()` is made. The parameters that are passed to `LocationManager.addProximityAlert()` are listed in Table 4-1.

The code in Listing 4-2 sets a proximity alert that never expires for the location and radius that have been specified by the user.

To turn off the proximity alert, the app provides a Clear Proximity Alert button. This is necessary since the proximity alert that is created has no expiration. `ProximityAlertActivity` `.onClearProximityAlertClick()` is the handler for the click event of the button. The method clears the proximity alert with a call to `LocationManager.removeProximityAlert()`. The implementation of the method is shown in Listing 4-3.

TABLE 4-1: LocationManager.addProximityAlert() Parameters

TYPE	NAME	EXPLANATION
double	latitude	Latitude coordinate.
double	longitude	Longitude coordinate.
float	radius	The radius (in meters) around the location that should trigger a proximity alert.
long	expiration	The time limit for the expiration. After the given amount of time, the proximity alert will no longer be triggered. A value of –1 indicates that the proximity alert has no expiration.
PendingIntent	intent	The intent to broadcast when the proximity alert is triggered.

LISTING 4-3: Clearing a proximity alert

```
public void onClearProximityAlertClick(View view)
{
    if (androidProximityTypeRadioButton.isChecked())
    {
        locationManager.removeProximityAlert(pendingIntent);
    }

    setProximityAlert.setEnabled(true);
    clearProximityAlert.setEnabled(false);
}
```

One thing to note in Listing 4-3 is the pendingIntent that is passed to removeProximityAlert(). That is the same intent that was used to create the proximity alert. Because the intent needs to be used in multiple areas through the class, it is created in the onCreate() method and stored in a member variable. Listing 4-4 shows the implementation of the onCreate() method and the creation of the PendingIntent that is used to both set and clear the proximity alert.

LISTING 4-4: onCreate() that creates and sets the PendingIntent used by the proximity alert

```
@Override
protected void onCreate(Bundle savedInstanceState)
{
    super.onCreate(savedInstanceState);
    setContentView(R.layout.proximity_alert);

    locationManager = (LocationManager) getSystemService(LOCATION_SERVICE);

    pendingIntent = ProximityPendingIntentFactory.createPendingIntent(this);
```

```
        preferences = getPreferences(MODE_PRIVATE);
        androidProximityTypeRadioButton =
                (RadioButton)findViewById(R.id.androidProximityAlert);

        setProximityAlert = (Button) findViewById(R.id.setProximityAlert);
        clearProximityAlert = (Button) findViewById(R.id.clearProximityAlert);
    }
```

The app has now successfully added a proximity alert and will be notified when the device is within the radius of the specified location. To receive the registered intent that will be broadcast, the app needs to have a BroadcastReceiver.

Responding to a Proximity Alert

Once set, a proximity alert broadcasts an intent when it detects that a device has either entered the region defined by the location coordinates and the radius, or left that region. This means that to process a proximity alert, the example app will need a broadcastreceiver that is configured to receive the intent that was passed to LocationManager.addProximityAlert(). The broadcastreceiver that is used in the example app extends the LocationBroadcastReceiver that was used in previous chapters. Once again, the LocationBroadcastReceiver saves this app some trouble by determining the why the intent was broadcast and which handler method should be invoked. Listing 4-5 shows the implementation of the LocationBroadcastReceiver.onReceive() method and highlights the code that is responsible for processing an Intent sent on behalf of a proximity alert.

Available for
download on
Wrox.com

LISTING 4-5: LocationBroadcastReceiver.onReceive()

```
@Override
public void onReceive(Context context, Intent intent)
{
    Log.d(TAG, "Received Intent");

    if (intent.hasExtra(LocationManager.KEY_LOCATION_CHANGED))
    {
        Log.d(TAG, "Received KEY_LOCATION_CHANGED");

        Location location =
                (Location) intent.
                getExtras().
                get(LocationManager.KEY_LOCATION_CHANGED);

        onLocationChanged(context, location);
    }
    else if (intent.hasExtra(LocationManager.KEY_PROVIDER_ENABLED))
    {
        Log.d(TAG, "Received KEY_PROVIDER_ENABLED");

        if (intent.
                getExtras().
                getBoolean(LocationManager.KEY_PROVIDER_ENABLED))
        {
            onProviderEnabled(null);
```

continues

LISTING 4-5 *(continued)*

```
        }
        else
        {
            onProviderDisabled(null);
        }
    }
    else if (intent.hasExtra(LocationManager.KEY_PROXIMITY_ENTERING))
    {
        Log.d(TAG, "Received KEY_PROXIMITY_ENTERING");

        if (intent.getBooleanExtra(LocationManager.KEY_PROXIMITY_ENTERING,
                false))
        {
            onEnteringProximity(context);
        }
        else
        {
            onExitingProximity(context);
        }
    }
}
```

code snippet LocationBroadcastReceiver.java

In Listing 4-5, the intent is checked for the LocationManager.KEY_PROXIMITY_ENTERING extra. This extra indicates why the proximity alert was fired. Proximity alerts can be fired because the device is entering the target area, or because the device is exiting the target area. The boolean value of the LocationManager.KEY_PROXIMITY_ENTERING extra indicates whether the device is entering or leaving the defined area.

The concrete implementations for onEnteringProximity() and onExitingProximity() can be found in ProximityAlertBroadcastReceiver. In both cases, the example app simply displays a notification to alert the user that the proximity alert has been received. Both methods are displayed in Listing 4-6.

LISTING 4-6: ProximityAlertBroadcastReceiver

```
public class ProximityAlertBroadcastReceiver extends LocationBroadcastReceiver
{
    private static final int NOTIFICATION_ID = 9999;

    @Override
    public void onEnteringProximity(Context context)
    {
        displayNotification(context, "Entering Proximity");
    }

    @Override
```

```
        public void onExitingProximity(Context context)
        {
            displayNotification(context, "Exiting Proximity");

        }

        private void displayNotification(Context context, String message)
        {
            String systemService = Context.NOTIFICATION_SERVICE;
            NotificationManager notificationManager =
                        (NotificationManager)context.getSystemService(systemService);

            PendingIntent pi =
                        PendingIntent.getActivity(context, 0, new Intent(), 0);

            Notification notification =
                        new Notification(R.drawable.icon,
                                message,
                                System.currentTimeMillis());

            notification.setLatestEventInfo(context, "GAST", "Proximity Alert", pi);

            notificationManager.notify(NOTIFICATION_ID, notification);
        }
    }
```

The example app will now display a notification when the device enters the defined location and when it exits the location.

PROXIMITY ALERT LIMITATIONS

So far, this chapter has presented the mechanics of implementing proximity alerts in Android. Though proximity alerts can be a useful tool in an Android developer's toolbox, it is important to understand the limitations and side effects of using them. Utilizing proximity alerts can have adverse effects on battery life as well as require additional permissions.

Battery Life

Although Android's default proximity alert implementation may be simple to use, it can also be costly in terms of battery life. Notice that neither ProximityAlertActivity nor GeocodeActivity contains a call to LocationManager.requestLocationUpdates(). Recall from previous chapters that the parameters to LocationManager.requestLocationUpdate() include values that control the frequency of location updates and desired location providers. Remember that requesting frequent location updates, especially with the GPS location provider, consumes a lot of battery power. The fact that the default proximity implementation does not require a call to LocationManager.requestLocationUpdates() means that the app does not have control over location update frequency or the location providers that will be used. Under the hood (at least at the time this book was written), Android sets up a LocationListener for each proximity alert that is set. Each proximity alert will use every location provider on a device and make a call to

`LocationManager.requestLocationUpdates()` with both the minimum distance and minimum time parameters set to a value of one. This means that a proximity alert with a long expiration will consume large amounts of battery power because the device will receive location updates frequently and continuously use the GPS location provider. Although this may be acceptable for proximity alerts with a short expiration, it can be problematic for proximity alerts with a long expiration.

Permissions

Remember from Chapter 2 that an app needs to include the `android.permission.ACCESS_FINE_LOCATION` permission in order to use the GPS provider. Because Android's proximity alert implementation uses the GPS provider, an app needs to include this permission in its manifest. Failure to do so causes a `SecurityException` to be thrown when the `LocationManager.addProximityAlert()` method is called.

Though this is not inherently a problem, it does not give the app developer much flexibility. With regards to permissions in Android, the general rule of thumb is to limit the list of required permissions as much as possible. With the default proximity alert implementation, an app is required to have the `android.permission.ACCESS_FINE_LOCATION` permission even if it needs only coarse-grained location data.

MORE EFFICIENT PROXIMITY ALERT

Because of the limitations of the default proximity alert functionality, the example app provides an alternative implementation that the user can select. The `ProximityAlertActivity` screen provides radio buttons that allows the user to toggle between the default proximity alert implementation and the custom implementation (described shortly). The idea behind the custom implementation is to reduce the number of location updates needed to determine how close a device is to a target location, as well as limit the amount of time the GPS location provider is active. By explicitly making the call to `LocationManager.requestLocationUpdates()`, the app has more control over which location providers are used as well as how often location updates should be received.

ProximityAlertService

The example app uses `ProximityAlertService` to notify the user of proximity alerts in a more efficient manner than the default Android implementation. As expected, the `ProximityAlertService` extends the `Service` class and overrides the `onCreate()` and `onStart()` methods. As shown in the following code snippet, the `onCreate()` method is pretty simple and just initializes a `LocationManager` member variable that will provide access to the location service:

```
@Override
public void onCreate()
{
    super.onCreate();
    locationManager = (LocationManager) getSystemService(LOCATION_SERVICE);
}
```

The remainder of the initialization happens when the service is stated in the `onStartCommand()` method, which is shown in Listing 4-7.

Available for
download on
Wrox.com

LISTING 4-7: ProximityAlertService.onStartCommand()

```java
public int onStartCommand(Intent intent, int flags, int startId)
{
    Location bestLocation = null;

    latitude = intent.getDoubleExtra(LATITUDE_INTENT_KEY, Double.MIN_VALUE);
    longitude = intent.getDoubleExtra(LONGITUDE_INTENT_KEY, Double.MIN_VALUE);
    radius = intent.getFloatExtra(RADIUS_INTENT_KEY, Float.MIN_VALUE);

    for (String provider : locationManager.getProviders(false))
    {
        Location location = locationManager.getLastKnownLocation(provider);

        if (bestLocation == null)
        {
            bestLocation = location;
        }
        else
        {
            long locationStaleness =
                    System.currentTimeMillis() - location.getTime();

            if (locationStaleness < AlarmManager.INTERVAL_HOUR * 3
                    && location.getAccuracy() < bestLocation.getAccuracy())
            {
                bestLocation = location;
            }
        }
    }

    if (bestLocation != null)
    {
        if (getDistance(bestLocation) <= radius)
        {
            inProximity = true;
        }
        else
        {
            inProximity = false;
        }
    }

    locationManager.requestLocationUpdates(LocationManager.NETWORK_PROVIDER,
            0,
            0,
            this);

    return START_STICKY;
}
```

code snippet ProximityAlertService.java

Once started, the service initialization reads the extras that were passed in the intent that started the service. In the intent, the caller must set the latitude, longitude, and radius for the proximity alert. These values define the proximity alert in the same way that they would for `LocationManager.addProximityAlert()`. In the example app, these extras are set in the `else` clause of `ProximityAlertActivity.onSetProximityAlertClick()`.

Once the member data is initialized, the service attempts to determine if the device is within the target area or outside the target area by calling `LocationManager.getLastLocation()` for each activated location provider. The accuracy of each provider's last location is compared. The location with the best accuracy is used to determine if the device is currently in the target area.

The `LocationManager.getLastLocation()` method should not be used blindly. Although the method is a convenient way to get location information immediately, the location information that is returned is cached. This may result in stale location data if the device has not received any location updates for a long period of time. It is possible for a user to turn off all location providers and then move several miles away before re-enabling the providers. To combat the possibility of stale data, the service checks the time on each cached location returned from `LocationManager.getLastLocation()` via the `Location.getTime()` method. If the location was received within the last three hours, it is probably safe to use it in this case.

Once the service is started, it starts receiving location updates from the network provider as often as the device can supply them. Because the service implements `LocationListener`, it needs to implement the `onLocationChanged()` method. This is where the core business logic is located. `onLocationChanged()` is displayed in Listing 4-8.

LISTING 4-8: ProximityAlertService.onLocationChanged() and ProximityAlertService.getDistance()

Available for
download on
Wrox.com

```
@Override
public void onLocationChanged(Location location)
{
    float distance = getDistance(location);

    if (distance <= radius && !inProximity)
    {
        inProximity = true;
        Log.i(TAG, "Entering Proximity");

        Intent intent =
                new Intent(ProximityPendingIntentFactory.PROXIMITY_ACTION);
        intent.putExtra(LocationManager.KEY_PROXIMITY_ENTERING, true);
        sendBroadcast(intent);
    }
    else if (distance > radius && inProximity)
    {
        inProximity = false;
        Log.i(TAG, "Exiting Proximity");

        Intent intent =
                new Intent(ProximityPendingIntentFactory.PROXIMITY_ACTION);
        intent.putExtra(LocationManager.KEY_PROXIMITY_ENTERING, true);
```

```
            sendBroadcast(intent);
        }
        else
        {
            float distanceFromRadius = Math.abs(distance - radius);

            // Calculate the distance to the edge of the user-defined radius
            // around the target location
            float locationEvaluationDistance =
                    (distanceFromRadius - location.getAccuracy()) / 2;

            locationManager.removeUpdates(this);
            float updateDistance = Math.max(1, locationEvaluationDistance);

            String provider;
            if (distanceFromRadius <= location.getAccuracy()
                    || LocationManager.GPS_PROVIDER.equals(location.getProvider()))
            {
                provider = LocationManager.GPS_PROVIDER;
            }
            else
            {
                provider = LocationManager.NETWORK_PROVIDER;
            }

            locationManager.requestLocationUpdates(provider,
                    0,
                    updateDistance,
                    this);
        }
    }

    private float getDistance(Location location)
    {
        float[] results = new float[1];

        Location.distanceBetween(latitude,
                longitude,
                location.getLatitude(),
                location.getLongitude(),
                results);

        return results[0];
    }
```

code snippet ProximityAlertService.java

The service achieves improved battery life with two optimizations over the default proximity alert implementation. First, it limits the usage of the GPS. Second, it reduces the frequency of requested location updates.

The last line in the onStartCommand() method in Listing 4-7 registers the service to receive location updates from the network provider. The goal is to use the network provider as long as possible and enable the GPS provider only when the accuracy of the network provider can no longer provide an accurate estimate of the device's distance from the target area. `onLocationChanged()` starts off by computing the distance between the newest location and the target location by making a call to `getDistance()`, which is displayed in the following code snippet:

```
private float getDistance(Location location)
{
    float[] results = new float[1];

    Location.distanceBetween(latitude,
            longitude,
            location.getLatitude(),
            location.getLongitude(),
            results);

    return results[0];
}
```

Once the distance is calculated, `onLocationChanged()` can compare the current distance with the radius that was supplied to the service to determine if an intent should be broadcast to signal a proximity alert. If no alert needs to be broadcast, the method cancels the current request for location updates, calculates a new minimum distance, and re-registers for location updates using the new minimum distance.

The minimum distance calculation is shown here:

```
float distanceFromRadius = Math.abs(distance - radius);

// Calculate the distance to the edge of the user-defined radius
// around the target location
float locationEvaluationDistance =
        (distanceFromRadius - location.getAccuracy()) / 2;
```

To make the calculation, the method first computes the distance to the radius that encloses the target area. The absolute value for this calculation is needed to support both entering and exiting the target area defined by the radius. Once the distance to the radius of the target area is made, the new minimum distance can be computed as the (`distanceFromRadius` – location accuracy) / 2. Halving the distance from the location to the radius (after subtracting out the accuracy) allows the method request more frequent location updates as the device approaches the target area. This alone should produce better battery life than the default proximity alert implementation included in Android because the location update frequency will be drastically reduced for proximity alerts that need to span large distances.

To improve battery life further, the service also limits when the GPS location provider is used. Before re-registering for location updates, the service compares the accuracy of the latest point with the distance from the radius. Only when the accuracy of the latest point is greater than the distance from the target area, is the GPS provider enabled. In other words, even though the network provider has less accuracy than the GPS provider, it is still good enough if the device is far away from the target area.

This should allow the service to enable the GPS provider only when the network provider is no longer precise enough to any additional proximity determinations. If the newest location came from the GPS provider, the GPS provider will continue to be used because the device is probably close enough to the target location to warrant its use.

SUMMARY

This chapter discussed parts of the location API that tend to get less attention than the parts discussed in previous chapters. The geocoding and proximity alert functionality can be an invaluable tool in a developer's Android toolbox.

Geocoding allows a user to communicate location information to an app in a way that is natural to a human. The ability to transform location and latitude and longitude coordinate information in both directions gives developers another way to communicate location information with a human outside of just a map.

The proximity alert API provides a quick way for Android to notify an app when the device is approaching or departing from a given location. Although it may have negative effects on battery life, the simple API allows it to be useful under the right conditions.

The alternative proximity alert implementation provided in this chapter provides a robust (and more complicated) solution that will reduce the cost of battery life for an app.

PART II
Inferring Information from Physical Sensors

5

Overview of Physical Sensors

WHAT'S IN THIS CHAPTER?

➤ Understanding the available sensors and how they actually work.

➤ Explaining the physical values the sensors measure and providing a physical intuition for what these values mean.

➤ Understanding potential applications of each sensor and code for common use cases.

Before the introduction of smartphones, people would interact with a range of narrowly focused sensors in daily life. Each sensor usually resided in a single device, and was usually designed for a single purpose (oven temperature sensors, tire pressure sensors, television remote control systems, and so on). The introduction of smartphones put an exciting range of sensors in the hands of users and developers. Previously, sensors rarely existed in such quantities, or in such close and continuous proximity to the user. The availability of the multiple sensors on a single device adds a wide array of uses for the device.

Starting with Android 1.5 (API level 3), a standard set of sensors and the associated sensor API has been made available. In Android 2.3 (API level 9), new sensors and tools were added to the Android developer's toolbox. The standard sensors now include the accelerometer, gyroscope, magnetometer (compass), light sensor, proximity sensor, relative humidity sensor and pressure sensor. The tools added in API level 9 include methods to get rotation matrices, quaternions (an alternate representation of rotations), and "synthetic" sensors. These provide developers with a rich array of options for physical navigation, gaming control, augmented reality, and many other uses.

Understanding the sensor API is useful, but not enough to develop innovative applications. To avoid pitfalls and common misconceptions, the developer must go beyond the typical "black box" approach where a sensor's data is digested by an app with little understanding of what the data represents or how it is produced. Fully understanding how the sensors work allows you to select the right sensor for an app's task, which can be difficult because there are sensors with overlapping capabilities and devices with different sensors. It also helps you to use the sensors better by allowing you to know how to interpret the sensor output properly. In addition, understanding how the sensors work allows you to identify new ways to use sensors in your app.

The goal of this chapter is to provide a deeper understanding of how Android sensors work and what type of data they produce.

 Portions of this chapter are reproduced from work created and shared by the Android Open Source Project and used according to terms described in the Creative Commons 2.5 Attribution License.

DEFINITIONS

Before getting into the discussion of sensors, some of the terms used throughout the chapter need to be introduced.

➤ *Microelectromechanical sensors (MEMS)* are sensors that have been made on a tiny scale, usually on silicon chips using techniques borrowed from computer-chip manufacturing. All Android sensors are made using these techniques, but technically, the term MEMS sensor refers to the ones that incorporate some part of their design that physically moves or vibrates: the pressure sensor, accelerometer, gyroscope, and possibly the compass are true MEMS sensors.

The sensors referenced through the `Sensor` class may be of two types: a *raw sensor* or a *synthetic* (or *composite* or *virtual*) sensor. Raw sensors give raw data from a sensor, and one raw sensor corresponds to one actual physical component inside the Android device. Synthetic sensors provide an abstraction layer between application code and low-level device components by either combining the raw data of multiple raw sensors, or by modifying the raw sensor data to make it easier to consume. They may report a physical quantity by referring to two or three sensors (such as reporting orientation by referring to the compass, which gives a north-south-east-west bearing and the accelerometer, which gives tilt). Synthetic sensors may manipulate the sensor reading before reporting it; for example, by integrating the gyroscope data before using it in addition to magnetometer and accelerometer to get a better determination of orientation. Regardless of the sensor type, the programmer accesses any type of sensor in the same way using the sensor API.

➤ Raw sensors:

➤ `Sensor.TYPE_LIGHT`

➤ `Sensor.TYPE_PROXIMITY`

➤ `Sensor.TYPE_PRESSURE`

➤ `Sensor.TYPE_TEMPERATURE` (deprecated)

➤ `Sensor.TYPE_ACCELEROMETER`

➤ `Sensor.TYPE_GYROSCOPE`

➤ `Sensor.TYPE_MAGNETIC_FIELD`

➤ Sensor.TYPE_RELATIVE_HUMIDITY

➤ Sensor.TYPE_AMBIENT_TEMPERATURE

➤ Synthetic sensors:

➤ Sensor.TYPE_ROTATION_VECTOR

➤ Sensor.TYPE_LINEAR_ACCELERATION

➤ Sensor.TYPE_GRAVITY

➤ Sensor.TYPE_ORIENTATION (deprecated)

Synthetic sensors do not necessarily have consistent implementation across different devices. For example, some devices may use the gyroscope to determine rotation vector values while others do not. Differences in hardware or sensor synthesis implementations can cause synthetic sensors on some devices to provide better readings than synthetic sensors on other devices. Although these differences exist, it is still generally preferable to utilize synthetic sensor data over raw sensor data. Sensors tend to be designed to provide good results for a device's specific sensor hardware.

However, not all synthetic sensors exist on all versions of Android. Versions of Android earlier than 2.3 do not support the Sensor.TYPE_ROTATION_VECTOR, Sensor.TYPE_LINEAR_ACCELERATION, or Sensor.TYPE_GRAVITY sensors.

➤ A *binary sensor* is a sensor that reports only one of two values. Most proximity sensors and some light sensors are binary sensors, reporting only a near and far measurement.

➤ A *continuous sensor* measures any of a range of values from its minimum to its maximum.

➤ *Dynamic range* is the range of values the sensor can measure. For instance, the dynamic range of a light sensor may be 1 to 10,000 lux.

➤ *Saturation* occurs when a sensor attempts to sense an input greater than its maximum measurable value. For example, a bright halogen light can saturate the light sensor in an Android device. In that case the sensor just reports the maximum value. When the stimulation is removed, the signal returns values close to zero (sensor noise prevents a constant value of zero).

➤ In many other situations, resolution means the smallest detectable difference between actual physical values. This detectable difference is limited by noise. However, in Android, *resolution* (as reported by Sensor.getResolution()) refers to the smallest difference between possible numbers that may be reported by the sensor, even if the noise is greater. For example, an 8-bit accelerometer with a maximum range of 39.24 m/s^2 will report a resolution of 39.24 / 2^8 = 0.15328126 m/s^2.

➤ *Sampling frequency* is the reciprocal of the time between measurements, and is measured in Hertz (which is equivalent to 1/s, where s is the unit of seconds). In Android, a sensor's highest possible sampling frequency is measured using the public method Sensor.getMinDelay() which measures the minimum time between two measurements in microseconds. The *minimum* delay is reported because the device may not necessarily take measurements as quickly as physically possible, but this minimum delay represents the maximum sampling frequency possible by the sensor. Minimum delay can also vary across different hardware sensor implementations and therefore may vary from device to device.

Now that some of the basic sensor concepts and definitions have been presented, the chapter will turn its focus to the different sensors Android supports.

ANDROID SENSOR API

The Android Sensor API consists of classes for requesting and processing sensor information from a device's hardware. This section outlines the classes within the Android Sensor API and illustrates how to use the classes by providing examples in the form of code.

The entry point to the API is the `SensorManager` class, which allows an app to request sensor information and register to receive sensor data. When registered, sensor data values are sent to a `SensorEventListener` in the form of a `SensorEvent` that contains information produced from a given `Sensor`.

SensorManager

`SensorManager` is the Android system service that gives an app access to hardware sensors. Like other system services, it allows apps to register and unregister for sensor-related events. Once registered, an app will receive sensor data from the hardware.

In addition to allowing an app to register for sensor data, the `SensorManager` also provides methods that process sensor data. `SensorManager.getOrientation()` is an example of such a method that uses sensor data to generate device orientation information.

Sensor

The `Sensor` class is the Android representation of a hardware sensor on a device. This class exposes information about the sensor, such as:

- ➤ Maximum range
- ➤ Minimum delay
- ➤ Name
- ➤ Power
- ➤ Resolution
- ➤ Type
- ➤ Vendor
- ➤ Version

`SensorManager` provides two methods to access `Sensor` objects: `getSensorList()` and `getDefaultSensor()`. The `getSensorList()` method retrieves all the sensors of a given type while `getDefaultSensor()` returns the default sensor for the specified type. The sensor returned from `getDefaultSensor()` may be either a raw sensor or a synthetic sensor that manipulates raw sensor data.

It is import for an app to examine the output from these methods because devices may or may not support a particular sensor that an app needs. The following code sample is a generally foolproof method for checking for an accelerometer with `getSensorList()`. Checks for other sensors follow a similar pattern.

```
public static boolean isAccelerometerSupported(Context context)
{
    SensorManager sm =
            (SensorManager) context
                    .getSystemService(Context.SENSOR_SERVICE);
    List<Sensor> sensors = sm.getSensorList(Sensor.TYPE_ACCELEROMETER);
    return sensors.size() > 0;
}
```

Sensor Rates

When you register a listener, you specify the delay or measurement rate for the listener. The predefined rates are:

➤ SENSOR_DELAY_FASTEST

➤ SENSOR_DELAY_GAME

➤ SENSOR_DELAY_UI (Suitable for usual user interface functions, like rotating the screen orientation.)

➤ SENSOR_DELAY_NORMAL (The default value.)

In Android 4.0.3, these are hard-coded to be 0, 20, 67, and 200 milliseconds, respectively. You can also specify your own delay in microseconds by passing a sensor rate value to the registration that is not one of the aforementioned constants. However, these rates are only intended to be hints to the system, as events may be received faster or slower than the specified delay. Events are usually received faster if the hardware and garbage collection can keep up.

Device configuration may also affect the rate at which events are fired. For example, the accelerometer on a Nexus S running Android 2.3 with a sensor rate of SENSOR_DELAY_GAME may fire rapidly when the device orientation changes rapidly and slowly when the device orientation changes slowly. However, the accelerometer on Droid 2 running the same version of Android (2.3) and using the same sensor rate (SENSOR_DELAY_GAME) produces sensor events at an approximately constant rate. In many cases, this inconsistency in firing times across different devices is actually a benefit to the developer. The timing of the sensor events is optimized for the particular device and returns sensor data as often as needed for different classes of applications (as suggested by the names of the sensor rate constants) without causing undue lag. This allows for the sensor polling procedure to be device-agnostic and future-proofed even as newer and better sensor hardware is released.

Because the data values are not necessarily evenly spaced in time, the `SensorEvent.timestamp` field is important, and allows you to access the timestamp associated with the data (which is held in the `SensorEvent.values` field) in nanoseconds.

To find the minimum delay allowed between two events in microseconds, use the `Sensor.getMinDelay()` method. This returns zero if this sensor returns a value only when the data it is measuring changes (for example, for a binary proximity sensor).

Sensor Range and Resolution

Perhaps the most useful methods of the `Sensor` class are `Sensor.getMaximumRange()` and `Sensor.getResolution()`, both of which take no arguments and return a floating-point number.

`getMaximumRange()` returns the maximum range the sensor can measure in the regular units reported by the sensor. A measured value of 19.6133 m/s^2 (equivalent to 2 g, where g is a unit of acceleration) — as in STMicroelectronics' KR3DM 3-axis accelerometer, for instance — means the sensor can measure accelerations from +2g to –2g. If a sensor is subjected to a larger signal than the maximum range reported here, it will simply saturate and report this maximum range value.

Binary sensors, such as binary proximity sensors that report only a near or far measurement, should report their maximum range value in the far state and a lesser value in the near state (this value is usually either identically 0.0 or some small number like 2E-6). While this is true is most cases, the value from `getMaximumRange()` is not always reported as the far measurement on a binary proximity sensor. For example, the OSRAM SFH7743 proximity sensor (in the Motorola Droid 2) has a maximum range of 6 cm but reports a "far" value of 2.38 x 107 cm! To catch this, generally an app may sense a near measurement as anything near zero (where near zero may be some number less than approximately 1/100th of `getMaximumRange()`) and detect a far measurement as anything equal to or greater than `getMaximumRange()`.

`getResolution()` reports the resolution of the sensor, in the regular units reported by the sensor. As described previously, resolution is a word sometimes used to describe the minimum detectable difference between two signals, which is a description that takes into account the noise in the system. However, the resolution here is a digital resolution figure that is independent of the sensor noise. Android sensors output digital signals, for example, 8-bit (256 possible values), 10-bit (1024 possible values), and 12-bit (4096 possible values) accelerometers are common. The maximum range divided by the number of possible values gives the resolution reported here.

Other methods are also available that give access to the generic type of the sensor, the sensor's name string, vendor and version, and the power it consumes when active. This data is typically less useful to developers and is not covered here.

Before moving on, it is important to understand that more data is not always better data. In general apps should collect data only as quickly as necessary, and only let it affect the display (if applicable) as often as necessary. This may sound obvious, but apps can be significantly helped or hurt by consideration of this point. Some sensors produce data faster than the GUI can display it. If an app updates the GUI on every event, the app's responsiveness will suffer and the app may crash.

For example, if an app needs to update its UI only on events received every 500 milliseconds or more (regardless of when the sensor events are actually received), it can use the following approach. Remember that an app can also specify the sensor rate as described in the "Sensor Rates" section. The number specified, however, is only a guideline to the system and an app cannot be assured of receiving events at that rate.

```
public void onSensorChanged(SensorEvent event)
   {
       if (event.sensor.getType() == Sensor.TYPE_ACCELEROMETER)
       {
           long actualTime = System.currentTimeMillis();
```

```
        if (actualTime - lastUpdate > 500)
        {
            lastUpdate = actualTime;
            // update values for app
        }
    }
}
```

SensorEventListener

The `SensorEventListener` is an interface that provides the callbacks to alert an app to sensor-related events. To be made aware of these events, an app registers a concrete class that implements `SensorEventListener` with the `SensorManager`.

SensorEvent

The `SensorEvent` is the data structure that contains the information that is passed to an app when a hardware sensor has information to report. A `SensorEvent` object is passed from the sensor system service to callback methods on `SensorEventListener`. The listener then processes the data in a `SensorEvent` object in an application-specific manner. The data members of the `SensorEvent` are described next.

➤ `SensorEvent.accuracy`: Each sensor reports its accuracy as one of four levels. In this case, *accuracy* refers to how reliable or "trustable" the reported values are, not necessarily how close each value actually is to the physical value.

  ➤ A `SensorEvent` can have the following values for `SensorEvent.accuracy`:

    ➤ `SensorManager.SENSOR_STATUS_ACCURACY_HIGH`

    ➤ `SensorManager.SENSOR_STATUS_ACCURACY_MEDIUM`

    ➤ `SensorManager.SENSOR_STATUS_ACCURACY_LOW`

    ➤ `SensorManager.SENSOR_STATUS_UNRELIABLE`

  An unreliable accuracy does not mean the sensor is broken. For example, the magnetometer reports an unreliable status if it needs calibration, and changes accuracy level relatively often.

  If the sensor is a binary sensor, and therefore cannot give an absolute measurement, it reports SensorManager.SENSOR_STATUS_UNRELIABLE. For example, the binary proximity sensor may report a near and far measurement of approximately 0.0 cm and 5.0 cm respectively, but these probably don't correspond to reality because the nearest object may be any distance away and not just those two values. Instead, a near or far measurement simply signifies that a proximity threshold has been reached. Thus a binary sensor always reports an unreliable accuracy.

➤ `SensorEvent.sensor`: An instance of the `Sensor` class that generated the `SensorEvent`.

➤ `SensorEvent.timestamp`: The time in milliseconds when the `SensorEvent` occurred.

➤ `SensorEvent.values`: An array of values that represent sensor data. The size of the array and the meaning of the array values depend on the type of the sensor that produced the data.

Sensor List

To utilize the Sensor API described in previous sections, an app needs to register a `SensorEventListener` to receive sensor data, extract data from `SensorEvent` depending on the sensor type, and ensure that an app unregisters at the right time. Each type of sensor requires similar code. This section describes the boilerplate code you need by explaining an app called Sensor List. Sensor List collects and displays the data it gets from all available sensors. Beyond highlighting how to operate the sensor API, it is also an excellent way to explore the data the sensors produce and the effect of different delay rates.

`SensorListActivity` uses two screens to interact with the user and the screens are illustrated below. The screen illustrated in Figure 5-2 presents the user with the list of sensors that are on the device. Once a sensor is clicked, the screen illustrated in Figure 5-3 displays the details for the selected sensor.

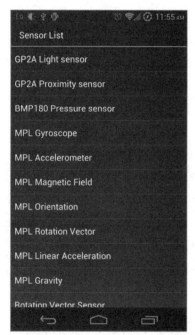

FIGURE 5-1: Showing the list of sensors on a device

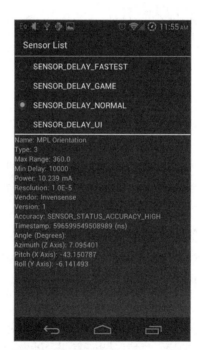

FIGURE 5-2: Screenshot showing the details of a selected sensor

The Manifest File

The first step in implementing the example app is to declare the intent to use specific sensors in the manifest file. This is done with the `<uses-feature>` declaration, and may include an optional `android:required` attribute indicating whether the app prefers to have the feature or whether it cannot function without a feature. The purpose of this declaration is to inform any external entity of the sensors an app will use. This is informational only: the OS will not check for features before installing an app, but other services such as Google Play will check an application's `<uses-feature>` declaration, so it is best to declare all the sensors an app will use. (Google Play will not show apps that are not compatible with a user's device). Each sensor must be specified in a separate tag. A snippet of the `AndroidManifest.xml` for the example app is shown here:

```
<uses-feature android:name="android.hardware.sensor.accelerometer"
        android:required="true" />
    <uses-feature android:name="android.hardware.sensor.compass"
        android:required="false" />
```

The default for the `android:required` attribute is `true`, meaning the app cannot run without it. A value of `false` means that an app prefers to use the feature if available but is designed to run without it.

Here are some of the possible arguments for the `android:name` attribute that apply to Android sensors:

➤ `android.hardware.sensor.accelerometer`

➤ `android.hardware.sensor.barometer`

➤ `android.hardware.sensor.compass`

➤ `android.hardware.sensor.gyroscope`

➤ `android.hardware.sensor.light`

➤ `android.hardware.sensor.proximity`

If an app requires the synthetic sensors `GRAVITY` or `LINEAR_ACCELERATION`, the app should also make `android.hardware.sensor.accelerometer` required. If an app requires the synthetic sensor `ROTATION_VECTOR`, it should also make the accelerometer and compass required and the gyroscope optional, because the gyroscope is sometimes but not always used to calculate this. (The gyro should be used if available, but its presence alone does not require it to be implemented in the rotation vector sensor.)

SensorListActivity

`SensorListActivity` lets the user choose a sensor to inspect and then shows the data it produces interactively. To implement this, `SensorListActivity` uses two `Fragment`s. It uses `SensorSelectorFragment` to allow the user to select a sensor from a list, and `SensorDisplayFragment` to show the data values from a selected sensor.

The `SensorListActivity` class has a short implementation. The code creates the `Fragment`s and then wires them together so that when the user selects a sensor, `SensorSelectorFragment` can show `SensorDisplayFragment`. Listing 5-1 shows the code for `SensorListActivity`.

Available for
download on
Wrox.com

LISTING 5-1: Sets up Fragments for selecting sensors and viewing their data

```
public class SensorListActivity extends FragmentActivity
{
    @Override
    protected void onCreate(Bundle savedInstanceState)
    {
        super.onCreate(savedInstanceState);
```

continues

LISTING 5-1 *(continued)*

```
        setContentView(R.layout.sensor_main);

        // wire up the fragments so selector
        // can call display
        SensorDisplayFragment sensorDisplay =
                (SensorDisplayFragment) getSupportFragmentManager()
                        .findFragmentById(R.id.frag_sensor_view);
        SensorSelectorFragment sensorSelect =
                (SensorSelectorFragment) getSupportFragmentManager()
                        .findFragmentById(R.id.frag_sensor_select);
        sensorSelect.setSensorDisplay(sensorDisplay);
    }
}
```

code snippet SensorListActivity.java

SensorSelectorFragment

When it starts, `SensorSelectorFragment` displays a list of sensors to the user. To build this list, it obtains all the available sensors from `SensorManager` during the `setSensorDisplay()` method. `setSensorDisplay()` also creates a `SensorListAdapter` to display the sensor's name and register an `OnClickListener`. When the user clicks, the `OnClickListener` calls `showSensorFragment()` to properly show `SensorDisplayFragment`. The implementation for `SensorSelectorFragment` is shown in listing 5-2.

Available for
download on
Wrox.com

LISTING 5-2: Allows the user to select a sensor to inspect

```
public class SensorSelectorFragment extends ListFragment
{
    private static final String TAG = "SensorSelectorFragment";

    private SensorDisplayFragment sensorDisplay;

    /**
     * connect with a display fragment to call later when user clicks a sensor
     * name, also setup the ListAdapter to show all the Sensors
     */
    public void setSensorDisplay(SensorDisplayFragment sensorDisplay)
    {
        this.sensorDisplay = sensorDisplay;

        SensorManager sensorManager =
                (SensorManager) getActivity().getSystemService(
                        Activity.SENSOR_SERVICE);
        List<Sensor> sensors = sensorManager.getSensorList(Sensor.TYPE_ALL);
        this.setListAdapter(new SensorListAdapter(getActivity()
                .getApplicationContext(), android.R.layout.simple_list_item_1,
                sensors));
    }
```

```java
/**
 * hide the list of sensors and show the sensor display fragment
 * add these changes to the backstack
 */
private void showSensorFragment(Sensor sensor)
{
    sensorDisplay.displaySensor(sensor);
    FragmentTransaction ft =
            getActivity().getSupportFragmentManager().beginTransaction();
    ft.hide(this);
    ft.show(sensorDisplay);
    ft.addToBackStack("Showing sensor: " + sensor.getName());
    ft.commit();
}

/**
 * list view adapter to show sensor names and respond to clicks.
 */
private class SensorListAdapter extends ArrayAdapter<Sensor>
{
    public SensorListAdapter(Context context, int textViewResourceId,
            List<Sensor> sensors)
    {
        super(context, textViewResourceId, sensors);
    }

    /**
     * create a text view containing the sensor name
     */
    @Override
    public View getView(final int position, View convertView,
            ViewGroup parent)
    {
        final Sensor selectedSensor = getItem(position);
        if (convertView == null)
        {
            convertView =
                    LayoutInflater.from(getContext()).inflate(
                            android.R.layout.simple_list_item_1, null);
        }

        ((TextView) convertView).setText(selectedSensor.getName());

        convertView.setOnClickListener(new View.OnClickListener()
        {
            @Override
            public void onClick(View v)
            {
                if (BuildConfig.DEBUG)
                {
                    Log.d(TAG,
                            "display sensor! " + selectedSensor.getName());
                }
```

continues

LISTING 5-2 *(continued)*

```
                        showSensorFragment(selectedSensor);
                }
        });
        return convertView;
    }
  }
}
```

code snippet SensorSelectFragment.java

SensorDisplayFragment

SensorDisplayFragment receives the selected sensor, starts listening for data, and displays the data it receives. The onCreateView() method does most of the initialization work, such as getting a reference to the SensorManager. Once onCreateView() is complete, SensorDisplayFragment is ready for SensorSelectorFragment to call displaySensor() with the user's selected sensor.

To receive sensor data, SensorDisplayFragment registers a SensorEventListener with the SensorManager. Because SensorDisplayFragment implements SensorEventListener, it can register itself to receive sensor events. In order to implement SensorEventListener, SensorDisplayFragment provides concrete implementations for onAccuracyChanged(), and onSensorChanged(). Both methods update the display whenever a sensor reports new data or its accuracy changes.

Because SensorDisplayFragment should receive updates only while it is being displayed, it registers itself with the SensorManager in displaySensor() and unregisters itself when it is not being displayed. SensorDisplayFragment will no longer be displayed when SensorSelectorFragment hides it, or when Android pauses SensorListActivity. Because hiding the fragment does not trigger a call to onPause(), the call to SensorManager.unregisterListener() must occur in both the onPause() (to handle any pauses, such as when the user presses the Home button) and onHiddenChanged() (to handle being hidden). Some apps may need to restart listening for sensors when part of it returns from being hidden or paused. To do so, an app may want to restart the sensing by re-registering the SensorEventListener in the onResume() method and possibly onHiddenChanged().

It is important to remember to unregister sensor listeners whenever they are not in use. Not doing so drains the battery and uses system resources including the garbage collector. Android does not take care of this by itself when another Activity comes to the foreground or when the screen is turned off — it is in the hands of the app developer to control listeners wisely. If Android kills the app, however, it also unregisters listeners.

After registering, SensorManager passes data periodically to the onSensorChanged() method in the form of a SensorEvent. The onSensorChanged() method implementation in SensorDisplayFragment updates the display with the data in SensorEvent. Since the *SensorEvent.values* array holds different data based on the sensor that produced it, onSensorEvent()

must first determine which sensor was the source of this data. Once it determines the source, it shows the sensor data by setting the values and labels of the appropriate TextViews.

Listing 5-3 shows the complete implementation for SensorDisplayFragment.

Available for download on Wrox.com

LISTING 5-3: Collects and displays data for a particular Sensor.

```java
public class SensorDisplayFragment extends Fragment implements SensorEventListener
{
    private static final String TAG = "SensorDisplayFragment";
    private static final String THETA = "\u0398";
    private static final String ACCELERATION_UNITS = "m/s\u00B2";

    private SensorManager sensorManager;
    private Sensor sensor;
    private TextView name;
    private TextView type;
    private TextView maxRange;
    private TextView minDelay;
    private TextView power;
    private TextView resolution;
    private TextView vendor;
    private TextView version;
    private TextView accuracy;
    private TextView timestampLabel;
    private TextView timestamp;
    private TextView timestampUnits;
    private TextView dataLabel;
    private TextView dataUnits;
    private TextView xAxis;
    private TextView xAxisLabel;
    private TextView yAxis;
    private TextView yAxisLabel;
    private TextView zAxis;
    private TextView zAxisLabel;
    private TextView singleValue;
    private TextView cosLabel;
    private TextView cos;

    @Override
    public View onCreateView(LayoutInflater inflater, ViewGroup container,
            Bundle savedInstanceState)
    {
        View layout = inflater.inflate(R.layout.sensor_view, null);

        sensorManager =
                (SensorManager) getActivity().getSystemService(Context.SENSOR_SERVICE);

        name = (TextView) layout.findViewById(R.id.name);
        type = (TextView) layout.findViewById(R.id.type);
        maxRange = (TextView) layout.findViewById(R.id.maxRange);
        minDelay = (TextView) layout.findViewById(R.id.minDelay);
        power = (TextView) layout.findViewById(R.id.power);
```

continues

LISTING 5-3 *(continued)*

```java
resolution = (TextView) layout.findViewById(R.id.resolution);
vendor = (TextView) layout.findViewById(R.id.vendor);
version = (TextView) layout.findViewById(R.id.version);
accuracy = (TextView) layout.findViewById(R.id.accuracy);
timestampLabel = (TextView) layout.findViewById(R.id.timestampLabel);
timestamp = (TextView) layout.findViewById(R.id.timestamp);
timestampUnits = (TextView) layout.findViewById(R.id.timestampUnits);
dataLabel = (TextView) layout.findViewById(R.id.dataLabel);
dataUnits = (TextView) layout.findViewById(R.id.dataUnits);
xAxis = (TextView) layout.findViewById(R.id.xAxis);
xAxisLabel = (TextView) layout.findViewById(R.id.xAxisLabel);
yAxis = (TextView) layout.findViewById(R.id.yAxis);
yAxisLabel = (TextView) layout.findViewById(R.id.yAxisLabel);
zAxis = (TextView) layout.findViewById(R.id.zAxis);
zAxisLabel = (TextView) layout.findViewById(R.id.zAxisLabel);
singleValue = (TextView) layout.findViewById(R.id.singleValue);
cosLabel = (TextView) layout.findViewById(R.id.cosLabel);
cos = (TextView) layout.findViewById(R.id.cos);

layout.findViewById(R.id.delayFastest).setOnClickListener(new OnClickListener()
{
    @Override
    public void onClick(View v)
    {
        sensorManager.unregisterListener(SensorDisplayFragment.this);
        sensorManager.registerListener(SensorDisplayFragment.this,
                sensor,
                SensorManager.SENSOR_DELAY_FASTEST);
    }
});

layout.findViewById(R.id.delayGame).setOnClickListener(new OnClickListener()
{
    @Override
    public void onClick(View v)
    {
        sensorManager.unregisterListener(SensorDisplayFragment.this);
        sensorManager.registerListener(SensorDisplayFragment.this,
                sensor,
                SensorManager.SENSOR_DELAY_GAME);
    }
});

layout.findViewById(R.id.delayNormal).setOnClickListener(new OnClickListener()
{
    @Override
    public void onClick(View v)
    {
        sensorManager.unregisterListener(SensorDisplayFragment.this);
        sensorManager.registerListener(SensorDisplayFragment.this,
                sensor,
                SensorManager.SENSOR_DELAY_NORMAL);
```

```
            }
        });

        layout.findViewById(R.id.delayUi).setOnClickListener(new OnClickListener()
        {
            @Override
            public void onClick(View v)
            {
                sensorManager.unregisterListener(SensorDisplayFragment.this);
                sensorManager.registerListener(SensorDisplayFragment.this,
                        sensor,
                        SensorManager.SENSOR_DELAY_UI);
            }
        });

        return layout;
    }

    public void displaySensor(Sensor sensor)
    {
        if (BuildConfig.DEBUG)
        {
            Log.d(TAG, "display the sensor");
        }

        this.sensor = sensor;

        name.setText(sensor.getName());
        type.setText(String.valueOf(sensor.getType()));
        maxRange.setText(String.valueOf(sensor.getMaximumRange()));
        minDelay.setText(String.valueOf(sensor.getMinDelay()));
        power.setText(String.valueOf(sensor.getPower()));
        resolution.setText(String.valueOf(sensor.getResolution()));
        vendor.setText(String.valueOf(sensor.getVendor()));
        version.setText(String.valueOf(sensor.getVersion()));

        sensorManager.registerListener(this,
                sensor,
                SensorManager.SENSOR_DELAY_NORMAL);
    }

    @Override
    public void onAccuracyChanged(Sensor sensor, int accuracy)
    {
        switch(accuracy)
        {
            case SensorManager.SENSOR_STATUS_ACCURACY_HIGH:
                this.accuracy.setText("SENSOR_STATUS_ACCURACY_HIGH");
                break;
            case SensorManager.SENSOR_STATUS_ACCURACY_MEDIUM:
                this.accuracy.setText("SENSOR_STATUS_ACCURACY_MEDIUM");
                break;
            case SensorManager.SENSOR_STATUS_ACCURACY_LOW:
                this.accuracy.setText("SENSOR_STATUS_ACCURACY_LOW");
```

continues

LISTING 5-3 *(continued)*

```java
                break;
            case SensorManager.SENSOR_STATUS_UNRELIABLE:
                this.accuracy.setText("SENSOR_STATUS_UNRELIABLE");
                break;
        }
    }

    @Override
    public void onSensorChanged(SensorEvent event)
    {
        onAccuracyChanged(event.sensor, event.accuracy);

        timestampLabel.setVisibility(View.VISIBLE);
        timestamp.setVisibility(View.VISIBLE);
        timestamp.setText(String.valueOf(event.timestamp));
        timestampUnits.setVisibility(View.VISIBLE);

        switch (event.sensor.getType())
        {
            case Sensor.TYPE_ACCELEROMETER:
                showEventData("Acceleration - gravity on axis",
                        ACCELERATION_UNITS,
                        event.values[0],
                        event.values[1],
                        event.values[2]);
                break;

            case Sensor.TYPE_MAGNETIC_FIELD:
                showEventData("Abient Magnetic Field",
                        "uT",
                        event.values[0],
                        event.values[1],
                        event.values[2]);
                break;
            case Sensor.TYPE_GYROSCOPE:
                showEventData("Angular speed around axis",
                        "radians/sec",
                        event.values[0],
                        event.values[1],
                        event.values[2]);
                break;
            case Sensor.TYPE_LIGHT:
                showEventData("Ambient light",
                        "lux",
                        event.values[0]);
                break;
            case Sensor.TYPE_PRESSURE:
                showEventData("Atmospheric pressure",
                        "hPa",
                        event.values[0]);
                break;
            case Sensor.TYPE_PROXIMITY:
```

```
            showEventData("Distance",
                    "cm",
                    event.values[0]);
        break;
    case Sensor.TYPE_GRAVITY:
        showEventData("Gravity",
                ACCELERATION_UNITS,
                event.values[0],
                event.values[1],
                event.values[2]);
        break;
    case Sensor.TYPE_LINEAR_ACCELERATION:
        showEventData("Acceleration (not including gravity)",
                ACCELERATION_UNITS,
                event.values[0],
                event.values[1],
                event.values[2]);
        break;
    case Sensor.TYPE_ROTATION_VECTOR:

        showEventData("Rotation Vector",
                null,
                event.values[0],
                event.values[1],
                event.values[2]);

        xAxisLabel.setText("x*sin(" + THETA + "/2)");
        yAxisLabel.setText("y*sin(" + THETA + "/2)");
        zAxisLabel.setText("z*sin(" + THETA + "/2)");

        if (event.values.length == 4)
        {
            cosLabel.setVisibility(View.VISIBLE);
            cos.setVisibility(View.VISIBLE);
            cos.setText(String.valueOf(event.values[3]));
        }

        break;
    case Sensor.TYPE_ORIENTATION:
        showEventData("Angle",
                "Degrees",
                event.values[0],
                event.values[1],
                event.values[2]);

        xAxisLabel.setText(R.string.azimuthLabel);
        yAxisLabel.setText(R.string.pitchLabel);
        zAxisLabel.setText(R.string.rollLabel);

        break;
    case Sensor.TYPE_RELATIVE_HUMIDITY:
        showEventData("Relatice ambient air humidity",
                "%",
                event.values[0]);
        break;
```

continues

LISTING 5-3 *(continued)*

```java
            case Sensor.TYPE_AMBIENT_TEMPERATURE:
                showEventData("Ambien temperature",
                        "degree Celcius",
                        event.values[0]);
                break;
        }
    }

    private void showEventData(String label, String units, float x, float y, float z)
    {
        dataLabel.setVisibility(View.VISIBLE);
        dataLabel.setText(label);

        if (units == null)
        {
            dataUnits.setVisibility(View.GONE);
        }
        else
        {
            dataUnits.setVisibility(View.VISIBLE);
            dataUnits.setText("(" + units + "):");
        }

        singleValue.setVisibility(View.GONE);

        xAxisLabel.setVisibility(View.VISIBLE);
        xAxisLabel.setText(R.string.xAxisLabel);
        xAxis.setVisibility(View.VISIBLE);
        xAxis.setText(String.valueOf(x));

        yAxisLabel.setVisibility(View.VISIBLE);
        yAxisLabel.setText(R.string.yAxisLabel);
        yAxis.setVisibility(View.VISIBLE);
        yAxis.setText(String.valueOf(y));

        zAxisLabel.setVisibility(View.VISIBLE);
        zAxisLabel.setText(R.string.zAxisLabel);
        zAxis.setVisibility(View.VISIBLE);
        zAxis.setText(String.valueOf(z));
    }

    private void showEventData(String label, String units, float value)
    {
        dataLabel.setVisibility(View.VISIBLE);
        dataLabel.setText(label);

        dataUnits.setVisibility(View.VISIBLE);
        dataUnits.setText("(" + units + "):");
```

```java
        singleValue.setVisibility(View.VISIBLE);
        singleValue.setText(String.valueOf(value));

        xAxisLabel.setVisibility(View.GONE);
        xAxis.setVisibility(View.GONE);

        yAxisLabel.setVisibility(View.GONE);
        yAxis.setVisibility(View.GONE);

        zAxisLabel.setVisibility(View.GONE);
        zAxis.setVisibility(View.GONE);
    }

    @Override
    public void onHiddenChanged(boolean hidden)
    {
        super.onHiddenChanged(hidden);

        if (hidden)
        {
            if (BuildConfig.DEBUG)            {
                Log.d(TAG, "Unregistering listener");
            }

            sensorManager.unregisterListener(this);
        }
    }

    @Override
    public void onPause()
    {
        super.onPause();

        if (BuildConfig.DEBUG)
        {
            Log.d(TAG, "onPause");
            Log.d(TAG, "Unregistering listener");
        }

        sensorManager.unregisterListener(this);
    }
}
```

code snippet SensorDisplayFragment.java

So far, this chapter has discussed the Sensor API in Android. The rest of the chapter will be dedicated to discussion of the actual sensors and the data they provide.

TRY THIS

Select the Sensor List button to run `SensorListActivity` and observe live sensor values.

SENSING THE ENVIRONMENT

This section introduces the sensors that can be used to sense properties of the physical environment that a device is currently in. The next section describes how to sense device movement and orientation in the environment.

Sensor.TYPE_LIGHT

The light sensor is often visible on the face of the device, under a small opening in the black coloring on the glass. It is simply a photodiode, which operates on the same physical principle as an LED (light-emitting diode) but in reverse. Instead of generating light when a voltage is applied, it generates a voltage when light is incident on it.

The light sensor reports its values in lux, and has a typical dynamic range between 1 and 30,000 lux. The light sensor also has a resolution of 1 lux. A value of 0.25 lux is like the indirect brightness from a full moon; bright enough to see things, but a basic camera without a flash wouldn't capture enough light to take a photograph. An overcast day is 10,000 lux, full daylight (indirect sun) is around 20,000 lux, and direct sunlight is around 110,000 lux. These values span a wide range and cannot be accurately represented by a qualitative human measure such as "an overcast day" (which may vary in brightness depending on the thickness of cloud cover, the height of the sun in the sky, and so on). However, these numbers do represent the values that can be expected. Here are the constant values (in lux) for the light sensor.

➤ `SensorManager.LIGHT_NO_MOON`: 0.001

➤ `SensorManager.LIGHT_FULLMOON`: 0.25

➤ `SensorManager.LIGHT_CLOUDY`: 100

➤ `SensorManager.LIGHT_SUNRISE`: 400

➤ `SensorManager.LIGHT_OVERCAST`: 10000

➤ `SensorManager.LIGHT_SHADE`: 20000

➤ `SensorManager.LIGHT_SUNLIGHT`: 110000

➤ `SensorManager.LIGHT_SUNLIGHT_MAX`: 120000

The light sensor is mostly used to adjust screen brightness according to ambient light. Because screen brightness is managed by the OS and Android's settings, this is not often something developers typically need to access.

Some earlier devices do not have a proximity sensor, and therefore some developers have written programs to use the light sensor as a proximity sensor to lock and blank the screen during calls.

Sensor.TYPE_PROXIMITY

The proximity sensor is usually visible on the face of the device only in bright sunlight. It typically looks like a dark hole underneath the blackened part of the glass, usually at the top of the front face of a smartphone. It consists of a weak infrared LED (light-emitting diode) next to a photodetector. When something (such as the ear of a person making a phone call) comes close enough to the sensor, the photodetector detects the reflected infrared light.

The LED does not shine continuously, but pulses on and off. The photodetector locks in to this frequency of pulsing in order to make the sensor insensitive to any light that is not changing at that exact frequency. For example, the sensor doesn't care if you move from a bright room to a dark room because the bright and dark are just background light levels and aren't picked out by the locked-in photodetector system. The photodector is looking for light that is pulsing at the exact frequency of the LED. The pulsing frequency is not available for control, because the proximity detector is usually a third-party piece of hardware that internally measures the photodetector's signal, decides on the proximity state, and only makes a near or far state available to the app.

Some proximity sensors report the distance to an object in centimeters. Others are not designed to measure the *distance* to an object, but only the presence or absence of an object at a distance closer than some threshold (this is the case with proximity sensors in many smartphones today). A typical dynamic range for a binary sensor (reported by the `getMaximumRange()` method) is around 5 cm; however, a more valuable number is the approximate threshold distance, which is usually around 2–4 cm.

Because the proximity detector is designed to detect reflections, the actual distance reported depends on the reflectivity of the object. For those sensors that report only the presence or absence of an object, the combination of the brightness of the LED, the sensitivity of the detector, and the reflectivity of the object gives a range of around 2–3 cm. For measurements outside of that range, the sensor should report its maximum value (this number can be compared to the maximum range using the method `getMaximum-Range()`). For measurements within that range, the sensor will report a lesser number as discussed earlier.

Proximity sensors that have only binary output are interrupt-based and are not polled apps that make use of these types of sensors will receive an `onSensorChanged()` callback when a proximity state transition occurs (near-to-far or far-to-near).

The main application of a proximity sensor is detecting the ear of the user in order to shut down or lock the screen during calls.

To prevent rapid back-and-forth state switching when an object is exactly positioned at the distance threshold, the threshold for the sensor switching from far to near state is typically designed to be closer to the device than the threshold for switching from near to far state.

Typical proximity sensor LEDs operate at a wavelength of around 900 nanometers (nm), which is longer than humans can see (typically 750 nm) but shorter than many remote controls (around 1000 nm), and can travel through the black coloring on the glass.

Some people have reported that very bright light can saturate the detector and trick the sensor into giving a false reading. However, this is not usually a problem unless you are looking for it. If it is found to be a problem, it can be circumvented by appealing to the separate light sensor for a secondary reading, assuming it is not saturated.

Sensor.TYPE_PRESSURE

This constant refers to a MEMS barometer, which measures air pressure. Its primary use is for determining altitude in places where the device cannot get a GPS fix, such as locations inside a building. This sensor is currently available only in a few devices.

> *There is some misunderstanding around whether this sensor measures pressure of a finger on the screen or the ambient air pressure. This misunderstanding probably stems from the fact that there is also a* MotionEvent. getPressure() *method, which is designed to return the pressure of a finger on the screen.*

In their simplest incarnation, MEMS pressure sensors look like a drum skin over a chamber with a known pressure inside. As the outside pressure changes, the drum skin bulges in or out with the differential pressure. More accurate MEMS pressure sensors involve a drum skin or other structure that is set into resonant motion, and the amount that the air impedes its motion is measured. This is related to air density, which is related to air pressure at a given temperature.

It is normal for pressure to drift by approximately 0.5 millibar (mbar) in an hour. An intensifying storm may cause pressure to drift by 1 mbar per hour in the same direction for a few consecutive hours. Pressure cycles up and down usually twice daily due to atmospheric tides and other effects such as changes in temperature.

Altitude can be calculated from air pressure using the SensorManager.getAltitude() method, which returns the altitude above sea level in meters. This uses a standard physics formula to calculate the altitude (elevation) based on the measured pressure p and the pressure at sea level $p0$. The pressure at sea level can be either:

➤ The standard pressure given by the associated constant PRESSURE_STANDARD_ATMOSPHERE, which gives decent results for relative elevations but not for absolute elevation.

➤ The *effective* (or mean) sea-level pressure reported by an airport or other weather-reporting station, which gives the best results for both relative and absolute elevation measurements.

Because the latter option is significantly harder to implement, it is advisable to use PRESSURE_STANDARD_ATMOSPHERE for most cases and use the latter option only when higher absolute accuracy and precision is necessary. However, the latter option is covered with plenty of detail in the "Mean Sea-Level Pressure" section to get you started.

Absolute Altitude

`SensorManager.getAltitude()` uses the formula shown in Figure 5-3.

$$h(p_0, p) = \frac{T_0}{L}\left(1 - \left(\frac{p}{p_0}\right)^{\frac{RL}{gM}}\right) = 44330 * \left(1 - \left(\frac{p}{p_0}\right)^{\frac{1}{5.255}}\right)$$

FIGURE 5-3: Computing altitude from atmospheric pressure

In the equation shown in Figure 5-3, h is altitude, $T0$ is sea-level standard temperature, L is temperature lapse rate, R is the universal gas constant, g is gravitational acceleration, and M is the molar mass of dry air. You can look up these constants online if necessary, but in general you shouldn't need to look them up because the simplified formula appears on the right-hand side of the equation.

Relative Altitude

Using the formula from the preceding section, you can calculate relative altitude differences such as the difference in altitude between floors in a shopping mall. Because pressure drifts over time, the app should look for relative differences that happen over a short enough timescale (such as the timescale corresponding to a person ascending a flight of stairs). It is important to calculate the altitudes first and then subtract them rather than trying to compare pressures. This will work quite well even if the absolute altitudes are not accurate. For example:

```
float altitudeDifference =
    getAltitude(SensorManager.PRESSURE_STANDARD_ATMOSPHERE,pressureAtPoint2)
    -
    getAltitude(SensorManager.PRESSURE_STANDARD_ATMOSPHERE,pressureAtPoint1);
```

For instance, a pressure change from 1010 to 1011 mbar corresponds to descending by 8.34 m, and (inverting the formula) an altitude change of 10 m corresponds to 1.2 mbar pressure change at sea level.

Mean Sea-Level Pressure (MSLP)

Assume you don't want to use `PRESSURE_STANDARD_ATMOSPHERE`, so you need to find effective sea-level pressure. First, what *is* effective (or mean) sea-level pressure (MSLP)?

Consider a particular weather station in Chicago that measures an atmospheric pressure of 1000.0 mbar. It will calculate and report an MSLP (sometimes just called sea-level pressure, or SLP) of 1010.0 mbar. MSLP is calculated to be what the air pressure *would* be if the Chicago station were actually sitting at sea level. We expect it to be higher because pressure gets higher as you go down in altitude. This latter pressure is actually the pressure usually given in weather reports on television, newspapers, and online, because then you can show weather patterns across a country despite the differing terrain and elevations. In addition, home barometers are usually calibrated by the user to track the MSLP rather than report the actual measured pressure — so a home barometer in this example would measure 1010 mbar if the user has calibrated it against MSLP as is usually the case. This can lead to some confusion because the MEMS barometer in Android is a raw sensor and would return 1000 mbar in Chicago (assuming it is a good sensor and responds to air pressure in the same way as the Chicago reporting station). To avoid confusion, ignore any home barometers that may be lying around and trust the value from the Android device, referenced to the reported MSLP of the nearest reporting station to calculate altitude. The following code shows how to calculate altitude:

```
float altitude =
    mSensorManager.getAltitude(pressure_localReportingStationMSLP,
                        pressure_measuredOnDevice);
```

Where to Find MSLP

You can find many sources of meteorological station data online. For example, for the United States go to the ADDS website (http://aviationweather.gov/adds/metars/). A simple web request can be sent (see the details on the website), and a string received for a given station. For instance, the main Chicago station may return the following:

```
KMDW 171851Z 25014G23KT 10SM SCT150 BKN200 BKN250 12/M01 A2984 RMK AO2 SLP106 T01221006
```

You will need to parse that string to find the effective sea-level pressure. You can find a detailed interpretation on the ADDS website, but briefly: KMDW is a code that uniquely identifies a particular station in Chicago (you can find latitude and longitude at http://aviationweather.gov/adds/metars/stations.txt), "SLP" stands for sea-level pressure, and 106 is a truncated 1010.6 mbar. Notice that the decimal point and the first two digits are dropped — this is standard notation. To know whether the first two digits that were dropped were a 09 or a 10, use the number that is closest to 1000, because the other number would be unphysical.

Sensor Units

Although the pressure sensor reports pressure in millibars (mbar), many different units of pressure may be encountered. For instance, all United States reporting stations will report the pressure in inches of mercury (inHg). Other common units of pressure are: 1 mbar (millibar) = 0.001 bar = 0.1 kPa (kilopascal) = 1 hPa (hectopascal) = 1,000 dyn/cm2 (dynes per square cm) = 0.000987 atm (atmospheres) = 0.0295 inHg (inches of mercury) = 0.750 mmHg (mm of mercury) = 0.0145 psi (pounds per square inch).

Sensor Range

A typical dynamic range of a MEMS pressure sensor is 300–1100 mbar and a typical resolution is 0.01 mbar (for the Bosch BMP085 in the Motorola Xoom, for example). The pressure sensor has one constant, SensorManager.PRESSURE_STANDARD_ATMOSPHERE, with a value (in mbar) of 1013.25.

Common Use Cases

The main area of anticipated use for pressure sensors is in measuring elevation. This can be for either an absolute elevation measurement (meaning the measurement of absolute height above sea level) or relative elevation measurement (meaning the measurement of relative elevation due to fast but small changes in elevation — for instance, detecting floor changes, for indoor navigation such as in a shopping mall or other areas where use of GPS would be problematic).

➤ **Absolute elevation measurement:** GPS can take a long time to get a fix. Reading the pressure sensor is quick, so an app could use a less accurate elevation measurement from the pressure sensor and use the (possibly) more accurate GPS-based elevation value when it is available. Alternatively, you may just be interested in finding the absolute altitude when GPS is turned off or GPS signals are not available.

➤ **Relative elevation measurement:** Although GPS provides altitude data, GPS signal is not always available. Using the pressure sensor, however, you may be able to determine which floor in a building a device is on instead of just which building the device is in. Current MEMS pressure sensors are sensitive enough to detect air pressure differences between different floors in a building (typically on the order of 0.3–0.4 mbar differences for typical residential buildings and larger for buildings like shopping malls, calculable from the formula given previously), especially buildings like shopping malls where each story is taller than in a residential building. Air pressure may naturally fluctuate by more than 0.3–0.4 mbar over time, however air pressure changes due to going upstairs or downstairs are usually faster changes and can be detected. Depending on location, pressure may vary over the course of a year from approximately 995 to 1030 mbar with an average value of 1013 mbar. However, pressure usually drifts by less than 1 mbar over the course of an hour.

➤ **Sensing weather:** Although barometers are usually associated with weather measurements, this is actually not as useful for users or developers as it might initially seem. National weather reporting systems have better barometers, Android devices can usually check such data over the Internet, and weather doesn't vary on a small enough spatial scale to make barometric measurement for weather measurement very useful.

Sensor.TYPE_RELATIVE_HUMIDITY

The relative humidity sensor provides the current ambient humidity as the percent of water vapor in the air. More specifically, *relative humidity* is the amount of water vapor in the air compared to the maximum amount of water vapor that the air can hold at a given temperature. A value of 100% indicates that the air is fully saturated. The value returned by this sensor is humidity commonly used in weather reports.

The relative humidity can be used, along with the ambient temperature, to calculate the dew point and the absolute humidity. *Dew point* is the temperature at which water vapor condenses. Absolute humidity is the mass of water in a given volume of air.

Sensor.TYPE_AMBIENT_TEMPERATURE

The ambient temperature sensor provides the room temperature in degrees Celsius. This sensor is meant to replace the use of `Sensor.TYPE_TEMPERATURE`, which has been deprecated.

Sensor.TYPE_TEMPERATURE

The temperature sensor in Android devices is designed to detect the temperature of the CPU for internal hardware calibration. It is not designed for measuring environmental temperature, and is therefore not generally useful to developers. As of release 4.0, the sensor has been deprecated in favor of the ambient temperature sensor.

Although the online documentation may not list the temperature sensor as deprecated, the official Android 4.0 Compatibility Definition states:

> *Device implementations MAY but SHOULD NOT include a thermometer*
> *(i.e. temperature sensor.) If a device implementation does include a thermometer,*
> *it MUST measure the temperature of the device CPU. It MUST NOT measure any*
> *other temperature. (Note that this sensor type is deprecated in the Android 4.0 APIs.)*
> *(Source:* `http://source.android.com/compatibility/android-4.0-cdd.pdf`.*)*

The reason for deprecation appears to be that it is an internal system sensor and has no general-purpose use in apps.

Thus far, this chapter has discussed the various concepts surrounding sensors and the Android platform, as well as enumerated the sensors that may be available on a given Android device. The remainder of the chapter will be dedicated to implementing application code that makes use of the sensor data.

SENSING DEVICE ORIENTATION AND MOVEMENT

This section goes into depth describing Android inertial sensors. *Inertial* is just a term that refers to motion measurement. These are different than the sensors in the previous section in that they describe what the device is doing in its environment as opposed to describing the environment itself.

Coordinate Systems

When using orientation and movement sensors in Android, two coordinate systems are defined: the *global coordinate system* x_E, y_E, z_E, and a *device coordinate system* x, y, z. Both coordinate systems are illustrated in Figure 5-4. This figure shows the device positioned at the equator of Earth, with some tilt with respect to Earth. All coordinate systems for three-axis sensors obey these coordinate systems, except Sensor.TYPE_ORIENTATION, which is deprecated.

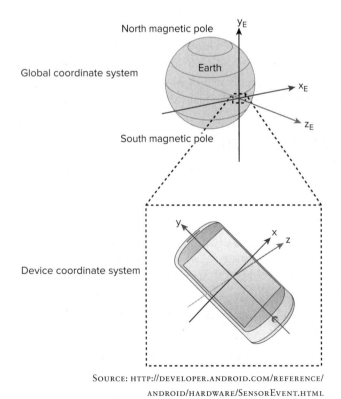

SOURCE: HTTP://DEVELOPER.ANDROID.COM/REFERENCE/
ANDROID/HARDWARE/SENSOREVENT.HTML

FIGURE 5-4: Android coordinate systems

Note that `SensorManager.getOrientation()` has reversed x and z axes with respect to the global coordinate system shown here.

Global Coordinate System

All sensors and methods that refer to an absolute orientation with respect to Earth (except the orientation sensor) use the global coordinate system. These include:

➤ The rotation vector sensor, which uses the accelerometer, magnetometer, and possibly the gyroscope to sense device orientation relative to Earth.

➤ `getRotationMatrix()`, `getRotationMatrixFromVector()`, and `getQuaternionFromVector()`, which get the rotation matrix or quaternion that can map the device coordinate system on to the global coordinate system.

➤ `getOrientation()`, which takes a rotation matrix generated from `getRotationMatrix()` and returns an orientation vector.

➤ `getInclination()`, which takes a rotation matrix from the `getOrientation()` method and returns the magnetic inclination. Magnetic inclination is how much a compass needle would deviate vertically from a plane horizontal to Earth's surface.

In the global coordinate system:

➤ y_E points toward magnetic north, which is approximately true north.

➤ x_E points approximately east — parallel to Earth's surface but 90 degrees from y_E.

➤ z_E points away from the center of the earth.

Device Coordinate System

Raw three-axis inertial sensors (accelerometer, magnetometer, and gyroscope) report values corresponding to the device coordinate system. The device coordinate system is partially defined by the default orientation, which differs depending on the type of the device. For example, phones have a portrait default orientation while tables have a landscape default orientation. When the device is viewed in its default orientation, the axes are directed as follows

➤ The x-axis is horizontal with positive values to the right.

➤ The y-axis is vertical with positive values upward.

➤ The z-axis is positive values in front of the screen.

The coordinate system is fixed to the device — the axis orientations are not changed when the device goes from portrait to landscape mode.

The Android 2D APIs use a different coordinate system, where the origin is in the top-left corner rather than at the center of the screen.

Angles

Angular quantities around axes are given by either a 3-vector, rotation matrix, or quaternion that maps the device coordinate system on to the global coordinate system. Quaternions are an alternate representation of rotation matrices and are beyond the scope of this book. For example, a 3-vector gyroscope reading of (0.1, −0.2, 0.0) indicates that the rotation rate is +0.1 radians per second around the x-axis, −0.2 radians per second around the y-axis, and not rotating around the z-axis.

The direction of angular three-vectors is determined by the so-called *right-hand rule*: if the thumb of your right hand points along the positive direction of the axis, your fingers will curl around in the direction of positive angle. The components of angular three-vectors may also be called azimuth (or heading or yaw), pitch, and roll. This is covered in more detail later.

Sensor.TYPE_ACCELEROMETER, .TYPE_GRAVITY, and .TYPE_LINEAR_ACCELERATION

MEMS accelerometers (Figure 5-5) are tiny masses on tiny springs. These devices can sense:

➤ Speeding up or slowing down in a straight line (such as the act of throwing or catching the device, during the short time period just before you release it or just after you catch it)

➤ Shaking the device

➤ Holding the device while going around a sharp corner in a car

➤ Earth's gravity, which is 1 g downward (g is a unit of acceleration and is equal to 9.8 m/s²)

Because acceleration is often associated with the feeling of being pushed into a car seat when the gas pedal in a car is depressed, it can be difficult to see why there is a constant downward acceleration due to gravity when a mass is standing still. However, remember that $F=ma$ shows that an acceleration a is just the same thing as a force F, related through the proportionality constant m, for mass. So *whenever there is a force there will be a proportional acceleration too*, even if acceleration may not be what we call it in everyday terms. How are forces acting on masses measured? By attaching the masses to springs and seeing how far the springs are deformed (see Figure 5-5).

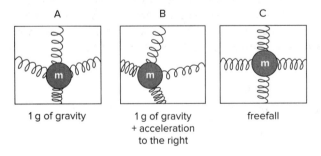

A — 1 g of gravity

B — 1 g of gravity + acceleration to the right

C — freefall

FIGURE 5-5: Force being applied to a mass attached to springs

Acceleration is measured by attaching a mass to springs and seeing how far the mass deviates from its equilibrium position. In Figure 5-5, A would correspond to the device sitting on a table. B would correspond to the device being thrown to the right, in the instant before it leaves the user's hand. C would correspond to the user dropping the device, during its free-fall motion. With this in mind it is easy to see why accelerometers measure both the force of gravity and also linear acceleration. It is also easy to see why an accelerometer in free-fall will report zero acceleration even though it is still subject to Earth's gravity — this is because both the mass and the frame it is suspended from have the same acceleration acting on them, so the springs do not deform.

Every particle on Earth feels the downward force of gravity and is held against gravity through springy molecular forces and possibly macroscopic springs. MEMS masses are also pulled downward by gravity and their tiny springs deform, allowing acceleration due to gravity to be measured.

The same inertial forces act, and the MEMS springs bend, when the device is shaken or swung around in a circle (though in the latter case the acceleration is inward, and due to the force applied to pull the device inward), so that is measured as acceleration.

Because force and the physics definition of acceleration are related, accelerometers can be thought of as *force-meters* that measure the force acting on the MEMS mass. At rest, they measure the force of gravity downward. When accelerating, they measure the force that caused them to accelerate (added to the force of gravity by vector addition).

During free-fall, the force of gravity still acts downward, however the MEMS mass and the surrounding frame to which it is attached (by springs) both have this same gravitational acceleration acting equally on them, therefore the MEMS springs no longer bend and the accelerometer measures 0 g.

From Android 2.3 onward, for convenience, developers also have the synthetic sensors `Sensor.TYPE_GRAVITY` and `Sensor.TYPE_LINEAR_ACCELERATION` available. These sensors factor out the force due to gravity and other accelerations. The sum of the values from the gravity and linear acceleration sensors equals the value from the accelerometer `Sensor.TYPE_ACCELEROMETER`.APS

Sensor Units and Resolution

Android reports acceleration in m/s^2. Earth's gravity is 9.8 m/s^2 or 1 g (gee, a unit of gravity) downwards. However when at rest the sensor reports its z-value to be +9.8 m/s^2, because it reports positive values for downwards accelerations. For all three accelerations, the convention is:

➤ *values[0]*: Minus gx on the x-axis

➤ *values[1]*: Minus gy on the y-axis

➤ *values[2]*: Minus gz on the z-axis

where gx, gy, and gz are the three components of the measured acceleration vector.

A typical dynamic range is 0 ± 2 or ± 4 g, and a typical resolution is 0.1 m/s^2. A device at rest will often report noise of around 1/20th of a g. Vibration of the internal device vibrator (the notification vibrator) may shake it at an amplitude of 1 g. Shaking the device vigorously by hand will result in changes of around 1–10 g. Here are the associated constants for the accelerometer and their corresponding values in m/s^2:

➤ `SensorManager.GRAVITY_EARTH`: 9.80665

➤ `SensorManager.STANDARD_GRAVITY`: 9.80665

A few other constants also exist, such as `SensorManager.GRAVITY_SATURN`, *but these are typically not very useful.*

Sensor.TYPE_GYROSCOPE

MEMS gyroscopes are also tiny masses on tiny springs, but instead of measuring acceleration, they are designed to measure a different force — the so-called *Coriolis force* due to rotation. The Coriolis force is the tendency for a free object to veer off course when viewed from a rotating reference frame. For instance, when you are sitting on a merry-go-round and roll a ball away from you, the ball appears to veer away from a straight line as if there is a force acting on it. This fictitious force is called the Coriolis force. It is a "fictitious force" because when viewed from someone standing next to the merry-go-round, no force acts on the ball — it is simply rolling in a straight line as you would expect from Newtonian physics.

In the MEMS world, the gyroscope works by pushing a tiny mass back-and-forth along one axis. When the gyroscope is rotated, the Coriolis force makes the mass veer away from the direction it was vibrating, and it starts to move along a different axis. Movement along this new axis is sensed electrically, using capacitor plates — one capacitor plate is fixed to the frame and one is fixed to the moving mass.

The Coriolis force acts only when the device is rotating, therefore gyroscopes measure only *angular velocity*, or, the *speed* at which the device is rotating. When the device is stationary, regardless of which direction the device is pointing, all three axes of the gyroscope will measure zero.

You cannot directly measure angle using a gyroscope. However, often the gyroscope values are integrated over time to calculate an angle. The gyroscope noise and offset will introduce large errors in the calculated angle, which if not addressed would make the integrated data be useless within a second or so. These errors may be compensated using the information from other sensors, and are covered in Chapter 6.

Sensor Units

Android reports values in radians per second around the standard x, y, and z axes shown in Figure 5-4. The standard mathematical convention is followed: if the axis in question is pointing toward you, positive values indicate counterclockwise rotations. This is given by the right-hand rule, discussed previously.

Sensor Range

A typical maximum range to expect is around 35 degrees/second (0.61 rad/s), and a typical resolution is around 0.001 degrees/second (2E-5 rad/s).

Sensor.TYPE_MAGNETIC_FIELD

Magnetic field sensors may operate under a variety of different methods depending on the manufacturer and architecture — they may use the Hall effect, magneto-resistive materials, or the Lorentz force. Hall effect sensors currently comprise the largest market share of magnetometers and work by simply passing a current through a wire. A magnetic field component perpendicular to that wire causes the electrons to have higher density on one side of the wire compared to the other, which results in a voltage across the width of the wire that is proportional to the magnetic field. Lorentz force sensors are similar but measure a mechanical deflection of the wire rather than voltage across the wire's width. Regardless of the physical mechanism, magnetic field sensors will report the magnetic field in x, y, and z (by having three separate sensors, one aligned along each axis).

You may notice that the magnetic field readout is quite jumpy and may seem less accurate than other sensors. Magnetometers will undoubtedly continue to improve, but at the time of writing, creating a low-noise, sensitive, accurate, inexpensive MEMS magnetic field sensor is still an open problem in the field of MEMS.

Sensor Units, Range, and Resolution

Android reports magnetic fields in microtesla. A typical dynamic range is around 2000 microtesla. The resolution for the magnetic field sensor is 0.1 microtesla. Earth's magnetic field can vary from 30 microtesla to 60 microtesla, and over the U.S. the value varies from around 58 microtesla in North Dakota to around 48 microtesla in southern Texas, and these values drift over time. However, the absolute value does not matter much, and these should be only taken to be ballpark estimates — MEMS-based magnetometers have both poor absolute accuracy and will vary based on the local environment. The local environment (the presence of nearby metal, even many nonmagnetic metals), hysteretic effects (the effect of environmental history; for example, if a metal body or magnet was close to the sensor and then removed, it may have changed the reading on the sensor), and drift cause measured values to change over time.

If better accuracy for the magnitude of the measurement is desired, the class `android.hardware.GeomagneticField` will estimate the magnetic field magnitude and direction at a given point on Earth. You supply a latitude, longitude, altitude, and time to instantiate it, and then have access to the following fields:

➤ `float getDeclination()` (Declination is the angle between magnetic north and true north for a given location.)

➤ `float getFieldStrength()`

➤ `float getHorizontalStrength()`

➤ `float getInclination()` (Inclination is how far downward or upward the magnetic field should point, compared to the horizon.)

➤ `float getX()`, `float getY()`, `float getZ()` (These give the northward, eastward, and downward components of the expected magnetic field in *nanoteslas* [multiply by 1000 to get microteslas].)

Here are the associated constants for `Sensor.TYPE_MAGNETIC FIELD` and their values (in microtesla):

➤ `SensorManager.MAGNETIC_FIELD_EARTH_MAX`: 60.0

➤ `SensorManager.MAGNETIC_FIELD_EARTH_MIN`: 30.0

Ideally, MEMS magnetometers would always measure the absolute magnetic field of Earth. In reality, the measured values change over time based on both the current local magnetic environment and the history of the device. For instance, the presence of a nearby magnet or nonmagnetic metal object distorts Earth's magnetic fields and results in readings that differ from magnetic north (see Figure 5-6).

Because the magnetic field sensor can be influenced by nearby metal, some people have used the sensor to make an Android device into a crude metal detector. These apps watch for large changes in the magnetic field as you move a piece of metal over your stationary Android device.

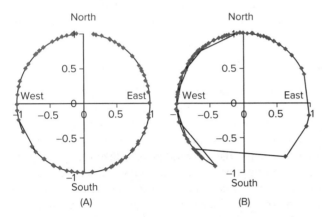

FIGURE 5-6: (A) Device rotated by hand at approximately constant rate, magnetic sensor readings plotted (normalized azimuth plot)
(B) Device rotated in the same way, but with a metal object nearby

The sensor may report different values before the introduction of a nearby metal object or magnet compared with after it is removed (an effect known as *hysteresis* — where the sensor reading depends on the *history* of the sensor's environment and not always the real value you wish to measure).

Sometimes when interrogating the compass, there may be some "jumpiness" or a large offset in the data. Waving the device in a figure eight (away from any metal objects) will usually cause the magnetometer to report better readings. There is nothing special about a figure eight other than that it ensures a wide range of rapid data changes, which allows the magnetometer to get back on track. The figure eight should not be performed in just one plane (it's not just like driving a toy racecar around a flat figure eight track), but the user should to wave it in all three axes to calibrate all axes of the magnetometer.

To determine when the figure eight calibration is needed, monitor the accuracy using `SensorEventListener.onAccuracyChanged(Sensor sensor, int accuracy)`. As previously mentioned, there are four levels of accuracy: `SENSOR_STATUS_ACCURACY_HIGH`, `SENSOR_STATUS_ACCURACY_MEDIUM`, `SENSOR_STATUS_ACCURACY_LOW`, and `SENSOR_STATUS_UNRELIABLE`. Some apps remind the user to do this when the magnetometer reports an unreliable status, whereas others assume the accuracy is always sufficient or that the user knows the calibration procedure and when to calibrate. (Another method of calibration may have the user place the device flat on a table and pointing toward magnetic north, and thereafter using that reading as a constant offset from subsequent measurements; however, it is unlikely that users will perform this procedure.)

Lastly, some people who have reported a stuck compass (stuck pointing in one direction) have said that by waving a magnet around the device, the magnetometer can get unstuck. The magnetic field sensor is often located near the top of a smartphone. The sensor can be found by moving a weak magnet (such as a small piece of flexible fridge magnet) over the device and watching the sensor readings.

Sensor.TYPE_ROTATION_VECTOR

Available since API level 9, Sensor.TYPE_ROTATION_VECTOR is a synthetic sensor that calculates rotation angle of the global coordinate system with respect to the device coordinate system using the accelerometer, the magnetometer, and possibly the gyroscope if available.

The output of this sensor is in a form similar to a quaternion, which is an alternate representation of a rotation. Quaternions have certain mathematical advantages over expressing rotations in typical Euclidean terms, but they are not easily visualized. To get a true normalized quaternion from the output of this sensor, use the SensorManager.getQuaternionFromVector() method. However, quaternions are beyond the scope of this book, so we will simply skirt the issue by staying with the Euclidean representation, and convert the output immediately to a rotation matrix using the get-RotationMatrixFromVector() method, as shown in the following snippet:

```
private float[] rotationMatrix = new float[16];
private float[] rotationVector = new float[3];
public void onSensorChanged(SensorEvent event){
    switch (event.sensor.getType()){
        case Sensor.TYPE_ROTATION_VECTOR:{
            rotationVals = event.values.clone();
            break;
        }
        case ...
    }
    getRotationMatrixFromVector (rotationMatrix, rotationVector);
};
```

As described, rotation matrices can be thought of as just another representation of an orientation vector — in other words, you can specify the orientation using rotationVector, or using the rotationMatrix that maps rotationVector on to the global coordinate system. As such, it may be used in, for example, an augmented reality app to calculate at what angle a virtual reality object should appear on the screen.

SensorManager.getRotationMatrixFromVector() takes two arguments. The first is a 9 or 16 element matrix to hold the desired rotation matrix. The second is the output of the rotation vector sensor. The matrix rotationMatrix describes the rotation necessary to rotate the global coordinate system to the device coordinate system (see Figure 5-4) — thus, it describes the orientation of the device.

This synthetic sensor may be heavily processed depending on the implementation, and you can expect more processing in future devices. The section on "Sensor Fusion Schemes" later in this chapter will go into more detail.

When performing intensive three-dimensional vector calculations for graphical purposes (for example, an augmented reality app), check out OpenGL (Open Graphics Library) — also beyond the scope of this book, but worth learning because it has been designed for such calculations.

SensorManager.getOrientation()

A rotation matrix can be obtained from `getRotationMatrix()` or `getRotationMatrixFromVector()`, and can then be passed `getOrientation()` to get the orientation (azimuth, pitch, and roll in radians). Note that here orientation means both the north-south-east-west bearing and the tilt angle. It is a vector describing how the device is oriented with respect to Earth. It is different than screen orientation (the portrait or landscape orientation) defined in the `getResources().getConfiguration().orientation` field.

Use of the deprecated `Sensor.TYPE_ORIENTATION`, which reports azimuth, pitch, and roll in degrees, should be avoided. However, `Sensor.TYPE_ORIENTATION` is still fairly widely implemented by developers and will probably still work on most devices for some time.

The coordinate system used here is shown in Figure 5-7. Annoyingly, the x and z axes are inverted with respect to the regular global coordinate system in Figure 5-4. The reported values are all given by the right-hand rule: if your right-hand thumb points along the positive direction of an axis, your fingers will curl around in the direction of increasing angle.

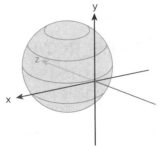

SOURCE: HTTP://DEVELOPER.ANDROID. COM/REFERENCE/ANDROID/HARDWARE/ SENSORMANAGER.HTML.

FIGURE 5-7: The axes for `getOrientation()`. The sphere represents Earth and the device is positioned at the equator. The y-axis points toward magnetic north, x points west, and z points to the center of the earth. (The x and z axes are inverted with respect to Figure 5-4.) Pitch, roll, and azimuth are defined by the right-hand rule around the x, y, and z axes, respectively

`getOrientation()` returns the following values:

➤ **values[0] = Azimuth (or heading or yaw) = Rotation about z-axis:** Assume the device is flat on its back in portrait mode, with the top pointing toward north. The device reports 0 radians in this orientation, Π/2 radians when pointing east, –Π/2 radians when pointing west, and Π radians when pointing south.

➤ **values[1] = Pitch = Rotation about x-axis:** Assume the device is flat on its back in portrait mode. The device reports 0 radians in this orientation, –Π/2 radians when you lift the top upward so it is standing upright with the screen facing toward you, +Π/2 radians when you lower the top so it is standing upright with the screen facing away from you, and Π radians when the device is face down.

➤ **values[2] = Roll = Rotation about y-axis:** Assume the device is flat on its back in portrait mode. The device reports 0 radians in this orientation, –Π/2 radians when you lift the right side so it is standing upright on its side with the screen facing west, Π/2 radians when you lift the left side so it is standing upright with the screen facing east, and Π radians when the device is face down.

The procedure for determining device orientation is given in Listing 5-3.

LISTING 5-4: DETERMINING DEVICE ORIENTATION

```
private SensorManager sm;
private float[] accelVals;
private float[] magVals;
private float[] rotationMatrix = new float[16];
private float[] orientationVals = new float[3];

/*
 * Construct the SensorManager objects and register sensor listeners. Not
 * shown here.
 */

// Sensor reading
public void onSensorChanged(SensorEvent event)
{
    switch (event.sensor.getType())
    {
        case Sensor.TYPE_ACCELEROMETER:
        {
            accelVals = event.values.clone();
            break;
        }
        case Sensor.TYPE_MAGNETIC_FIELD:
        {
            magVals = event.values.clone();
            break;
        }
    }

    SensorManager.getRotationMatrix(rotationMatrix, null, accelVals,
            magVals);
    SensorManager.getOrientation(rotationMatrix, orientationVals);

    // Optionally convert the result from radians to degrees
    orientationVals[0] = (float) Math.toDegrees(orientationVals[0]);
    orientationVals[1] = (float) Math.toDegrees(orientationVals[1]);
    orientationVals[2] = (float) Math.toDegrees(orientationVals[2]);
};
```

The code in Listing 5-4 passes the accelerometer and magnetometer measurements into getRotationMatrix(), which populates rotation Matrix. The generated rotation matrix is then passed into getOrientation() to get yaw, pitch, and roll. In most cases (but not in this example), an app may need to check that getRotationMatrix() returns true — it will return true if it succeeded and false if it failed.

For this example, the call to getRotationMatrix() is passed a null inclination matrix as the second parameter. This is because the inclination matrix is not needed for the calculation and this can save execution time.

`rotationMatrix` is the matrix that fulfills:

`[0 0 g] =` `rotationMatrix` `*` `accelVals` and the inclination matrix `inclinationMatrix` (which we consider in the following section) is the matrix that fulfills:

`[0 m 0] =` `inclinationMatrix` `*` `rotationMatrix` `*` `magVals`, where g = 9.8 m/s² and m = the magnitude of the magnetometer reading (to get the magnitude you add the squares of mx, my, and mz, and then take the square root).

In other words, `rotationMatrix` assumes no significant external acceleration other than 1 g downward toward Earth (this means that it assumes the device is not being shaken), and simply maps `accelVals` (which are taken in the device's coordinate system, which is fixed to the device) on to the coordinate system in Figure 5-4 which is fixed to Earth. When the device is lying flat on its back with the top of the device in portrait mode pointing to the north, the device's coordinate system and Earth's coordinate system align, and `rotationMatrix` is just the identity matrix.

This method returns `true` on success, `false` on failure. Failure will occur if the device is in free fall because the accelerometer's downward measurement is not defined. (Failure will also occur if the device is close to the magnetic north or south of Earth, although admittedly this is not likely to happen.) On failure the output matrices are not modified.

`orientationVals` is the vector that will hold the azimuth, pitch, and roll in radians.

Notice that the values passed into `onSensorChanged()` are cloned before they are assigned the class member data. This is because the `SensorEvent` object that is passed to `onSensorChanged()` may be reused on subsequent calls. The use of `clone()` is needed to avoid the values getting overridden as the array points to a reference.

This method for getting the orientation will not fail, but may give incorrect results if the device is accelerating or a nearby magnet is affecting the magnometer.

Once you have found `rotationMatrix`, `remapCoordinateSystem()` can be used to cast `rotationMatrix` into a more convenient form. For instance, the matrix that `getRotationMatrix()` returns is defined to have the y-axis pointing out the top of the device, so when the device is sitting flat on a table pointing north, it will read (0,0,0). If a particular application needs it to read (0,0,0) when pointing north but sitting vertical, the app simply remaps the coordinate system so the x-axis is negative. This can be implemented with the following code right after `getRotationMatrix()` in `onSensorChanged()`. The matrix *outR* holds the result, but an app can make this be `rotationMatrix` instead if you simply want to overwrite `rotationMatrix` with the result. So, in other words, the following code takes `rotationMatrix`, remaps the coordinate system as just described, and spits out the resulting rotation matrix into *outR*. In subsequent code, *outR* can be used in the place of `rotationMatrix`, as if the global coordinate axes have been redefined as shown in Figure 5-4:

```
SensorManager.remapCoordinateSystem(rotationMatrix,
        SensorManager.AXIS_Y,
        SensorManager.AXIS_MINUS_X,
        outR);
```

The difference between using the rotation vector sensor and the `getOrientation()` method is that `getOrientation()` has no data smoothing, whereas the rotation vector sensor may have some smoothing. In general, if the orientation of a device is needed, some smoothing is generally also needed.

SensorManager.getInclination()

Earth's magnetic field is not perfectly horizontal at each point on Earth — a compass needle will point downward on the northern hemisphere and upward on the southern hemisphere, though it is not noticed because compass needles are constrained to move in a horizontal plane. *Magnetic inclination* or *magnetic dip* is the angle that a compass needle will make with the horizontal and is given by the `getInclination()` method. In the continental United States, inclination may be anywhere from about 60 degrees in Texas to about 70 degrees in North Dakota.

From the definition of `getInclination()` provided in the preceding section, it is clear that if the device is flat on its back with the top of the screen (in portrait mode) pointing toward magnetic north, then `inclinationMatrix` will be the identity matrix. In general, `inclinationMatrix` maps the magnetic field vector (expressed as `rotationMatrix * magVals`, which is therefore expressed in the global coordinate and not the device coordinate system) onto [0 m 0].

The magnetometer will always be found to point in the global y_E-z_E plane in Figure 5-4, because the only way the device knows which direction y_E is, is to consult the magnetometer. In other words, the global y_E axis in Figure 5-4 is actually set by the magnetometer's measurement of magnetic north and not of the actual magnetic north. Inclination, then, is the magnetometer's deviation from the y_E axis in the y_E-z_E plane.

Sensor Fusion Schemes

Sensor fusion describes the process of combining more than one sensor to get better results. For example, the accelerometer responds quickly to changes but is noisy. Smoothing it results in response lag. The gyroscope measurement, when integrated over time, provides a low-noise angle measurement but it is useless alone because gyroscope drift means that the integrated gyroscope data quickly becomes unphysical (unphysical meaning it doesn't correspond to the actual orientation of the device). Therefore, a sensor fusion system may use primarily the integrated gyroscope data, and stop it from drifting by constantly comparing it with the accelerometer (which does not drift).

Invensense, a manufacturer of accelerometers and gyroscopes, has worked with hardware manufacturers that use its sensors (for example, the Samsung Galaxy Tab 10.1, HTC Sensation, EVO 3D, and Galaxy Nexus) to implement its proprietary sensor fusion algorithms on the `ROTATION_VECTOR` sensor. (The `GRAVITY` and `LINEAR_ACCELERATION` sensors are also heavily processed.) Other vendors may soon follow suit, and open source sensor fusion algorithms may one day become available. Until then, if you need to determine if a device uses Invensense's sensor fusion algorithms, you can detect the manufacturer of the gyroscope (using the `Sensor.getVendor()` method) — if it is Invensense then it is probably implemented. You can find more details about sensor fusion in Chapter 6.

The take-home message is to use the synthetic sensors rather than the raw sensors whenever possible, because these will improve over time as sensor fusion algorithms are implemented in various hardware devices.

SUMMARY

This chapter provided detailed information about the physical sensors on Android devices to help you use physical sensors properly. The chapter described how to collect sensor data with the Sensor API. It also described how the sensor hardware works. Finally, this chapter described what the sensor values mean and how to interpret them.

The next chapters in this part describe sensor applications. The applications go into detail about how to apply the information in this chapter to create useful features that use physical sensors.

Errors and Sensor Signal Processing

➤ Outlining the errors that occur in sensor data

➤ Explaining algorithms for filtering data

➤ Understanding sensor fusion schemes

Sensors do not measure values perfectly. Instead, they can often produce data that is incorrect due to noise or because of degradation that occurs over time. Both of these problems may introduce errors in the resulting data.

Fortunately, algorithms and techniques exist to address these errors. To reduce errors, an app can filter output from individual sensor readings or fuse results from multiple sensors. Additionally, some of Android's synthetic sensors execute filtering algorithms or perform the sensor fusion for you.

This chapter first explores what kinds of errors can occur. Then, it describes filtering techniques that can help remove errors from individual sensor readings. Finally, it describes some sensor fusion schemes to combine outputs of multiple sensors to create improved results.

If Android does not provide a synthetic sensor you need, this chapter gives you the understanding you need to develop an approach and improve the quality of sensor data output. If Android does provide a synthetic sensor you need, this chapter helps you understand how such sensors work.

DEFINITIONS

Before describing filtering algorithms or sensor fusion schemes, it is useful to understand different terminology to describe errors, what types of errors can occur, and what kinds of techniques exist to address them.

Accuracy and Precision

To judge a sensor's accuracy and precision you need two relevant numbers. One is the actual value (such as the actual humidity or actual acceleration) that the sensor is trying to measure, and one is the measured value that the sensor reports. High accuracy means that the measured value is close to the actual value. In contrast, high precision means that measurements are more tightly clustered around a particular value, regardless of whether it is close to the actual value.

Figure 6-1 shows how the data values would appear under different accuracy and precision conditions. Notice the cluster of values in either high accuracy or low accuracy situations that have high precision, while low precision measurements scatter the data points.

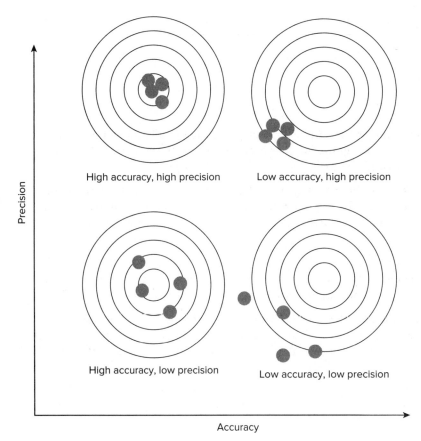

FIGURE 6-1: Accuracy vs. precision

The word precision *may sometimes be used to describe the total number of digits a measurement returns; however, in the present usage it is related only to the number of significant digits in a measurement.*

Types of Errors

When reading sensor data it is important to understand the types of errors you may encounter. Being familiar with why a sensor reading might return bad data may play a key role in developing algorithms to detect and process the erroneous data. Common causes of error in sensor data are discussed in the following sections.

Human Error, Systematic Error, and Random Error

Human errors are mistakes made by humans in making a measurement (such as incorrectly reading a value from a graph) and are not addressed in this book. Systematic errors are errors that affect the accuracy of a measurement — they are a constant offset from the true value (for instance, taking a measurement with the magnetometer with a magnet nearby). In some cases they can be predicted or removed by calibration or by changing the measurement scheme. On the other hand, random errors such as noise result in imprecise measurements and cannot be removed by these techniques.

Noise

Noise is the random fluctuation of a measured value. Although noise can be categorized (brown noise, white noise, and so on) and statistically quantified, these details are not usually necessary for programming with Android sensors and are not covered here. Instead, this chapter introduces you to low-pass filters to mitigate the effects of noise when necessary.

Drift

Drift describes slow, long-term wandering of data away from the real-world value. Drift may occur due to the sensor reading itself degrading over time. It can also occur if a sensor value is integrated. In such cases, a small offset (see the next section) will add up in each iteration of the integration to cause the resulting reading to drift away from the real measurement.

Zero Offset (or "Offset," or "Bias")

If the output signal is not zero when the measured property is zero, the sensor has an offset or bias. For example, if the average accelerometer measurement when the device is flat on a table is not exactly $(0, 0, -9.80665$ m/s$^2)$, the accelerometer has an offset.

If a gyroscope does not measure exactly $(0, 0, 0)$ rad/s when stationary, even a small zero offset will show up as an integration error when the gyro data is integrated to find the angle.

Time Delays and Dropped Data

Because Android is not a real-time operating system (RTOS), some measured data values can be delayed, resulting in incorrect timestamps. Data may even sometimes be dropped when the device is busy. Usually this is not a concern to developers, but is worth noting in a chapter about errors.

Integration Error

The gyroscope reports angular rotation rate in radians per second, however it would be more useful in many applications to know the amount by which the device has rotated. To find this quantity, you can integrate the gyroscope's readings and find a rotation angle in radians.

Listing 6-1 shows the code required to find the rotation angle in radians. `event.values` reports the rate of rotation as angle-per-second. First, the code calculates the time change between sensor readings, converts it from nanoseconds to seconds, and stores it in dT. To convert the angle-per-second value into just angle, the code multiplies each angle in `event.values` by dT. This conversion works because multiplying the angle-per-second value by a time in seconds results in a measurement with angle units. The resulting output is how far, in terms of angle, the gyroscope has rotated over the time period during dT.

LISTING 6-1: Integrates gyroscope readings to determine rotation angle in radians

```
//NS2S converts nanoseconds to seconds
private static final float NS2S = 1.0f / 1000000000.0f;

private float timestamp;
public void onSensorChanged(SensorEvent event)
{
    float[] valuesClone = event.values.clone();

    if (timestamp != 0)
    {
        final float dT = (event.timestamp - timestamp) * NS2S;
        angle[0] += valuesClone[0] * dT;
        angle[1] += valuesClone[1] * dT;
        angle[2] += valuesClone[2] * dT;
    }
    timestamp = event.timestamp;
}
```

However, the zero offset and drift in the gyroscope measurements mean that simple integration will give poor results. Over time, it will quickly explode to give large unphysical numbers even with no actual rotation, because offset and drift are accumulated under the integral, each time the integration executes. If you want to use gyroscope data to find orientation angle, these errors must be compensated for using the readings from other sensors using a "sensor fusion" approach discussed later.

The accumulated offset and drift is one reason why you can't measure distance by double-integrating the accelerometer measurement. Another reason is that, unless the device is accelerating or decelerating at all points in time, a constant nonzero velocity and a constant zero velocity will both contribute nothing to the double integral and, therefore, you can't tell a nonzero velocity from zero velocity, so a calculated distance is meaningless. For example, if you measure acceleration while a device is sitting on the table, it will measure 0,0,-g, where g is the constant acceleration due to gravity. If you measure it while it is traveling at a constant speed of 5 meters per second in the x direction, it will also measure 0,0,-g, because it is not "accelerating." Instead, it is traveling at a constant speed and therefore not accelerating. So the part of its travel where it is traveling at a constant speed contributes nothing to any integrated measurement.

Techniques to Address Error

The previous section discussed the types of errors that may be encountered when using Android sensor data. In most cases, an app will also need to handle the cases where a sensor error is present. The next sections discuss some of the methods that can be used to address sensor error.

Re-zeroing

If there is an offset present that is affecting your application, it may be useful to re-zero the sensor measurements. This is as simple as storing a calibrated value (potentially stored when the user clicks a Calibrate button) and subtracting it from each measured value. For instance, the device may be placed flat on a surface and the "downward" direction as measured by the accelerometer can be calibrated. This is simple enough that it doesn't need a code example; however, the trick is getting the user to actually perform the calibration, and know how and when to do so.

Filters

Low-pass filters filter out any high-frequency signal or noise and have a "smoothing" effect on data. High-pass filters filter out slow drift and offset and just give the higher frequency changes. The "cut-off frequency" is the approximate transition frequency above or below which the data is filtered out. Bandpass filters reject both low-frequency and high-frequency data and just keep the data in some frequency range of interest.

Sensor Fusion

Sensor fusion refers to using more than one sensor to take advantage of the strengths of each sensor and mitigate the effects of the weaknesses. For example, the accelerometer can give a relatively accurate measurement of the "downward" direction, but it has the disadvantage that it can never tell us the north-south-east-west yaw of the device. However, the compass can supplement that measurement to give yaw. A more complicated sensor fusion approach might be to also add integrated gyroscope data to give an app access to faster and lower-noise changes than the accelerometer and compass can give, but use the accelerometer and compass to reduce the effects of normal gyroscope drift. In effect, an app would primarily use the high-quality gyroscope data to get orientation information, but "nail it down" and prevent it from drifting by continually comparing it to the zero-drift accelerometer and compass data.

FILTERS

Filtering sensor data is another technique that can be used to overcome erroneous data. The following sections discuss a few filtering approaches.

Low-Pass

Although the sensors found in mobile devices are continually improving, in many cases an app may rely on some form of smoothing or averaging, also known as *low-pass filtering* (because it filters out high-frequency noise and "passes" low-frequency or slowly varying changes).

If all you want to do is get the gravity component of the accelerometer's measurement, use `Sensor.TYPE_GRAVITY` instead. This is a synthetic sensor that consists of low-pass-filtered accelerometer data. It is preferable to use the Gravity sensor rather than to filter the accelerometer data yourself because it is easier and chances are it has been optimized for the particular accelerometer on each device that will run your app.

Weighted Smoothing

A common method of implementing a low-pass filter to smooth data involves weighting the newest value against the old mean. A smoothing parameter (or weighting value) a is used such that:

(New value) = (Last value) + x_i * a – (Last value) * a

In other words, the last calculated value is added to x_i (the most recently collected value), which is weighted by a, with the weighted previous value being subtracted from the sum. If a is close to 1, the new value will be x_i, and if a is close to 0 the new value will not change with the calculation — this allows x_i to have any desired level of influence on the new value. More concisely for programming purposes but perhaps less clearly for understanding, the algorithm may be written as:

(New mean) – (Last value) * (1– a) + x_i * a

Or in Java as:

```
float a = 0.1f;

public void onSensorChanged(SensorEvent event
{
    x = event.values[0];
    y = event.values[1];
    z = event.values[2];
    mLowPassX = lowPass(x, mLowPassX);
    mLowPassY = lowPass(y, mLowPassY);
    mLowPassZ = lowPass(z, mLowPassZ);
}

// simple low-pass filter
float lowPass(float current, float last)
{
    return last * (1.0f - a) + current * a;
}
```

The value of a may need to be adjusted to find the best value for an app. However, a is defined here to be 0.1, which is often a decent choice for typical sampling rates when using the accelerometer to control a character in a game, for instance. As you can see in the code snippet, `a = 0` results in the mean never changing (the newest data has no effect), whereas `a = 1` results in the mean becoming equal to the newest data point each time it is computed (the newest data completely controls the mean). Values between 0 and 1 result in smoothed data.

Simple Moving Average (SMA)

A few extra lines of code to calculate the simple moving average (SMA) will provide a better smoothing against single-data-point spikes. The SMA is sometimes called the rolling average or running average. This simply finds the arithmetic mean of the most recent k data values in a stream. The integer k denotes the size of the averaging "window."

This method doesn't work until *k* values have been collected. For the first *k−1* values, arbitrary values may be supplied for the average (0, for example), or the SMA calculation can be deferred until *k* values have been collected.

Listing 6-2 is an example of the SMA implemented as its own object. To use it, push the newly collected sensor value using pushValue() and then get the averaged value using getValue().

LISTING: 6-2: SMA implementation

```
public class MovingAverage
{

    private float circularBuffer[];
    private float avg;
    private int circularIndex;
    private int count;

    public MovingAverage(int k)
    {
        circularBuffer = new float[k];
        count = 0;
        circularIndex = 0;
        avg = 0;
    }

    /* Get the current moving average. */
    public float getValue()
    {
        return avg;
    }

    public void pushValue(float x)
    {
        if (count++ == 0)
        {
            primeBuffer(x);
        }
        float lastValue = circularBuffer[circularIndex];
        avg = avg + (x - lastValue) / circularBuffer.length;
        circularBuffer[circularIndex] = x;
        circularIndex = nextIndex(circularIndex);
    }

    public long getCount()
    {
        return count;
    }

    private void primeBuffer(float val)
    {
        for (int i = 0; i < circularBuffer.length; ++i)
        {
            circularBuffer[i] = val;
        }
```

```
        avg = val;
    }

    private int nextIndex(int curIndex)
    {
        if (curIndex + 1 >= circularBuffer.length)
        {
            return 0;
        }
        return curIndex + 1;
    }
}
```

This code is available under the Apache 2.0 license from http://code.google.com/p/bigwords.

The effect of an SMA and weighted smoothing is shown in Figure 6-2.

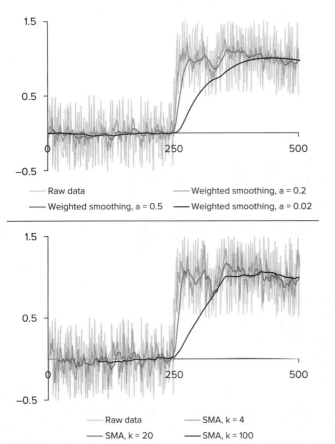

FIGURE 6-2: The effect of low-pass filtering on simulated accelerometer data for the weighted smoothing and SMA approaches. Notice the trade-off between response time and smoothness. Notice also that the weighted smoothing (a = 0.02) has a curving response after the step, versus the linear response of the SMA (k = 100).

Choosing the Smoothing Parameter

The time constant of a filter gives the duration of a signal it will act on. A low-pass filter will filter out signals much shorter than the time constant and a high-pass filter will filter out signals much longer than the time constant. The time constant of the first low-pass filter that was discussed,

*(New mean) = (Last value) * (1– a) + x_i * a*

with coefficient *a* and sample period *dt* is:

$$\tau = \frac{a\,dt}{1-a} \Leftrightarrow a = \frac{\tau}{\tau + dt}$$

If the desired time constant and sample rate are known, the filter constant *a* can be picked. Though the sample rates for a sensor can be specified (as discussed in Chapter 5), Android will treat the requested sample rate as a suggestion and does not guarantee that sensor data will be delivered at the specified rate. However, the approximate sample rate is good enough for our purposes because the cutoff frequency is a soft limit too.

Averaging: Smoothness vs. Response Time

It is clear from Figure 6-1 that choosing a smoothing parameter or window size involves a trade-off. On one hand, a large smoothing parameter or window size means that sudden changes in data values may take too long to be reflected in the moving average, and on the other hand, the smoothing parameter and window size should be chosen to be large enough to adequately smooth the data. Additionally, an overly large window size may reduce response time by requiring a longer calculation. A large window size also means that an app cannot get a reading until there is sufficient data to fill the window. Thus, if it takes one minute to fill the window size with data, the app has to wait that long before it has a measurement.

Also, data values may not be evenly spaced in time and the time spacing may vary from device to device. Hence, when defining a suitable window size, it is better to smooth all data values collected in a given *time period* rather than just the last, say, 20 values.

Simple Moving Median (SMM)

The simple moving median is, not surprisingly, the median of the most recent *k* data points. You can find the median by sorting the values in order of size and selecting the value closest to the center. This will give better tolerance for sharp data spikes than the SMA — sharp spikes in data don't even show up if they are much narrower than *k* data points. On the other hand, it is significantly more difficult to code, relatively processor-intensive, and not usually worth it, so is not shown here.

High-Pass

A *high-pass filter* de-emphasizes the static or slowly varying background and emphasizes the higher-frequency or transient components. Note that if all you want to do is to filter out the constant downward gravity component of the accelerometer data and keep the higher-frequency transient changes, use `Sensor.TYPE_LINEAR_ACCELERATION` instead. The Linear Acceleration sensor is a synthetic sensor that consists of high-pass-filtered accelerometer data, and has already been optimized for the particular hardware sensors in each device that will run your app.

Inverse Low-Pass Filter

The simplest way perform high-pass filtering is to do a low-pass filter and then subtract the result from the sensor data. For example, to filter the accelerometer data, the components of the data might be separated and adjusted using the code in Listing 6-3.

LISTING 6-3: Applies low-pass-filter to sensor data

```
public void onSensorChanged(SensorEvent event
{
    final float alpha = 0.8;

    gravity[0] = a * gravity[0] + (1 - a) * event.values[0];
    gravity[1] = a * gravity[1] + (1 - a) * event.values[1];
    gravity[2] = a * gravity[2] + (1 - a) * event.values[2];

    linear_acceleration[0] = event.values[0] - gravity[0];
    linear_acceleration[1] = event.values[1] - gravity[1];
    linear_acceleration[2] = event.values[2] - gravity[2];
}
```

This code snippet was derived from http://developer.android.com/reference/android/hardware/SensorEvent.html, which is available under the Apache 2.0 License.

You can choose the parameter *a* as described in the "Weighted Smoothing" section. Also, you need to start with an initial measurement or discard any initial measurements that used the initial zero value. One way to do this would be to initialize values with the first measurement.

A simple implementation of a high-pass filter is shown in Listing 6-4.

LISTING 6-4: Applies high-pass filter to sensor data

```
public void onSensorChanged(SensorEvent event
{
    x = event.values[0];
    y = event.values[1];
    z = event.values[2];
    mHighPassX = highPass(x, mLastX, mHighPassX);
    mHighPassY = highPass(y, mLastY, mHighPassY);
    mHighPassZ = highPass(z, mLastZ, mHighPassZ);
    mLastX = x;
    mLastY = y;
    mLastZ = z;
}

// simple high-pass filter
float highPass(float current, float last, float filtered)
{
    return a * (filtered + current - last);
}
```

To understand how this works, notice that if there is some background offset, this will be common to both *current* and *last* and will be filtered out. If there is some slow background drift, *current* will still approximately equal *last* and it will be filtered out. However, if there is some rapid change in the value, *current* will not equal *last*, and the fluctuation will survive through the filter.

You need to maintain connection with the previous value (so you need the *filtered* variable to appear in the `return` statement), but you also need for the contribution from *filtered* to dissipate to zero over time. To make the contribution dissipate over time and for the data to ultimately be centered around zero over long time scales as high-pass-filtered data should, you need to multiply *filtered* by *a*, which is some number between 0 and 1.

The effect of high-pass filtering is shown in Figure 6-3.

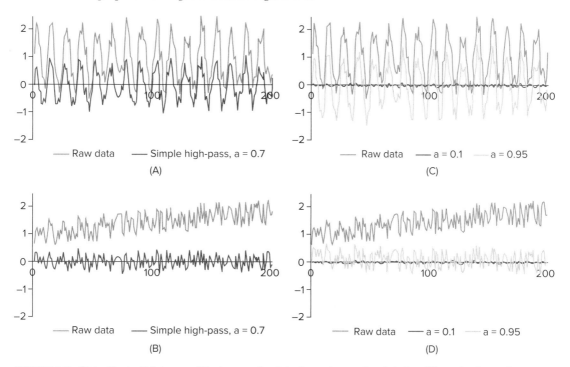

FIGURE 6-3: The effect of high-pass filtering on simulated accelerometer data for different values of *a*. Notice that high-frequency shaking in (A) passes through but low-frequency drift and offset in (A) and (B) do not pass. (C) and (D) give two extreme values of *a* for comparison, plotted on a separate graph from (A) and (B) for clarity.

Bandpass

A *bandpass filter* (or its inverse, the band-reject or notch filter) is useful to emphasize (or de-emphasize) a certain frequency signal and de-emphasize (or emphasize) higher and lower frequencies.

In its simplest incarnation, and in the form most useful for most Android sensor applications, it is simply a combination of a low-pass and high-pass filter. Data is first filtered to keep the higher-frequency components, and then the very high-frequency noise is filtered out with a low-pass smoothing filter.

Introducing Kalman Filters

A Kalman filter can provide excellent signal processing results, but is complicated to implement for all but the simplest examples. To use a Kalman filter, prior knowledge about the source of the data is needed. The algorithm is fed noisy measurements, some predictions about how the measurement's true value is behaving, maybe some knowledge about forces that are causing the system to change, and a Kalman filter algorithm can efficiently find an accurate estimate of something's true value. Kalman filters are extremely flexible and can be used to smooth high-frequency noise or to isolate a periodic signal such as a pedometer signal.

Entire textbooks have been written on the subject, and it is easy to get lost in the linear algebra. This chapter includes a simple introduction to present some exposure to a Kalman filter. In this example, a signal that originated from a pressure sensor (either an internal Sensor.TYPE_PRESSURE or external sensor via Android Open Accessory) will be processed. However, Kalman filters can be applied to any signal from any sensor.

For this example, let the actual current air pressure be approximately 1010.0 mbar, plus or minus 0.5 mbar, and the pressure sensor gives uniformly random results within a range of ±1.5 mbar of the true pressure. A Kalman filter picks a weighted average of the guess and the actual measurement. The weight is computed by the following formula:

```
weight = guess_variance / (guess_variance + sensor_variance);
```

In this case, the weight computes to 0.5 / (0.5 + 1.5) = 0.25. A weight approaching 1 would mean that the sensor's readings can be trusted, and a value approaching 0 means the guess is trusted. A value of 0.25 makes sense because the sensor variance is larger than the guess variance, so the guess should be trusted more.

Assume the pressure sensor provides a measurement of 1011.0 mbar. First the weighted average is computed:

```
estimate = guess + weight * (measurement - guess);
```

or equivalently:

```
estimate = (1-weight) * guess + weight * measurement;
```

You compute 1010 + 0.25 * (1011 − 1010) = 1010.25 mbar. Notice this value is 25 percent of the way from 1010 to 1011 mbar, as expected.

Second, the confidence of the 1010.25 mbar value is computed:

```
estimate_variance = guess_variance*sensor_variance / (guess_variance+sensor_variance)
```

This is 0.5 * 1.5 / (0.5 + 1.5) = 0.375 mbar. The algorithm now has a guess that the pressure is 1010.25 ± 0.375 mbar, and a sensor indicating that the pressure is plus or minus 1.5 mbar. The algorithm is now essentially back to where it started, and can run again. Say another measurement read to be 1010.5 mbar. The algorithm then calculates the three quantities again:

```
weight = 0.375 / (0.375 + 1.5) = 0.2
estimate = 1010.25 + 0.2 * (1010.5 - 1010.25) = 1010.3
estimate_variance = 0.375 * 1.5 / (0.375 + 1.5) = 0.3
```

So now it guesses that the pressure is 1010.3 ± 0.3 mbar.

In practice, such a simple example offers little advantage over simply smoothing the data using a low-pass filter, and doesn't include any external "forces" that would cause the actual air pressure to change (such as air pressure drift, or the twice-daily air pressure fluctuation due to atmospheric tides). However, it does provide insight into how a Kalman filter compares measurements to an expected physical model that you define with your estimates and weights. A full explanation would fill a textbook, but if functionality beyond simple smoothing and simple high-pass filtering is needed, a Kalman filter will give the best results.

A BETTER DETERMINATION OF ORIENTATION BY USING SENSOR FUSION

Several apps need to know the current orientation of a device. The angular velocity of the device might be useful too, so the problem is to map the sensor outputs onto these desired quantities (see Figure 6-4). The sensor outputs can indicate which direction is "north" and "down" (and therefore provide pitch, roll, and yaw) and an angular velocity, so it is natural to think that the problem is solved (see Figure 6-5). However, the accelerometer and compass are inherently noisy and give poor results. Note that the GPS can be used to get the heading, instead of the compass, if the device is moving — a device in a car dock in a moving car is a good example.

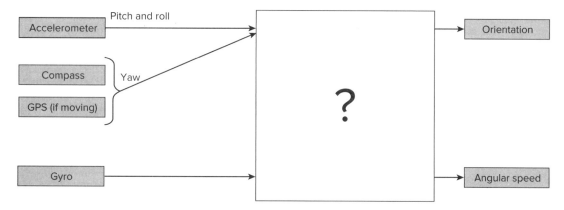

FIGURE 6-4: Graphical representation of the problem of using sensor fusion to determine orientation

Sensor Fusion: Simple vs. Proprietary

Since API level 9, `SensorManager` has had a `getOrientation()` method and there has been a "Rotation sensor" (referenced by `Sensor.TYPE_ROTATION`) that allows a developer to easily find the orientation of the device (see Chapter 5). However, the actual implementation of these synthetic sensors can be different depending on the hardware sensors and the device manufacturer. For instance, devices since around 2010 that incorporate an Invensense brand gyroscope (and possibly also an Invensense accelerometer) such as the Galaxy Nexus, Samsung Galaxy Tab 10.1, and HTC EVO 3D, are likely to also incorporate Invensense's Sensor Fusion algorithms. In short, this means that they get low-noise orientation data primarily from integrated gyroscope data, but mitigate the effects of gyro drift by constantly comparing that data to the pitch, roll, and yaw reported by the accelerometer and compass, which do not drift.

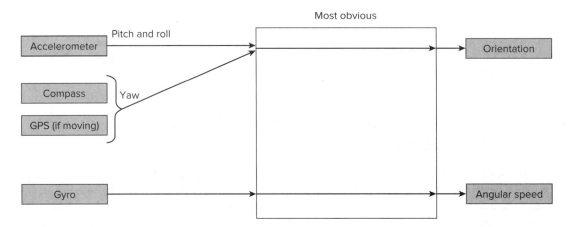

FIGURE 6-5: Determining orientation by directly mapping sensor inputs to the desired outputs

Proprietary Sensor Fusion

Invensense's Sensor Fusion algorithms are proprietary — Invensense as a company works with smartphone manufacturers to get their sensors and algorithms implemented — and the action happens behind the scenes during product development, so these algorithms are not available for developers to use. Developers just use `Sensor.TYPE_ROTATION` on participating devices. Older devices, non-participating devices, or devices using a different brand of gyroscope (which includes most devices today) use the algorithms depicted in Figure 6-5 or Figure 6-6 to find orientation. However, the presence of `SensorManager.getOrientation()` and `Sensor.TYPE_ROTATION` in the API and the success of Invensense's approach means that other gyroscope and Android device manufacturers will follow suit, and comparable open source Android sensor fusion algorithms will probably become available. This means that it is always a good idea to use the rotation sensor or `getOrientation()` whenever possible, rather than use raw accelerometer and compass data, so that in future devices your app will use superior sensor fusion algorithms without any work on your part.

`SensorManager.getOrientation()` requires a rotation matrix as a parameter. In the Android API, there are multiple ways to produce the rotation matrix. However, for the use of `getOrientation()`, a rotation matrix should not be produced by passing the sensor readings from the accelerometer and magnetic field sensor to the `getRotationMatrix()` method. The reason to avoid this method for producing a rotation matrix is that orientation should be relatively static. An app usually wants to know which way the phone is pointing, and not take into account any rapid shaking of the phone. Any readings from the accelerometer will include shaking of the device.

Because the sensor fusion algorithms are not available to most developers, developers continue to consider other methods to determine orientation. They may naively expect that, knowing the initial orientation, if they integrate the gyro measurement (see Figure 6-7) they can compute any final orientation. Unfortunately, if the gyro doesn't read perfectly zero when stationary (and it doesn't), this offset and drift will keep adding to the computed angle, and within a second or so, a completely unphysical answer may be produced.

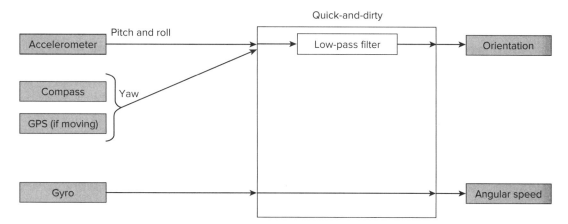

FIGURE 6-6: Quick and dirty use of a low-pass filter to determine orientation

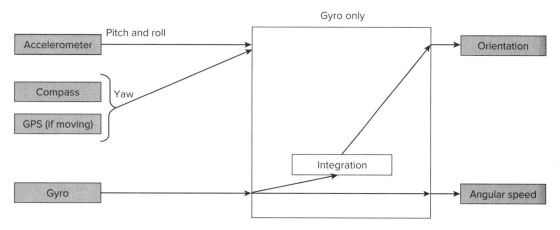

FIGURE 6-7: Integrating gyroscope readings to determine orientation

Simple Sensor Fusion: The Balance Filter

A simple sensor fusion algorithm called a *balance filter* or *complementary filter* (though it is not a complementary filter in the technical sense) has been promoted by Shane Colton at MIT (see Figure 6-8). This integrates the gyroscope to get angle, then high-pass filters the result to remove drift, and adds it to the smoothed accelerometer and compass results. The integrated, high-pass-filtered gyro data and the accelerometer/compass data are added in such a way that the two parts add to one, so that the output is an accurate estimate in units that make sense.

For the balance filter, the time constant may be tweaked to tune the response. The shorter the time constant, the better the response but the more acceleration noise will be allowed to pass through.

To see how this works, imagine you have the newest gyro data point (in rad/s) stored in `gyro`, the newest angle measurement from the accelerometer is stored in `angle_acc`, and `dt` is the time from the last gyro data until now. Then your new angle would be calculated using

```
angle = b * (angle + gyro*dt) + (1 - b) *(angle_acc);
```

You may start by trying b = 0.98 for instance, because you want to primarily use the gyroscope data. You will also probably want to use a fast gyroscope measurement time `dt` so the gyro doesn't drift more than a couple of degrees before the next measurement is taken.

The balance filter is useful and simple to implement, but is not the ideal sensor fusion approach. Invensense's approach involves some clever algorithms and probably some form of Kalman filter (see Figure 6-9) and will provide superior orientation results.

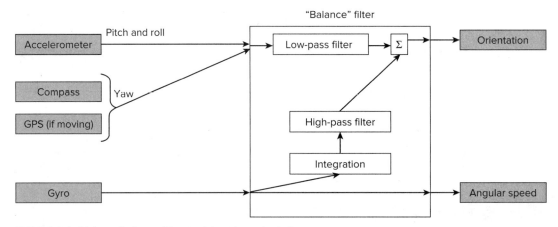

FIGURE 6-8: Using a balance filter to determine orientation

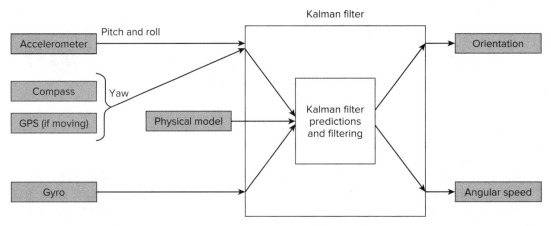

FIGURE 6-9: Use of Kalman filters to determine device orientation

SUMMARY

Sensors produce various types of errors from different sources. In order to use the data that a sensor provides, an app must be able to detect and work around this erroneous data. This chapter provided some techniques for dealing with sensor error in the form of filtering and sensor fusion techniques.

Understanding the difference between various filtering algorithms will allow you to determine when the use of each algorithm is appropriate. For example, high-pass and low-pass filters behave differently and are used in different scenarios. Being able to identify when the various filtering algorithms and fusion techniques are appropriate is an important part of utilizing the data that sensors provide.

Furthermore, understanding when proprietary sensor fusion techniques might be "baked" in to an existing Android API call can prevent an author from implementing or using a fusion technique that is home grown like a balance filter.

The approaches in the chapter are useful in a wide range of scenarios for interpreting physical sensor data. However, the approaches can also be used on any sensor data that an app is processing. Chapters 7–10 describe processing different kinds of the sensor data for various tasks and use the algorithms and concepts described in this chapter when appropriate.

Determining Device Orientation

➤ Using the gravity sensor to determine orientation

➤ Using the accelerometer and magnetometer to determine device orientation

➤ Using the rotation vector synthetic sensor to determine device orientation

➤ Using OpenGL to perform simple screen drawing

Determining the orientation of a device is something that is useful to many apps. Games, for example, can use changes in a device's orientation as a way of allowing humans to interact and control a device. A human can change the orientation of a device and an app can react to that change in orientation. The sensors used to determine device orientation were introduced in Chapter 5. This chapter goes into more detail on how to effectively use some of these sensors and provides an example app to further demonstrate their usage.

The example app functionality described in this chapter determines whether a device is face up or face down. Multiple sensors can be used to determine device orientation of this nature, and the code presented in this chapter makes use of multiple sensors to detect the desired changes in orientation.

PREVIEWING THE EXAMPLE APP

When the device senses a change in the device orientation (with respect to the face of the device), the example app for this chapter uses the Text-To-Speech (TTS) facilities to announce that the device is face up or face down, as well as display the current orientation on the screen. In addition to the current orientation, the app also displays the sensor data on the screen to allow the user to see how manipulating the device affects the sensor data.

The app allows the user to select different sensors to detect the change in orientation and provides a group of radio buttons that the user can toggle to select the desired sensor.

Because audio feedback is not always convenient (especially while working in a coffee shop), the app also allows the user to disable the TTS alerts as well as control their volume with the standard Android volume keys. The main screen for the app is shown in Figure 7-1.

FIGURE 7-1: The Determine Orientation screen

Now that what the example app will do has been discussed, this chapter will move on to how the example app will perform its task of determining device orientation.

DETERMINING DEVICE ORIENTATION

As discussed in the previous section, the example app uses multiple different sensors to determine the device orientation. The app allows the user to choose one of the following sensors to determine device orientation:

➤ Gravity sensor

➤ Accelerometer and magnetometer

➤ Gravity sensor and magnetometer

➤ Rotation sensor

You might notice that the TYPE_ORIENTATION sensor is missing. This sensor has been deprecated and therefore will not be used in the example app.

The next few sections discuss how each of the sensors listed will be used.

Gravity Sensor

Using the gravity sensor (available in API level 9 and greater) to determine whether the device is face up or face down can be one of the easier approaches discussed in this chapter. However, it yields less data on the overall orientation of the device. The gravity sensor yields the force due to gravity on the X, Y, and Z axes. Refer to Figure 5-4 to see how the X, Y, and Z axes are defined with respect to an Android device.

One important note about Figure 5-4 is that the depiction is of a device in its default orientation. The default orientation for phones is portrait, but this is not true of most tablets. However, even for a device that has a default orientation of landscape, the axes will still be orientated as Y pointing up, X pointing to the right, and Z pointing out of the screen.

From Figure 5-4, you can see that to determine if the device is face up or face down, the values of the Z axis need to be considered. The arrow of the Z axis indicates the direction of positive values. So, when the device is face up, the values are positive, and the values are negative when the device is face down.

The magnitude of the gravity sensor is defined by the force of gravity that is being applied to a device. Technically, this is based on where the device is located. Chances are that the device will be located on Earth where the force of gravity is roughly 9.8 m/sec^2. So, when the device is lying face up on a table, the gravity sensor should report a magnitude of 9.8 on the Z axis. When the device is face down on a table, the gravity sensor should report a magnitude of –9.8 on the Z axis.

As discussed in Chapter 5, the values reported by the sensor will be affected by noise, so the code that uses the sensor will need to account for the noise when attempting to determine device orientation. For this application of the gravity sensor, this means that values reported when the device is lying face up or face down will not be exactly 9.8 and –9.8 m/sec^2. Furthermore, hardware offsets may also prevent the value of 9.8 m/sec^2 from being reported by the sensor.

Accelerometer and Magnetometer

The accelerometer and magnetometer can be used together to determine device orientation. The data provided from both of these sensors can be used to generate a rotation matrix via a call to `SensorManager.getRotationMatrix()`. The generated rotation matrix can then be passed to `SensorManager.getOrientation()`, which will compute rotation around the X, Y, and Z axes.

As mentioned in Chapter 5, nearby magnets can influence the magnetometer. The magnetometer can also be exceedingly noisy and may not be calibrated correctly. All of these scenarios can lead to incorrect sensor data.

The output from the `SensorManager.getOrientation()` call is a list of values that contains the azimuth, pitch, and roll for the device. Refer to Figure 5-9 to see how the Earth's axes are defined for the `SensorManager.getOrientation()` call.

In Figure 5-9, the azimuth is the Z axis, the pitch is the X axis, and the roll is the Y axis. To determine if the device is face up or face down, only the X and Y axes (pitch and roll values) need to be considered. The Z axis (azimuth) gives the orientation of the top of the device with respect to north. Although this can be useful, the application does not care about that orientation.

The values from the X axis indicate how much the device is rotated up or down on its short edges. Because the device needs to be flat to be considered in a face-up or face-down position, the code looks for small values. A value of $\pi/2$ radians or $-\pi/2$ radians indicates that the device is standing perpendicular to the ground on either its top or bottom, respectively.

Similarly, the Y axis values indicate whether or not the device is standing on one of its long edges. A value of $-\pi/2$ radians indicates that the device is standing perpendicular to the ground on its left edge, and a value of $\pi/2$ radians indicates that the device is standing on its right side perpendicular to the ground. Values of 0 or $-\pi$ indicate that the device is lying flat.

For this app, the device is considered to be in a face-up or face-down position only if it is lying relatively flat on a surface. Therefore, the pitch needs to have a value of 0 radians and the roll needs to have a value of 0 radians when face up and π radians when face down. Once again, the sensors used for the calculations will be affected by noise, which the app will need to consider.

While the values provided by the accelerometer can be used to generate a rotation matrix that can be fed to `SensorManager.getRotationMatrix()`, accelerometer data may not be the best choice. This is because the orientation should be something relatively static, meaning that an app usually wants to know which way the phone is pointing and not take into account any rapid shaking of the phone. Therefore, instead of using the accelerometer, which would include that fast shaking, use of the gravity sensor may be a better choice because it would isolate the overall orientation of the phone.

Gravity Sensor and Magnetometer

Using the gravity sensor and magnetometer sensors to determine orientation is similar to using the accelerometer and magnetometer. In both cases, a rotation matrix is generated with a call to `SensorManager.getRotationMatrix()` and the generated rotation matrix is passed to `SensorManager.getRotationMatrix()`. The only difference is that values obtained from the gravity sensor are passed to the `SensorManager.getRotationMatrix()` call instead of values originating from the accelerometer

Rotation Vector

As discussed in Chapter 5, the rotation vector sensor is a synthetic sensor that makes use of the accelerometer, magnetometer, and possibly the gyroscope to produce device orientation information. Because of the raw sensors used by the rotation vector sensor, its output can be used in much the same way as the output of the accelerometer and magnetometer that was discussed in the previous section. The rotation vector returned from the sensor can be converted to a rotation matrix with a call to `SensorManager.getRotationMatrixFromVector()` and the resulting rotation matrix can be passed to `SensorManager.getOrientation()`.

Using the rotation vector is often simpler than using the accelerometer and magnetometer to determine device orientation. The rotation vector synthetic sensor hides some of the complexity of using multiple sensors together to produce the data needed to generate a rotation matrix to pass to `SensorManager.getOrientation()`. Thus, it is often preferable to use the rotation matrix synthetic sensor over the accelerometer and magnetometer to determine device orientation.

While the angles produced by `SensorManager.getOrientation()` can be a convenient representation of device rotation, there are related limitations. The Euclidean representation of rotation may not be suitable for more complex apps where problems such as Gimbal lock may occur. Because of these limitations, a quaternion representation of the current rotation may be preferable. For such cases, the `SensorManager.getQuaternionFromVector()` can be used to generate the quaternion representation.

Implementation Details

Now it's time to jump into more of the implementation details of the app. The implementation for this part of the example app is located entirely in `DetermineOrientationActivity`.

The layout used for the `DetermineOrientationActivity` presents the user with a set of radio buttons as well as displays the data returned from the selected sensor in the screen. Listing 7-1 shows the layout for the activity.

Available for
download on
Wrox.com

LISTING 7-1: Layout for DetermineOrientationActivity

```xml
<?xml version="1.0" encoding="utf-8"?>
<RelativeLayout xmlns:android="http://schemas.android.com/apk/res/android"
    android:layout_width="match_parent"
    android:layout_height="match_parent"
    android:orientation="vertical" >

    <RadioGroup android:id="@+id/sensorSelector"
        android:layout_width="match_parent"
        android:layout_height="wrap_content"
        android:layout_alignParentTop="true" >

        <RadioButton android:id="@+id/gravitySensor"
            android:layout_width="match_parent"
            android:layout_height="wrap_content"
            android:text="@string/gravitySensorLabel"
            android:checked="true"
            android:onClick="onSensorSelectorClick" />

        <RadioButton android:id="@+id/accelerometerMagnetometer"
            android:layout_width="match_parent"
            android:layout_height="wrap_content"
            android:text="@string/accelerometerMagnetometerLabel"
            android:checked="false"
            android:onClick="onSensorSelectorClick" />

        <RadioButton android:id="@+id/gravityMagnetometer"
            android:layout_width="match_parent"
            android:layout_height="wrap_content"
            android:text="@string/gravityMagnetometerLabel"
            android:checked="false"
            android:onClick="onSensorSelectorClick" />

        <RadioButton android:id="@+id/rotationVector"
            android:layout_width="match_parent"
            android:layout_height="wrap_content"
            android:text="@string/rotationVectorLabel"
            android:checked="false"
```

continues

LISTING 7-1 *(continued)*

```xml
            android:onClick="onSensorSelectorClick" />
</RadioGroup>

<ToggleButton android:id="@+id/ttsNotificationsToggleButton"
    android:layout_width="wrap_content"
    android:layout_height="wrap_content"
    android:text="@string/speakOrientationLabel"
    android:checked="true"
    android:layout_below="@id/sensorSelector"
    android:textOn="@string/ttsNotificationsOn"
    android:textOff="@string/ttsNotificationsOff"
    android:onClick="onTtsNotificationsToggleButtonClicked" />

<TextView android:id="@+id/selectedSensorLabel"
    android:layout_width="wrap_content"
    android:layout_height="wrap_content"
    android:text="@string/selectedSensorLabel"
    android:layout_below="@id/ttsNotificationsToggleButton"
    android:layout_marginRight="5dip" />

<TextView android:id="@+id/selectedSensorValue"
    android:layout_width="wrap_content"
    android:layout_height="wrap_content"
    android:layout_toRightOf="@id/selectedSensorLabel"
    android:layout_alignTop="@id/selectedSensorLabel"
    android:layout_alignBottom="@id/selectedSensorLabel" />

<TextView android:id="@+id/orientationLabel"
    android:layout_width="wrap_content"
    android:layout_height="wrap_content"
    android:text="@string/orientationLabel"
    android:layout_below="@id/selectedSensorValue"
    android:layout_marginRight="5dip" />

<TextView android:id="@+id/orientationValue"
    android:layout_width="wrap_content"
    android:layout_height="wrap_content"
    android:layout_toRightOf="@id/orientationLabel"
    android:layout_alignTop="@id/orientationLabel"
    android:layout_alignBottom="@id/orientationLabel" />

<TextView android:id="@+id/sensorXLabel"
    android:layout_width="wrap_content"
    android:layout_height="wrap_content"
    android:layout_below="@id/orientationValue"
    android:layout_marginRight="5dip" />

<TextView android:id="@+id/sensorXValue"
    android:layout_width="wrap_content"
    android:layout_height="wrap_content"
    android:layout_toRightOf="@id/sensorXLabel"
    android:layout_alignTop="@id/sensorXLabel"
```

```
            android:layout_alignBottom="@id/sensorXLabel" />

    <TextView android:id="@+id/sensorYLabel"
        android:layout_width="wrap_content"
        android:layout_height="wrap_content"
        android:layout_below="@id/sensorXLabel"
        android:layout_marginRight="5dip" />

    <TextView android:id="@+id/sensorYValue"
        android:layout_width="wrap_content"
        android:layout_height="wrap_content"
        android:layout_toRightOf="@id/sensorYLabel"
        android:layout_alignTop="@id/sensorYLabel"
        android:layout_alignBottom="@id/sensorYLabel" />

    <TextView android:id="@+id/sensorZLabel"
        android:layout_width="wrap_content"
        android:layout_height="wrap_content"
        android:layout_below="@id/sensorYLabel"
        android:layout_marginRight="5dip" />

    <TextView android:id="@+id/sensorZValue"
        android:layout_width="wrap_content"
        android:layout_height="wrap_content"
        android:layout_toRightOf="@id/sensorZLabel"
        android:layout_alignTop="@id/sensorZLabel"
        android:layout_alignBottom="@id/sensorZLabel" />

</RelativeLayout>
```

code snippet determine_orientation.xml

The initialization steps that need to be performed by the DetermineOrientationActivity are:

➤ Get a reference to the SensorManager

➤ Initialize the Text-To-Speech facility (to notify the user of the device's orientation)

As with most activities, this is done in DetermineOrientationActivity.onCreate(), which is shown in Listing 7-2.

LISTING 7-2: DetermineOrientationActivity.onCreate()

```
@Override
protected void onCreate(Bundle savedInstanceState)
{
    super.onCreate(savedInstanceState);
    super.setContentView(R.layout.determine_orientation);

    // Keep the screen on so that changes in orientation can be easily
    // observed
    getWindow().addFlags(WindowManager.LayoutParams.FLAG_KEEP_SCREEN_ON);

    // Set up stream to use for Text-To-Speech
```

continues

LISTING 7-2 *(continued)*

```
ttsParams = new HashMap<String, String>();
ttsParams.put(Engine.KEY_PARAM_STREAM, String.valueOf(TTS_STREAM));

// Set the volume control to use the same stream as TTS which allows
// the user to easily adjust the TTS volume
this.setVolumeControlStream(TTS_STREAM);

// Get a reference to the sensor service
sensorManager = (SensorManager) getSystemService(SENSOR_SERVICE);

// Initialize references to the UI views that will be updated in the
// code
sensorSelector = (RadioGroup) findViewById(R.id.sensorSelector);
selectedSensorValue = (TextView) findViewById(R.id.selectedSensorValue);
orientationValue = (TextView) findViewById(R.id.orientationValue);
sensorXLabel = (TextView) findViewById(R.id.sensorXLabel);
sensorXValue = (TextView) findViewById(R.id.sensorXValue);
sensorYLabel = (TextView) findViewById(R.id.sensorYLabel);
sensorYValue = (TextView) findViewById(R.id.sensorYValue);
sensorZLabel = (TextView) findViewById(R.id.sensorZLabel);
sensorZValue = (TextView) findViewById(R.id.sensorZValue);
ttsNotificationsToggleButton =
        (ToggleButton) findViewById(R.id.ttsNotificationsToggleButton);

// Retrieve stored preferences
preferences = getPreferences(MODE_PRIVATE);
ttsNotifications =
        preferences.getBoolean(TTS_NOTIFICATION_PREFERENCES_KEY, true);
}
```

After the initialization is complete, the next step is to register for the appropriate sensors based on the user's preferences. Recall from Figure 7-1 that the user can toggle the method that is used to determine the orientation of the device. The code needs to register for the proper sensor events based on the user's selection. The DetermineOrientationActivity.updateSelectedSensor() method is responsible for enabling and disabling the appropriate sensors based on the user's selection. The method is called from both DetermineOrientationActivity.onResume() and the code that handles the clicks to the radio buttons. Listing 7-3 shows the implementation of the updateSelectedSensor() method.

Available for
download on
Wrox.com

LISTING 7-3: DetermineOrientationActivity.UpdateSelectedSensor()

```
private void updateSelectedSensor()
{
    // Clear any current registrations
    sensorManager.unregisterListener(this);

    // Determine which radio button is currently selected and enable the
    // appropriate sensors
    selectedSensorId = sensorSelector.getCheckedRadioButtonId();
    if (selectedSensorId == R.id.accelerometerMagnetometer)
    {
```

```
        sensorManager.registerListener(this,
                sensorManager.getDefaultSensor(Sensor.TYPE_ACCELEROMETER),
                RATE);

        sensorManager.registerListener(this,
                sensorManager.getDefaultSensor(Sensor.TYPE_MAGNETIC_FIELD),
                RATE);
    }
    else if (selectedSensorId == R.id.gravityMagnetometer)
    {
        sensorManager.registerListener(this,
                sensorManager.getDefaultSensor(Sensor.TYPE_GRAVITY),
                RATE);

        sensorManager.registerListener(this,
                sensorManager.getDefaultSensor(Sensor.TYPE_MAGNETIC_FIELD),
                RATE);
    }
    else if ((selectedSensorId == R.id.gravitySensor))
    {
        sensorManager.registerListener(this,
                sensorManager.getDefaultSensor(Sensor.TYPE_GRAVITY),
                RATE);
    }
    else
    {
        sensorManager.registerListener(this,
                sensorManager.getDefaultSensor(Sensor.TYPE_ROTATION_VECTOR),
                RATE);
    }

    // Update the label with the currently selected sensor
    RadioButton selectedSensorRadioButton =
            (RadioButton) findViewById(selectedSensorId);
    selectedSensorValue.setText(selectedSensorRadioButton.getText());
}
```

code snippet DetermineOrientationActivity.java

Notice that the method first makes a call to `SensorManager.unregister()` to turn off any sensor updates that may already be registered. This is done so that the users can update the method used to determine the orientation as often as they desire and the app will respond appropriately.

Because `updateSelectedSensor()` registers the current instance of `DetermineOrientationActivity`, the class must implement `SensorEventListener` and contain implementation for both `onSensorChanged()` and `onAccuracyChanged()`.

This implementation for determining the device's orientation does not use the sensor accuracy, so the implementation of `onAccuracyChanged()` is left blank other than a logging comment.

The `onSensorChanged()` method must process `SensorEvents` from multiple different sensors. The actual sensor data that is received is dependent on the user's selection. Because the sensor registrations are updated when the user selects a different sensor, the `onSensorChanged()` method does not need to concern itself with what the user's selection. The method will receive only the relevant sensor data.

The sensor data is located in the `SensorEvent.values` array. Because the data can represent different quantities depending on what sensor generated it, `onSensorChanged()` must determine the source of the data before it can determine how to process the data.

Processing Gravity Sensor Data

For the gravity sensor, the `SensorEvent.values` array contains the magnitude of gravity as applied to the X, Y, and Z axes in the zeroth, first, and second slots in the array, respectively. Because the Z axis goes through the screen of the device and out of the back of the device, the code needs to use the third (offset 2) value in the array. When the device is on its back, the force of gravity being applied to the Z axis should equal the 1 G (9.8 m/sec²), which is stored in the constant `SensorManager.STANDARD_GRAVITY`. When the phone is on its face, the force of gravity on the Z axis should be –1 * `SensorManager.STANDARD_GRAVITY` (–9.8 m/sec²). However, remember that the sensor does generate a fair amount of noise, causing the actual values reported by the sensor to fluctuate. To combat the noise, the app uses a value of `SensorManager.STANDARD_GRAVITY/2` as the threshold for determining if the device is face up or face down. This provides the added bonus of allowing the user to trigger the face-up and face-down handlers without the device being perfectly parallel to the ground, making it easier for the user to get the triggers to fire.

The code snippet that processes the gravity sensor data is presented in Listing 7-4.

LISTING 7-4: Determining orientation with the gravity sensor

Available for download on Wrox.com

```
private static final double GRAVITY_THRESHOLD =
            SensorManager.STANDARD_GRAVITY / 2;
...
case Sensor.TYPE_GRAVITY:
    ...
    if (event.values[2] >= GRAVITY_THRESHOLD)
    {
        onFaceUp();
    }
    else if (event.values[2] <= (GRAVITY_THRESHOLD * -1))
    {
        onFaceDown();
    }

    break;
...
```

code snippet DetermineOrientationActivity.java

Processing Accelerometer and Magnetic Field Data

The values from the accelerometer and the magnetic sensors are passed to `SensorManager` `.getRotationMatrix()` to generate a rotation matrix that is used as input to `SensorManager` `.getOrientation()` to produce the device orientation.

Because both sets of values are needed to determine the device orientation, `DetermineOrientationActivity` maintains the most recent array of values from both sensors as member data for the class. When reading sensor data that may not be consumed before a subsequent call to onSensorEvent(), it is important to copy the event.values instead of just assigning another reference. This is because app code does not "own" the SensorEvent and cannot be sure that the values will not be changed. Cloning the event.values array ensures that app code will maintain the value of the event.values array passed to onSensorEvent() even if it should be overwritten by Android.

When onSensorChanged() is called with updated sensor information from either the accelerometer or the magnetic sensor, the method updates the correct member data to generate a rotation matrix with a call to generateRotationMatrix(). Once the rotation matrix is computed, it is passed to determineOrientation(), which computes the orientation. Being dependent on sensor data from two different sources can make using SensorManager.getOrientation() less convenient than using data from a single sensor (like the gravity sensor) to detect simple device orientation changes.

Listing 7-5 shows the implementation for generateRotationMatrix(). The method uses the latest accelerometer and magnetometer values to compute a rotation matrix only if both sets of values have been populated with sensor data.

LISTING 7-5: generateRotationMatrix()

Available for download on Wrox.com

```java
private float[] generateRotationMatrix()
{
    float[] rotationMatrix = null;

    if (accelerationValues != null && magneticValues != null)
    {
        rotationMatrix = new float[16];
        boolean rotationMatrixGenerated;
        rotationMatrixGenerated =
                SensorManager.getRotationMatrix(rotationMatrix,
                null,
                accelerationValues,
                magneticValues);

        if (!rotationMatrixGenerated)
        {
            Log.w(TAG, getString(R.string.rotationMatrixGenFailureMessage));

            rotationMatrix = null;
        }
    }

    return rotationMatrix;
}
```

code snippet DetermineOrientationActivity.java

After verifying that accelerationValues and magneticValues (which are updated in onSensor-Changed()) are non-null, generateRotationMatrix() passes the acceleration and magnetic value arrays to SensorManager.getRotationMatrix(). The initial null check of the acceleration and magnetic values ensures that they both have been updated in onSensorChanged(), meaning that the class has received data from both sensors. The call to `SensorManager.getRotationMatrix()` takes four parameters. The first two parameters are float arrays that hold the computed rotation matrix and the inclination matrix. For this app, `null` is passed for the inclination matrix (parameter two) because those values are not needed. The third and fourth parameters are the acceleration and magnetic values that were set in the `onSensorChanged()` method.

Once the call to `getRotationMatrix()` returns, the array passed as the first parameter will contain the rotation matrix that can be used to compute the device orientation. It is good practice to check the return value of `getRotationMatrix()`. If a value of `false` is returned, the output arrays will be left untouched.

Processing Rotation Vector Data

The sensor data received from the rotation vector sensor gets processed in much the same way as the data from the accelerometer and magnetometer. The major differences are that there is only one sensor used, eliminating the need to preserve cloned member data, and the rotation matrix is generated differently.

The complete implementation for `onSensorChanged()`, which processes the `SensorEvents` for the accelerometer and the gravity and magnetic field sensors, is shown in Listing 7-6.

LISTING 7-6: DetermineOrientationActivity.onSensorChanged()

Available for download on Wrox.com

```java
@Override
public void onSensorChanged(SensorEvent event)
{
    float[] rotationMatrix;

    switch (event.sensor.getType())
    {
        case Sensor.TYPE_GRAVITY:
            sensorXLabel.setText(R.string.xAxisLabel);
            sensorXValue.setText(String.valueOf(event.values[0]));

            sensorYLabel.setText(R.string.yAxisLabel);
            sensorYValue.setText(String.valueOf(event.values[1]));

            sensorZLabel.setText(R.string.zAxisLabel);
            sensorZValue.setText(String.valueOf(event.values[2]));

            sensorYLabel.setVisibility(View.VISIBLE);
            sensorYValue.setVisibility(View.VISIBLE);
            sensorZLabel.setVisibility(View.VISIBLE);
            sensorZValue.setVisibility(View.VISIBLE);

            if (selectedSensorId == R.id.gravitySensor)
            {
                if (event.values[2] >= GRAVITY_THRESHOLD)
                {
```

```
                onFaceUp();
            }
            else if (event.values[2] <= (GRAVITY_THRESHOLD * -1))
            {
                onFaceDown();
            }
        }
        else
        {
            accelerationValues = event.values.clone();
            rotationMatrix = generateRotationMatrix();

            if (rotationMatrix != null)
            {
                determineOrientation(rotationMatrix);
            }
        }

        break;
    case Sensor.TYPE_ACCELEROMETER:
        accelerationValues = event.values.clone();
        rotationMatrix = generateRotationMatrix();

        if (rotationMatrix != null)
        {
            determineOrientation(rotationMatrix);
        }
        break;
    case Sensor.TYPE_MAGNETIC_FIELD:
        magneticValues = event.values.clone();
        rotationMatrix = generateRotationMatrix();

        if (rotationMatrix != null)
        {
            determineOrientation(rotationMatrix);
        }
        break;
    case Sensor.TYPE_ROTATION_VECTOR:

        rotationMatrix = new float[16];
        SensorManager.getRotationMatrixFromVector(rotationMatrix,
                event.values);
        determineOrientation(rotationMatrix);
        break;
    }
}
```

code snippet DetermineOrientationActivity.java

When the user toggles either the accelerometer and magnetometer or the rotation vector sensors, determineOrientation() is called to compute the orientation from a given rotation matrix. Listing 7-7 shows the implementation of determineOrientation().

Available for
download on
Wrox.com

LISTING 7-7: DetermineOrientationActivity.determineOrientation()

```java
private void determineOrientation(float[] rotationMatrix)
{
    float[] orientationValues = new float[3];
    SensorManager.getOrientation(rotationMatrix, orientationValues);

    double azimuth = Math.toDegrees(orientationValues[0]);
    double pitch = Math.toDegrees(orientationValues[1]);
    double roll = Math.toDegrees(orientationValues[2]);

    sensorXLabel.setText(R.string.azimuthLabel);
    sensorXValue.setText(String.valueOf(azimuth));

    sensorYLabel.setText(R.string.pitchLabel);
    sensorYValue.setText(String.valueOf(pitch));

    sensorZLabel.setText(R.string.rollLabel);
    sensorZValue.setText(String.valueOf(roll));

    sensorYLabel.setVisibility(View.VISIBLE);
    sensorYValue.setVisibility(View.VISIBLE);
    sensorZLabel.setVisibility(View.VISIBLE);
    sensorZValue.setVisibility(View.VISIBLE);

    if (pitch <= 10)
    {
        if (Math.abs(roll) >= 170)
        {
            onFaceDown();
        }
        else if (Math.abs(roll) <= 10)
        {
            onFaceUp();
        }
    }
}
```

code snippet DetermineOrientationActivity.java

SensorManager.getOrientation() takes two parameters: a float[] containing the rotation matrix, and a second float[] that will contain the computed values when the method returns. Once the call returns, the app has the values that it needs to determine the orientation of the device.

The float[] populated by the SensorManager.getOrientation() call contains the azimuth, pitch, and roll in slots 0, 1, and 2 of the array. The values will all be in radians. Mainly for display purposes, the app will convert the values to degrees with calls to Math.toDegrees(). The converted values will be written to the UI views so that the user can see the changes in values while changing the orientation of the device. The converted values will also be used to determine if the device is face up or face down.

As discussed earlier in this chapter, the only values that are needed to determine if the device is face up or face down are the pitch and the roll. The pitch should be zero if the device is perpendicular to the ground. However, just like with the gravity sensor, the noise from the sensors must be factored into the algorithm. Additionally, it may be desirable to widen the window when the face-up handler and the face-down handler will be invoked so that the user can easily trigger the handlers. Because of this, a pitch threshold of 10 degrees is used when processing the pitch value. Also, because this app does not care in which direction the device is tilted, the absolute value of the pitch is used.

For similar reasons, the threshold for the roll value is also a value of 10 degrees. This means that the device can be considered face up when the absolute value of the roll is less than or equal to 10 degrees. The device can be considered face down when the absolute value of the roll is greater than or equal to 170 degrees.

The previous sections explained how the sensor data for determining device orientation was received and how it was processed to determine if the device was face up or face down. The only thing left is to notify the user when the orientation changes. DetermineOrientationActivity contains two methods, onFaceDown() and onFaceUp(), which are called when the device changes orientation.

Notifying the User of Orientation Changes

Once the app has determined that the device is either face up or face down, it uses Text-To-Speech (TTS) to alert the user. This makes it easy for a user to be alerted of orientation changes without having to view the screen. Other, more common use cases may have the handler disable ringers or enable/disable other device functionality. Speaking the orientation just makes operating the app easy for the user. Listing 7-8 shows the implementation for onFaceUp() and onFaceDown().

Available for download on Wrox.com

LISTING 7-8: onFaceUp() and onFaceDown()

```
/**
 * Handler for device being face up.
 */
private void onFaceUp()
{
    if (!isFaceUp)
    {
        if (tts != null && ttsNotificationsToggleButton.isChecked())
        {
            tts.speak(getString(R.string.faceUpText),
                    TextToSpeech.QUEUE_FLUSH,
                    ttsParams);
        }

        orientationValue.setText(R.string.faceUpText);
        isFaceUp = true;
    }
}

/**
 * Handler for device being face down.
 */
```

continues

LISTING 7-8 *(continued)*

```java
private void onFaceDown()
{
    if (isFaceUp)
    {
        if (tts != null && ttsNotificationsToggleButton.isChecked())
        {
            tts.speak(getString(R.string.faceDownText),
                    TextToSpeech.QUEUE_FLUSH,
                    ttsParams);
        }

        orientationValue.setText(R.string.faceDownText);
        isFaceUp = false;
    }
}
```

code snippet DetermineOrientationActivity.java

Thusfar, only the parts of DetermineOrientationActivity that deal with Android sensor data or initialization have been discussed. The activity has a few other tricks up its sleeve to keep the screen on and allow the volume buttons to control the volume of the TTS output stream. Because these are out of scope of the discussion of Android sensors, the chapter does not explain that code.

To support the use of TTS, DetermineOrientationActivity extends SpeechRecognizingAndSpeakingActivity, which allows DetermineOrientationActivity to easily support multiple languages. SpeechRecognizationAndSpeechActivity is discussed in Chapter 18.

Listing 7-9 shows the complete DetermineOrientationActivity implementation.

LISTING 7-9: Complete DetermineOrientationActivity implementation

Available for download on Wrox.com

```java
public class DetermineOrientationActivity
extends SpeechRecognizingAndSpeakingActivity implements SensorEventListener
{
    private static final String TAG = "DetermineOrientationActivity";
    private static final int RATE = SensorManager.SENSOR_DELAY_NORMAL;
    private static final int TTS_STREAM = AudioManager.STREAM_NOTIFICATION;
    private static final String TTS_NOTIFICATION_PREFERENCES_KEY =
            "TTS_NOTIFICATION_PREFERENCES_KEY";
    private static final double GRAVITY_THRESHOLD =
            SensorManager.STANDARD_GRAVITY / 2;

    private SensorManager sensorManager;
    private float[] accelerationValues;
    private float[] magneticValues;
    private TextToSpeech tts;
    private boolean isFaceUp;
    private RadioGroup sensorSelector;
```

```java
private TextView selectedSensorValue;
private TextView orientationValue;
private TextView sensorXLabel;
private TextView sensorXValue;
private TextView sensorYLabel;
private TextView sensorYValue;
private TextView sensorZLabel;
private TextView sensorZValue;
private HashMap<String, String> ttsParams;
private ToggleButton ttsNotificationsToggleButton;
private SharedPreferences preferences;
private boolean ttsNotifications;
private int selectedSensorId;

@Override
protected void onCreate(Bundle savedInstanceState)
{
    super.onCreate(savedInstanceState);
    super.setContentView(R.layout.determine_orientation);

    // Keep the screen on so that changes in orientation can be easily
    // observed
    getWindow().addFlags(WindowManager.LayoutParams.FLAG_KEEP_SCREEN_ON);

    // Set up stream to use for Text-To-Speech
    ttsParams = new HashMap<String, String>();
    ttsParams.put(Engine.KEY_PARAM_STREAM, String.valueOf(TTS_STREAM));

    // Set the volume control to use the same stream as TTS which allows
    // the user to easily adjust the TTS volume
    this.setVolumeControlStream(TTS_STREAM);

    // Get a reference to the sensor service
    sensorManager = (SensorManager) getSystemService(SENSOR_SERVICE);

    // Initialize references to the UI views that will be updated in the
    // code
    sensorSelector = (RadioGroup) findViewById(R.id.sensorSelector);
    selectedSensorValue = (TextView) findViewById(R.id.selectedSensorValue);
    orientationValue = (TextView) findViewById(R.id.orientationValue);
    sensorXLabel = (TextView) findViewById(R.id.sensorXLabel);
    sensorXValue = (TextView) findViewById(R.id.sensorXValue);
    sensorYLabel = (TextView) findViewById(R.id.sensorYLabel);
    sensorYValue = (TextView) findViewById(R.id.sensorYValue);
    sensorZLabel = (TextView) findViewById(R.id.sensorZLabel);
    sensorZValue = (TextView) findViewById(R.id.sensorZValue);
    ttsNotificationsToggleButton =
            (ToggleButton) findViewById(R.id.ttsNotificationsToggleButton);

    // Retrieve stored preferences
    preferences = getPreferences(MODE_PRIVATE);
    ttsNotifications =
            preferences.getBoolean(TTS_NOTIFICATION_PREFERENCES_KEY, true);
}
```

continues

LISTING 7-9 *(continued)*

```java
@Override
protected void onResume()
{
    super.onResume();

    ttsNotificationsToggleButton.setChecked(ttsNotifications);
    updateSelectedSensor();
}

@Override
protected void onPause()
{
    super.onPause();

    // Unregister updates from sensors
    sensorManager.unregisterListener(this);

    // Shutdown TTS facility
    if (tts != null)
    {
        tts.shutdown();
    }
}

@Override
public void onSensorChanged(SensorEvent event)
{
    float[] rotationMatrix;

    switch (event.sensor.getType())
    {
        case Sensor.TYPE_GRAVITY:
            sensorXLabel.setText(R.string.xAxisLabel);
            sensorXValue.setText(String.valueOf(event.values[0]));

            sensorYLabel.setText(R.string.yAxisLabel);
            sensorYValue.setText(String.valueOf(event.values[1]));

            sensorZLabel.setText(R.string.zAxisLabel);
            sensorZValue.setText(String.valueOf(event.values[2]));

            sensorYLabel.setVisibility(View.VISIBLE);
            sensorYValue.setVisibility(View.VISIBLE);
            sensorZLabel.setVisibility(View.VISIBLE);
            sensorZValue.setVisibility(View.VISIBLE);

            if (selectedSensorId == R.id.gravitySensor)
            {
                if (event.values[2] >= GRAVITY_THRESHOLD)
                {
                    onFaceUp();
                }
```

```
                else if (event.values[2] <= (GRAVITY_THRESHOLD * -1))
                {
                    onFaceDown();
                }
            }
            else
            {
                accelerationValues = event.values.clone();
                rotationMatrix = generateRotationMatrix();

                if (rotationMatrix != null)
                {
                    determineOrientation(rotationMatrix);
                }
            }

            break;
        case Sensor.TYPE_ACCELEROMETER:
            accelerationValues = event.values.clone();
            rotationMatrix = generateRotationMatrix();

            if (rotationMatrix != null)
            {
                determineOrientation(rotationMatrix);
            }
            break;
        case Sensor.TYPE_MAGNETIC_FIELD:
            magneticValues = event.values.clone();
            rotationMatrix = generateRotationMatrix();

            if (rotationMatrix != null)
            {
                determineOrientation(rotationMatrix);
            }
            break;
        case Sensor.TYPE_ROTATION_VECTOR:

            rotationMatrix = new float[16];
            SensorManager.getRotationMatrixFromVector(rotationMatrix,
                    event.values);
            determineOrientation(rotationMatrix);
            break;
    }
}

@Override
public void onAccuracyChanged(Sensor sensor, int accuracy)
{
    Log.d(TAG,
            String.format("Accuracy for sensor %s = %d",
            sensor.getName(), accuracy));
}

private float[] generateRotationMatrix()
{
```

continues

LISTING 7-9 *(continued)*

```java
        float[] rotationMatrix = null;

        if (accelerationValues != null && magneticValues != null)
        {
            rotationMatrix = new float[16];
            boolean rotationMatrixGenerated;
            rotationMatrixGenerated =
                    SensorManager.getRotationMatrix(rotationMatrix,
                    null,
                    accelerationValues,
                    magneticValues);

            if (!rotationMatrixGenerated)
            {
                Log.w(TAG, getString(R.string.rotationMatrixGenFailureMessage));

                rotationMatrix = null;
            }
        }

        return rotationMatrix;
    }

    private void determineOrientation(float[] rotationMatrix)
    {
        float[] orientationValues = new float[3];
        SensorManager.getOrientation(rotationMatrix, orientationValues);

        double azimuth = Math.toDegrees(orientationValues[0]);
        double pitch = Math.toDegrees(orientationValues[1]);
        double roll = Math.toDegrees(orientationValues[2]);

        sensorXLabel.setText(R.string.azimuthLabel);
        sensorXValue.setText(String.valueOf(azimuth));

        sensorYLabel.setText(R.string.pitchLabel);
        sensorYValue.setText(String.valueOf(pitch));

        sensorZLabel.setText(R.string.rollLabel);
        sensorZValue.setText(String.valueOf(roll));

        sensorYLabel.setVisibility(View.VISIBLE);
        sensorYValue.setVisibility(View.VISIBLE);
        sensorZLabel.setVisibility(View.VISIBLE);
        sensorZValue.setVisibility(View.VISIBLE);

        if (pitch <= 10)
        {
            if (Math.abs(roll) >= 170)
            {
                onFaceDown();
            }
```

```
            else if (Math.abs(roll) <= 10)
            {
                onFaceUp();
            }
        }
    }

    private void onFaceUp()
    {
        if (!isFaceUp)
        {
            if (tts != null && ttsNotificationsToggleButton.isChecked())
            {
                tts.speak(getString(R.string.faceUpText),
                        TextToSpeech.QUEUE_FLUSH,
                        ttsParams);
            }

            orientationValue.setText(R.string.faceUpText);
            isFaceUp = true;
        }
    }

    private void onFaceDown()
    {
        if (isFaceUp)
        {
            if (tts != null && ttsNotificationsToggleButton.isChecked())
            {
                tts.speak(getString(R.string.faceDownText),
                        TextToSpeech.QUEUE_FLUSH,
                        ttsParams);
            }

            orientationValue.setText(R.string.faceDownText);
            isFaceUp = false;
        }
    }

    private void updateSelectedSensor()
    {
        // Clear any current registrations
        sensorManager.unregisterListener(this);

        // Determine which radio button is currently selected and enable the
        // appropriate sensors
        selectedSensorId = sensorSelector.getCheckedRadioButtonId();
        if (selectedSensorId == R.id.accelerometerMagnetometer)
        {
            sensorManager.registerListener(this,
                    sensorManager.getDefaultSensor(Sensor.TYPE_ACCELEROMETER),
                    RATE);

            sensorManager.registerListener(this,
```

continues

LISTING 7-9 *(continued)*

```java
                sensorManager.getDefaultSensor(Sensor.TYPE_MAGNETIC_FIELD),
                RATE);
    }
    else if (selectedSensorId == R.id.gravityMagnetometer)
    {
        sensorManager.registerListener(this,
                sensorManager.getDefaultSensor(Sensor.TYPE_GRAVITY),
                RATE);

        sensorManager.registerListener(this,
                sensorManager.getDefaultSensor(Sensor.TYPE_MAGNETIC_FIELD),
                RATE);
    }
    else if ((selectedSensorId == R.id.gravitySensor))
    {
        sensorManager.registerListener(this,
                sensorManager.getDefaultSensor(Sensor.TYPE_GRAVITY),
                RATE);
    }
    else
    {
        sensorManager.registerListener(this,
                sensorManager.getDefaultSensor(Sensor.TYPE_ROTATION_VECTOR),
                RATE);
    }

    // Update the label with the currently selected sensor
    RadioButton selectedSensorRadioButton =
            (RadioButton) findViewById(selectedSensorId);
    selectedSensorValue.setText(selectedSensorRadioButton.getText());
}

public void onSensorSelectorClick(View view)
{
    updateSelectedSensor();
}

public void onTtsNotificationsToggleButtonClicked(View view)
{
    ttsNotifications = ((ToggleButton) view).isChecked();
    preferences.edit()
        .putBoolean(TTS_NOTIFICATION_PREFERENCES_KEY, ttsNotifications)
        .commit();
}

@Override
public void onSuccessfulInit(TextToSpeech tts)
{
    super.onSuccessfulInit(tts);
    this.tts = tts;
}
```

```
    @Override
    protected void receiveWhatWasHeard(List<String> heard,
                                       float[] confidenceScores)
    {
        // no-op
    }
}
code snippet DetermineOrientationActivity.java
```

code snippet DetermineOrientationActivity.java

NORTHFINDER

The NorthFinder app illustrates how to use the rotation vector sensor to implement an augmented reality app, and how to use OpenGL to change the screen color. When the rear camera is pointed within 20 degrees of north, the app changes the screen's color from red to green. Because the app knows which direction the user is pointing the camera, it could add camera views or other overlays and make a full augmented reality app.

Getting the correct orientation requires two steps: acquire the rotation vector of the device and remap the rotation vector's coordinates to be along the camera's axes. The onSensorChanged() method performs these two steps using SensorManager.getRotationMatrixFromVector() and SensorManager.remapCoordinateSystem(). If the call to remapCoordinateSystem() is removed, the app will measure when the top of the device is pointing north instead of when the device's rear camera is pointing north. Listing 7-10 contains the full implementation.

Available for download on Wrox.com

LISTING 7-10: NorthFinder

```java
public class NorthFinder extends Activity implements SensorEventListener
{
    private static final int ANGLE = 20;

    private TextView tv;
    private GLSurfaceView mGLSurfaceView;
    private MyRenderer mRenderer;
    private SensorManager mSensorManager;
    private Sensor mRotVectSensor;
    private float[] orientationVals = new float[3];

    private final float[] mRotationMatrix = new float[16];

    @Override
    protected void onCreate(Bundle savedInstanceState)
    {
        super.onCreate(savedInstanceState);

        setContentView(R.layout.sensors_north_main);

        mRenderer = new MyRenderer();
        mGLSurfaceView = (GLSurfaceView) findViewById(R.id.glsurfaceview);
```

continues

LISTING 7-10 *(continued)*

```
        mGLSurfaceView.setRenderer(mRenderer);

        tv = (TextView) findViewById(R.id.tv);

        mSensorManager = (SensorManager) getSystemService(SENSOR_SERVICE);
        mRotVectSensor =
                mSensorManager.getDefaultSensor(Sensor.TYPE_ROTATION_VECTOR);

    }

    @Override
    protected void onResume()
    {
        super.onResume();
        mSensorManager.registerListener(this, mRotVectSensor, 10000);
    }

    @Override
    protected void onPause()
    {
        super.onPause();
        mSensorManager.unregisterListener(this);
    }

    @Override
    public void onSensorChanged(SensorEvent event)
    {
        // It is good practice to check that we received the proper sensor event
        if (event.sensor.getType() == Sensor.TYPE_ROTATION_VECTOR)
        {
            // Convert the rotation-vector to a 4x4 matrix.
            SensorManager.getRotationMatrixFromVector(mRotationMatrix,
                    event.values);
            SensorManager
                    .remapCoordinateSystem(mRotationMatrix,
                            SensorManager.AXIS_X, SensorManager.AXIS_Z,
                            mRotationMatrix);
            SensorManager.getOrientation(mRotationMatrix, orientationVals);

            // Optionally convert the result from radians to degrees
            orientationVals[0] = (float) Math.toDegrees(orientationVals[0]);
            orientationVals[1] = (float) Math.toDegrees(orientationVals[1]);
            orientationVals[2] = (float) Math.toDegrees(orientationVals[2]);

            tv.setText(" Yaw: " + orientationVals[0] + "\n Pitch: "
                    + orientationVals[1] + "\n Roll (not used): "
                    + orientationVals[2]);
```

```java
        }
    }

    @Override
    public void onAccuracyChanged(Sensor sensor, int accuracy)
    {
        // no-op
    }

    class MyRenderer implements GLSurfaceView.Renderer
    {
        public void onDrawFrame(GL10 gl)
        {
            // Clear screen
            gl.glClear(GL10.GL_COLOR_BUFFER_BIT);

            // Detect if the device is pointing within +/- ANGLE of north
            if (orientationVals[0] < ANGLE && orientationVals[0] > -ANGLE
                    && orientationVals[1] < ANGLE
                    && orientationVals[1] > -ANGLE)
            {
                gl.glClearColor(0, 1, 0, 1); // Make background green
            }
            else
            {
                gl.glClearColor(1, 0, 0, 1); // Make background red
            }
        }

        @Override
        public void onSurfaceChanged(GL10 gl, int width, int height)
        {
            // no-op
        }

        @Override
        public void onSurfaceCreated(GL10 gl, EGLConfig config)
        {
            // no-op
        }
    }
}
```

code snippet NorthFinder.java

The rotation vector sensor can be used to control a game or in an augmented reality application. OpenGL (Open Graphics Library) can also be used in both cases. This example included the basic example showing how to use OpenGL to perform the simple task of changing the screen from red to green.

SUMMARY

This chapter provided an example of how to make a simple orientation determination, whether the device is face up or face down. To accomplish this, the example in the chapter made use of multiple sensors including the accelerometer, magnetometer, rotation vector, and gravity sensor.

In addition to using TTS to notify the user when the device orientation changes from face up to face down, the `DetermineOrientationActivity` also displays the values that are used to make the determination to the screen. This also allows the user to see how the values change as the phone is moved. Taking some time to run the app and see the values change would be a good use of time before trying to use the sensors. Becoming familiar with how the different axes' rotation values change when the device is moved can save a lot of time during implementation.

8

Detecting Movement

WHAT'S IN THIS CHAPTER?

➤ Explaining the difference between the accelerometer and the linear acceleration sensor

➤ Introducing some of the issues involved with using acceleration data in Android

➤ Providing a method to smooth acceleration data

➤ Providing a functional example of acceleration data being collected and processed to detect device movement

Chapter 7 discussed ways to determine the current orientation of a device using the gravity sensor and `SensorManager.getOrientation()`. This chapter discusses methods to detect device movement using the accelerometer and the linear acceleration sensor. Although both sensors provide acceleration data, the data has differences that may make one sensor preferable over the other in certain situations. This chapter illustrates the differences in how the acceleration data is represented for each sensor.

To aid in illustrating the use of these sensors, this chapter provides an example in the form of a motion detector that uses Text-To-Speech to indicate when device movement is detected. The example app in this chapter will be provided sensor information in a similar manner to the way sensor data was read in Chapter 7. The main difference is the actual sensors that are used in this chapter—the accelerometer and the linear acceleration sensor. As explained in Chapter 5, the accelerometer provides raw acceleration data for the X, Y, and Z axes, and the linear acceleration is a synthetic sensor that performs processing on the raw sensor data before providing it to an app.

The example provided in this chapter will detect linear movement and, similar to the example in Chapter 7, use the Android TTS facility to announce that the device has detected movement. In addition to the audio cues that the device is moving, the example app will also plot the X, Y, and Z axes values as well as the net acceleration value on a graph in real time. The data for the plot will also be stored on the external storage area so that the data can be analyzed (outside of the app) after the app has finished.

Though plotting the data has nothing to do with the detection of movement, it does help tell the story of the data the accelerometer and linear acceleration sensors provide. Being able to analyze the change in component acceleration values (X, Y, and Z axes) and how they affect net acceleration can be extremely useful when attempting to use the data. Figure 8-1 shows a screen shot of the example app collecting and plotting acceleration data.

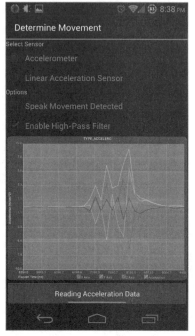

FIGURE 8-1: Running and plotting acceleration data

Whereas Chapter 5 gave a broad overview of these two sensors, this chapter dives into the details of using the sensors and making sense of the data they provide.

ACCELERATION DATA

Both the accelerometer and the linear acceleration sensor provide acceleration data for the X, Y, and Z axes. The acceleration data not only provides the magnitude of the acceleration (in m/sec^2), but also the direction of the acceleration. For each axis, a positive acceleration indicates acceleration in one direction and a negative value indicates acceleration in the opposite direction. Refer to Figure 5-4 to see how the axes are defined for a device.

As an example, if the device is lying flat on a surface and is moved from left to right, a positive acceleration for the X axis would be generated. Conversely, if the device is moved from right to left, a negative acceleration value will be generated. The same logic can be applied to the Y and Z axes as well.

Though both the accelerometer and the linear acceleration sensor produce acceleration data, the major difference between the two is how gravity affects the data values. The accelerometer produces raw acceleration data and is affected by the force of gravity, whereas the linear acceleration sensor factors out the acceleration due to gravity.

Accelerometer Data

Figure 8-2 shows a plot of raw acceleration data that was received from the accelerometer while the device was lying flat on a table with its screen pointing up. Notice that the value of the Z axis is continuously reading a value of ≈9.8 m/sec^2. This is because even when the device is lying motionless, it is being affected by gravity.

If the device is rotated up such that the Y axis forms a 90° angle with the ground, the acceleration value along the Z axis will drop to 0, while the acceleration along the Y axis will jump to 9.8 m/sec^2. In this way, the raw accelerometer data is related to data that was provided by the gravity sensor in Chapter 7.

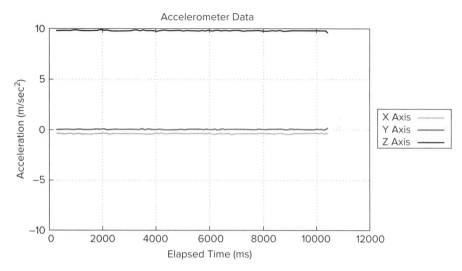

FIGURE 8-2: Accelerometer data of a device lying in its back

To remove the effect of gravity on the acceleration values, a high-pass filter can be applied to the raw accelerometer data. A high-pass filter will reduce the offset that is caused by the constant force of gravity being applied to the device. When using the accelerometer data, this is probably a necessity for an app because including gravity can lead to erroneous calculations. Figure 8-3 shows a plot of accelerometer data where a high-pass filter has been applied to the raw data. Notice that with the high-pass filter applied, all axes values are ≈0 while the device is lying motionless.

Chapter 6 dives much deeper into the details of filtering sensor data.

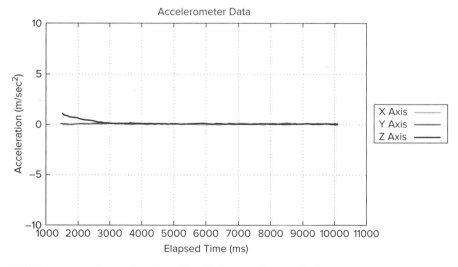

FIGURE 8-3: Accelerometer plot with a high-pass filter applied

Linear Acceleration Sensor Data

Compare Figure 5-4 to Figure 8-4, which shows unfiltered data plotted from the linear acceleration sensor. The data was again collected while the device was lying motionless on its back. Notice that the X, Y, and Z axes all show continuous values close to zero. This is because the linear acceleration sensor factors out the acceleration due to gravity without the need to apply any additional filtering.

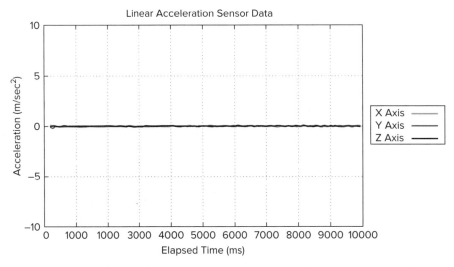

FIGURE 8-4: Linear acceleration sensor plotted data

To reiterate a point made in Chapter 5, if your app needs access to acceleration data that is not influenced by gravity, it is better to use the linear acceleration sensor and allow it to filter the data, than to use the raw accelerometer data.

Though data received when the device is motionless illustrates the differences between raw accelerometer data and data received from the linear acceleration sensor (and the need to filter it), it is data while the device is accelerating/decelerating that the example app is really concerned with. Because the linear acceleration sensor data and the filtered accelerometer data are similar, most of the images of plots that follow only depict data received from only one of the sensors.

Data While Device Is in Motion

When using either the accelerometer or the linear acceleration sensor, an app will typically be interested in the data that is received while the device is accelerating or decelerating. For example, the example for this chapter will monitor one of the sensors (which the user can select) and use the data provided by that sensor to detect changes in device movement. Figure 8-5 shows a plot of data that was recorded while the device went through the following sequence of events:

1. Lay the device flat on its back for 10 seconds.

2. Move the device left to right along the X axis.

3. Leave the device motionless for 10 seconds.

4. Move the device right to left along the X axis.

5. Leave the device motionless for 10 seconds.

6. Move the device left to right along the X axis.

7. Leave the device motionless for 10 seconds.

8. Move the device right to left on the X axis.

9. Leave the device motionless for 10 seconds.

From Figure 8-5, you can see the "spikes" where the device went from motionless to moving. The acceleration values on the X axis went from a value of ≈0 to values greater than or less than 0.

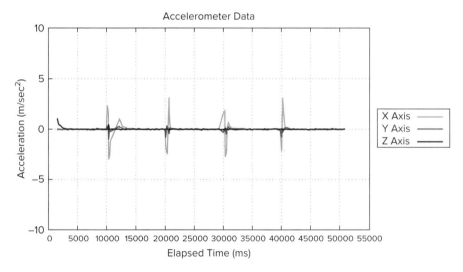

FIGURE 8-5: Acceleration data from moving device along the X axis

Remember that both acceleration sensors not only provide the magnitude of the acceleration, but also the direction as determined by the sign of the acceleration. In Figure 8-5, a move from left to right is shown to have a sharp change in the acceleration value in the positive direction followed by a sharp change in the negative direction. The positive value indicates a force being applied in the positive direction of the X axis as the device accelerates, and the negative value indicates a force being applied in the negative direction of the X axis as the device decelerates. Conversely, when the device is moved from right to left, first a negative acceleration value is provided from the sensor followed by a positive value.

The same logic can be applied to the Y and Z axes and is depicted in Figure 8-6, which shows plotted data that was recorded by the example app. The data generated for this plot came from a device where the following actions were applied:

1. Lay the device flat on its back motionless for 10 seconds.

2. Shake the device left and right along the X axis for 10 seconds.

3. Lay the device flat on its back motionless for 10 seconds.

4. Shake the device forward and back along the Y axis for 10 seconds.

5. Lay the device flat on its back motionless for 10 seconds.

6. Shake the device up and down along the Z axis for 10 seconds.

7. Lay the device flat on its back motionless for 10 seconds.

From Figure 8-6, you can see the drastic change in the acceleration values along each axis when the device is being shaken. This provides the foundation for what is needed to detect motion.

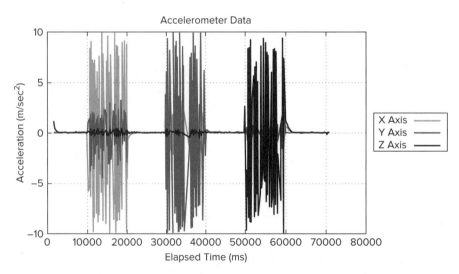

FIGURE 8-6 Data plot from moving the device in the direction of all three axes

The accelerometer and the linear acceleration sensors provide the acceleration in each direction over a three-dimensional space. The next section describes how to compute the total acceleration.

Total Acceleration

The example in this chapter is not concerned with the direction in which the device is accelerating, but the fact that it *is* accelerating. To determine if the device is accelerating, the acceleration values from the X, Y, and Z axes can be used to compute total acceleration by calculating the square root of the sum of the squares for the axes values.

To detect general device acceleration, this is a better approach than simply looking at each axis individually because this will allow you to set a threshold on the acceleration that your app will respond to. This would allow an app to differentiate between the incidental acceleration produced from a person bumping a sitting device from the intentional acceleration produced by a person shaking a device.

Now that some of the concepts have been introduced, it is time to jump into the details of the code.

IMPLEMENTATION

The classes that implement the movement detection part of the example app are located in the `root.gast.playground.movement` package, which contains `DetermineMovementActivity` and `AccelerationEventListener`. `DetermineMovementActivity` is responsible for loading the UI, getting a handle to the `SensorManager`, and registering for sensor updates. `AccelerationEventListener` implements `SensorEventListener` and will receive and respond to updates from the acceleration sensors.

DetermineMovementActivity

Recall from Figure 8-1 that the example app for this chapter allows users to select which sensor they want to utilize in order to detect movement, indicate whether or not to filter the data, and display a graph of the acceleration data across the X, Y and Z axes. A third-party library (`http://androidplot.com`) is used to generate the graph, but that is not the focus of this chapter. However, for those who are interested, the entire source code is available at this book's companion website at `www.wrox.com`.

Once users have selected which sensor to use to report acceleration data, and configured the options for processing the sensor data, they can touch the toggle button at the bottom of the screen to start receiving acceleration data. The handler for the toggle button click event starts or stops the data collection based on the button's current state. The code for the toggle button click handler is shown in Listing 8-1.

LISTING 8-1: Toggle button handler

```
public void onReadAccelerationDataToggleButtonClicked(View view)
{
    ToggleButton toggleButton = (ToggleButton)view;

    if (toggleButton.isChecked())
    {
```

```
        startReadingAccelerationData();
    }
    else
    {
        stopReadingAccelerationData();
    }
}
```

The plotting operation is started in the startReadingAcceleration() method, which is shown in Listing 8-2. In Listing 8-2, the member variable *sensorSelector* is a reference to the RadioGroup that allows the user to select the desired sensor. The member variable *useHighPass-Filter* reflects whether the user has checked the Use High-Pass Filter on the main screen of the activity (see Figure 8-1).

Available for download on Wrox.com

LISTING 8-2: Initialize the AccelerationSensorEventListeners

```
private void startReadingAccelerationData()
{
    if (!readingAccelerationData)
    {
        // Clear any plot that may already exist on the chart
        xyPlot.clear();
        xyPlot.redraw();

        // Disable UI components so they cannot be changed while plotting
        // sensor data
        for (int i = 0; i < sensorSelector.getChildCount(); i++)
        {
            sensorSelector.getChildAt(i).setEnabled(false);
        }
        ttsNotificationsCheckBox.setEnabled(false);
        highPassFilterCheckBox.setEnabled(false);

        // Data files are stored on the external cache directory so they can
        // be pulled off of the device by the user
        File accelerometerDataFile =
                new File(getExternalCacheDir(), "accelerometer.csv");
        File linearAcceclerationDataFile =
                new File(getExternalCacheDir(), "linearAcceleration.csv");

        if (selectedSensorType == Sensor.TYPE_ACCELEROMETER)
        {
            xyPlot.setTitle("Sensor.TYPE_ACCELEROMETER");
            accelerometerListener =
                    new AccelerationEventListener(xyPlot,
                            useHighPassFilter,
                            accelerometerDataFile,
                            (useTtsNotification ? tts : null),
                            ttsParams,
                            getString(R.string.movementDetectedText));
```

```
        linearAccelerationListener =
                new AccelerationEventListener(null,
                        useHighPassFilter,
                        linearAcceclerationDataFile,
                        (useTtsNotification ? tts : null),
                        ttsParams,
                        getString(R.string.movementDetectedText));
    }
    else
    {
        xyPlot.setTitle("Sensor.TYPE_LINEAR_ACCELERATION");
        accelerometerListener =
                new AccelerationEventListener(null,
                        useHighPassFilter,
                        accelerometerDataFile,
                        (useTtsNotification ? tts : null),
                        ttsParams,
                        getString(R.string.movementDetectedText));

        linearAccelerationListener =
                new AccelerationEventListener(xyPlot,
                        useHighPassFilter,
                        linearAcceclerationDataFile,
                        (useTtsNotification ? tts : null),
                        ttsParams,
                        getString(R.string.movementDetectedText));
    }

    sensorManager.registerListener(accelerometerListener,
            sensorManager.getDefaultSensor(Sensor.TYPE_ACCELEROMETER),
            RATE);

    sensorManager.registerListener(linearAccelerationListener,
            sensorManager.getDefaultSensor(Sensor.TYPE_LINEAR_ACCELERATION),
            RATE);

    readingAccelerationData = true;

    Log.d(TAG, "Started reading acceleration data");
}
```

code snippet DetermineMovementActivity.java

Listing 8-2 shows `startReadingAcceleration()` creating two instances of `AccelerationEventListener` and registering them both with `SensorManager.registerListener()`. There is a listener for the accelerometer *and* the linear acceleration sensor because both sensors will be receiving acceleration data at the same time and writing the data to two different CSV files. However, the data of only one sensor will be plotted to the chart, or be used to detect movement.

The CSV files that are written can be used to analyze the sensor data after the app has been closed. It was these CSV files that were used to generate the charts displayed earlier in the chapter.

From a sensor standpoint, the only other interesting method in `DetermineMovementActivity` is `stopReadingAccelerationData()`, which is called when the user touches an activated toggle button or presses the back button. `stopReadingAccelerationData()` is where the app makes the call to `SensorManager.unregisterListener()` to stop receiving acceleration data and clean up after itself. Listing 8-3 shows the implementation of `stopReadingAccelerationData()`.

LISTING 8-3: Stop app from receiving acceleration data

```
private void stopReadingAccelerationData()
{
    if (readingAccelerationData)
    {
        // Re-enable sensor and options UI views
        for (int i = 0; i < sensorSelector.getChildCount(); i++)
        {
            sensorSelector.getChildAt(i).setEnabled(true);
        }
        ttsNotificationsCheckBox.setEnabled(true);
        highPassFilterCheckBox.setEnabled(true);

        sensorManager.unregisterListener(accelerometerListener);
        sensorManager.unregisterListener(linearAccelerationListener);

        // Tell listeners to clean up after themselves
        accelerometerListener.stop();
        linearAccelerationListener.stop();

        readingAccelerationData = false;

        Log.d(TAG, "Stopped reading acceleration data");
    }
}
```

`DetermineMovementActivity` contains the boilerplate code for initializing the app to receive sensor data. The code is similar to the code that was provided in previous chapters for setting up a `SensorEventListener`, which includes retrieving a reference to the `SensorManager` and registering a `SensorEventListener` to receive updated sensor data. Both of these topics were discussed at length in Chapter 5, so an in-depth discussion of the code is not included in this chapter.

Instead, the chapter moves on to the specific details for handling and processing acceleration data to accomplish the task at hand — detecting movement — the details for which are in the `AccelerationEventListener` class.

AccelerationEventListener

The `AccelerationEventListener` is responsible for receiving and processing the acceleration data. For the example app, this entails filtering the data, computing the total acceleration, writing the data to a CSV file, plotting the data on the graph, and detecting movement.

Because the `AccelerationEventListener` needs to receive sensor data, it implements `SensorEventListener`. Therefore, it must provide an implementation for the `onSensorChanged()`

and onAccuracyChanged() methods. For the example app, onAccuracyChanged() has an empty implementation. onSensorChanged() is where the main business logic of the app is located and is shown in Listing 8-4.

Available for
download on
Wrox.com

LISTING 8-4: onSensorChanged()

```java
private static final int THRESHHOLD = 2;
@Override
public void onSensorChanged(SensorEvent event)
{
    float[] values = event.values.clone();

    // Pass values through high-pass filter if enabled
    if (useHighPassFilter)
    {
        values = highPass(values[0],
                values[1],
                values[2]);
    }

    // Ignore data if the high-pass filter is enabled, has not yet received
    // some data to set it
    if (!useHighPassFilter || (++highPassCount >= HIGH_PASS_MINIMUM))
    {
        double sumOfSquares = (values[0] * values[0])
                + (values[1] * values[1])
                + (values[2] * values[2]);
        double acceleration = Math.sqrt(sumOfSquares);

        // Write to data file
        writeSensorEvent(printWriter,
                    values[0],
                    values[1],
                    values[2],
                    acceleration,
                    event.timestamp);

        // If the plot is null, the sensor is not active. Do not plot the
        // data or used the data to determine if the device is moving
        if (xyPlot != null)
        {
            long current = SystemClock.uptimeMillis();

            // Limit how much the chart gets updated
            if ((current - lastChartRefresh) >= CHART_REFRESH)
            {
                long timestamp = (event.timestamp / 1000000) - startTime;

                // Plot data
                addDataPoint(xAxisSeries, timestamp, values[0]);
                addDataPoint(yAxisSeries, timestamp, values[1]);
                addDataPoint(zAxisSeries, timestamp, values[2]);
```

continues

LISTING 8-4 *(continued)*

```
                    addDataPoint(accelerationSeries, timestamp, acceleration);

                    xyPlot.redraw();

                    lastChartRefresh = current;
                }

                // A "movement" is only triggered of the total acceleration is
                // above a threshold
                if (acceleration > THRESHHOLD)
                {
                    Log.i(TAG, "Movement detected");

                    if (tts != null)
                    {
                        tts.speak(movementText,
                                TextToSpeech.QUEUE_FLUSH,
                                ttsParams);
                    }
                }
            }
        }
    }
}
```

code snippet AccelerationEventListener.java

The data that is passed to onSensorChanged() resides in SensorEvent.values. The values member contains a three-element float array, which contains the values of the X, Y, and Z axes, respectively. Both the accelerometer and the linear acceleration sensor pass data that is formatted the same way, which allows the example app to process the data from the different sources in the same manner (even using the same class).

The first step is to apply the high-pass filter if the user has enabled it. If the user has enabled the high-pass filter, the values in SensorEvent.values are passed to highPass(), which will apply the high-pass filter and return the results. The high-pass filter algorithm that is used in this chapter is the one that is presented in the Android javadoc for the SensorEvent class that is provided by Google. Recall from Chapter 6 that a simple way to perform high-pass filtering is to perform a low-pass filter and then subtract the result from the sensor data. Listing 8-5 shows the implementation for the highPass() method that performs the high-pass filtering operation.

LISTING 8-5: Google's high-pass filter algorithm

```
private static final float ALPHA = 0.8f;
private float[] highPass(float x, float y, float z)
{
    float[] filteredValues = new float[3];

    gravity[0] = ALPHA * gravity[0] + (1 - ALPHA) * x;
    gravity[1] = ALPHA * gravity[1] + (1 - ALPHA) * y;
```

```
      gravity[2] = ALPHA * gravity[2] + (1 - ALPHA) * z;

      filteredValues[0] = x - gravity[0];
      filteredValues[1] = y - gravity[1];
      filteredValues[2] = z - gravity[2];

      return filteredValues;
   }
```

This code snippet was derived from http://developer.android.com/reference/android/hardware/SensorEvent.html

which is available under the Apache 2.0 License.

The discussion of how the high-pass filter works is discussed in detail in Chapter 6.

Once the data has been (conditionally) filtered, the total acceleration can be computed using the square root of the sum of the squares of the X, Y, and Z axes' acceleration values. The values of the three axes and the acceleration are then written to the data file.

If the listener has a reference to a graph, it will additionally graph the data and then use the acceleration to determine of the device is moving. Once the total acceleration is computed, a simple comparison to a threshold can be used to detect movement. If movement is detected, the TTS is used to indicate the detected movement to the user.

SUMMARY

This chapter discussed how acceleration data can be obtained in Android via the accelerometer and the linear acceleration synthetic sensor. Additionally, the differences in the data provided by each sensor, mainly how gravity affects the data, were also discussed.

Detecting general motion is the foundation for performing many more complex tasks with the acceleration data. From the data provided in this chapter, it is easy see that detecting the device being shaken is the same as detecting general motion with the total acceleration threshold set to a higher value.

Using the real-time graph to see how moving the device affects the acceleration sensors in real time can be incredibly useful in understanding how the acceleration sensors work. The reader is encouraged to spend some time running the example app and examining both the in-app graph and the data CSV files that are saved to become more familiar with how the acceleration sensors work.

Sensing the Environment

WHAT'S IN THIS CHAPTER?

➤ Providing an example implementation of how to use the barometer to produce altitude

➤ Comparing the altitude produced by GPS and the altitude produced using barometric pressure

➤ Showing how to acquire external sea-level pressure data from a web service

➤ Explaining use cases for barometric data

The past few chapters have discussed how to determine how a device is oriented in its environment and whether it is moving. This chapter discusses how a device can make sense of the environment itself. As stated in Chapter 5, Android supports many different sensors that can be used to make sense of the environment. This chapter focuses on one of the newest environment sensors supported by Android, the barometer.

Recall from Chapter 5 that the main purpose for the barometer is to detect the altitude of a given device. This sensor is useful when a device cannot obtain a GPS signal and still needs to provide altitude data.

To showcase the barometer sensor, this chapter adds altimeter functionality to the book's example app. The altimeter provides the ability to determine a device's current altitude as well as compute the relative altitude as the device's altitude changes. Because it does not rely solely on GPS data (which also provides altitude data), the altimeter will remain fully functional indoors where a GPS signal would probably be lost.

As explained in Chapter 5, altitude can be calculated by passing a barometer reading to the `SensorManager.getAltitude()` method. `SensorManager.getAltitude()` takes two float parameters, which represent the current atmospheric pressure at sea level and the atmospheric pressure as reported by the barometer and returns the altitude in meters. The pressure at sea level can be obtained by using the `SensorManager.PRESSURE_STANDARD_ATMOSPHERE` constant, or by getting the information from an external source. The example app will compute the altitude using both the standard atmospheric pressure constant and by retrieving the current pressure from a web service. Using both values for the altitude computation showcases the difference between the two values as well as illustrates how to obtain and process both values.

BAROMETER VS. GPS FOR ALTITUDE DATA

Although receiving altitude from the GPS is convenient from a coding perspective, it may not always be possible. For example, should the device be in a location where it cannot get a GPS fix (indoors, for example), an app will not receive a call to onLocationChanged(). Furthermore, because it can take a significant amount of time to get a GPS fix, GPS altitude data may not be available in a timely fashion. Use of GPS can also consume more battery power than the barometer, which alone can make the barometer an attractive choice for receiving altitude information.

The barometer, on the other hand, reports pressure readings almost immediately and is almost always able to produce relatively accurate readings. Though it might not be the ideal source of altitude data in all cases, the sensor is certainly useful in a large number of cases where altitude is needed by an app.

EXAMPLE APP OVERVIEW.

Figure 9-1 shows a screen capture of the altimeter activity, DetermineAltitudeActivity, in the book's companion app.

The altimeter displays the absolute altitude and relative altitude using data from both the GPS and the barometer. Because the altitude can be calculated from barometer readings using the standard pressure constant and an externally provided sea-level pressure reading, the activity makes both calculations and shows them in the UI.

Retrieving barometer data is similar to retrieving data from other sensors on a device; the activity will get a handle for the SensorManager and register a SensorEventListener to receive callbacks when the sensor data is ready to be consumed. When the barometer data is received, it can be passed to SensorManager.getAltitude() in order to compute the altitude that can be displayed in the screen.

DetermineAltitudeActivity also provides the altitude that is provided by the location service so that a comparison can be made between the barometer-based altitude values and the location service–based values. To accomplish this, the activity also needs a reference to the location service and must register a LocationListener to receive location updates.

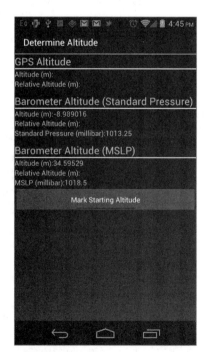

FIGURE 9-1: The DetermineAltitudeActivity screen

In addition to calculating the absolute altitude, DetermineAltitudeActivity also calculates a relative altitude. Relative altitude is the difference between the altitude values at two points in time. To calculate relative altitude, users first press the "Mark Starting Altitude" button. Doing so records the device's current altitude using the GPS and barometer values. When users are ready to calculate relative altitude, they again press the toggle button. The relative altitude is calculated using the GPS and barometer and displayed to the screen.

Implementation Details

Listing 9-1 shows the layout that is used by DetermineAltitudeActivity. The layout has TextViews for each piece of data that will be displayed to the user, as well as a toggle button that is used to compute relative altitude.

LISTING 9-1: DetermineAltitudeActivity layout

Available for
download on
Wrox.com

```xml
<?xml version="1.0" encoding="utf-8"?>
<RelativeLayout xmlns:android="http://schemas.android.com/apk/res/android"
    android:layout_width="match_parent"
    android:layout_height="match_parent"
    android:orientation="vertical" >

    <!-- GPS Altitude -->
    <TextView android:id="@+id/gpsAltitudeSectionHeading"
        style="@style/apptext"
        android:text="@string/gpsAltitudeLabel"
        android:layout_alignParentTop="true" />

    <TextView android:id="@+id/gpsAltitudeSectionDivider"
        style="@style/line_separator"
        android:layout_below="@id/gpsAltitudeSectionHeading" />

    <TextView android:id="@+id/gpsAltitudeLabel"
        android:layout_width="wrap_content"
        android:layout_height="wrap_content"
        android:text="@string/altitudeLabel"
        android:layout_below="@id/gpsAltitudeSectionDivider"/>

    <TextView android:id="@+id/gpsAltitude"
        android:layout_width="wrap_content"
        android:layout_height="wrap_content"
        android:layout_alignTop="@id/gpsAltitudeLabel"
        android:layout_alignBottom="@id/gpsAltitudeLabel"
        android:layout_toRightOf="@id/gpsAltitudeLabel"
        android:text="@string/notAvailable"/>

    <TextView android:id="@+id/gpsRelativeAltitudeLabel"
        android:layout_width="wrap_content"
        android:layout_height="wrap_content"
        android:text="@string/relativeAltitudeLabel"
        android:layout_below="@id/gpsAltitude"/>

    <TextView android:id="@+id/gpsRelativeAltitude"
        android:layout_width="wrap_content"
        android:layout_height="wrap_content"
```

continues

LISTING 9-1 *(continued)*

```
        android:layout_alignTop="@id/gpsRelativeAltitudeLabel"
        android:layout_alignBottom="@id/gpsRelativeAltitudeLabel"
        android:layout_toRightOf="@id/gpsRelativeAltitudeLabel"
        android:text="@string/notAvailable"/>

    <!-- Standard Pressure Barometer Altitude -->
    <TextView android:id="@+id/barometerAltitudeSectionHeading"
        style="@style/apptext"
        android:text="@string/barometerAltitudeLabel"
        android:layout_below="@id/gpsRelativeAltitudeLabel"
        android:layout_marginTop="10dip" />

    <TextView android:id="@+id/barometerAltitudeSectionDivider"
        style="@style/line_separator"
        android:layout_below="@id/barometerAltitudeSectionHeading" />

    <TextView android:id="@+id/barometerAltitudeLabel"
        android:layout_width="wrap_content"
        android:layout_height="wrap_content"
        android:text="@string/altitudeLabel"
        android:layout_below="@id/barometerAltitudeSectionDivider"/>

    <TextView android:id="@+id/barometerAltitude"
        android:layout_width="wrap_content"
        android:layout_height="wrap_content"
        android:layout_alignTop="@id/barometerAltitudeLabel"
        android:layout_alignBottom="@id/barometerAltitudeLabel"
        android:layout_toRightOf="@id/barometerAltitudeLabel"/>

    <TextView android:id="@+id/barometerRelativeAltitudeLabel"
        android:layout_width="wrap_content"
        android:layout_height="wrap_content"
        android:text="@string/relativeAltitudeLabel"
        android:layout_below="@id/barometerAltitude"/>

    <TextView android:id="@+id/barometerRelativeAltitude"
        android:layout_width="wrap_content"
        android:layout_height="wrap_content"
        android:layout_alignTop="@id/barometerRelativeAltitudeLabel"
        android:layout_alignBottom="@id/barometerRelativeAltitudeLabel"
        android:layout_toRightOf="@id/barometerRelativeAltitudeLabel"/>

    <TextView android:id="@+id/standardPressureLabel"
        android:layout_width="wrap_content"
        android:layout_height="wrap_content"
        android:text="@string/standardPressureLabel"
        android:layout_below="@id/barometerRelativeAltitude"/>

    <TextView android:id="@+id/standardPressure"
        android:layout_width="wrap_content"
        android:layout_height="wrap_content"
        android:layout_alignTop="@id/standardPressureLabel"
        android:layout_alignBottom="@id/standardPressureLabel"
```

```
        android:layout_toRightOf="@id/standardPressureLabel"
        android:text="@string/notAvailable"/>

<!-- MSLP Barometer Altitude -->
<TextView android:id="@+id/mslpBarometerAltitudeSectionHeading"
    style="@style/apptext"
    android:text="@string/mslpBarometerAltitudeLabel"
    android:layout_below="@id/standardPressureLabel"
    android:layout_marginTop="10dip" />

<TextView android:id="@+id/mslpBarometerAltitudeSectionDivider"
    style="@style/line_separator"
    android:layout_below="@id/mslpBarometerAltitudeSectionHeading" />

<TextView android:id="@+id/mslpBarometerAltitudeLabel"
    android:layout_width="wrap_content"
    android:layout_height="wrap_content"
    android:text="@string/altitudeLabel"
    android:layout_below="@id/mslpBarometerAltitudeSectionDivider"/>

<TextView android:id="@+id/mslpBarometerAltitude"
    android:layout_width="wrap_content"
    android:layout_height="wrap_content"
    android:layout_alignTop="@id/mslpBarometerAltitudeLabel"
    android:layout_alignBottom="@id/mslpBarometerAltitudeLabel"
    android:layout_toRightOf="@id/mslpBarometerAltitudeLabel"
    android:text="@string/notAvailable"/>

<TextView android:id="@+id/mslpRelativeAltitudeLabel"
    android:layout_width="wrap_content"
    android:layout_height="wrap_content"
    android:text="@string/relativeAltitudeLabel"
    android:layout_below="@id/mslpBarometerAltitude"/>

<TextView android:id="@+id/mslpBarometerRelativeAltitude"
    android:layout_width="wrap_content"
    android:layout_height="wrap_content"
    android:layout_alignTop="@id/mslpRelativeAltitudeLabel"
    android:layout_alignBottom="@id/mslpRelativeAltitudeLabel"
    android:layout_toRightOf="@id/mslpRelativeAltitudeLabel"
    android:text="@string/notAvailable"/>

<TextView android:id="@+id/mslpLabel"
    android:layout_width="wrap_content"
    android:layout_height="wrap_content"
    android:text="@string/mslpLabel"
    android:layout_below="@id/mslpBarometerRelativeAltitude"/>

<TextView android:id="@+id/mslp"
    android:layout_width="wrap_content"
    android:layout_height="wrap_content"
    android:layout_alignTop="@id/mslpLabel"
    android:layout_alignBottom="@id/mslpLabel"
    android:layout_toRightOf="@id/mslpLabel"
    android:text="@string/notAvailable"/>
```

continues

LISTING 9-1 *(continued)*

```xml
    <ToggleButton
        android:layout_width="match_parent"
        android:layout_height="wrap_content"
        android:layout_below="@id/mslpLabel"
        android:onClick="onToggleClick"
        android:textOff="Mark Starting Altitude"
        android:textOn="Compute Relative Altitude" />

</RelativeLayout>
```

code snippet determine_altitude.xml

Listing 9-2 shows the member data and constants used throughout DetermineAltitudeActivity. These are presented and referenced in the rest of the code listings throughout the chapter.

LISTING 9-2: DetermineAltitudeActivity member data and constants

```java
    private static final String TAG = "DetermineAltitudeActivity";
    private static final int TIMEOUT = 1000; //1 second
    private static final long NS_TO_MS_CONVERSION = (long)1E6;

    // System services
    private SensorManager sensorManager;
    private LocationManager locationManager;

    // UI Views
    private TextView gpsAltitudeView;
    private TextView gpsRelativeAltitude;
    private TextView barometerAltitudeView;
    private TextView barometerRelativeAltitude;
    private TextView mslpBarometerAltitudeView;
    private TextView mslpBarometerRelativeAltitude;
    private TextView mslpView;

    // Member state
    private Float mslp;
    private long lastGpsAltitudeTimestamp = -1;
    private long lastBarometerAltitudeTimestamp = -1;
    private float bestLocationAccuracy = -1;
    private float currentBarometerValue;
    private float lastBarometerValue;
    private double lastGpsAltitude;
    private double currentGpsAltitude;
    private boolean webServiceFetching;
    private long lastErrorMessageTimestamp = -1;
```

Listing 9-3 shows the onCreate() method for DetermineAltitudeActivity. Most of the code in onCreate() should be familiar by now because it follows the same pattern that has been used throughout the book. The method acquires references to the UI views that will be updated and retrieves a handle to both the location and sensor services.

LISTING 9-3: DetermineAltitudeActivity.onCreate()

```
@Override
protected void onCreate(Bundle savedInstanceState)
{
    super.onCreate(savedInstanceState);
    setContentView(R.layout.determine_altitude);
    getWindow().addFlags(WindowManager.LayoutParams.FLAG_KEEP_SCREEN_ON);

    sensorManager =
            (SensorManager) getSystemService(Context.SENSOR_SERVICE);
    locationManager = (LocationManager) getSystemService(LOCATION_SERVICE);

    gpsAltitudeView = (TextView) findViewById(R.id.gpsAltitude);

    gpsRelativeAltitude =
            (TextView) findViewById(R.id.gpsRelativeAltitude);

    barometerAltitudeView = (TextView) findViewById(R.id.barometerAltitude);
    barometerRelativeAltitude =
            (TextView) findViewById(R.id.barometerRelativeAltitude);
    mslpBarometerAltitudeView =
            (TextView) findViewById(R.id.mslpBarometerAltitude);
    mslpBarometerRelativeAltitude =
            (TextView) findViewById(R.id.mslpBarometerRelativeAltitude);
    mslpView = (TextView) findViewById(R.id.mslp);

    webServiceFetching = false;

    TextView standardPressure =
            (TextView)findViewById(R.id.standardPressure);
    String standardPressureString =
            String.valueOf(SensorManager.PRESSURE_STANDARD_ATMOSPHERE);
    standardPressure.setText(standardPressureString);
}
```

The last three statements of the onCreate() method display the value of the standard atmospheric pressure constant to the user. Recall from Figure 9-1 that in addition to the altitude values, the activity also displays the values that were used for sea level. Because the standard atmospheric pressure is a constant, the view can be set once when the activity is created because it will not need to be updated (this is not the case for the externally accessed sea-level value, which will need to be updated later in the activity).

Because both sensor data and location data are needed by DetermineAltitudeActivity, the activity implements both LocationListener and SensorEventListener. This allows the activity to register itself to receive location and sensor updates and conveniently update the UI. The registration for both location and sensor data happens in the onResume() method, which is shown in Listing 9-4.

LISTING 9-4: DetermineAltitudeActivity.onResume()

```
@Override
protected void onResume()
{
    super.onResume();

    List<String> enabledProviders = locationManager.getProviders(true);

    if (enabledProviders.isEmpty()
            || !enabledProviders.contains(LocationManager.GPS_PROVIDER))
    {
        Toast.makeText(this,
                R.string.gpsNotEnabledMessage,
                Toast.LENGTH_LONG).show();
    }
    else
    {
        // Register every location provider returned from LocationManager
        for (String provider : enabledProviders)
        {
            // Register for updates every minute
            locationManager.requestLocationUpdates(provider,
                    60000,  // minimum time of 60000 ms (1 minute)
                    0,      // Minimum distance of 0
                    this,
                    null);
        }
    }

    Sensor sensor = sensorManager.getDefaultSensor(Sensor.TYPE_PRESSURE);

    // Only make registration call if device has a pressure sensor
    if (sensor != null)
    {
        sensorManager.registerListener(this,
                sensor,
                SensorManager.SENSOR_DELAY_NORMAL);
    }
}
```

Because the user can disable location providers, the onResume() method registers only active location providers by iterating through the array returned from the call to getProviders(true). Passing the value of true ensures that only active location providers are returned. In addition, the code checks that the GPS location provider is present. At the time of this writing, the GPS provider is the only location provider that can provide altitude information.

Care must be taken when registering for updates from the barometer because not every device has a barometer. To compensate for this, the method makes a call to getDefaultSensor(), passing the constant for the pressure sensor (barometer). If the method returns a value of null, the device does not contain a barometer and the registration can be skipped.

Now that the activity is registered to receive location and sensor information, it will receive call-backs when updated location and/or barometer readings are available. The next sections will dive into the details of processing the information that is received.

GPS-Based Altitude

The altitude that is provided by the GPS location provider can be read with a simple call to `Location.getAltitude()`. The method call returns the altitude in meters. In the example for this chapter, the GPS altitude is read when `onLocationChanged()` is called. Listing 9-5 shows the implementation of `DetermineAltitudeActivity.onLocationChanged()`.

LISTING 9-5: Retrieving the altitude provided by GPS

```
@Override
public void onLocationChanged(Location location)
{
    if (LocationManager.GPS_PROVIDER.equals(location.getProvider())
            && (lastGpsAltitudeTimestamp == -1
                || location.getTime() - lastGpsAltitudeTimestamp > TIMEOUT))
    {
        double altitude = location.getAltitude();
        gpsAltitudeView.setText(String.valueOf(altitude));
        lastGpsAltitudeTimestamp = location.getTime();
        currentGpsAltitude = altitude;
    }

    float accuracy = location.getAccuracy();
    boolean betterAccuracy = accuracy < bestLocationAccuracy;
    if (mslp == null || (bestLocationAccuracy > -1 && betterAccuracy))
    {
        bestLocationAccuracy = accuracy;

        if (!webServiceFetching)
        {
            webServiceFetching = true;
            new MetarAsyncTask().execute(location.getLatitude(),
                    location.getLongitude());
        }
    }
}
```

Before the altitude is read, the method verifies that the location object contains altitude information with a call to `Location.hasAltitude()`. This check is needed because the activity will register all enabled location providers when it's brought to the foreground (see Listing 9-4), but not every location provider provides altitude data. The reason for using location providers that do not provide altitude data is explained later in the chapter.

Along with verifying that altitude data is present, the code checks to see if `lastGpsAltitudeTimestamp` contains a value of –1, indicating that it has never been set (Listing 9-2 shows the variable's declaration and initialization to a value of –1). Furthermore, the code compares the difference of the current location's timestamp with the timestamp that was set the last time the UI was updated with the location-based altitude data. If the difference is greater than the value of TIMEOUT (a constant representing 1 sec.), the UI is updated with the current altitude value, and the current altitude is stored in a class member variable (currentGpsAltitude). This check ensures that the screen is not updated more than once a second with location service altitude data.

In Listing 9-5, only the highlighted code deals with location-based altitude. The rest of the method supports retrieving sea-level pressure externally, which is discussed later in the chapter.

Barometric Pressure–Based Altitude

Computing the altitude using the barometer is relatively straightforward. To get a fairly good reading of the altitude, an app only needs to read the barometer in a similar fashion to other sensors and pass the values that were read to SensorManager.getAltitude(). SensorManager.getAltitude() encapsulates the formula needed to perform the actual calculation and returns the altitude in meters.

In the example, the reading of the barometer and call to SensorManager.getAltitude() happens on the onSensorEvent() method that is called when sensor data is available. The method is shown in Listing 9-6.

LISTING 9-6: Reading barometer data and calculating altitude

```
@Override
public void onSensorChanged(SensorEvent event)
{
    float altitude;
    currentBarometerValue = event.values[0];

    double currentTimestamp = event.timestamp / NS_TO_MS_CONVERSION;
    double elapsedTime = currentTimestamp - lastBarometerAltitudeTimestamp;
    if (lastBarometerAltitudeTimestamp == -1 || elapsedTime > TIMEOUT)
    {
        altitude =
                SensorManager
                    .getAltitude(SensorManager.PRESSURE_STANDARD_ATMOSPHERE,
                        currentBarometerValue);
        barometerAltitudeView.setText(String.valueOf(altitude));

        if (mslp != null)
        {
            altitude = SensorManager.getAltitude(mslp,
                    currentBarometerValue);
            mslpBarometerAltitudeView.setText(String.valueOf(altitude));
            mslpView.setText(String.valueOf(mslp));
        }

        lastBarometerAltitudeTimestamp = (long)currentTimestamp;
    }
}
```

The method first reads the *event.values* array to retrieve the raw barometer reading. *event. values* is an array of floats, and for the barometer, the sensor data is located in the first (zero-eth) position.

Listing 9-6 makes two calls to `SensorManager.getAltitude()`. The first call uses the `SensorManager.PRESSURE_STANDARD_ATMOSPHERE` constant, and the second call passes the *mslp* variable as the first parameter. Recall from earlier in the chapter that the first parameter of `SensorManager.getAltitude()` is the altitude at sea level. The first call makes use of the standard pressure constant that will yield fairly accurate altitude results when computing relative altitude.

However, if more accurate altitude data is desired, the mean sea-level pressure (MSLP) should be used. As explained in Chapter 5, the MSLP is the pressure that is reported by an external source such as a weather station. Though using the MSLP can provide increased accuracy when computing altitude, it must first be retrieved from that external source. Luckily, many places on the Internet supply MSLP information through a web service.

`DetermineAltitudeActivity` makes use of one such web service to retrieve MSLP based on the device's current location. Once the value is set, it can be used on `onSensorChanged()` to update the UI with the MSLP-computed altitude. Because web services should be accessed asynchronously (and off the main thread), `onSensorChanged()` needs to verify that the *mslp* variable has been set before accessing it. Hence, the check for a null *mslp* before its value is used.

The next section discusses how to retrieve the MSLP values.

Retrieving MSLP Values

To use the MSLP, the `DetermineAltitudeActivity` connects to a remote web service supplying the device's current location as parameters to the web service call. The web service responds with weather data that includes the MSLP for the location it was sent. To facilitate access to the web service, `DetermineAltitudeActivity` contains a private inner class, `MetarAsyncTask`, that makes the call to the web service in another thread (to avoid blocking the main thread, which can cause an "Application Not Responding" error) and process the response. Listing 9-7 shows the implementation of the `MetarAsyncTask`.

LISTING 9-7: Class to access weather web service and retrieve MSLP data

Available for
download on
Wrox.com

```
private class MetarAsyncTask extends AsyncTask<Number, Void, Float>
{
    private static final String WS_URL =
            "http://ws.geonames.org/findNearByWeatherJSON";
    private static final String SLP_STRING = "slp";

    @Override
    protected Float doInBackground(Number... params)
    {
        Float mslp = null;
        HttpURLConnection urlConnection = null;
```

continues

LISTING 9-7 *(continued)*

```
try
{
    // Generate URL with parameters for web service
    Uri uri =
            Uri.parse(WS_URL)
            .buildUpon()
            .appendQueryParameter("lat", String.valueOf(params[0]))
            .appendQueryParameter("lng", String.valueOf(params[1]))
            .build();

    // Connect to web service
    URL url = new URL(uri.toString());
    urlConnection = (HttpURLConnection) url.openConnection();

    // Read web service response and convert to a string
    InputStream inputStream =
            new BufferedInputStream(urlConnection.getInputStream());

    // Convert InputStream to String using a Scanner
    Scanner inputStreamScanner =
            new Scanner(inputStream).useDelimiter("\\A");
    String response = inputStreamScanner.next();
    inputStreamScanner.close();

    Log.d(TAG, "Web Service Response -> " + response);

    JSONObject json = new JSONObject(response);

    String observation =
            json
                .getJSONObject("weatherObservation")
                .getString("observation");

    // Split on whitespace
    String[] values = observation.split("\\s");

    // Iterate of METAR string until SLP string is found
    String slpString = null;
    for (int i = 1; i < values.length; i++)
    {
        String value = values[i];

        if (value.startsWith(SLP_STRING.toLowerCase())
                || value.startsWith(SLP_STRING.toUpperCase()))
        {
            slpString =
                    value.substring(SLP_STRING.length());
            break;
        }
    }
```

```java
            // Decode SLP string into numerical representation
            StringBuffer sb = new StringBuffer(slpString);

            sb.insert(sb.length() - 1, ".");

            float val1 = Float.parseFloat("10" + sb);
            float val2 = Float.parseFloat("09" + sb);

            mslp =
                    (Math.abs((1000 - val1)) < Math.abs((1000 - val2)))
                        ? val1
                        : val2;
        }
        catch (Exception e)
        {
            Log.e(TAG, "Could not communicate with web service", e);
        }
        finally
        {
            if (urlConnection != null)
            {
                urlConnection.disconnect();
            }
        }

        return mslp;
    }


    @Override
    protected void onPostExecute(Float result)
    {
        long uptime = SystemClock.uptimeMillis();

        if (result == null
                && (lastErrorMessageTimestamp == -1
                    || ((uptime - lastErrorMessageTimestamp) > 30000)))
        {
            Toast.makeText(DetermineAltitudeActivity.this,
                    R.string.webServiceConnectionFailureMessage,
                    Toast.LENGTH_LONG).show();

            lastErrorMessageTimestamp = uptime;
        }
        else
        {
            DetermineAltitudeActivity.this.mslp = result;
        }

        DetermineAltitudeActivity.this.webServiceFetching = false;
    }
}
```

code snippet DetermineAltitudeActivity.java

The web service used in the chapter example is provided by www.geonames.org. GeoNames provides a simple web service (among other things) that takes coordinate values (latitude and longitude) as parameters and returns weather data. The GeoNames web service can return data in both XML and JSON formats. For this example, the web service returns a response in JSON. For more information on what other services GeoNames provides, take a look at its website.

The GeoNames weather web service returns weather data encoded as a METAR string. METAR is a commonly used standard for formatting weather data. It is used among pilots and meteorologists to make weather predictions, and is standardized through the International Civil Aviation Organization (ICAO).

A typical METAR string containing weather data looks like:

```
KNUQ 021756Z 30004KT 10SM CLR 13\/07 A3017 RMK AO2 SLP218 T01280072 10128
20050 58004
```

A METAR string is separated by white space and contains various components of weather data. The first string, KNUQ in this case, is the unique identifier of the reporting station that was the source of the data. The reporting station is followed by encoded weather data. The complete contents of a METAR string are out of the scope of the chapter. For now it is enough to know that the part of a METAR string that contains sea-level pressure begins with SLP. For the preceding METAR string, the encoded sea-level pressure is SLP218.

Although METAR is standardized, various regions around the world do make locale-specific additions to the standard. For example, the SLP data located in the preceding METAR string is unique to North America and may not be present in METAR strings in other parts of the world.

To receive METAR-encoded weather data from the GeoNames web service, the MetarAsyncTask must generate an HTTP request and send it to the web service. It does this in the first part of MetarAsyncTask.doInBackground() with the following code:

```
// Generate URL with parameters for web service
Uri uri =
        Uri.parse(WS_URL)
        .buildUpon()
        .appendQueryParameter("lat", String.valueOf(params[0]))
        .appendQueryParameter("lng", String.valueOf(params[1]))
        .build();

// Connect to web service
URL url = new URL(uri.toString());
urlConnection = (HttpURLConnection) url.openConnection();

// Read web service response and convert to a string
InputStream inputStream =
        new BufferedInputStream(urlConnection.getInputStream());

// Convert InputStream to String using a Scanner
Scanner inputStreamScanner =
        new Scanner(inputStream).useDelimiter("\\A");
String response = inputStreamScanner.next();
inputStreamScanner.close();
```

After the code is executed, the response from the web service is located in the variable name *response*. A typical response from the GeoNames web service is presented in Listing 9-8.

LISTING 9-8: GeoNames METAR web service response

```
{
    "weatherObservation": {
        "weatherCondition": "n\/a",
        "clouds": "n\/a",
        "observation": "KNUQ 021756Z 30004KT 10SM CLR 13\/07 A3017 RMK A02 SLP218",
        "windDirection": 300,
        "ICAO": "KNUQ",
        "elevation": 12,
        "seaLevelPressure": 1021.8,
        "countryCode": "US",
        "lng": -122.03333333333333,
        "dewPoint": "7.2",
        "temperature": "12.8",
        "windSpeed": "04",
        "humidity": 68,
        "datetime": "2012-02-02 17:56:00",
        "stationName": "Mountain View, Moffett Field",
        "lat": 37.416666666666664
    }
}
```

The response from the web service contains more than just a METAR string. In fact, it contains the decoded sea-level pressure in the field name `seaLevelPressure`. Though this field does represent the sea-level pressure, this chapter focuses on how to decode the METAR string. Knowing how to decode the SLP part of a METAR string will allow an app to make use of many different weather data sources that may not return the decoded sea-level pressure.

The weather METAR string is located in the "observation" field of the JSON web service response. After receiving the response, the `MetarAsyncTask.doInBackground()` method uses the JSON library in Android to parse the METAR string and locate the sea-level pressure data. It does this in the following code:

```
JSONObject json = new JSONObject(response);

String observation =
        json
            .getJSONObject("weatherObservation")
            .getString("observation");

// Split on whitespace
String[] values = observation.split("\\s");

// Iterate of METAR sting until SLP string is found
String slpString = null;
for (int i = 1; i < values.length; i++)
{
```

```
        String value = values[i];

        if (value.startsWith(SLP_STRING.toLowerCase())
                || value.startsWith(SLP_STRING.toUpperCase()))
        {
            slpString =
                    value.substring(SLP_STRING.length());
            break;
        }
    }
}
```

Upon completion of the code, the sea-level portion of the METAR string is located in the *slpString* variable. As can be verified by the sample JSON response in Listing 9-8, the `slpString` should have a value of `218`, which is the encoded value of the sea-level pressure.

To decode the sea-level pressure, the code adds a decimal point before the last character and prepends the string with either 10 or 09. The determination of what to prepend the string with is made by determining which value would make the sea-level pressure closer to 1000. The following code snippet decodes the SLP METAR string:

```
// Decode SLP string into numerical representation
StringBuffer sb = new StringBuffer(slpString);

sb.insert(sb.length() - 1, ".");

float val1 = Float.parseFloat("10" + sb);
float val2 = Float.parseFloat("09" + sb);

mslp =
        (Math.abs((1000 - val1)) < Math.abs((1000 - val2)))
            ? val1
            : val2;
```

At this point `MetarAsyncTask.doInBackground()` is finished processing the sea-level pressure from the GeoNames web service, and has parsed the response. The Android `AsynTask` handles passing the return value to `MetarAsynTask.postExecute()`, which either stores the mean sea-level pressure as part of the `DetermineAltitudeActivity` member data, or displays a toast to the user if there was an error.

Launching MetarAsyncTask

Because device location is needed to retrieve MSLP data from the GeoNames web service, a web service request cannot be made until the app has received location data. Recall from previous chapters that some location providers (especially the GPS provider) may take minutes to return a single location fix. It is often not desirable to block a user from performing a task in an app until a location is received. To combat long time to first fix (TTFF) times, `DetermineAltitudeActivity` makes use of all location providers that are currently enabled (shown in Listing 9-4). Assuming that the user has a location provider other than the GPS provider enabled, the app should receive a location from the location service in a relatively small amount of time. Once a location is received in `DetermineAltitudeActivity.onLocationChanged()`, the method makes the determination on whether or not a request needs to be sent to the web service to refresh MSLP. In addition to processing location service altitude data, `onLocationChanged()` also initiates the call to the web service. Listing 9-9 again shows the implementation of `DetermineAlltitudeActivity.onLocation-Changed()`, but this time highlights the portion of the method that makes the call to the web service.

LISTING 9-9: Making the web service call from onLocationChanged()

```
@Override
public void onLocationChanged(Location location)
{
    if (LocationManager.GPS_PROVIDER.equals(location.getProvider())
            && (lastGpsAltitudeTimestamp == -1
                || location.getTime() - lastGpsAltitudeTimestamp > TIMEOUT))
    {
        double altitude = location.getAltitude();
        gpsAltitudeView.setText(String.valueOf(altitude));
        lastGpsAltitudeTimestamp = location.getTime();
        currentGpsAltitude = altitude;
    }

    float accuracy = location.getAccuracy();
    boolean betterAccuracy = accuracy < bestLocationAccuracy;
    if (mslp == null  || (bestLocationAccuracy > -1 && betterAccuracy))
    {
        bestLocationAccuracy = accuracy;

        if (!webServiceFetching)
        {
            webServiceFetching = true;
            new MetarAsyncTask().execute(location.getLatitude(),
                    location.getLongitude());
        }
    }
}
```

Listing 9-9 shows the conditional call to `MetarAsynTask.execute()` (which makes the call to `MetarAsyncTask.doInBackground()` on another thread) only if the MSLP had not yet been retrieved, or if the latest location has a better accuracy than the previous location used to retrieve the MSLP. There is also a check to ensure that only one call to the web service is made at a time.

Thus far, the main topic of this chapter has been computing absolute altitude. This is useful in some use cases, but a more common use case for the barometer is to calculate relative altitude.

Relative Altitude

Relative altitude is used to determine the change in altitude. For example, by computing the difference between an ending altitude and a starting altitude, an app can determine if a device has changed floors in a building. This can be another useful piece of information when performing tasks such as navigation. An app can use GPS to provide a user with general directions to a building, then use the barometer to produce fine-grained navigation within the building. Although the

GPS can also provide altitude information, it is unlikely to produce any position information while indoors.

Recall from Figure 9-1 that the screen for `DetermineAltitudeActivity` has a toggle button that allows the user to mark a starting altitude when it is pressed, and computes relative altitude when the button is pressed again. The relative altitude calculation is made in the handler for the toggle button click. The layout (shown in Listing 9-1) defines the click handler to be `DetermineAltitudeActivity.onToggleClick()`, which is shown in Listing 9-10.

LISTING 9-10: Calculating relative altitude

```
public void onToggleClick(View view)
{
    if (((ToggleButton)view).isChecked())
    {
        lastGpsAltitude = currentGpsAltitude;
        lastBarometerValue = currentBarometerValue;
        gpsRelativeAltitude.setVisibility(View.INVISIBLE);
        barometerRelativeAltitude.setVisibility(View.INVISIBLE);

        if (mslp != null)
        {
            mslpBarometerRelativeAltitude.setVisibility(View.INVISIBLE);
        }
    }
    else
    {
        double delta;

        delta = currentGpsAltitude - lastGpsAltitude;
        gpsRelativeAltitude.setText(String.valueOf(delta));
        gpsRelativeAltitude.setVisibility(View.VISIBLE);

        delta = SensorManager
                .getAltitude(SensorManager.PRESSURE_STANDARD_ATMOSPHERE,
                    currentBarometerValue)
            - SensorManager
                .getAltitude(SensorManager.PRESSURE_STANDARD_ATMOSPHERE,
                    lastBarometerValue);

        barometerRelativeAltitude.setText(String.valueOf(delta));
        barometerRelativeAltitude.setVisibility(View.VISIBLE);

        if (mslp != null)
        {
            delta = SensorManager.getAltitude(mslp, currentBarometerValue)
                - SensorManager.getAltitude(mslp, lastBarometerValue);
            mslpBarometerRelativeAltitude.setText(String.valueOf(delta));
            mslpBarometerRelativeAltitude.setVisibility(View.VISIBLE);
        }
    }
}
```

The first `if` block of the method is executed when the user wants to mark the current altitude. Marking the current altitude is as simple as assigning *lastGpsAltitude* the value of *currentGpsAltitude* for the GPS-based altitude and *lastBarometerValue* the value of *currentBarometerValue* for the barometer data. Both *currentGpsAltitude* and *currentBarometerValue* are constantly updated when new calls are made to `onLocationChanged()` and `onSensorEvent()`, respectively. This means that both values always maintain the current values for their respective sensors.

The `else` block is executed when the user presses the toggle button after the app has marked the starting altitude. Because `DetermineAltitudeActivity` maintains the current GPS and barometer values as part of its member data, computing relative altitude is as simple as computing the difference between the current and starting altitudes for both GPS and barometer data.

In a similar fashion to `onSensorEvent()`, `onToggleClick()` computes the altitude using both the standard pressure constant and the MSLP if it has been populated. Once all the calculations are made, the UI is updated with the values to inform the user.

Figure 9-2 shows a screen capture of `DetermineAltitudeActivity` after the user has marked the current altitude, walked up a flight of stairs, and computed the relative altitude. Figure 9-3 also shows a screen capture of `DetermineAltitudeActivity`, but this time the relative altitude was calculated as the user walked down that same flight of stairs.

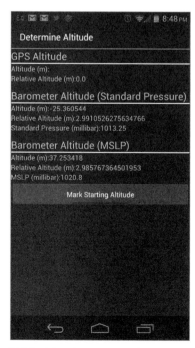

FIGURE 9-2: Increasing relative altitude

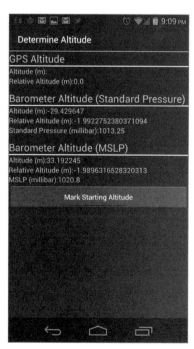

FIGURE 9-3: Decreasing relative altitude

Notice that the relative altitude values are positive as the altitude increases and negative as the altitude decreases.

For the sake of completeness, Listing 9-11 shows the complete implementation of DetermineAltitudeActivity. The code is also available on the book's companion website.

Available for download on Wrox.com

LISTING 9-11: Complete implementation of DetermineAltitudeActivity

```java
public class DetermineAltitudeActivity extends Activity
    implements SensorEventListener, LocationListener
{
    private static final String TAG = "DetermineAltitudeActivity";
    private static final int TIMEOUT = 1000; //1 second
    private static final long NS_TO_MS_CONVERSION = (long)1E6;

    // System services
    private SensorManager sensorManager;
    private LocationManager locationManager;

    // UI Views
    private TextView gpsAltitudeView;
    private TextView gpsRelativeAltitude;
    private TextView barometerAltitudeView;
    private TextView barometerRelativeAltitude;
    private TextView mslpBarometerAltitudeView;
    private TextView mslpBarometerRelativeAltitude;
    private TextView mslpView;

    // Member state
    private Float mslp;
    private long lastGpsAltitudeTimestamp = -1;
    private long lastBarometerAltitudeTimestamp = -1;
    private float bestLocationAccuracy = -1;
    private float currentBarometerValue;
    private float lastBarometerValue;
    private double lastGpsAltitude;
    private double currentGpsAltitude;
    private boolean webServiceFetching;
    private long lastErrorMessageTimestamp = -1;

    @Override
    protected void onCreate(Bundle savedInstanceState)
    {
        super.onCreate(savedInstanceState);
        setContentView(R.layout.determine_altitude);
        getWindow().addFlags(WindowManager.LayoutParams.FLAG_KEEP_SCREEN_ON);

        sensorManager =
                (SensorManager) getSystemService(Context.SENSOR_SERVICE);
        locationManager = (LocationManager) getSystemService(LOCATION_SERVICE);

        gpsAltitudeView = (TextView) findViewById(R.id.gpsAltitude);
```

```java
        gpsRelativeAltitude =
                (TextView) findViewById(R.id.gpsRelativeAltitude);

        barometerAltitudeView = (TextView) findViewById(R.id.barometerAltitude);
        barometerRelativeAltitude =
                (TextView) findViewById(R.id.barometerRelativeAltitude);
        mslpBarometerAltitudeView =
                (TextView) findViewById(R.id.mslpBarometerAltitude);
        mslpBarometerRelativeAltitude =
                (TextView) findViewById(R.id.mslpBarometerRelativeAltitude);
        mslpView = (TextView) findViewById(R.id.mslp);

        webServiceFetching = false;

        TextView standardPressure =
                (TextView)findViewById(R.id.standardPressure);
        String standardPressureString =
                String.valueOf(SensorManager.PRESSURE_STANDARD_ATMOSPHERE);
        standardPressure.setText(standardPressureString);
    }

@Override
protected void onResume()
{
    super.onResume();

    List<String> enabledProviders = locationManager.getProviders(true);

    if (enabledProviders.isEmpty()
            || !enabledProviders.contains(LocationManager.GPS_PROVIDER))
    {
        Toast.makeText(this,
                R.string.gpsNotEnabledMessage,
                Toast.LENGTH_LONG).show();
    }
    else
    {
        // Register every location provider returned from LocationManager
        for (String provider : enabledProviders)
        {
            // Register for updates every minute
            locationManager.requestLocationUpdates(provider,
                    60000,  // minimum time of 60000 ms (1 minute)
                    0,      // Minimum distance of 0
                    this,
                    null);
        }
    }

    Sensor sensor = sensorManager.getDefaultSensor(Sensor.TYPE_PRESSURE);

    // Only make registration call if device has a pressure sensor
    if (sensor != null)
    {
        sensorManager.registerListener(this,
```

continues

LISTING 9-11 *(continued)*

```
                    sensor,
                    SensorManager.SENSOR_DELAY_NORMAL);
    }
}

@Override
protected void onPause()
{
    super.onPause();

    sensorManager.unregisterListener(this);
    locationManager.removeUpdates(this);
}

@Override
public void onSensorChanged(SensorEvent event)
{
    float altitude;
    currentBarometerValue = event.values[0];

    double currentTimestamp = event.timestamp / NS_TO_MS_CONVERSION;
    double elapsedTime = currentTimestamp - lastBarometerAltitudeTimestamp;
    if (lastBarometerAltitudeTimestamp == -1 || elapsedTime > TIMEOUT)
    {
        altitude =
                SensorManager
                    .getAltitude(SensorManager.PRESSURE_STANDARD_ATMOSPHERE,
                        currentBarometerValue);
        barometerAltitudeView.setText(String.valueOf(altitude));

        if (mslp != null)
        {
            altitude = SensorManager.getAltitude(mslp,
                    currentBarometerValue);
            mslpBarometerAltitudeView.setText(String.valueOf(altitude));
            mslpView.setText(String.valueOf(mslp));
        }

        lastBarometerAltitudeTimestamp = (long)currentTimestamp;
    }
}

@Override
public void onAccuracyChanged(Sensor sensor, int accuracy)
{
    // no-op
}

@Override
public void onLocationChanged(Location location)
{
    if (LocationManager.GPS_PROVIDER.equals(location.getProvider())
```

```
                && (lastGpsAltitudeTimestamp == -1
                    || location.getTime() - lastGpsAltitudeTimestamp > TIMEOUT))
    {
        double altitude = location.getAltitude();
        gpsAltitudeView.setText(String.valueOf(altitude));
        lastGpsAltitudeTimestamp = location.getTime();
        currentGpsAltitude = altitude;
    }

    float accuracy = location.getAccuracy();
    boolean betterAccuracy = accuracy < bestLocationAccuracy;
    if (mslp == null  || (bestLocationAccuracy > -1 && betterAccuracy))
    {
        bestLocationAccuracy = accuracy;

        if (!webServiceFetching)
        {
            webServiceFetching = true;
            new MetarAsyncTask().execute(location.getLatitude(),
                    location.getLongitude());
        }
    }
}


@Override
public void onProviderDisabled(String provider)
{
    // no-op
}


@Override
public void onProviderEnabled(String provider)
{
    // no-op
}

@Override
public void onStatusChanged(String provider, int status, Bundle extras)
{
    // no-op
}

public void onToggleClick(View view)
{
    if (((ToggleButton)view).isChecked())
    {
        lastGpsAltitude = currentGpsAltitude;
        lastBarometerValue = currentBarometerValue;
        gpsRelativeAltitude.setVisibility(View.INVISIBLE);
        barometerRelativeAltitude.setVisibility(View.INVISIBLE);

        if (mslp != null)
```

continues

LISTING 9-11 *(continued)*

```
            {
                mslpBarometerRelativeAltitude.setVisibility(View.INVISIBLE);
            }
        }
        else
        {
            double delta;

            delta = currentGpsAltitude - lastGpsAltitude;
            gpsRelativeAltitude.setText(String.valueOf(delta));
            gpsRelativeAltitude.setVisibility(View.VISIBLE);

            delta = SensorManager
                    .getAltitude(SensorManager.PRESSURE_STANDARD_ATMOSPHERE,
                        currentBarometerValue)
                - SensorManager
                    .getAltitude(SensorManager.PRESSURE_STANDARD_ATMOSPHERE,
                        lastBarometerValue);

            barometerRelativeAltitude.setText(String.valueOf(delta));
            barometerRelativeAltitude.setVisibility(View.VISIBLE);

            if (mslp != null)
            {
                delta = SensorManager.getAltitude(mslp, currentBarometerValue)
                        - SensorManager.getAltitude(mslp, lastBarometerValue);
                mslpBarometerRelativeAltitude.setText(String.valueOf(delta));
                mslpBarometerRelativeAltitude.setVisibility(View.VISIBLE);
            }
        }
    }

    private class MetarAsyncTask extends AsyncTask<Number, Void, Float>
    {
        private static final String WS_URL =
                "http://ws.geonames.org/findNearByWeatherJSON";
        private static final String SLP_STRING = "slp";

        /**
         * @see android.os.AsyncTask#doInBackground(Params[])
         */
        @Override
        protected Float doInBackground(Number... params)
        {
            Float mslp = null;
            HttpURLConnection urlConnection = null;

            try
            {
                // Generate URL with parameters for web service
                Uri uri =
```

```java
        Uri.parse(WS_URL)
        .buildUpon()
        .appendQueryParameter("lat", String.valueOf(params[0]))
        .appendQueryParameter("lng", String.valueOf(params[1]))
        .build();

// Connect to web service
URL url = new URL(uri.toString());
urlConnection = (HttpURLConnection) url.openConnection();

// Read web service response and convert to a string
InputStream inputStream =
        new BufferedInputStream(urlConnection.getInputStream());

// Convert InputStream to String using a Scanner
Scanner inputStreamScanner =
        new Scanner(inputStream).useDelimiter("\\A");
String response = inputStreamScanner.next();
inputStreamScanner.close();

Log.d(TAG, "Web Service Response -> " + response);

JSONObject json = new JSONObject(response);

String observation =
        json
            .getJSONObject("weatherObservation")
            .getString("observation");

// Split on whitespace
String[] values = observation.split("\\s");

// Iterate of METAR string until SLP string is found
String slpString = null;
for (int i = 1; i < values.length; i++)
{
    String value = values[i];

    if (value.startsWith(SLP_STRING.toLowerCase())
            || value.startsWith(SLP_STRING.toUpperCase()))
    {
        slpString =
                value.substring(SLP_STRING.length());
        break;
    }
}

// Decode SLP string into numerical representation
StringBuffer sb = new StringBuffer(slpString);

sb.insert(sb.length() - 1, ".");
```

continues

LISTING 9-11 *(continued)*

```java
                float val1 = Float.parseFloat("10" + sb);
                float val2 = Float.parseFloat("09" + sb);

                mslp =
                        (Math.abs((1000 - val1)) < Math.abs((1000 - val2)))
                            ? val1
                            : val2;
            }
            catch (Exception e)
            {
                Log.e(TAG, "Could not communicate with web service", e);
            }
            finally
            {
                if (urlConnection != null)
                {
                    urlConnection.disconnect();
                }
            }

            return mslp;
        }

        @Override
        protected void onPostExecute(Float result)
        {
            long uptime = SystemClock.uptimeMillis();

            if (result == null
                    && (lastErrorMessageTimestamp == -1
                        || ((uptime - lastErrorMessageTimestamp) > 30000)))
            {
                Toast.makeText(DetermineAltitudeActivity.this,
                        R.string.webServiceConnectionFailureMessage,
                        Toast.LENGTH_LONG).show();

                lastErrorMessageTimestamp = uptime;
            }
            else
            {
                DetermineAltitudeActivity.this.mslp = result;
            }

            DetermineAltitudeActivity.this.webServiceFetching = false;
        }
    }
}
```

code snippet DeterminAltitudeActivity.java

SUMMARY

This chapter expanded on the information that was presented in Chapter 5 about the barometer and provided an implementation that made use of pressure data to calculate altitude. This is just one use of the barometer, but will probably end up being one of the most common use cases for pressure data.

Using barometer-based altitude data can add another dimension to location data because it allows devices to provide finer-grained location information without the use of the GPS.

The app displayed in the chapter is robust enough to enable users to start experimenting with the barometer right away, assuming they have a device with the sensor. Between the sensor API, the standard atmospheric pressure constant, and the `SensorManager.getAltitude()` method, making use of barometric data is fairly straightforward.

The next chapter covers the Android Open Accessory Development Kit (AOA). AOA allows external hardware to communicate with an Android device via USB.

10
Android Open Accessory

WHAT'S IN THIS CHAPTER?

➤ Introducing AOA

➤ Explaining how AOA works and why developers may want to use it

➤ Presenting some of the limitations of AOA

➤ Providing an example of code that uses AOA

Android Open Accessory (AOA) is a protocol that allows an Android device to interact with external sensors and actuators via USB. This addition to the Android SDK is exciting for both electronics hobbyists and mobile professionals because it opens up the possibilities of reacting to real-world inputs like temperature changes and controlling real-world objects such as lights without being limited to the current form-factor of a mobile phone or its current hardware sensors.

A SHORT HISTORY OF AOA

AOA is a relatively new and underutilized feature of the Android SDK, having only been announced by Google at the Google I/O developer conference in May 2011. Official Android SDK support for external hardware such as USB devices (and, to some extent, NFC) is still in the early phases and the infancy of the APIs may help explain why some idiosyncrasies such as power requirements (to be described in a later section) exist.

At the same time as announcing the AOA APIs in the Android SDK, Google also announced the availability of an Android Development Kit (ADK) microcontroller based on the popular Arduino hardware platform. In conjunction with external hardware, it is easy to see how mobile phones have shifted away from simply being cellular-enabled phones to "little computers in your pocket," which can act as the brains for applications ranging from wearable computing to home automation.

Currently AOA projects have remained mostly in the realm of hobbyists, but, as the AOA platform matures and the open source hardware movement grows, we should start to see more commercial projects built on this protocol much like Apple's MFi (Made for iPhone/iPad/iPod Touch) program which allows third-party developers to create 30-pin dock connector accessories. And, unlike Apple's MFi program, AOA is free to use, there are no licensing fees, and no non-disclosure agreements to sign. Based on our experiences, it would seem that there are two main barriers to AOA development: lack of Android devices that support AOA and lack of Android developers with electronics experience; hopefully this chapter will help address the latter problem!

USB Host Versus USB Accessory

Without AOA, due to the nature of USB protocols, most Android devices' USB ports cannot act as a USB host and are therefore incapable of sending commands to an external accessory. AOA uses a clever workaround: the Android device enters a special *accessory mode* where, although it is technically acting as an accessory to the external hardware, it sends information to the external hardware, which is interpreted by the hardware as commands. Meanwhile, the external hardware can send sensor information to the Android device.

In the actual physical configuration, the external hardware is the *USB host* (it powers the bus and enumerates connected devices) and the Android device is the *USB accessory*. However, in order to avoid confusion, this book refers to the external hardware as the *accessory* and the Android device as the *device* even though the master-slave roles are essentially reversed.

Electrical Power Requirements

The accessory must provide 500mA at 5V for charging power to the Android device. Though it may seem strange that a small external device like a temperature sensor is required to charge an Android smartphone or tablet while connected to it, this is a limitation of the underlying USB protocols rather than an oversight by the AOA developers. This is one part of AOA that will almost certainly change in the future as protocol workarounds are developed, or as more devices are released that can natively act as a USB host.

Supported Android Devices

Though most future Android devices will support AOA, Android hardware is not *required* to support Accessory Mode even if it has a sufficient OS version. Although AOA was released starting with Android 3.1 for tablets and backported to version 2.3.4 for phones, the decision to include AOA into the OS is made by the device manufacturer. Many custom Android ROMs built by popular firmware distributors such as CyanogenMod don't support AOA (although some versions of CyanogenMod do support it).

To guarantee AOA support, a Google Nexus line of phones running 2.3.4, 3.1, 4.0, and higher is recommended. If you have a non-Nexus phone or an Android tablet, a quick way to check for compatibility is to search for the *Basic Accessory Demo* app by Microchip Technology, Inc., in the Android Market. (Direct links: `https://play.google.com/store/apps/details?id=com.microchip.android.BasicAccessoryDemo_API12` for tablets and `https://play.google.com/store/apps/details?id=com.microchip.android.BasicAccessoryDemo` for phones.) If you are unable to view or install this app, it is an indicator that your phone does not support AOA. Microchip also maintains a list of compatible devices on their website: `http://microchip.com/android`.

So while this may seem like Android fragmentation at its worst, there are alternative external hardware microcontrollers that can be used such as the SparkFun IOIO, which is backwards compatible to Android 1.5. Or you can consider eschewing a hardwired USB connection and the current AOA API and instead communicate over Bluetooth or WiFi using the proper Arduino shield. Continue reading for more information about what microcontrollers are supported by Android and when you should look for other solutions.

THE ANDROID DEVELOPMENT KIT (ADK)

As mentioned earlier in this chapter, Google announced an Arduino-based ADK alongside the release of AOA support in the Android SDK. Arduino is an open-source single-board micro-controller system that has become popular among hobbyists because it simplifies the process of using electronics in multidisciplinary projects due to its easy to learn, high level programming language and non-intimidating IDE. Arduinos come in many varying sizes and form factors which add to its desirability as a microntroller platform. Refer to Figure 10-1 for examples of various Arduinos.

FIGURE 10-1: Various Arduino form factors. The LilyPad (left) for wearable and soft electronics projects, a typical Uno (top right), and the Mega ADK (bottom right). Only the Mega ADK is compatible with AOA.

The easiest to use AOA compatible Arduino is the Mega ADK. However, while its mainstream popularity may make the Arduino "brand" synonymous with electronics tinkering, it's important to understand that an ADK is also an open-source platform (the protocols for making an Android compatible development kit are licensed under Creative Commons and Apache 2.0 licenses) so anyone can create their own custom hardware. As long as the hardware has integrated USB host support and implements the *Android Accessory Protocol* as outlined by Google to establish communication to a USB connected Android device and to indicate to the device to use a special AOA accessory mode, then it can be considered ADK-compatible.

The Android developer portal lists some of the vendors on their ADK information page (`http://accessories.android.com`) but the following are some development kits of note:

➤ **Arduino Mega ADK** (`http://store.arduino.cc`): By today's standards, a "typical" Arduino is an Arduino Uno. An Arduino Mega 2560 is programmed by a developer in exactly the same manner as an Uno but a Mega 2560 is double the physical size and has more flash memory, SRAM, and EEPROM to perform faster. A step up, the Mega ADK is a Mega 2560 with integrated USB host controllers.

The instructions and code examples from this chapter will use a Mega ADK.

➤ **Seeed Studio Seeeduino** (`www.seeedstudio.com/depot/seeeduino-adk-main-board-p-846.html`), **SparkFun Electric Sheep** (`www.sparkfun.com/products/10745`), and **Modern Device Freeduino USB Host Board** (`http://shop.moderndevice.com/products/freeduino-usb-host-board`): The Arduino specifications are open-source so anyone can make Arduino compatible hardware and use the Arduino IDE to program it without learning a new programming language for each microcontroller. These boards are a great example of the advantages of open source hardware since it means that various ADKs can be offered with different specs, be competitively priced, or even be simultaneously backwards compatible for 1.5+ Android devices using non-AOA APIs.

➤ **Microchip *PIC24F Accessory Development Starter Kit*** (`www.microchip.com/stellent/idcplg?IdcService=SS_GET_PAGE&nodeId=1406&dDocName=en553673`): Microchip Technology has been in the semiconductor chip business for a long time. Comparatively speaking, Arduino is still a new kid on the block at seven years of age (created 2005) and Microchip is a grizzled veteran at 25 (created in 1987 as a spinoff of now defunct General Instrument).

Microchip's line of PIC microcontrollers are widely used in the embedded systems industry and possibly show up in some commercial electronic gadgets you use today. However, this long history may explain why most new electronics hobbyists have never heard of a PIC chip before — Microchip caters to electrical engineers and hasn't changed their website much to reflect the growing popularity of the open source hardware movement. Shopping on the Microchip website can be confusing and the PIC development environment (the C programming language and Microchip's IDE called MPLAB) isn't as welcoming as the Arduino IDE.

So while there can be an argument made for the PIC24F and upcoming PIC32, because they are superior spec-wise due to a better and more tightly integrated USB host support, many other factors make it hard to recommend PIC chips to newcomers to electronics. However, if you are already familiar with PIC chips, this would be a great development board to pick up.

On the bright side, hardware developers with more experience have being doing all the "hard work" for us and many derivative ADKs have been created based on the PIC chipset such as the IOIO to be discussed next and soon-to-be ADK compatible boards such as the Pinguino (http://pinguino. cc/) which allow you to write firmware code in BASIC or C, and even a language that matches the Arduino programming language.

ARDUINO COMPATIBLE

Wondering what the difference between an official Arduino product is and one that is labeled as "Arduino compatible" is? An official Arduino board is still designed and manufactured by various companies but they pay a licensing fee to fund continued work on the Arduino platform. They also work with the Arduino team to ensure compatibility and quality. However, having stated that, do not assume that it means that non-official Arduino boards are necessarily inferior products — they are simply part of the open source ecosystem.

➤ **Sparkfun IOIO** (www.sparkfun.com/products/10748): The IOIO (pronounced "yo-yo") is a very interesting Android-compatible microcontroller because it pre-dated the Google AOA announcement by a month and uses a completely different communication protocol. Instead of using the Android Accessory Protocol required for an ADK, the IOIO cleverly uses the information transferred by the Android Debug Bridge (ADB) commonly used for logging debug messages while testing Android applications connected to a computer. More recently, beta AOA support has been added and apps built for the IOIO will attempt to use AOA first and then gracefully fall back to ADB for non-AOA phones and tablets.

Price-wise, the IOIO is $50 USD compared to $80 USD for a Mega ADK, which can make it very appealing to the wallet. The IOIO is based on the Microchip PIC chipset discussed in the bullet point immediately above, which partially accounts for the price difference. Firmware has already been pre-installed in the IOIO board (unlike the Arduino based ADKs) so the only code that you need to write is Java code in your Android app.

For all these reasons, IOIO may sound clearly better than AOA, however there are two main drawbacks to IOIO. The first is that ADB is incredibly powerful – you can do almost anything by ADB. An accessory could do damage to the Android device via ADB, either maliciously or through bad coding. Therefore I, for one, would not be comfortable connecting my device to a IOIO-based accessory that I had not built myself. This poses a serious problem if you want to mass-produce and sell your Android accessory. Secondly, in order to connect to a IOIO-based accessory, the user must open Settings ➪ Applications ➪ Development, and check the box to allow USB debugging (though this only needs to be done once). To sell a IOIO-based product to the non-technically-inclined public you would have to show them how to turn on that feature and have them comfortable enabling it. Google could change ADB to get around these problems, but at this stage that seems unlikely and probably unwise.

For a more thorough comparison, please refer to this blog entry by Ytai Ben-Tsvi, the creator of the IOIO: http://ytai-mer.blogspot.com/2011/06/ioio-over-openaccessory-adk-available. html.

In addition to these devices, it's possible to set up almost any microcontroller to be AOA compatible by adding a pre-assembled USB host shield such as these listed on the Circuits@Home website: www.circuitsathome.com/products-page/arduino-shields/. Refer to Figure 10-3 for how an breadboard shield sits on top of an Arduino Mega.

Hardware Components

The Arduino microcontroller board (see Figure 10-2) usually consists of the microcontroller chip, USB or other connectivity interface, and supporting circuitry with notification LEDs (light-emitting diodes). Sensors can be interfaced with the board's *pin headers*, often by using a *shield*. Shields may either be bare *breadboards* (no electronic components, but an array of holes to solder components on), or have pre-soldered components. (See Figure 10-3.) For example, shields may provide Ethernet/WiFi/USB/XBee connectivity, provide SD card storage, or hold a wide range of sensors and actuators. Although the possible voltage supply levels from microcontrollers are low, larger devices (such as large motors) may be controlled using *relays*. Relays are electronic switches — they allow the controller to turn on or off a large external current with just a small control voltage signal.

FIGURE 10-2: A close up view of the Arduino ADK board

FIGURE 10-3: An Arduino Mega "breadboard" shield. Shields interface with the pin headers and sit atop a microcontroller board. Sensors or other devices may sit on a shield.

Software Components

For Android Open Accessory, you need two programs: an Android program running on your Android device, and another program running on your Arduino. The program running on the Arduino is referred to as *firmware* in the online Android SDK documentation but most Arduino users will refer to this program as a *sketch*. (The term sketch is analogous to the idea of being able to pick up a pencil and quickly draw something; Arduino development is meant to be fast and easy.)

After the Arduino board is connected to the Android device, communication begins immediately and the relevant application launches (or the user will be taken to the Google Play to download the app if it is not installed).

The Arduino platform is both hardware and software. The Arduino software component consists of a simplified IDE with a standard programming language compiler and the boot loader that runs on the board. Arduino sketches are written in the Arduino programming language, which is a thin layer on top of C++. Programmers with previous experience in C, C++, Java, or a similar open-source project called Processing (www.processing.org) should find Arduino syntax very easy to learn.

Sketches are uploaded to the board by clicking the Upload button on the Arduino IDE. (The Arduino IDE is not part of Eclipse, it is a separate program that needs to be downloaded from www.arduino.cc.) Once uploaded, sketches run a setup function first and then will loop infinitely as long as the Arduino is receiving electrical power and there are no errors in the code. If power is removed, the board will retain the sketch next time it is powered up. Figure 10-4 shows the Arduino IDE and a barebones sketch with two required methods unsurprisingly named setup() and loop().

FIGURE 10-4: The Arduino IDE and a basic Arduino sketch

More information about the Arduino environment will be discussed in the "Getting Started with the Arduino Software" section later in this chapter.

AOA SENSORS VERSUS NATIVE DEVICE SENSORS

A developer can do many things using only native sensors, such as the accelerometer, in an Android device. However, at times the sensors on a device cannot provide the data needed for an application. The device may not have a sensor to provide the data, or the sensor on the device may not provide enough precision and/or sensitivity in the data it reports. For instance, there is no good way to measure wind speed, blood alcohol level, or ambient temperature with an Android device. (The temperature sensor in Android devices measures CPU temperature — if you want room temperature you need an external sensor.) In addition, though in-device sensor sensitivity improves with newer devices, there will always be cases where far more sensitive sensors exist but cannot be integrated into an Android device. For instance, MEMS gyroscopes are nowhere near as good as large, bulky, fiber-optic gyroscopes, and external light sensors may detect broader levels of light than the built-in light sensor is capable of measuring. In general, AOA sensors have vastly greater sensing possibilities.

AOA BEYOND SENSORS

Common sensors that are easily interfaced with AOA include temperature, light, capacitive (touch) sensors, accelerometers, gyroscopes, and magnetometers. Joysticks or other input devices are also common.

Of course, Arduino isn't just limited to collecting sensor information — it can also act on the environment. The counterpart to a sensor is an *actuator*. Actuators include motors, lights, and buzzers, and many larger components that may be switched using relays.

AOA LIMITATIONS

Arduino has a finite sampling frequency, which limits the ability to handle sensor signals that rapidly vary. This frequency is different for analog (waveform-like) and digital (step-like) inputs, and varies by the brand and model of the Arduino board. For example, Arduino Mega analog inputs may sample up to 10 kHz (10,000 times per second), whereas its digital inputs can read once per instruction cycle, or 16 MHz (6 million times per second). It is, of course, impossible to measure a signal that varies faster than your sampling frequency (or even one fifth or one tenth of your sampling frequency, because you often require several data points to adequately define a rapid value fluctuation). This means, for instance, that the analog input cannot be directly used to sense FM radio wave frequencies (~100 MHz) or even high-pitched audible sounds via microphone (the frequency limit of human hearing is around 20 kHz). The problems caused by sampling at a slower frequency than the frequency you are trying to measure are called *aliasing errors*. You can imagine, for instance, that if waves are crashing on a beach every 10 seconds and I only take a measurement of the wave height of the nearest wave every 60 seconds, I'm not going to be able to know exactly where each wave is, nor even know that they crash every 10 seconds — I'd have no idea. Clever electrical engineering workarounds can be used, but these are advanced topics that are not covered here.

In addition, although AOA can directly sense the outputs of many digital and some analog sensors, not all sensors can simply be plugged into a microcontroller. Often some kind of circuit is needed to interface the sensor with Arduino. These circuits may scale or otherwise operate on the signal from the sensor in order to convert it into voltages that Arduino can handle.

AOA AND SENSING TEMPERATURE

As a simple example of how to use AOA, this chapter discusses how to use AOA to collect readings from an external temperature sensor. In the example, an Arduino board with a 10-bit analog-to-digital converter is used. This means that when the sensor applies a voltage of between 0 and 5 volts on one of the analog input pins, it will be mapped to a value between 0 and 1023. This yields a resolution between readings of 5 volts / 1024 units, or 0.0049 volts (4.9 mV) per unit.

Assume you are using an MCP9701/9701A temperature sensor manufactured by Microchip (www. microchip.com/wwwproducts/Devices.aspx?dDocName=en022290). If you are buying this component, you will want the one suffixed TO and not LT or TT. These refer to the package and form factor – the TO has long leads that are easy to connect for our purposes, whereas the other ones are surface-mount and only have short stubby legs. You may verify this by searching for images of these components (e.g. on a component vendor site like http://digikey.com).

Next, download the datasheet from the microchip webpage by looking immediately underneath the blue Data Sheets header in the Documentation section of that webpage (the download link is named MCP9700/01 - Low-Power Linear Active Thermistor ICs) or by doing a web search with the model number of the component. If you are unfamiliar with technical datasheets, there is a brief tutorial on the Sparkfun website (www.sparkfun.com/tutorials/223).

Looking at the datasheet, there is a picture of the sensor (the one with long leads, called 3-Pin TO-92 on the datasheet, is the one you want). The pins are labeled VDD, VOUT, and GND. The VDD pin is where it gets its electrical power — connect +5 volts to that by connecting it to any of the +5V outputs labeled on the Arduino board. The GND pin is the ground pin, or the other end of the electrical circuit — you connect it to the GND pin header on the Arduino board. The VOUT pin is where the signal comes out. This signal is a voltage that you will measure and then map back to a real-world temperature as described later. You can connect this pin to any of the numbered pin headers labeled Analog In. For this example, you can connect it to pin number A3.

To make these three electrical connections, you may clip or solder three long wires to the leads and push the free end into the pin headers. Or, if you have a board where +5V, GND, and an analog input pin are close enough together, you may just push the three leads of the unmodified sensor into the pin headers (you may do this on the Arduino Mega, for instance, using Analog Input number 0).

On the datasheet you will notice that the voltage is scaled to a temperature coefficient of 19.5 mV/°C (this is listed as the typical value — you can calibrate your individual sensor if you wish). The output voltage at 0°C is also scaled to 400 mV (typical). Therefore, the voltage coming out of the sensor is $V_{out}[mV] = k[mV/°C] * T[°C] + V0 [mV]$ (the units are written in square brackets), where k is the temperature coefficient, T is the temperature you want to measure, and V0 is the output voltage at 0 C.

In other words, the voltage coming out of the temperature sensor when the actual room temperature is 25°C is $V_{out}[mV] = 19.5 * 25 + 400 = 887.5$ mV. If you convert that from millivolts to volts, 887.5

mV = 0.8875 V. Next, assume this temperature sensor is directly plugged into the analog input pin described in the first paragraph of this section. You find that 0.8875 volts / (5 volts / 1024 units) = 181.8. So 887.5 mV is between the possible digital values of 181 and 182, and closer to 182. So on a scale of 0 to 1023 units, the microcontroller will register the signal coming from the sensor as being at 182 units. Finding temperature in the code is as simple as getting that 182 number from the microcontroller and calculating backward to find that the temperature is 25°C.

Implementation

Now that this chapter has introduced the example app, it is time to discuss the actual implementation. The implementation includes the Arduino sketch code as well as code that runs on the Android device. The code is based on the ADK package that is available as a download from `http://developer.android.com/guide/topics/usb/adk.html`. The ADK package contains code to interact with many kinds of input and output. This section simplifies the ADK package's app so that it can explain a complete, simple code example that collects data from a specific temperature sensor. Before discussing code, a quick discussion on what is required to use AOA and how to get the Arduino software running is needed.

Requirements

The following is a list of the minimum requirements needed to use AOA:

➤ An AOA-compatible Android device. To test compatibility before trying this example, please refer to the "Supported Android Devices" section for links to the Microchip AOA demonstration apps available on the Google Play.

➤ An Arduino-compatible microcontroller board as discussed in the "The Android Development Kit (ADK)" section previously. We recommend the Arduino Mega ADK if you are unsure.

➤ A "breadboard" or breadboard shield (see Figure 10-3). Breadboard shields are available from many vendors; just search for "prototyping breadboard shield for Arduino Mega." For example, the "ProtoShield with breadboard" shown at `www.bizoner.com/prototype-shield-protoshield-with-bread-board-for-arduino-mega-p-183.html` has pin headers already attached, and has the option to solder components to the bare board, or to push them (without solder) into holes in a white prototyping breadboard allowing for quick prototyping before components are semi-permanently soldered in place.

➤ A temperature sensor. This example uses a Microchip MCP9701/9701A temperature sensor. If you choose a different temperature sensor, you may need to adjust your calculations.

Getting Started with the Arduino Software

Before using AOA, you must download the Arduino IDE. You can find the Arduino development software under the Download tab at `http://arduino.cc`. An important warning is that Arduino recently had a 1.0 release and saw many major upgrades; some API method names have changed. The Android AOA libraries supplied by Google have not been upgraded so they are out-of-sync and the Arduino compiler will produce many errors in version 1.0. You should download version 0023 of the Android IDE instead of the Android 1.0 version for these examples — on the downloads page, scroll down to the Previous IDE Versions section.

Install the Arduino IDE to your Mac, Windows, or Linux machine based your specific computer platform instructions linked from the Getting Started page: `http://arduino.cc/en/Guide/ HomePage`. The driver installation for Windows can be a bit tricky so pay special attention to that part of the instructions.

Arduino is very beginner friendly and comes pre-packaged with code samples available from within the IDE by looking under File ➪ Examples from the top menu bar. Additional tutorials and reference guides are also available on the Arduino website. Once you are comfortable with uploading one of the example sketches to your board, read on.

The next step is to set up the Android development environment to use with AOA. You can do this by following the instructions at `http://developer.android.com/guide/topics/usb/adk.html` under the "Installing the Arduino software and necessary libraries" section of the webpage.

Now that you have the development environment set up, the discussion moves to the actual implementation. The Arduino code (see Listing 10-1) is discussed first and then the Android code. For the remainder of the implementation, it is assumed that the temperature sensor is connected to pin.

Arduino Sketch

Create an Arduino project by selecting File ➪ New from the top menu of the Arduino IDE. A new, blank window will appear. Save this file as `Arduino_Temp_Sensor.pde`.

All Arduino projects must have a `setup()` and a `loop()` method declared. You should run each one once initially to ensure the microcontroller is clear of previous programs, and the `loop()` method will also check for presence of the board.

```
/* The two essential methods for any Arduino sketch:
setup() and loop(). Run both of them once to ensure a
clear and functional board. */
void setup();
void loop();

/* Now declare setup() for real. This method will run
once after the board has been powered on or reset. */
void setup()
{
}

/* Now declare loop() for real. This method will continue
to loop until Arduino is powered down or reset. */
void loop()
{
}
```

For debugging and message logging, use Arduino's serial communications monitor. When your Arduino is hooked up to your computer via USB, you can get useful information from the microcontroller using the `Serial.print()` or `Serial.println()` commands. To open the serial monitor, select Tools ⇨ Serial Monitor from the top menu and make sure that it matches the baud rate that you have defined in your Arduino sketch using the `Serial.begin()` command. For more information about serial communications, visit the Arduino documentation: `http://arduino.cc/en/Serial/Begin`. For more information about the `Serial.print()` command, visit: `http://arduino.cc/en/Serial/Print`.

The following is an updated `setup()` method:

```
void setup()
{
    // start serial debugging
    Serial.begin(115200);
    Serial.print("\r\nADK has run setup().");
    Serial.println("Ready to start reading the temp...");
}
```

As noted previously, we'll be plugging the temperature sensor's input pin into the Analog In pin of the Arduino ADK marked A3. Constants are useful because if you ever reorganize the layout of your circuit, it's only a matter of changing one number. The following line of code defines a constant named `TEMP_SENSOR` and sets it to be pin A3. Much like Java programming, Arduino constants are typically declared at the beginning of a file.

```
#define TEMP_SENSOR A3 // the temperature sensor pin
```

To get data from the sensor, within the `loop()` method, use the Arduino `analogRead()` method to read the voltage of the temperature sensor's analog input pin and store it as an unsigned 16 bit variable (`uint16`).

A reading may take 100 microseconds depending on the microcontroller, so in that case, the maximum reading rate would be 10kHz. You can look up the analog pin read speed for your particular Arduino on the manufacturer's website. However, temperature doesn't change much in a fraction of a second so if you don't want to get data at the maximum reading rate you can slow it down with a time delay using the `delay()` method. Using a delay is also beneficial in order to not use system resources unnecessarily; however, the Android device will expect a certain timeliness in order to maintain the AOA connection so a delay of 100 ms is ideal.

The following is an updated `loop()` method with serial debugging:

```
void loop()
{
    // Read the voltage from the sensor
    uint16_t val;
    val = analogRead(TEMP_SENSOR);
    Serial.println(val,HEX);
    Serial.write(val);
    // Delay for 100 milliseconds.
    delay(100);
}
```

And that's all it takes to get data from a temperature sensor! Listing 10-1 shows the full Arduino sketch. As you can see, this is why they are called sketches!

To test the sketch, upload to your Arduino ADK and open up the Arduino serial monitor. You will see the monitor output ADK has run setup(), followed by Ready to start reading the temp..., then a series of "val=##" where ## will be a number from 0 to 1023. This is a not the actual temperature but a number based on the temperature coefficient of your sensor. The Android app discussed in an upcoming section section will take care of the math to convert the sensor data into Celsius readings.

Touch the temperature sensor or shine a warm light bulb on your circuit to see the temperature coefficient increase. Remove the source of heat and watch the val variable decrease. If you do not see this change, confirm that your circuit is wired correctly. It's very easy to confuse the pins for 5V and GND based on the direction you plugged them into the breadboard, or to confuse the slot for pin A3 with a nearby pin.

LISTING 10-1: The Arduino sketch Arduino_Temp_Sensor.pde for reading temperature data without an AOA device

```
#define TEMP_SENSOR A3 // the temperature sensor pin

/* The two essential methods for any Arduino sketch:
setup() and loop(). Run both of them once to ensure a
clear and functional board. */
void setup();
void loop();

/* Now declare setup() for real. This method will run
once after the board has been powered on or reset. */
void setup()
{
    // start serial debugging
    Serial.begin(115200);
    Serial.println("\r\nADK has run setup().");
    Serial.println("Ready to start reading the temp...");
}

/* Now declare loop() for real. This method will continue
to loop until Arduino is powered down or reset. */
void loop()
{
    // Read the voltage from the sensor
    uint16_t val;
    val = analogRead(TEMP_SENSOR);
    Serial.print("val=");
    Serial.println(val,HEX);


    // Delay for 100 milliseconds.
    delay(100);
}
```

Building on the previous sketch, let's add AOA capabilities. First you must include some Arduino libraries and classes using the #include directive. You should already have installed these libraries as part of the setup. These statements go at the very top of the sketch. The `Max3421e` and `Usb` libraries are for USB Host controlling:

```
// the USB Host libraries
#include <Max3421e.h>
#include <Usb.h>
```

`AndroidAccessory` is the Google-supplied, C++ class for instantiating the Android Accessory protocol:

```
// the AOA library
#include <AndroidAccessory.h>
```

Now you are ready to implement AOA features in your Arduino code! Instantiate a new instance of the `AndroidAccessory` class named *acc* and define the metadata associated with the board.

```
// create an instance of the AndroidAccessory class
AndroidAccessory acc("Manufacturer name",
        "Model",
        "Description",
        "1.0",
        "http://www.example.com",
        "Serial number");
```

Through the use of Android intent filters, this metadata can be read by the Android device to determine which app to launched when the phone or tablet is plugged into the ADK board via USB. The Android app will only use the manufacturer, model, and version information to determine when the accessory is connected; description, URI, and serial number are not used by the intent filters.

Continuing on, if you recall from much earlier in this chapter, the Arduino is acting as a USB host to the Android device so the Arduino is obligated to supply 5V of power to the phone. The `powerOn()` method of the `AndroidAccessory` class is a convenience method that simply calls the `powerOn()` method in the `Max3421e` library. Call `powerOn()` in your `setup()` method:

```
void setup()
{
    // start serial debugging
    Serial.begin(115200);
    Serial.println("\r\nADK has run setup().");
    Serial.println("Ready to start reading the temp...");

    // Power up the USB host controller
    acc.powerOn();
}
```

To check if the Android device is connected via USB and that the Android app has been launched, use the `isConnected()` method of the `AndroidAccessory` class your `loop()`. For our temperature sensor example code, if the AOA device is connected, start reading the temperature sensor. Otherwise, do nothing.

```
void loop()
{
    if (acc.isConnected())
    {
        // Read the voltage from the sensor
```

```
            uint16_t val;
            val = analogRead(TEMP_SENSOR);
            Serial.print("val=");
            Serial.println(val,HEX);
    }

    // Delay for 100 milliseconds.
    delay(100);
}
```

For other Arduino projects, you may wish to use the `else` condition to detect a recently disconnected device and reset the Arduino circuit to its default state. For example, if a button on your Android app turns on a LED, it makes sense to turn the LED off if the device is disconnected from the Arduino board.

```
if (acc.isConnected())
{
    // turn on LED
}
else {
    // device may have been disconnected so turn off LED
}
```

Finally, get the Arduino and Android to send data back and forth. There are two methods available in the `AndroidAccessory` class that do as their names imply: `read()` and `write()`. For the temperature sensor, the data is packaged into three bytes. The reason for this is that the value reported by the analog input pin will be a number from 0 to 1023, so we need at least two bytes to hold a value up to 1023. (One byte (8 bits) can hold a maximum value of $2^8 - 1 = 255$.) The method of packaging and unpackaging of the two smaller bytes into the larger number are shown in the Arduino sketch and Android code, respectively. The third byte (actually, the first byte we send) is simply to specify which sensor or actuator the reading refers to. We only have one sensor, so in this simple example we set this byte to be zero, however it is clear how we may choose other numbers to refer to other sensors or actuators.

```
if (acc.isConnected())
{
    // Read the voltage from the sensor
    uint16_t val;
    val = analogRead(TEMP_SENSOR);
    Serial.print("val=");
    Serial.println(val,HEX);

    // Declare a message to be sent to the Android device
    byte msg[3];

    // default to 0 for the first sensor
    msg[0] = 0x0;

    /* Repackage val into two bytes. (This is unpackaged
    by the composeInt method in the Android code.)
    >> is a right-shift operator, so >> 8 moves all the
    bits in val to the right by 8 places.
    For more information, look up bitwise operations in
```

```
   the C programming language. */
   msg[1] = val >> 8;
   msg[2] = val & 0xff;

   // Finally, send the message to the Android device
   acc.write(msg, 3);
}
```

The temperature sensor example doesn't use read() but, for your other Arduino projects, you could use it to read input from the Android phone such as an on/off press on a UI button, a range of numbers from a UI slider, or anything else your app wants to send to the Arduino.

LISTING 10-2: The Arduino sketch Arduino_Temp_Sensor_with_AOA.pde for reading temperature data without an AOA device

```
// the USB Host libraries
#include <Max3421e.h>
#include <Usb.h>

// the AOA library
#include <AndroidAccessory.h>

#define TEMP_SENSOR A3 // the temperature sensor pin

// create an instance of the AndroidAccessory class
AndroidAccessory acc("Manufacturer name",
      "Model",
      "Description",
      "1.0",
      "http://www.example.com",
      "Serial number");

/* The two essential methods for any Arduino sketch:
setup() and loop(). Run both of them once to ensure a
clear and functional board. */
void setup();
void loop();

/* Now declare setup() for real. This method will run
once after the board has been powered on or reset. */
void setup()
{
    // start serial debugging
    Serial.begin(115200);
    Serial.println("\r\nADK has run setup().");
    Serial.println("Ready to start reading the temp...");

    // Power up the Android device.
    acc.powerOn();
}

/* Now declare loop() for real. This method will continue
```

```
    to loop until Arduino is powered down or reset. */
void loop()
{
    if (acc.isConnected())
    {
        // Read the voltage from the sensor
        uint16_t val;
        val = analogRead(TEMP_SENSOR);
        Serial.print("val=");
        Serial.println(val,HEX);

        // Declare a message to be sent to the Android device
        byte msg[3];

        // default to 0 for the first sensor
        msg[0] = 0x0;

        /* Repackage val into two bytes. (This is unpackaged
        by the composeInt method in the Android code.)
        >> is a right-shift operator, so >> 8 moves all the
        bits in val to the right by 8 places.
        For more information, look up bitwise operations in
        the C programming language. */
        msg[1] = val >> 8;
        msg[2] = val & 0xff;

        // Finally, send the message to the Android device
        acc.write(msg, 3);
    }

    // Delay for 100 milliseconds.
    delay(100);
}
```

As you can see by the bolded area of code in Listing 10-2, implementing the Android Accessory Protocol in the Arduino firmware only takes about six lines of code — and three of the lines were imports of preexisting libraries. And communicating with the Android device simply uses `acc.write()` to send data or `acc.read()` to write data. It's that easy to get started on the Arduino end!

Compile the sketch by clicking on the Verify button and confirm that there are no errors. When the Arduino IDE's status bar indicates that it is done compiling, make sure that your Arduino is plugged into your computer and upload the sketch to the Arduino by clicking on the Upload button. When the status bar indicates that it is done uploading, it is time to move on to Android code.

Android Code

First an overview: The Android code is located in `BaseActivity`. Before `BaseActivity` can access any of the USB accessories, it must gain permission to do so. After receiving permission from the user, `BaseActivity` initializes the `USBManager` and uses it to connect to the temperature sensor. Once connected, `BaseActivity` reads the data from the sensor and updates the user interface.

To start, make an XML file called `accessory_filter.xml` that provides manufacturer, model, and version information to allow you to start the app when the correct accessory is connected.

Save this file to the res/xml folder of your project. This must be an exact match to the manufacturer, model, and version information metadata supplied in the Arduino sketch when you create a AndroidAccessory instance. The contents of the XML file are illustrated in Listing 10-3.

LISTING 10-3: xml/accessory_filter.xml

```xml
<?xml version="1.0" encoding="utf-8"?>
<resources>
    <usb-accessory manufacturer="Manufacturer name" model="Model" version="1.0" />
</resources>
```

If an accessory is not connected when the user runs the app, the app displays a prompt to connect the accessory. If an accessory is connected without the app running, Android runs the app.

Secondly, make sure the minimum SDK of the application is set to at least API level 10. If you're deploying to a 2.3.4+ Android phone only, double-check that you are targeting the 2.3.3 Google API libraries as seen in Figure 10-5 since AOA was backported from 3.1 via a library. (No checkbox exists for 2.3.4 in the settings panel!)

FIGURE 10-5: Make sure 2.3.3 Google libraries are checked off when deploying to phones.

In the manifest file, check that the device supports AOA. If you're using a 2.3.4+ Android phone, include both of these elements in the manifest:

```xml
<uses-sdk android:minSdkVersion="10" />
<uses-library android:name="com.android.future.usb.accessory" />
```

If you're using a 3.1+ Android phone or tablet, then the `<uses-library>` isn't necessary — instead, just set the minimum SDK to at least 12. In that case, the app will be using the platform APIs instead of the add-on library:

```
<uses-sdk android:minSdkVersion="12" />
<uses-feature android:name="android.hardware.usb.accessory" />
```

In addition, for all Android OS versions, add an intent filter to launch the app immediately when it's been connected via USB to a matching device listed in the accessory filter xml:

```
<intent-filter>
    <action android:name="android.hardware.usb.action.USB_ACCESSORY_ATTACHED"/>
</intent-filter>
<meta-data
    android:name="android.hardware.usb.action.USB_ACCESSORY_ATTACHED"
    android:resource="@xml/accessory_filter" />
```

Listing 10-4 shows the AndroidManifest.xml file in its entirety for a 3.1+ AOA compatible device with the variations for 2.3.4+ devices commented out for your reference.

LISTING 10-4: AndroidManifest.xml

```
<?xml version="1.0" encoding="utf-8"?>
<manifest xmlns:android="http://schemas.android.com/apk/res/android"
    package="com.example.temperaturesensor"
    android:versionCode="1"
    android:versionName="1.0">

    <!-- Android 2.3.4+ devices: -->
    <!--  <uses-sdk android:minSdkVersion="10"  />  -->

    <!-- Android 3.1+ devices -->
    <uses-sdk android:minSdkVersion="12"  />

    <!-- Android 3.1+ devices: -->
    <uses-feature android:name="android.hardware.usb.accessory" />

    <application android:icon="@drawable/icon" android:label="@string/app_name">

        <!-- Android 2.3.4+ devices: -->
        <!--  <uses-library android:name="com.android.future.usb.accessory" /> -->
        <activity android:name=".BaseActivity"
                android:label="@string/app_name">
            <intent-filter>
                <action android:name="android.intent.action.MAIN" />
                <category android:name="android.intent.category.LAUNCHER" />
            </intent-filter>
            <intent-filter>
                <action
                    android:name="android.hardware.usb.action.USB_ACCESSORY_ATTACHED"/>
            </intent-filter>
            <meta-data
                android:name="android.hardware.usb.action.USB_ACCESSORY_ATTACHED"
                (UsbAccessory) intent.getParcelableExtra(UsbManager.EXTRA_ACCESSORY);
```

continues

LISTING 10-4 *(continued)*

```
                android:resource="@xml/accessory_filter" />
        </activity>

    </application>
</manifest>
```

In the `BaseActivity` class, there are two other differences to between 2.3.4 and 3.1 devices, because the `android.hardware.usb` package is written in such a way that it must instantiate `UsbManager` and `UsbAccessory` objects differently from how you do it if you are using the library.

If you're using a 2.3.4+ Android phone, you should obtain a reference to `UsbManager` and `UsbAccessory` in the following way:

```
import com.android.future.usb.UsbAccessory;
import com.android.future.usb.UsbManager;
UsbManager manager = UsbManager.getInstance(this);
UsbAccessory accessory = UsbManager.getAccessory(intent);
```

If you're using a 3.1+ Android phone or tablet, you should obtain a reference to `UsbManager` and `UsbAccessory` in the following way:

```
import com.android.hardware.usb.UsbAccessory;
import com.android.hardware.usb.UsbManager;
UsbManager manager = (UsbManager) getSystemService(Context.USB_SERVICE);
UsbAccessory accessory = (UsbAccessory)
  intent.getParcelableExtra(UsbManager.EXTRA_ACCESSORY);
```

The full code follows in Listing 10-5 but here are some highlights that may need some elaboration for all AOA projects.

Communication between Arduino and Android

If you are wondering what the protocol is that allows the Arduino to speak to the Android device, and vice versa, you may be interested to know that it simply uses an instance of an Android `FileInputStream` when reading sensor data from a connected Arduino device (and `FileOutputStream` when writing commands to the Arduino device). This is very similar to using native OS protocols to read and write from a system file or buffer where, instead of a file, it's a microcontroller!

Because these code statements are not in the same method, the following are some statements to keep an eye out for in BaseActivity.java:

➤   In the `openAccessory()` method:

```
    mFileDescriptor = mUsbManager.openAccessory(accessory);
    // ...
FileDescriptor fd = mFileDescriptor.getFileDescriptor();
    mInputStream = new FileInputStream(fd);
```

➤   And in the `run()` method:

```
ret = mInputStream.read(buffer);
```

Available for
download on
Wrox.com

LISTING 10-5: BaseActivity.java

```java
package com.example.temperaturesensor;

import java.io.FileDescriptor;
import java.io.FileInputStream;
import java.io.IOException;
import java.text.DecimalFormat;

import android.app.Activity;
import android.app.PendingIntent;
import android.content.BroadcastReceiver;
import android.content.Context;
import android.content.Intent;
import android.content.IntentFilter;
import android.os.Bundle;
import android.os.Handler;
import android.os.Message;
import android.os.ParcelFileDescriptor;
import android.util.Log;
import android.widget.TextView;

//for Android 2.3.4+ devices:
/*
import com.android.future.usb.UsbAccessory;
import com.android.future.usb.UsbManager;
*/

//for Android 3.1+ devices
import android.hardware.usb.UsbAccessory;
import android.hardware.usb.UsbManager;


public class BaseActivity extends Activity implements Runnable
{
    private static final String TAG = "AOA,BaseActivity";
    private static final String ACTION_USB_PERMISSION =
            "com.example.aoaTempSensor.action.USB_PERMISSION";
    private static final int MESSAGE_TEMPERATURE = 2;
    private static final DecimalFormat TEMP_FORMATTER =
            new DecimalFormat("### " + (char) 0x00B0 + "C");

    private UsbManager mUsbManager;
    private PendingIntent mPermissionIntent;
    private boolean mPermissionRequestPending;
    private UsbAccessory mAccessory;
    private ParcelFileDescriptor mFileDescriptor;
    private FileInputStream mInputStream;
    private TextView temperatureValue;

    private Handler mHandler = new Handler()
    {
        @Override
```

continues

LISTING 10-5 *(continued)*

```java
        public void handleMessage(Message msg)
        {
            if (msg.what == MESSAGE_TEMPERATURE)
            {
                handleTemperatureMessage((Integer) msg.obj);
            }
        }
    };

    private final BroadcastReceiver mUsbReceiver = new BroadcastReceiver()
    {
        @Override
        public void onReceive(Context context, Intent intent)
        {
            String action = intent.getAction();
            if (ACTION_USB_PERMISSION.equals(action))
            {
                synchronized (this)
                {
                    // 2.3.4+ devices:
                    //UsbAccessory accessory = UsbManager.getAccessory(intent);

                    // 3.1+ devies:
                    UsbAccessory accessory = (UsbAccessory)
                    intent.getParcelableExtra(UsbManager.EXTRA_ACCESSORY);

                    boolean hasPermission =
                            intent.getBooleanExtra(UsbManager.EXTRA_PERMISSION_GRANTED,
                                    false);
                    if (hasPermission)
                    {
                        openAccessory(accessory);
                    }
                    else
                    {
                        Log.d(TAG,
                                "permission denied for accessory " + accessory);
                    }
                    mPermissionRequestPending = false;
                }
            }
            else if (UsbManager.ACTION_USB_ACCESSORY_DETACHED.equals(action))
            {
                // 2.3.4+ devices:
                //UsbAccessory accessory = UsbManager.getAccessory(intent);

                // 3.1+ devices
                UsbAccessory accessory = (UsbAccessory)
                intent.getParcelableExtra(UsbManager.EXTRA_ACCESSORY);

                if (accessory != null && accessory.equals(mAccessory))
                {
```

```java
                        closeAccessory();
                }
            }
        }
    }
};

@Override
public void onCreate(Bundle savedInstanceState)
{
    super.onCreate(savedInstanceState);
    setContentView(R.layout.aoa);

    temperatureValue = (TextView) findViewById(R.id.temperatureValue);

    // 2.3.4+ devices:
    //mUsbManager = UsbManager.getInstance(this);

    // 3.1+ devices:
    mUsbManager = (UsbManager) getSystemService(Context.USB_SERVICE);

    mPermissionIntent =
            PendingIntent.getBroadcast(this,
                    0,
                    new Intent(ACTION_USB_PERMISSION),
                    0);

    IntentFilter filter = new IntentFilter(ACTION_USB_PERMISSION);
    filter.addAction(UsbManager.ACTION_USB_ACCESSORY_DETACHED);
    registerReceiver(mUsbReceiver, filter);

    if (getLastNonConfigurationInstance() != null)
    {
        mAccessory = (UsbAccessory) getLastNonConfigurationInstance();
        openAccessory(mAccessory);
    }

    if (mAccessory != null)
    {
        showTemp();
    }
    else
    {
        hideTemp();
    }
}

@Override
public void onResume()
{
    super.onResume();

    UsbAccessory[] accessories = mUsbManager.getAccessoryList();
    UsbAccessory accessory = (accessories == null ? null : accessories[0]);
    if (accessory != null)
    {
```

continues

LISTING 10-5 *(continued)*

```java
            if (mUsbManager.hasPermission(accessory))
            {
                openAccessory(accessory);
            }
            else
            {
                synchronized (mUsbReceiver)
                {
                    if (!mPermissionRequestPending)
                    {
                        mUsbManager.requestPermission(accessory,
                                mPermissionIntent);

                        mPermissionRequestPending = true;
                    }
                }
            }
        }
        else
        {
            Log.d(TAG, "mAccessory is null");
        }
    }

    @Override
    public void onPause()
    {
        super.onPause();
        closeAccessory();
    }

    @Override
    public void onDestroy()
    {
        unregisterReceiver(mUsbReceiver);
        super.onDestroy();
    }

    @Override
    public Object onRetainNonConfigurationInstance()
    {
        if (mAccessory != null)
        {
            return mAccessory;
        }
        else
        {
            return super.onRetainNonConfigurationInstance();
        }
    }

    private void handleTemperatureMessage(Integer temperature)
```

```
{
    if (temperature != null)
    {
        // The calibration factors below (4.9, 400, 19.5) come from the
            temperature sensor's datasheet
        double voltagemv = temperature * 4.9;
        double kVoltageAtZeroCmv = 400;
        double kTemperatureCoefficientmvperC = 19.5;
        double temperatureC = ((double) voltagemv - kVoltageAtZeroCmv)
                / kTemperatureCoefficientmvperC;

        temperatureValue.setText(TEMP_FORMATTER.format(temperatureC));
    }
}

private Integer composeInt(byte hi, byte lo)
{
    int val = (int) hi & 0xff;
    val *= 256;
    val += (int) lo & 0xff;
    return val;
}

public void run()
{
    int ret = 0;
    // As explained on http://developer.android.com/guide/topics/usb/accessory.html,
    // "The Android accessory protocol supports packet buffers up to 16384 bytes,
    // so you can choose to always declare your buffer to be of this size for
    // simplicity."
    byte[] buffer = new byte[16384];
    int i;

    while (ret >= 0)
    {
        try
        {
            ret = mInputStream.read(buffer);
        }
        catch (IOException e)
        {
            break;
        }

        i = 0;
        while (i < ret)
        {
            int len = ret - i;

            switch (buffer[i])
            {
                case 0x0:
                    if (len >= 3)
                    {
                        Message m = Message.obtain(mHandler,
```

continues

LISTING 10-5 *(continued)*

```
                                    MESSAGE_TEMPERATURE);
                    m.obj = composeInt(buffer[i + 1], buffer[i + 2]);
                    mHandler.sendMessage(m);
                }
                i += 3;
                break;

            default:
                Log.d(TAG, "unknown msg: " + buffer[i]);
                i = len;
                break;
            }
        }
    }
}

private void openAccessory(UsbAccessory accessory)
{
    mFileDescriptor = mUsbManager.openAccessory(accessory);
    if (mFileDescriptor != null)
    {
        mAccessory = accessory;
        FileDescriptor fd = mFileDescriptor.getFileDescriptor();
        mInputStream = new FileInputStream(fd);
        new Thread(null, this, "AOATempSensor").start();
        Log.d(TAG, "accessory opened");
        showTemp();
    }
    else
    {
        Log.d(TAG, "accessory open fail");
    }
}

private void closeAccessory()
{
    hideTemp();

    try
    {
        if (mFileDescriptor != null)
        {
            mFileDescriptor.close();
        }
    }
    catch (IOException e)
    {
        Log.e(TAG, "Error closing file", e);
    }
    finally
    {
        mFileDescriptor = null;
```

```
            mAccessory = null;
        }
    }

    private void showTemp()
    {
        temperatureValue.setText("");
    }

    private void hideTemp()
    {
        temperatureValue.setText("Please connect the accessory.");
    }
}
```

code snippet <BaseActivity.java>

TAKING AN ANDROID ACCESSORY TO THE CONSUMER MARKET

So while the average price tag of an ADK is $80 USD, it may be easy to justify purchasing one to build that Android-powered cat litter box you've always dreamed about building, but it doesn't make sense to include a full ADK in a commercial project like a medical device or home automation system. An important point to keep in mind as you consider developing commercial, external hardware products for Android devices is that the ADK should be considered for prototyping only. If you have expectations to manufacture a run of more than a hundred items, shipping an ADK with each product is not cost effective.

The topic of taking a physical object to market is beyond the scope of this chapter but here are some tips to get you further along after you've prototyped on an ADK:

➤ First, make sure that your product has a viable business model and intended audience. To offset the steep start up costs of getting a production run ready for your cat litter box idea, make sure that more people than just your mom and dad are going to buy it.

➤ Figure out how to much the average person is willing to pay for your product at retail pricing. For example, a frequent jogger who wants to log their runs might be willing to pay $100 for an exercise accessory. However, together, a Nike+ sensor and adapter for an iPod is only $50 so make sure your product is competitive enough by either adjusting price or features.

➤ Related to the previous point, strip down your product into the essential components so you can produce it and still make a profit. And if you plan on selling your product via a retail outlet, subtract at least 50% from the expected retail price tag to get this breaking point number because a lot goes into markup.

➤ In terms of electronics, if you consider the Arduino Mega ADK, it has almost 60 pins on it and your product is unlikely to need all of them. The printed curcuit board should be a lot smaller; you also don't need the extra USB outlet that is used for programming the ADK. The brains of the Mega ADK is a chip called the ATmega2560 by Atmel and they can be bought individually for $20; however, buy 100 ATmega2560 chips in bulk and you only pay $10 each. If you instead go with the PICs from Microchip, you can get the price down to $4 each and also have integrated USB host controllers in the same chip. The idea is that you must be aggressive with cutting manufacturing costs. On the flip side, if you have a very unique product that would merit a high markup (e.g. a limited production run featuring artwork from a famous artist), then you can be more liberal with the cost cutting, but that is why the first two points are important — know your audience!

➤   This particular tip will be harder to accomplish without some previous experience first but you will need to find a manufacturer. Depending on your product, you may be able to get by with local creators or artisans, or send away designs to be 3D printed or laser cut. For some products, you may want to brush up on your Cantonese or Mandarin as Phillip Torrone, hardware developer and writer at *Make Magazine*, describes in his blog article entitled "Why Every Maker Should Learn Chinese": http://blog.makezine.com/2011/07/07/ why-every-maker-should-learn-chinese/.

➤   As an alternative to traditional manufacturing routes and production cycles, Kickstarter (www.kickstarter.com) type of sites are cropping up all the time and companies such as Quirky (www.quirky.com) are taking the crowd sourcing idea and actually putting their industrial design and manufacturing knowledge into popularly voted projects pitched by anyone.

So while these tips are not a comprehensive plan for monetizing your AOA app, they should get you started in thinking about taking AOA beyond a hobby activity.

SUMMARY

This chapter introduced the Android AOA. It discussed the how AOA works, what it can accomplish, and why it is relevant to Android sensor development. The goal of this chapter was to introduce you to the various parts required to create an Android Accessory. On the hardware end: you learned of several ADKs, including the Arduino Mega ADK, and how they differ from each other, alongside additional external hardware components such as a temperature sensor. On the software end: you learned about ADK firmware, namely Arduino sketches, and what APIs are required in the Android app.

Although this chapter did go into enough detail to provide an example of how to use AOA, it is far from a complete overview of all the things you can create using the AOA. Hopefully you have been enticed to increase your knowledge of basic electronics components including other actuators like motors and other sensors like the temperature sensor, and then combining it with the Android programming knowledge you have gained throughout this book.

This chapter completes the discussion of inferring information from physical sensors. It showed that there are various kinds of sensors available on Android devices that give it an awareness of its own state and its immediate environment. You can extend these capabilities using the AOA mechanism.

The next part of this book describes using some of Android's other sensing capabilities to increase its awareness further. By using the NFC scanner, camera, and microphone an Android app can find things in the world that emit or display identifying information and detect patterns that the device can see and hear.

PART III
Sensing the Augmented, Pattern-Rich External World

11

Near Field Communication (NFC)

WHAT'S IN THIS CHAPTER?

- ➤ Describing NFC and relationship to RFID
- ➤ Describing how NFCs work
- ➤ Explaining sample code

If you've ever waved your credit card in front of a grocery checkout terminal, entered into your apartment or office building with a tap of a key fob, or installed an electronic toll collector under your car to zoom past the lines at the toll booth, then you are familiar with this seemingly invisible technology called *radio frequency identification* (RFID) and its subset technology, *near field communication* (NFC).

With the NFC hardware on the Samsung Nexus S and Samsung Galaxy Nexus, you can sense electronically enabled objects that come within close range of your device and read data from these objects. In addition, when two NFC-enabled Android devices meet, they can use NFC to submit data peer-to-peer. The inclusion of NFC on Android devices enables developers to create *low friction* interactions, such as those that are described throughout this chapter.

This chapter also gives you an overview of what these two *contactless* technologies are, outlines the advantages and disadvantages of NFC with Android, walks you through the tools and code needed to build a small NFC-enabled inventory system with the Android SDK, and wraps up by discussing the future of NFC on Android. As a bonus, some suggested use case scenarios are listed at the end of the chapter to jump start your own NFC development.

WHAT IS RFID?

A discussion of NFC would not be possible without first exploring radio frequency identification, because NFC is a subset of RFID. Radio frequency identification tags come in many form factors, such as cards and key fobs, but you've probably encountered the very common *RFID sticker* while shopping at major drugstores such as Walgreens (U.S.) or Shoppers Drug Mart (Canada). They are usually 2.5 cm square white stickers attached to almost all the products on the shelves. Major retail stores use RFID for inventory tracking and theft prevention.

If you look closely enough by holding the sticker up to the light or peeling away the white plastic, you will see a flat, rectangular coil of metal strips much like that shown in Figure 11-1; these coils are the *antennas* that "listen" for radio frequency. Within the coils are other larger metal blocks; the circuit layouts vary, but these metal blocks are very small integrated circuits (IC) made of silicon. These ICs can store small amounts of manufacturer defined identification data and the logic to allow the tag to transmit data back to the RFID reader via the antenna.

FIGURE 11-1: The internal components of an RFID sticker

Many types of RFID tags exist, with the major categories being *active* or *passive*, or a combination of the two. Active RFID tags have built-in batteries and have the advantage of being able to receive and transmit from a much longer distance (up to 10 meters or more) than passive tags. Passive tags, as you might have already guessed, do not have an on-board power supply and are limited to only a few feet at most.

The benefits of passive tags mean that they can be cheaper, smaller, and can remain readable as long as the circuit remains in good condition (that is, not cut or severely bent).

Without on-board power, passive RFID tags get activated when they are "interrogated" by an RFID reader or scanner. The scanner (which must always have an electrical supply) emits short-range radio frequency signals that the antenna in the tags can detect and convert into power.

How does a seemingly innocuous object such as a sticker create power out of thin air? If that seems unbelievable, imagine back to your days in high school science class. An experiment your teacher may have had you try was to create a DIY power generator by wrapping magnetic wire around a magnet and connecting it to a light bulb. When you spin the wires around the magnet at high speed, it causes electrons to become excited and activate the light bulb. This electricity is created through a process called *electromagnetic* induction.

If you've never done this experiment before or just want a refresher, visit www.amasci.com/amateur/coilgen.html to watch a video of a DIY generator in action and read the instructions on how to make your own. Then have a look at the antenna coils in the RFID tag in Figure 11-2. Not that far off, right?

Invisible to the naked eye, the radio waves generated by the RFID scanner are enough to cause the coils of the RFID tag to oscillate, which can be converted to energy.

FIGURE 11-2: An RFID with clear plastic casing lets you see the wire coils easily.

If you own a Samsung Nexus S, take off the back battery cover. Glued onto the plastic is a gray rectangle; that is the hardware antenna of your phone's NFC reader, as shown in Figure 11-3. The back cover alone won't be able to scan anything, but when it's receiving power from the phone via the two metal contacts it has the energy to start scanning.

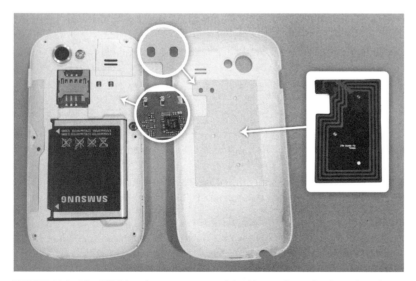

FIGURE 11-3: The NFC hardware antenna of the Nexus S can be found on the inside of the back cover.

In contrast, the Samsung Galaxy Nexus has the antenna built into the battery; peeling off the cover of the battery will reveal the NFC antenna. So if you ever replace your Galaxy Nexus's battery, ensure that the replacement has NFC capabilities!

FIGURE 11-4: The NFC antenna on the Galaxy Nexus comes as part of the battery (right).

The NFC controller (part number PN65N), developed by electronics component manufacturing company NXP Semiconductors, is soldered onto a printed circuit board with the rest of the internal phone components.

Most RFID tags only store a 40-bit unique identifier such as 0x12345678AB. When a scanner activates an RFID tag, the tag transmits this unique ID and the middleware of the scanner interprets it. The middleware may use this information to then pass it on to software that looks it up in an inventory system or, in the case of mall security systems, to trigger an alarm to indicate that you're carrying around a product whose tag was not deactivated. The read time of an RFID scanner to its tag can happen in less than 100 milliseconds!

WHAT IS NFC?

NFC tags share the same basic technology of those previously mentioned retail RFID stickers in that they are passive and are meant for short-range scanning, specifically at a frequency of 13.56MHz. The biggest comparisons to make between NFC and the wider spectrum of RFID tags is that near field communications, as its name would imply, is meant for very short range scanning of 1–4 cm. NFC tags are advertised to be scannable at up to a distance of 10 cm, but that would only occur under perfect conditions.

Another large difference between RFID and NFC is the size of the data transaction. As mentioned, most RFID tags contain a 40-bit unique identifier and are read-only. In comparison, a small NFC tag can store 48 bytes of data, average around 144 bytes, and go up to 8 kilobytes (8,152 bytes) for larger tags. Its data can also be rewritten by any reader if the tag is not write-protected.

The NDEF Data Format

Unlike RFID technology, which has many proprietary implementations for data exchange, the NFC standards are regulated by various bodies including the International Organization for Standardization (ISO), International Electrotechnical Commission (IEC), European Telecommunications Standards Institute (ETSI), and ECMA (the European association for standardizing information and communication systems). In addition, the NFC Forum (www.nfc-forum.org) is a consortium of manufacturers, applications developers, financial services institutions, and other stakeholders created to promote NFC technologies and develop NFC standards.

As defined by the NFC Forum, the standard data format for NFC-compliant devices and tags is a lightweight binary message format named *NFC Data Exchange Format*, or *NDEF* for short. This data format is comprised of an encompassing *NDEF message* container that can contain one or more NDEF records.

An *NDEF record* carries application data (commonly referred to as the *payload*) and additional meta data to help NFC applications quickly parse the payload during a data transaction. Alongside the payload, each NDEF record must define meta data values for the payload, such as type and length. An additional identifier URI is optional.

The following list summarizes these meta data fields with a brief explanation of how each relates to the Android NFC APIs. These parameters are discussed in the "NdefMessage and NdefRecord" section of the Building an Inventory Tracking System code example.

➤ **Payload length:** An unsigned integer indicating the size of the payload measured in octets. (An octet is 8 bits of computer storage.)

   The Android operating system takes care of generating the length value so you don't need to worry about defining it yourself.

➤ **Payload type:** An arbitrary type as declared by the developer for its specific application.

   Example types include: URIs such as web addresses; MIME media formats such as *text/plain-text* for plaintext or *text/x-vCard* for electronic business cards; or NFC-specific record types such as the NFC *Smart Poster* record type definition (the ability to encode URLs, SMSs, and phone numbers on an NFC tag) or the NFC *Signature* record type definition (for digitally signing NFC tags).

   The Android APIs expect payload type to be converted to a byte array. In addition, the Android APIs also request higher-level categorization of the payload type through the use of Type Name Format (TNF) values defined by the Android SDK. These TNF constants indicate to the interpreter what structure to expect from the payload type so it knows how to handle it. An example TNF might be NdefRecord.TNF_ABSOLUTE_URI for a URI or NdefRecord.TNF_WELL_KNOWN for plaintext.

➤ **Payload identifier:** An optional and arbitrary URI-based value set by the developer.

   Payload identifiers are rarely used in practice, however the ability for NDEF messages to contain multiple NDEF records means that you can cross-reference records should such a scenario arise.

   The Android API will accept anything encoded into a byte array for the identifier.

It should be noted that the NDEF specifications do not provide support for error handling, so it is up to the receiving application parser to determine the validity of the payload. For further information about the NDEF format, a 25-page PDF document entitled *NFC Data Exchange Format (NDEF) Technical Specification* is available on the NFC Forum website by filling out the form at www.nfc-forum.org/specs/spec_license.

Keep in mind that NFC is a 15-year-old evolving technology and the NDEF data specifications were defined after the creation of the NFC hardware; there exist NFC tags, especially legacy tags, which do not support NDEF and implement their own proprietary formats. You can write to a tag using a format other than NDEF, but that requires you to write your own custom protocol stack to handle reading and writing the raw data on tags. Therefore, NDEF and NDEF-compatible tags are recommended for quicker development and the widest Android support — especially when you want to take advantage of Android's powerful intent filter feature to launch the most appropriate app for the content stored on the tag.

How and Where to Buy NFC Tags

The type of NFC tag you should acquire depends on its intended usage. Three important questions are: How much data do you want to store on it? Do you want to be able to write-protect it? And what environment will the NFC tag be deployed to?

NDEF-compatible NFC Tags

See Table 11-1 for a chart of compatible, commercially available NFC tags. Each type's rewrite capability, available memory, communication speed, and price range are also indicated in the chart.

To be the most compatible with Android devices and the Android SDK, buy tags marked as NFC Forum Type 1, 2, 3, or 4 because they are the most compatible with the NDEF spec discussed in the previous section.

Storage Size versus Price versus Security Trade-off

Design your application with the lowest NFC tag storage footprint as possible considering the cost of the tags and their security features.

Consider a scenario in which you want to share a picture. Attempting to encode even a very small JPEG thumbnail photo would cause your storage requirements to skyrocket to 3000 bytes, which would increase the costs of the NFC sticker. Instead, it would be better to embed a link to an online resource that the Android application would then download after scanning the NFC tag.

Type 1 and Type 2 tags are very similar, however the least expensive and most widely available NFC chips are the NFC Forum Type 2 tags sold under the MIFARE UltraLights brand owned by NXP Semiconductors. Many online retailers will carry only the 48- and 144-byte variants, though. The smaller storage size makes the MIFARE UltraLights appropriate for links or plaintext. A shortened URL might consume 23 bytes, a plaintext sentence containing "The quick brown fox jumps over the lazy dog" uses 51 bytes, and a custom MIME type to deep-link to content within an app might use around 100 bytes.

TABLE 11-1: Compatible, Commercially Available NFC Tags

NFC FORUM TYPE	POPULAR PRODUCTS OF THIS TYPE	OPERATIONS SPECIFICATIONS	REWRITE CAPABILITIES	AVAILABLE MEMORY	COMMUNICATION SPEED	PRICE RANGE (PRICE PER UNIT)
1	Broadcom Topaz	ISO 14443A	User rewritable; can be marked as read-only by user	96 bytes, expandable to 2KB	106kbit/s	Low (~$1-2 USD)
2	MIFARE UltraLight	ISO 14443A	User rewritable; can be marked as read-only by user	48 bytes, 144 bytes is common, expandable to 2KB	106kbit/s	Low (~$1-2 USD)
3	Sony FeliCa	JIS X 6319-4	Manufacture pre-configured to be read-only or re-writable.	variable, theoretical 1MB	212kbit/s or 424kbit/s	High (~$8-10 USD or higher)
4	NXP DESFire, NXP SmartFX	ISO 14443A, ISO 14443B	Manufacture pre-configured to be read-only or rewritable.	4KB for DESFire, up to 32KB for SmartFX	Up to 424kbit/s	Medium-High (~$3-4 USD)

An electronic business card in vCard format with your contact information might use up to 300 bytes, so a typical Type 2 tag would not be sufficient. Two options to explore when you want more storage are to purchase Type 3 or 4 NFC cards or MIFARE Classic tags.

Type 3 Sony FeliCa (which is short for *Felicity Card*) tags have higher amounts of storage but they are harder to order off the shelf. FeliCa technology has been widely accepted as a secure form of NFC and is used in high-profile electronic payment systems such as the *Octopus* transit card system in Hong Kong. Extra security comes at a higher per-unit price tag, however.

Conversely, the Type 4 NXP DESFire can be purchased in 4k and 8k variants, but their encryption scheme was recently proven to be insecure so the additional costs are not worthwhile.

When you need more space but don't want to pay more, you can find some MIFARE tags sold under the "Classic" label (sometimes called MIFARE Standard) that are currently supported by the Nexus line of phones. They can hold up to 4KB but they may not be supported in the future by other Android devices or the SDK, because the MIFARE Classic tags use a proprietary protocol to format NDEF messages and this requires device manufacturers to pay licensing fees.

If you are controlling the environment and devices that your NFC application is deployed in, there shouldn't be any foreseeable issue with using MIFARE Classic tags for the time being. Table 11-2 contains a chart on the MIFARE Classic chips.

Write Protection

As indicated in the rewrite capabilities columns of Tables 11-1 and 11-2, some tags are more appropriate for prototyping or controlled environments because their data can be rewritten using any NFC reader/writer, including those found on mobile phones. If you are planning to release these tags into the wild, purchase Type 1 or Type 2 tags so you can set read-only privileges yourself. (Keep in mind the size limitations of these tags, though.)

MIFARE Classics can be write-protected only by the manufacturer. If you are past the prototyping phase, you could work directly with a manufacturer such as NXP or Sony to create tags that are shipped with read-only capabilities.

Form Factor

Another consideration to keep in mind when purchasing NFC stickers is the surface that you will be sticking them onto. Paper, fabric, wood, plastic, and other non-conductive materials shouldn't cause any problems, but take care if you are applying to metal surfaces. Because metal is conductive, you should look for "metal isolated" tags that are thicker than regular stickers.

For extra environmental protection of your NFC stickers, buy "outdoor" or "laundry" type tags that are water-resistant or waterproof. If you don't want to use stickers, plastic-encased NFC tags in the form factor of contactless credit cards and key fobs are also an alternative.

In very rare deployment scenarios, note that there exist fabrics and materials that can be coated with specific metals to shield out radio waves, including those from NFC tags and readers; this may act in your favor or against it. An example of this fabric in use is in special RFID-shielding passport wallets. Lastly, be conscious of deploying NFC in scientific or medical labs that may actively be trying to block out radio waves.

TABLE 11-2: Information about Classic MIFARE Chips

MIFARE TYPE	OPERATIONS SPECIFICATIONS	REWRITE CAPABILITIES	AVAILABLE MEMORY	COMMUNICATION SPEED	PRICE RANGE (PRICE PER UNIT)
Classic 1K	ISO 14443A compatible, but NDEF is formatted using a proprietary protocol	User rewritable; only manufacturer can mark as read-only	752 bytes	106kbit/s	Low (~$1 USD)
Classic 4K	ISO 14443A compatible, but NDEF is formatted using a proprietary protocol	User rewritable; only manufacturer can mark as read-only	3440 bytes	106kbit/s	Low-Medium (~$2 USD)

Retailers

For the hobbyist or newcomer, shopping for NFC tags might be a bit overwhelming, so here are some suggested online retailers:

➤ For U.S.-based developers, Tagstand (www.tagstand.com) offers NFC starter kits with 15 NFC stickers of four varying sizes. You can order custom logo NFC stickers with a minimum batch size of 50 stickers.

➤ For Europeans, Finnish company UPM also offers plain and custom-printed NFC stickers directly or through its TagAge website (www.tagage.net).

➤ You can order high-volume batches of NFC stickers or cards directly from NXP Semiconductors; especially worth exploring when you want to get MIFARE Classic tags write-protected.

➤ If you are an open source hardware tinkerer, Adafruit Industries sells NFC tags in card and key fob format. It also sells the *PN532 NFC/RFID controller breakout board*, which can be used for experimenting with NFC outside of your Android device, for example, with an Arduino microcontroller. You can find Adafruit's NFC inventory here: www.adafruit.com/category/55.

Many other online retailers sell NFC tags and you can find them by doing a web search. An important point to remember when buying NFC tags is that some retailers will simply list them as RFID tags, so keep an eye out for the specific NFC frequency of 13.56 MHz.

General Advantages and Disadvantages of NFC

Why choose NFC technology for your application? And when should you choose an alternative such as QR barcodes or Bluetooth? This section goes into the pros and cons of

NFC. References to any Android applications can be found and downloaded by searching in Google Play.

Low Power and Proximity Based

The biggest selling feature of NFC interactions is something Google likes to call "low friction" because the experience of using NFC should be one of instant gratification — just tap and go.

Turning on NFC scanning for your device is described in the "Enabling NFC in the Settings" section later and, once enabled, your device can be left to scan for tags whenever the screen is on with very little power draw on the battery.

The advantage of NFC tags over barcodes or QR codes (aka 3-D barcodes) is that you don't need line of sight. A 2-D barcode needs to be lined up with the laser or camera that's reading it and a QR code needs to be decently lit for a camera application to read it. As long as the Android device's screen is turned on and has been set to detect NFC tags in the Android settings, an NFC tag just needs to be held close to the reader (regardless of orientation) and can be detected through thin amounts of material such as the fabric of your wallet or the plastic on the back of a Samsung Nexus S.

Small, Short Data Bursts

Although NFC-enabled devices such as the Nexus S do enable peer-to-peer transactions, NFC is not to be used for verbose communications between two devices. For scenarios in which you want to transfer more than a kilobyte of data, consider using Bluetooth or Wi-Fi to do the heavy lifting and leave NFC to just get the interaction started.

The NFC standard currently supports data rates of 106kbit/s, 212kbit/s , and 424kbit/s, which is fine for data transactions below 4KB. Bluetooth is a mid-range wireless technology that works within a 10-meter range and transfers data at a rate of 2.1Mbps. This higher data transfer rate makes it ideal for ongoing, peer-to-peer communications such as syncing screens of the same app on two different Android phones in scenarios where there is no reliable Wi-Fi.

However, Bluetooth requires a pairing process that can be quite cumbersome, so it makes sense to use NFC to help quickly authenticate the pairing process and then hand it off to Bluetooth to continue the communications. One such example of this is the proposed two-player game mode of Fruit Ninja in which two NFC-enabled Android devices can tap and quickly launch into a head-to-head battle mode. (Sadly, this battle mode was only a demo proof of concept at the Google I/O 2011 developer conference; the Fruit Ninja found in Google Play does not use NFC.)

When Internet or 3G networks are available, NFC can do the device handshaking and the app can then continue on with the transaction in the cloud. For example, the Hashable mobile app lets you tap phones so you can immediately check in with others on `http://hashable.com`.

Singular Scanning

If you're considering using NFC for simultaneous inventory tracking of multiple items, or "push cart checkout" in which you are attempting to scan multiple items at once, you should be aware that only one NFC tag can be reliably scanned at a time; and considering the distance limitations of fewer than 10 cm or less, it's unlikely the scannable space would allow for more than one item to be within range unless it was stacked like a deck of cards.

Security

The short range of the NFC chip is its biggest security feature. Consider that some RFID tags are used for animal tracking over several miles, and therefore the tags can be read from far distances. In contrast, NFC chips must be held within centimeters of the reader, making it harder for "sniffers" to find out if you are carrying an NFC-enabled device. Manufacturers of NFC chips have also gone the extra step of shielding the tag to further reduce their ability to be read from specialized, long-distance RFID readers.

The NFC on your phone is also turned off when the screen is off so "sniffers" cannot just read the data on your phone.

The data on an NFC tag can also be encrypted before writing to it using your own encryption schema, such as using MD5 or AES, and certain tags can be made read-only by the user or the manufacturer.

Card Emulation

Card emulation is the capability of an NFC chip on a mobile device to act like a contactless smart-card, such as a PayPass™ or payWave™ credit card, when presented at retail store terminals. The PN65N NFC controller chip installed on the Nexus line of phones has a component called the *Secure Element* (or SmartMX), which is an embedded version of a smartcard.

Google Wallet uses the Secure Element, however, it is important to note that Google has reserved not to open up any public APIs to emulate cards on Android phones. Google advocates developers to design their application with peer-to-peer abilities instead of attempting to emulate cards using the device's Secure Element hardware.

Android-specific Advantage: Intents

The Android intent filter system is a huge advantage to building low-friction interactions with NFC. You don't need to be redirected to a URL like a QR code might. The detection of an NFC tag can deep-link into an app already installed on your phone or redirect you to Google Play to download the app.

A good example of this is an add-on app to Evernote called Touchanote that launches into specific Evernote entries. For example, you could stick an NFC sticker onto a textbook and use Evernote to type and record your notes. Now, every time you pull that book off the shelf, give it a scan to pick up where you left.

Required Hardware

The biggest disadvantage that NFC has in the Android ecosystem is the availability of phones and tablets that have built-in NFC readers at the moment. Android devices that can currently read and write NFC tags include: the Google Nexus line of phones (Samsung Nexus S and Samsung Galaxy Nexus), the Samsung Galaxy SII, and the HTC Amaze 4G, among others.

There currently exists no off-the-shelf ability to add NFC support to phones that were not shipped with NFC. As a developer, it is recommended to obtain either the Nexus S or Galaxy Nexus to fully test NFC interactions because there is no desktop emulation.

You may have heard of the ability to buy passive NFC stickers or NFC-enabled SIM cards for your phone but these add-ons only enable compatibility with NFC payment systems like Google Wallet, and do not enable your phone to read other NFC tags.

For extreme hardware tinkerers, you may be able to take advantage of the new Android Open Accessory APIs and an Android ADK to connect an Android phone to a custom, external USB NFC tag reader (such as a PN532), but this option is not for the faint of heart. (See Chapter 10 for more information on Android Open Accessory.)

It's unlikely that you would be able to purchase an NFC-enabled device running a version of Android below Gingerbread, but it's worth noting that the NFC APIs are available only on devices running Android 2.3 (API level 9) and higher.

BUILDING AN INVENTORY TRACKING SYSTEM

In this section you apply what you've read about NFC theory and start working on the example Android project.

The Scenario

Consider this scenario: You are an IT support professional. You handle the inventory of various computer systems, but you often swap out the RAM and other internal components and want to keep track of them. You want a custom app that will let you tag the cases of desktop computers so when you scan them, you can quickly see what's inside without ever pulling out a screwdriver.

The NFC Inventory Demonstration App

Figure 11-5 shows the screens from the NFC Inventory demo app supplied with this book's example source code and app.

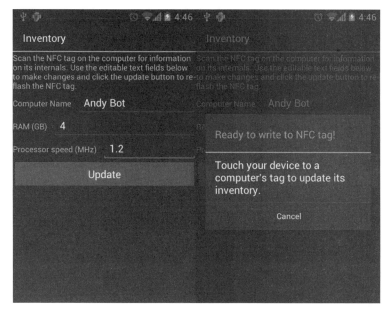

FIGURE 11-5: Main activity of the demo NFC app (left); updating an NFC tag with newer specs (right)

On the main `activity` screen, type in a computer name, the amount of RAM, and the processor speed of the computer you want to track. Clicking the Update button sets the phone into a mode that allows you to write NDEF data to a compatible NFC tag.

Scanning a tag with inventory NDEF data updates the three text fields with the currently recorded specs. If you ever upgrade the computer or swap out parts, scan the tag attached to the computer, edit the text fields, and click Update to overwrite the tag with the newest specs.

Enabling NFC in the Settings

In addition to enabling the usual Development Mode settings, you must turn on NFC. On a device running Gingerbread: go to Settings ⇨ Wireless & Network settings. Scroll down and look for the NFC list item toward the bottom. As Figure 11-6 shows, make sure the NFC checkbox is checked in order to read and exchange tags.

On a device running Ice Cream Sandwich: swipe down from the top of any screen to pull down the notification shade. Next to the date, click on the settings icon (the three sliders). Under the Wireless & Networks heading, click on More. As Figure 11-6 shows, make sure the NFC checkbox is checked off.

FIGURE 11-6: Turn on NFC in your settings. For both Gingerbread (left) and Ice Cream Sandwich (right), ensure that the NFC option is checked off

Once NFC has been enabled in the settings, and as long as the device's screen is on, NFC tags that come into range will be detected. For security reasons, the Android OS does not respond to NFC tags when the screen is turned off. Oddly, the Android OS will still scan tags even when the screen is on but locked.

The power draw of turning on the NFC option is negligible, so there's no need to turn off NFC when you're done developing.

Debugging Your Tags with Apps

As a test, you may want to download and try these two apps created by NXP Semiconductor to practice reading and writing to your tags:

➤ **NFC TagWriter by NXP** (`https://play.google.com/store/apps/details?id=com.nxp.nfc.tagwriter`) gives you an all-in-one interface to play around with reading NFC stickers and writing to tags that are not locked. TagWriter gives you four built-in NDEP record data types to write such as vCard, URL, plaintext, and SMS.

➤ **NFC TagInfo by NXP** (`https://play.google.com/store/apps/details?id=com.nxp.taginfolite`) gives you more information about the tag than the TagWriter app. In addition to showing you any available raw data saved to the sticker, TagInfo also summarizes the type of NFC tag (for example, MIFARE Classic), who the manufacturer is (for example, NXP), how much data is used/available, and other interesting tidbits like ISO/IEC compatibility and protocol information. You can also use this app to analyze your credit cards and other contactless smart tags you already own for NFC compatibility, although the data on them will likely be encrypted.

ANDROID APIS

Now that you're set up, this section dives into some code! The code in this section is based on `http://nfc.android.com/StickyNotes.zip`, which is under the Apache 2.0 license.

In Your AndroidManifest.xml File

Every Android project has a Manifest file and this one is no different. Here are some basic additions you will need to make to your project's `AndroidManifest.xml` to make your app NFC compatible.

Permissions and Minimum API Level

To target devices that support the NFC APIs, you must declare `android.hardware.NFC` as a feature. Depending on your application, you may want to also declare it as a required feature. You also need to indicate that your application requires permission to use the NFC reader hardware by adding code like this:

```
<uses-feature
    android:name="android.hardware.nfc"
    android:required="true" />

<uses-permission android:name="android.permission.NFC" />
```

If NFC is a required feature of your application, be sure to also declare a minimum SDK version of 2.3.3 (level 10) or 4.0 (level 14). Although API level 9 supports NFC, the tag dispatch options are limited and there is no tag writing support, so targeting level 9 is not recommended. API level 10 includes reader/writer support and foreground NDEF pushing.

The latest Ice Cream Sandwich Android SDK provides improved NDEF pushing to other Android devices via Android Beam and improved NDEF creation. You can find APIs specific to Android 4.0's Beam feature in the "Peer-to-Peer NFC Sharing" section later in this chapter.

This inventory example targets SDK version 2.3.3, so you will need the following code:

```
<uses-sdk android:minSdkVersion="10" />
```

Intent Filters

For your `Activity`, add an `IntentFilter` to handle the NFC tag scanning event. Three `Intents` are available and the Android tag dispatching system prioritizes them. From highest to lowest priority, they are:

➤ `android.nfc.action.NDEF_DISCOVERED`

➤ `android.nfc.action.ACTION_TECH_DISCOVERED`.

➤ `android.nfc.action.ACTION_TAG_DISCOVERED`

The highest-priority `IntentFilter`, `NDEF_DISCOVERED`, should be used for the majority of scenarios because it offers the most precise filter for matching the content of a tag to the application that should handle it.

The lowest-priority `IntentFilter`, `ACTION_TAG_DISCOVERED`, was introduced with NFC support in API level 9 and is more of a legacy `Intent`. If either `NDEF_DISCOVERED` or `ACTION_TECH_DISCOVERED` is set, the probability of an `ACTION_TAG_DISCOVERED` `IntentFilter` triggering your application when it is not in the foreground is unlikely, so its use in the manifest file is not recommended by the Google Android documentation.

The remaining `IntentFilter`, `ACTION_TECH_DISCOVERED`, is generally to be used as a fallback when the NFC tag is not formatted using NDEF. If you are controlling the content written to the tags and have chosen NDEF, you may never need to use `ACTION_TECH_DISCOVERED` in your manifest for your application. If you are working with legacy tags and/or non-NDEF data, please refer to the Advanced NFC documentation at `http://developer.android.com/guide/topics/nfc/advanced-nfc.html`.

Using the preferred `NDEF_DISCOVERED` `IntentFilter`, your declaration would look like this if your NFC tag contained plaintext:

```
<intent-filter>
    <action android:name="android.nfc.action.NDEF_DISCOVERED" />
    <category android:name="android.intent.category.DEFAULT" />
    <data android:mimeType="text/plain" />
</intent-filter>
```

However, listening for such a generic MIME type will not allow other NFC-enabled applications to be triggered by scanning this tag. Alternatively, if you leave out the `IntentFilter`, the scanning of the NFC tag will be handled by the preinstalled Tags application, which will attempt to read the content of your tag. And if multiple NFC-enabled applications are installed, there's a large possibility that the select-an-action Android OS Activity Chooser will pop up.

To create a friction-less scanning experience for the user, use the most precise `IntentFilter` as possible for your app. The best way to do that is to create your own custom MIME type for your `IntentFilter` instead of using something as generic as plaintext.

Custom MIME Type Intent Filters

For example, the following code is registering `IntentFilters` for the custom MIME type "`application/root.gast.playground.nfc`", which is specific to this chapter's demo application:

```
<intent-filter>
    <action android:name="android.nfc.action.NDEF_DISCOVERED" />
    <category android:name="android.intent.category.DEFAULT" />
    <data android:mimeType="application/root.gast.playground.nfc" />
</intent-filter>
```

Note that the MIME type `application/root.gast.playground.nfc` is arbitrarily defined by the developer. It can be anything, however you must be consistent between the `IntentFilters` defined in your Android Manifest and what you write to your tags.

The following is an example of creating an NDEF record with the custom `application/root.gast.playground.nfc` MIME type. This example was simplified for readability; the "NdefMessage and NdefRecord" section goes into this code in more detail.

```
String mimeType = "application/root.gast.playground.nfc";
byte[] mimeBytes = mimeType.getBytes(Charset.forName("UTF-8"));
//...
NdefRecord r = new NdefRecord(NdefRecord.TNF_MIME_MEDIA,
        mimeBytes, id, dataBytes);
```

URI-based Intent Filters

If you want to avoid locking NFC tag creation to your particular app, it's very useful to instead use the URI MIME type to register `IntentFilters`. The Foursquare app for Android uses this to its advantage by allowing individual venue owners to create their own NFC-enabled location check-in tags using any NFC writer (including the NFC TagWriter app mentioned previously in the "Debugging Your Tags with Apps" section).

As outlined in the Foursquare developer documentation (`https://developer.foursquare.com/client/`), a venue owner simply needs to make an NFC tag that links to its venue page, for example, `http://m.foursquare.com/venue/VENUE_ID` where `VENUE_ID` is an ID string such as 128530, which is the ID for the Foursquare head office in New York.

If you have the Foursquare app already installed and scan one of these tags, that specific venue page will automatically launch within the Foursquare app because of the power of `IntentFilters`. Using a URI MIME type also allows the interaction to gracefully fall back to using the preinstalled Tags app to read the URL and give the user an option to launch a web browser to view the mobile website.

When declaring a URI-based `IntentFilter` for everything within a domain name, set the scheme, host, and (when needed) port of your URI. For example:

```
<data
        android:scheme="http"
        android:host="localhost"
        android:port="8080" />
```

If there's even more specific content to filter by such as a web folder, you can add a `path`, `pathPattern`, or `pathPrefix` attribute to the data element. For more information about the data element, please visit the Android developer documentation: `http://developer.android.com/guide/topics/manifest/data-element.html`.

This is how the `IntentFilter` would appear in Foursquare's manifest file because the Foursquare app will want to react to all tags containing the URL `http://m.foursquare.com/venue/`:

```
<intent-filter>
    <action android:name="android.nfc.action.NDEF_DISCOVERED" />
    <category android:name="android.intent.category.DEFAULT" />
    <data
        android:host="m.foursquare.com"
        android:pathPrefix="/venue/"
        android:scheme="http" />
</intent-filter>
```

Because the NFC inventory demo app of this chapter is used mainly for reading and writing to NFC tags, a custom MIME type is used for this chapter's code examples. Listing 11-1 contains the full `AndroidManifest.xml` file for your reference.

Available for download on Wrox.com

LISTING 11-1: Manifest file needed to run NFC example

```xml
<?xml version="1.0" encoding="utf-8"?>
<manifest xmlns:android="http://schemas.android.com/apk/res/android"
    package="root.gast.playground.nfc"
    android:versionCode="1"
    android:versionName="1.0" >

    <uses-sdk android:minSdkVersion="10" />

    <uses-feature
        android:name="android.hardware.nfc"
        android:required="true" />

    <uses-permission android:name="android.permission.NFC" />

    <application
        android:icon="@drawable/icon"
        android:launchMode="singleTask"
        android:label="@string/app_name" >
        <activity
            android:label="@string/app_name"
            android:name=".NFCInventoryActivity" >
            <intent-filter>
                <action android:name="android.intent.action.MAIN" />
                <category android:name="android.intent.category.LAUNCHER" />
            </intent-filter>

            <!-- Handle NFC tags detected from outside our application -->
            <intent-filter>
                <action android:name="android.nfc.action.NDEF_DISCOVERED" />
                <category android:name="android.intent.category.DEFAULT" />
                <data android:mimeType="application/root.gast.playground.nfc" />
            </intent-filter>

        </activity>
    </application>
</manifest>
```

code snippet AndroidManifest.xml

Now that your Manifest file is set up, the next section examines the demo app's main `Activity` class.

In Your Main Activity Class

You can find the full main `Activity` code of this demonstration app in the `root.gast.playground` `.nfc.NFCInventoryActivity.java` file of this book's source code, but this section goes over some key NFC-related APIs.

NfcManager

NfcManager is a high-level manager used to obtain a reference to an instance of an NFC Adapter. This class is redundant, so continue to the next section for the real meat.

NfcAdapter

The NFC Adapter is your bridge to the NFC hardware. It lets you check if the NFC option is turned on and it controls the pushing of NDEF data to and from NFC tags.

You should not instantiate an NfcAdapter instance yourself; instead call the static helper method getDefaultAdapter(), which is a shortcut for getSystemService(), to leverage the context's cached NfcAdapter. See the following code for how it is used for the demo NFC Inventory app:

```
public class NFCInventoryActivity extends Activity
{
    //...

    NfcAdapter mNfcAdapter;

    //...

    /** Called when the activity is first created. */
    @Override
    public void onCreate(Bundle savedInstanceState)
    {
        //...

        // get an instance of the context's cached NfcAdapter
        mNfcAdapter = NfcAdapter.getDefaultAdapter(this);

        // check if NFC is enabled
        Boolean nfcEnabled = mNfcAdapter.isEnabled();
        if (nfcEnabled)
        {
            // show off your fancy NFC feature!
        } else
        {
            // let the user know how to turn NFC on in the Settings
        }

        //...
    }
    //...
}
```

In addition to isEnabled(), two main pairs of methods to be aware of in the NfcAdapter class are enableForegroundDispatch() and disableForegroundDispatch(), and enableForegroundNdefPush() and disableForegroundNdefPush(), which the next sections describe.

Foreground Dispatching

enableForegroundDispatch() and disableForegroundDispatch() turn on and off the foreground activity's priority to receive intent dispatches when NFC tags are scanned.

To illustrate this, say you have two NFC tags; one is encoded with a URI (`http://m.foursquare .com`) and the other is a custom MIME type (`application/root.gast.playground.nfc`). In addition, the main `Activity` class has created `IntentFilters` for the `root.gast.playground.nfc` custom MIME type only. When foreground dispatching is enabled, and the app is running and in focus, attempts to scan the tag with the URI will have no visible results — even the Activity Chooser will not be triggered.

Related, if an app such as TagInfo by NXP is listening for all types of tags to be scanned, when the TagInfo app is running and in focus on your device, it will redirect all NFC scanned tag events to itself because it has foreground dispatching enabled. Even if other apps are listening for `root.gast .playground.nfc` tag dispatch events, they will not be notified of them by the Android OS.

Where to Declare Intent Filters: Manifest File Versus Activity Class

You may be wondering: What's the difference between an NFC-related `IntentFilter` declared in the AndroidManifest.xml and `IntentFilter`s declared in an `Activity` class? Why declare two separate instances of them, especially if they are listening for the same thing?

The following are some scenarios for how NFC-related intents react in the Android operating system. All scenarios assume that an `NDEF_DISCOVERED` `IntentFilter` is set in the Android manifest of our demo app, and is registered to dispatch whenever a tag matches the MIME type `root.gast.playground.nfc` and no other types. All scenarios also have a main `Activity` class in which an `onResume()` method is defined and checks for an `ACTION_NDEF_DISCOVERED` Intent in order to populate a set of text fields.

Scenario #1: The Android device is turned on and is waiting on the homescreen. Foreground dispatching is not enabled:

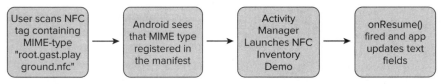

FIGURE 11-7: NFC Scenario #1

Scenario #2: Demo app is already open and foreground dispatching is not enabled:

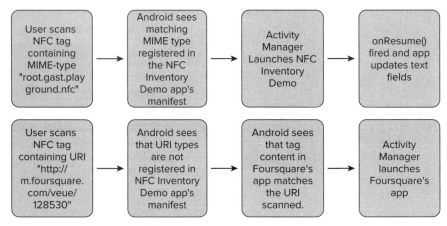

FIGURE 11-8: NFC Scenario #2

Scenario #3: Demo app is already open and foreground dispatching is enabled:

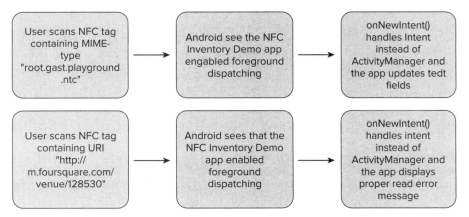

FIGURE 11-9: NFC Scenario #3

As you can see with Scenario #3, some subtle but important differences exist between allowing the Android operating system to handle the `Intents` declared in the manifest file versus handling them via foreground dispatching.

Implementing the Intent Filter in NFCInventoryActivity.java

It is best practice to disable foreground dispatches in your `Activity` class's `onPause()` method. Enable foreground dispatches in `onResume()`.

It is especially important to enable foreground dispatching when getting ready to write to a tag, otherwise hovering over the URI-based NFC tag would zip you over to the Foursquare app and you would never be able to write to that tag.

The following code example is a modified version (simplified for readability) of how the demo inventory app implements foreground dispatching:

```
public class NFCInventoryActivity extends Activity
{

    // NFC-related variables
    NfcAdapter mNfcAdapter;
    PendingIntent mNfcPendingIntent;
    IntentFilter[] mReadTagFilters;

    /* Called when the activity will start interacting with the user. */
    @Override
    protected void onResume()
    {
        //...

        // Handle foreground NFC scanning in this activity by creating a
        // PendingIntent with FLAG_ACTIVITY_SINGLE_TOP flag
        mNfcPendingIntent = PendingIntent.getActivity(this, 0, new Intent(this,
            getClass()).addFlags(Intent.FLAG_ACTIVITY_SINGLE_TOP), 0);

        // Create intent filter to handle NDEF NFC tags detected from inside our
        // application when in "read mode":
```

```
            IntentFilter ndefDetected = new IntentFilter(
                    NfcAdapter.ACTION_NDEF_DISCOVERED);
            try
            {
               ndefDetected.addDataType("application/root.gast.playground.nfc");
            } catch (MalformedMimeTypeException e)
            {
               throw new RuntimeException("Could not add MIME type.", e);
            }
            mReadTagFilters = new IntentFilter[] { ndefDetected };

            // Enable priority for current activity to detect scanned tags
            // enableForegroundDispatch( activity, pendingIntent,
            // intentsFiltersArray, techListsArray );
            mNfcAdapter.enableForegroundDispatch(this, mNfcPendingIntent,
                    mReadTagFilters, null);
            //...
        }

        /* Called when the system is about to start resuming a previous activity. */
        @Override
        protected void onPause() {
            //...
            mNfcAdapter.disableForegroundDispatch(this);
            //...
        }
        //...
    }
```

To summarize the preceding code:

1. Create an `IntentFilter` (ndefDetected) to listen for `root.gast.playground.nfc` NDEF NFC tags.

2. Create an array of `IntentFilters` (mReadTagFilters) and populate it with `ndefDetected` previously.

3. Create a `PendingIntent` (mNfcPendingIntent) with the `FLAG_ACTIVITY_SINGLE_TOP` flag set so each new NFC scan doesn't create multiple instances of the main `Activity`. (This makes it so the Android Back button exits the app immediately instead of having to dismiss several screens of recently scanned NFC tags.)

Related to setting the `FLAG_ACTIVITY_SINGLE_TOP` flag, you may or may not have noticed that the `Activity`'s launch mode was set to be `"singleTask"` to avoid multiple `Activity` instances.

```
<activity
           android:label="@string/app_name"
           android:launchMode="singleTask"
           android:name=".NFCInventoryActivity" >
```

For more information on the Android back stack, visit the Android developer site: `http://developer.android.com/guide/topics/fundamentals/tasks-and-back-stack.html`.

4. Enable foreground dispatching using the `enableForegroundDispatch()` method.

Filtering for generic tags

If you were instead looking to create an `IntentFilter` for generic tags, you could either add a wild-card data type (`*/*`) as illustrated in the following code, or use `null` for the `intentFiltersArray` parameter. The following two examples are almost equivalent except that the latter will default to `NfcAdapter.ACTION_TAG_DISCOVERED` instead of `NfcAdapter.ACTION_NDEF_DISCOVERED` and it will catch all tags.

Using a wildcard:

```
IntentFilter ndefDetected = new IntentFilter(
        NfcAdapter.ACTION_NDEF_DISCOVERED);
ndefDetected.addDataType("*/*"); //catch all MIME types
mNfcAdapter.enableForegroundDispatch(this, mNfcPendingIntent,
        mNdefExchangeFilters, null);
```

Using `null`:

```
mNfcAdapter.enableForegroundDispatch(this, mNfcPendingIntent,
        null, null);
```

Using `NDEF_DISCOVERED` is preferred in your manifest because `TAG_DISCOVERED` is the lowest-priority `IntentFilter` and will react to all scanned NFC tags. However, inside your `Activity` class (meaning that your app is running and has focus), it doesn't make much difference between the previous two `IntentFilter` examples because no other `Activity` can receive the intent when foreground dispatching is enabled.

If you were looking to create an `IntentFilter` on a URI such as the previously mentioned Foursquare examples, it may look something like this in your app:

```
IntentFilter ndefDetected = new IntentFilter(
        NfcAdapter.ACTION_NDEF_DISCOVERED);
ndefDetected.addDataScheme("http");
ndefDetected.addDataAuthority("m.foursquare.com", null);
ndefDetected.addDataPath("/venue/", 0);
```

Foreground NDEF Push

The methods `enableForegroundNdefPush()` and `disableForegroundNdefPush()` were made available in API level 10 for sharing NDEF data between Android devices. With the new features of Ice Cream Sandwich, these two methods have been deprecated in favor of `setNdefPushMessage()` or `setNdefPushCallbackMessage()` for newer devices. Both of these methods are explored later in the "Peer-to-Peer NFC Sharing" section.

Reacting to an NDEF Tag

As described in the "In Your AndroidManifest.xml File" section, you can create `IntentFilters` in your manifest for detecting NDEF tags, or you can create them within your application's main `Activity` as described in the "Foreground Dispatching" section.

To handle `Intent`s dispatched when your application is not in the foreground, use `getIntent()`. `getAction()` in your `onResume()` method to find out if `ACTION_NDEF_DISCOVERED` caused the app to start up.

To handle foreground `Intents`, create an `onNewIntent()` method in your `Activity`. The following code shows the logic flow for handling both NDEF tags using `ACTION_NDEF_DISCOVERED` and non-NDEF tags using the `ACTION_TAG_DISCOVERED` Intent.

```
public class NFCInventoryActivity extends Activity
{
    //...

    /* Called when the activity will start interacting with the user. */
    @Override
    protected void onResume()
    {
        //...

        // tag received when app is not running and not in the foreground:
        if (getIntent().getAction().equals(NfcAdapter.ACTION_NDEF_DISCOVERED))
        {
            NdefMessage[] msgs = getNdefMessagesFromIntent(getIntent());
            //do something with the NDEF messages here
        }

        //...
    }

    /*
     * This is called for activities that set launchMode to "singleTop" or
     * "singleTask" in their manifest package, or if a client used the
     * FLAG_ACTIVITY_SINGLE_TOP flag when calling startActivity(Intent).
     */
    @Override
    protected void onNewIntent(Intent intent)
    {
        //...

        if (intent.getAction().equals(NfcAdapter.ACTION_NDEF_DISCOVERED))
        {
            NdefMessage[] msgs = getNdefMessagesFromIntent(intent);
            // Do something with the NDEF messages here
        } else if (intent.getAction().equals(
                NfcAdapter.ACTION_TAG_DISCOVERED))
        {
            Toast.makeText(this,
              "This NFC tag currently has no inventory NDEF data.",
              Toast.LENGTH_LONG).show();
        }

        //...
    }
    //...
}
```

Note that `getNdefMessagesFromIntent()` is a custom method that is discussed in the next section on reading tags.

NdefMessage and NdefRecord

The `NdefMessage` and `NdefRecord` classes in the `android.nfc.tech` package of the Android SDK relate very closely to the NFC Forum's specifications discussed earlier in "The NDEF Data Format" section. As a refresher, an NDEF message is a container that can hold one or more NDEF records. An NDEF record has a payload and additional meta data such as type, length, and optional payload identifier.

Use `getParcelableArrayExtra()` on the `Intent` object with the item keyword name `NfcAdapter.EXTRA_NDEF_MESSAGES` to get the raw data in `Parcels`. Assuming that the raw data is not null, you can create an `NdefMessage` object by iterating over the raw `Parcelable` object. Or, because there is typically only one message when working with NDEF, use the value at the first index, for example, *msgs[0]*.

```
Parcelable[] rawMsgs = intent
        .getParcelableArrayExtra(NfcAdapter.EXTRA_NDEF_MESSAGES);

NdefMessage[] msgs = new NdefMessage[rawMsgs.length];
for (int i = 0; i < rawMsgs.length; i++) {
    msgs[i] = (NdefMessage) rawMsgs[i];
}
```

There are not many methods for `NdefMessage` but the most important one to know is `getRecords()`, which simply returns an array of `NdefRecords`. Again, for NDEF there is typically only one record so create an `NdefRecord` from the value in the first index unless you know otherwise.

`getPayload()` will likely be your most used `NdefRecord` method, but the following are some examples of common getter methods for `NdefRecord` and its usage:

```
NdefRecord record = msgs[0].getRecords()[0];

//Returns the variable length payload
byte[] payload = record.getPayload();
Log.d(TAG,new String(payload));

// Returns the optional variable length ID
byte[] id = record.getId();
Log.d(TAG, "id: " + new String(id));

// Returns the variable length Type field
byte[] type = record.getType();
Log.d(TAG, "type: " + new String(type));

// Returns the 3-bit TNF. TNF is the top-level type.
short tnf = record.getTnf();
Log.d(TAG, Short.toString(tnf));
```

So that is an example of reading NDEF data, but what about creating your own? In the case of the demo app, it has three editable text fields in which freeform text strings can be inputted. For readability, the demo app creates a JSON object out of the text field inputs before encoding the values into a byte array to become the NDEF record's payload.

```
JSONObject computerSpecs = new JSONObject();
// use computerSpecs.put("specTypeName", specTextFieldValue); to populate JSONObject
String data = computerSpecs.toString();
byte[] dataBytes = data.getBytes(Charset.forName("UTF-8"));
```

`NdefRecord`'s instantiation parameters are byte arrays, so you must also encode the custom MIME type into a byte array:

```
String mimeType = "application/root.gast.playground.nfc";
byte[] mimeBytes = mimeType.getBytes(Charset.forName("UTF-8"));
```

And because you are not going to use the optional NDEF record identifier, set it to be empty bytes:

```
byte[] id = new byte[0];
```

From there, it is as easy as instantiating a new `NdefRecord` and passing in:

➤ A 3-bit TNF constant, which is a higher-level constant to indicate what type of payload is being encoded. In this case, `Ndef.TNF_MIME_MEDIA` has a value of 0x00000002 and indicates that it will follow a standards-based MIME type specification. Other options include:

  ➤ `TNF_ABSOLUTE_URI` (0x00000003)

  ➤ `TNF_EMPTY` (0x00000000)

  ➤ `TNF_EXTERNAL_TYPE` (0x00000004)

  ➤ `TNF_UNKNOWN` (0x00000005)

  ➤ `TNF_WELL_KNOWN` (0x00000001)

➤ The MIME type as a byte array

➤ The ID as a byte array

➤ The payload data as a byte array

This code creates an `NdefMessage` by passing in the newly created `NdefRecord` as a parameter:

```
NdefRecord record = new NdefRecord(NdefRecord.TNF_MIME_MEDIA,
        mimeBytes, id, dataBytes);
NdefMessage m = new NdefMessage(new NdefRecord[] { record });
```

An example of creating an `NdefRecord` for a URI would look like the following:

```
byte[] uriBytes = "http://m.foursquare.com/venue/128530"
            .getBytes(Charset.forName("US-ASCII"));
byte[] id = new byte[0];
byte[] emptyPayload = new byte[0];
NdefRecord record = new NdefRecord(NdefRecord.TNF_MIME_MEDIA,
        uriBytes, id, emptyPayload);
NdefMessage m = new NdefMessage(new NdefRecord[] { record });
```

For your reference, Listing 11-2 provides the full `createNdefFromJson()` custom method.

Available for download on Wrox.com

LISTING 11-2: NDEF creation method

```
public class NFCInventoryActivity extends Activity {
    //...

    private NdefMessage createNdefFromJson()
```

```
        {
            // get the values from the form's text fields:
            Editable nameField = mName.getText();
            Editable ramField = mRAM.getText();
            Editable processorField = mProcessor.getText();

            // create a JSON object out of the values:
            JSONObject computerSpecs = new JSONObject();
            try
            {
                computerSpecs.put("name", nameField);
                computerSpecs.put("ram", ramField);
                computerSpecs.put("processor", processorField);
            } catch (JSONException e)
            {
                Log.d(TAG, "Could not create JSON");
            }

            // create a new NDEF record and containing NDEF message using the app's
            // custom MIME type:
            String mimeType = "application/root.gast.playground.nfc";
            byte[] mimeBytes = mimeType.getBytes(Charset.forName("UTF-8"));
            String data = computerSpecs.toString();
            byte[] dataBytes = data.getBytes(Charset.forName("UTF-8"));
            byte[] id = new byte[0];
            NdefRecord record = new NdefRecord(NdefRecord.TNF_MIME_MEDIA,
                    mimeBytes, id, dataBytes);
            NdefMessage m = new NdefMessage(new NdefRecord[] { record });

            // return the NDEF message
            return m;
        }

    //...
}
```

The preceding example uses a JSON object but you can define the data payload in any manner that is appropriate for your own unique applications. Just remember to keep in mind the storage size of the NFC tag you will be writing to and choose an appropriate payload schema to accommodate the size limitations.

Parsing and Reading NDEF Tags

When an NFC tag is scanned, the Android operating system automatically parses the tag meta data and payload data on the tag and encapsulates it into an `Intent`. Use `getParcelableExtra()` on the `Intent` object with the item keyword name `NfcAdapter.EXTRA_TAG` to read the `Tag` object.

```
Tag detectedTag = intent
        .getParcelableExtra(NfcAdapter.EXTRA_TAG);

Log.d(TAG, tag.getID()); //log tag identifier if one is available
```

To find out more information on this `Tag` object, such as its type, size, or read/write ability, you need to get an instance of an `Ndef` object for the given tag. If your tag was using non-NDEF data, you would instead get an instance of another supported tag technology such as IsoDep or NfcV as outlined in the Advanced NFC documentation online at `http://developer.android.com/guide/topics/nfc/advanced-nfc.html`.

The following code snippet shows an example of outputting some of the more useful property getters of an `Ndef` object such as `getType()`, `getMaxSize()`, `isWritable()`, and `canMakeReadOnly()`:

```
Ndef ndef = Ndef.get(detectedTag);

// Get the NDEF tag type (such as NFC_FORUM_TYPE_1 through
// NFC_FORUM_TYPE_4 and MIFARE_CLASSIC)
Log.d(TAG, ndef.getType().toString());

// Get the maximum NDEF message size in bytes
Log.d(TAG, Integer.toString(ndef.getMaxSize()));

// Determine if the tag is writable.
Log.d(TAG, ndef.isWritable() ? "true" : "false");

// Indicates whether a tag can be made read-only
Log.d(TAG, ndef.canMakeReadOnly() ? "true" : "false");
```

As an alternative to parsing the NDEF message from an `Intent` (for example, you are storing a reference to the tag and not the `Intent`), you could use the `getNdefMessage()` method on the `Ndef` instance, but it's more convenient to read the NDEF message immediately upon handling the `Intent` as you see in the next example. For your reference, the usage of `getNdefMessage()` is shown here:

```
Ndef ndef = Ndef.get(detectedTag);
// Read the current NdefMessage on this tag.
try {
    ndef.connect();
    NdefMessage ndefMessage = ndef.getNdefMessage();
    Log.d(TAG, ndefMessage.toString());
    NdefRecord record = ndefMessage.getRecords()[0];
byte[] payload = record.getPayload();
    Log.d(TAG, new String(payload));
    // Do something with the payload here
    ndef.close();
} catch (IOException e) {
    Log.e(TAG, "IOException reading tag");
} catch (FormatException e) {
    Log.e(TAG, "FormatException reading tag");
}
```

Getting Ready to Write to a Tag

Because the NFC chip on the Android phone is on a mobile device and mobile devices tend to move around, it is best to immediately attempt to write to an NFC sticker based on an `Intent` being fired when a tag has moved into scanning range. If a tag is out of range and you attempt to write to it, you will get an I/O error.

Instead of registering for the more specific `ACTION_NDEF_DISCOVERED` IntentFilter, you should listen for the more generic `ACTION_TAG_DISCOVERED` IntentFilter. This will give you the flexibility to format a tag that's not already in NDEF format.

Similar to what you already did to create a foreground dispatch for reading a tag, you will do something similar for preparing to write to a tag. The demo NFC Inventory app has an Update button that will turn on foreground dispatching.

The custom `createNdefFromJson()` method is covered in Listing 11-2 and the custom `writeTag()` method is covered in the section immediately following this code snippet.

```java
public class NFCInventoryActivity extends Activity {
    //...

    // NFC-related variables
    NfcAdapter mNfcAdapter;
    PendingIntent mNfcPendingIntent;
    IntentFilter[] mReadTagFilters;
    IntentFilter[] mWriteTagFilters;
    private boolean mWriteMode = false;

    /** Called when the activity is first created. */
    @Override
    public void onCreate(Bundle savedInstanceState)
    {
        //...

        // write_tag element is the Update button
        findViewById(R.id.write_tag).setOnClickListener(mTagWriter);

        // Handle foreground NFC scanning in this activity by creating a
        // PendingIntent with FLAG_ACTIVITY_SINGLE_TOP flag
        mNfcPendingIntent = PendingIntent.getActivity(this, 0, new Intent(this,
                getClass()).addFlags(Intent.FLAG_ACTIVITY_SINGLE_TOP), 0);

        // Create intent filter to detect any NFC tag when attempting to write
        // to a tag in "write mode"
        IntentFilter tagDetected = new IntentFilter(
                NfcAdapter.ACTION_TAG_DISCOVERED);

        // create IntentFilter arrays:
        mWriteTagFilters = new IntentFilter[] { tagDetected };
    }

    /*
     * This is called for activities that set launchMode to "singleTop" in their
     * package, or if a client used the FLAG_ACTIVITY_SINGLE_TOP flag when
     * calling startActivity(Intent).
     */
    @Override
    protected void onNewIntent(Intent intent)
    {
        //...

        if (intent.getAction().equals(NfcAdapter.ACTION_TAG_DISCOVERED))
        {
            Tag detectedTag = intent
                    .getParcelableExtra(NfcAdapter.EXTRA_TAG);
            writeTag(createNdefFromJson(), detectedTag);
```

```
        }

        //...
    }

    private void enableTagWriteMode()
    {
        mWriteMode = true;
        mNfcAdapter.enableForegroundDispatch(this, mNfcPendingIntent,
                mWriteTagFilters, null);
    }

    private View.OnClickListener mTagWriter = new View.OnClickListener()
    {
        @Override
        public void onClick(View arg0)
        {
            enableTagWriteMode();
        }

    };

    //...
}
```

Writing to the Tag

Once you have an `NdefMessage` object by either creating your own (refer to the "NdefMessage and NdefRecord" section) or storing the `NdefMessage` from a previously scanned NFC tag, writing to a tag is quite straightforward with the Android SDK.

First, you must open a connection to the `Ndef` object of a `Tag` using the `connect()` method to allow I/O operations on the NFC tag. Once the connection is made, you can write to the tag by using the `writeNdefMessage()` method and passing in an `NdefMessage` object. Optionally, you can use `makeReadOnly()` to write-protect the tag if the tag technology supports it. Finally, use the `close()` method to close the I/O connection.

The following is the workflow in its simplest form:

```
Ndef ndef = Ndef.get(detectedTag);
// Read the current NdefMessage on this tag.
try {
    ndef.connect();

    // Overwrite the NdefMessage on this tag
    ndef.writeNdefMessage(ndefMessage);

    // Make a tag read-only.
    ndef.makeReadOnly();

    ndef.close();
} catch (IOException e) {
    Log.e(TAG,"IOException reading tag");
```

```
    } catch (FormatException e) {
        Log.e(TAG,"FormatException reading tag");
    }
```

However, as with any operation that requires I/O communications, many scenarios can cause the write process to fail, such as:

➤ Attempting to write to a tag that's already read-only.

➤ Attempting to write to a tag that cannot fit the data in your NdefMessage object.

➤ Attempting to write to a tag that does not support NDEF.

➤ I/O errors such as moving the device away from the NFC tag during the write process.

Also, if the tag that you are writing to is not already formatted to accept NDEF data (such as a MIFARE Classic tag), it must be formatted first. Following is the custom writeTag() method used in the demo NFC Inventory app, which you can use for all of your projects, too:

LISTING 11-3: Write NDEF data to tag method

```
boolean writeTag(NdefMessage message, Tag tag)
{
    int size = message.toByteArray().length;

    try
    {
        Ndef ndef = Ndef.get(tag);
        if (ndef != null)
        {
            ndef.connect();

            if (!ndef.isWritable())
            {
                Toast.makeText(this,
                        "Cannot write to this tag. This tag is read-only.",
                        Toast.LENGTH_LONG).show();
                return false;
            }
            if (ndef.getMaxSize() < size)
            {
                Toast.makeText(
                        this,
                        "Cannot write to this tag. Message size (" + size
                                + " bytes) exceeds this tag's capacity of "
                                + ndef.getMaxSize() + " bytes.",
                        Toast.LENGTH_LONG).show();
                return false;
            }

            ndef.writeNdefMessage(message);
            Toast.makeText(this,
```

continues

LISTING 11-3 *(continued)*

```
                        "A pre-formatted tag was successfully updated.",
                        Toast.LENGTH_LONG).show();
                return true;
            } else
            {
                NdefFormatable format = NdefFormatable.get(tag);
                if (format != null)
                {
                    try
                    {
                        format.connect();
                        format.format(message);
                        Toast.makeText(
                                this,
                                "This tag was successfully formatted and updated.",
                                Toast.LENGTH_LONG).show();
                        return true;
                    } catch (IOException e)
                    {
                        Toast.makeText(
                                this,
                                "Cannot write to this tag due to I/O Exception.",
                                Toast.LENGTH_LONG).show();
                        return false;
                    }
                } else
                {
                    Toast.makeText(
                            this,
                            "Cannot write to this tag. This tag does not support NDEF.",
                            Toast.LENGTH_LONG).show();
                    return false;
                }
            }
        } catch (Exception e)
        {
            Toast.makeText(this,
                    "Cannot write to this tag due to an Exception.",
                    Toast.LENGTH_LONG).show();
        }

        return false;
    }
```

If you want to explore writing non-NDEF data, please refer to the Android SDK documentation for the `android.nfc.tech` classes located on `developer.android.com`.

Putting it All Together

Throughout this chapter you've been gathering the bits and pieces needed to put together a simple NFC inventory tracker, so here's a quick review.

In the Android manifest XML file, use the `<uses-feature android:name="android.hardware. nfc"/>` and `<uses-permission android:name="android.permission.NFC" />` options to allow your app to use NFC. Also, create an intent filter with an action name of `"android.nfc.action .NDEF_DISCOVERED"` to handle NDEF-formatted NFC tags when the application is not open on your device.

In your main `Activity`, get a reference to the `NfcAdapter` and enable foreground dispatching of scanned tags by passing in a `PendingIntent` and a set of `IntentFilter` arrays via the `enable-ForegroundDispatch()` method.

Scanned NFC tags automatically get encapsulated into `Intents`, so read the data on them by applying `getParcelableArrayExtra(NfcAdapter.EXTRA_NDEF_MESSAGES)` on those `Intents` to extract out the NDEF message. Because there's typically only one NDEF message and one NDEF record with the tags that you'll be writing, you can quickly get an `NdefRecord` payload by getting the first record of an `NdefMessage`, for example, `ndefMessage.getRecords()[0].getPayload();`.

Writing to a tag typically means encoding a TNF constant, a MIME type, and payload into separate byte arrays and creating an `NdefRecord` and `NdefMessage` out of them. Use the `writeNdefMessage()` method on an `Ndef` object of a `Tag` to write content to the tag.

The NFC Inventory demo application puts these all together and the only extra code is related to handling UI elements. Getting started with the NFC API is simple! Find the full manifest, main `Activity` code, and supporting layout and string XML files of the demonstration app in the supplied example source code and app of this book.

FUTURE CONSIDERATIONS

In addition to the previously covered Android APIs, what else should you put consideration into to make a successful NFC project?

NFC N-Mark

To make your NFC application or product more visible, you may want to download the N-Mark, shown in Figure 11-10, from the NFC Forum. This logo is used in much the same way you might use the WiFi or Bluetooth logos. Consider placing the N-Mark on the actual NFC sticker to help the users find the sweet spot for placing their mobile device for scanning.

FIGURE 11-10: NCF Forum's N-Mark. The "N-Mark" logo is a trademark or registered trademark of NFC Forum, Inc.

Visit `http://www.nfc-forum.org/resources/N-Mark/` for more information. You must agree to a click-through license in order to download a zip package of various image formats.

Peer-to-Peer NFC Sharing

With NXP Semiconductors announcing in a November 2011 press release that they have been designed into 90 mobile devices, the future for NFC-enabled interactions is only going to change from being novel to becoming mainstream.

As more devices become NFC enabled, we can move from simply thinking of NFC as being a passive, one-sided conversation into one that is peer-to-peer. Android Beam, released with the latest Android 4.0 release, should open up new possibilities for interactions on the go.

With the newest Android APIs, if a specified `activity` is in the foreground and it is touched to another NFC-enabled device with its screen unlocked, a prompt on the device running the `activity` will appear requesting to "beam" to the other device. The receiver can then accept or deny the beam request.

Depending on the data format, the receiving phone does not even need to be running Ice Cream Sandwich. It could be a Nexus S running Gingerbread!

Peer-to-Peer Android APIs

Iterating upon the inventory tracking example, imagine that you are in the middle of updating a computer, but you are interrupted by an emergency. You must leave immediately but don't want to lose your edits to the text fields you've already made. You have your coworker come over and beam him or her your current text field values.

You need to be aware of only a few new APIs to get your app enabled to send peer-to-peer NFC data, so if you already have an app NFC-ready, it should only be a few lines of code to get your NFC data sharing working.

In API level 10, a pair of methods were introduced in the `NfcAdapter` class for peer-to-peer sharing: `enableForegroundNdefPush()` and `disableForegroundNdefPush()`. These two methods have since been deprecated in API level 14 to make way for `setNdefPushMessage()` to automatically beam a predefined NDEF message and `setNdefPushMessageCallback()` to construct the `NdefMessage` object on demand before beaming.

To take advantage of Android Beam, your `activity` must implement the `android.nfc.NfcAdapter.CreateNdefMessageCallback` interface, which means you must implement a `createNdefMessage()` method in your `Activity`.

The following shows how little code you need to add to get the inventory demo working peer-to-peer by leveraging the already existing `createNdefFromJson()` method! The receiving phone will read the beaming phone exactly like a regular NFC sticker.

```
import android.nfc.NfcAdapter.CreateNdefMessageCallback;

public class NFCInventoryActivity extends implements
        CreateNdefMessageCallback
{
    //...

    NfcAdapter mNfcAdapter;

    //...

    /** Called when the activity is first created. */
    @Override
    public void onCreate(Bundle savedInstanceState) {
        //...
```

```
        // get an instance of the context's cached NfcAdapter
        // check if NFC is enabled

        // register the callback
        // usage: setNdefPushMessageCallback( callback, activity,
        // optionalExtraActivities)
        mNfcAdapter.setNdefPushMessageCallback(this,this);
        //...
    }

    @Override
    public NdefMessage createNdefMessage(NfcEvent event) {
        NdefMessage msg = createNdefFromJson();
        return msg;
    }
    //...
}
```

GO FORTH AND NFC!

This chapter touched upon some interesting implementations of NFC already out there such as Fruit Ninja's battle mode, Hashable's networking handshake, Touchanote's quick launch into Evernote feature, Foursquare check-ins, and Android Beam.

Here are some additional ideas to get you excited to build more NFC-enabled applications for Android!

➤ Other inventory tracking systems.

➤ Keyless door entry systems.

➤ Two-step verification authentication in which you require a passcode plus a physical NFC-enabled object such as phone or tag.

➤ Time tracking systems: imagine putting your phone next to your desk to sign in and removing it to sign out.

➤ Notification alarm diffuser: automatically deactivate extraneous sounds originating from your phone when you've already got e-mail and calendar notifications on your desktop computer.

➤ Money exchange applications: keep tabs with friends, or at bars or small businesses.

➤ Customer and table tracking applications: great for restaurants that use a number-based ordering system.

➤ Frequent shopper and loyalty card replacement using peer-to-peer mode.

➤ Secure coupons for high-end items to thwart counterfeiting.

➤ Innovative retail shopping experiences: Best Buy already attaches QR codes to its product displays that link to the product page on the Best Buy mobile website, so imagine if it added NFC stickers too. Other retailers should think about using stickers in-store to add meta data to their products to enable potential buyers to build side-by-side comparison charts for products, or to add products to online shopping carts and wish lists.

➤ Speed up location-based check-ins to services such as Foursquare, Gowalla, or Google Places.

➤ Interactive toys.

➤ NFC-enabled media (music and video) centers.

➤ "Smart" posters and advertisements.

➤ Special events promotions: imagine getting people to visit physical locations to unlock content such as game levels or free music tracks.

What will you make with these new NFC features?

SUMMARY

That was a long journey through the rocky landscape of RFID and NFC technology. Hopefully by now you should remember two key things about the technology itself:

➤ NFC is the special RFID radio frequency of 13.56MHz, and

➤ Always use NDEF data for ease of development on the Android platform!

In terms of implementing NFC in your Android applications, you should have a firm grasp on the multiple spots to add your intents filters and how to read/write to NFC tags. And, always remember the importance of enabling foreground dispatching.

Moving forward, keep in mind how easy it is to create peer-to-peer experiences with the Android NFC and get your app ready for the steady increase of NFC-enabled devices ready to hit the consumer market over the next 1–3 years. The future looks very bright for NFC!

Despite the potential usefulness of NFC technology, there will likely be some objects that an app needs to detect that are not augmented with NFC tags. The next two chapters describe how to detect such objects using the camera.

12

Using the Camera

WHAT'S IN THIS CHAPTER?

➤ Capturing images with the Android camera

➤ Creating your own `Activity` for controlling the camera

➤ Capturing images continuously during camera preview

➤ Creating a simple barcode reader that uses camera preview

The Android platform creates an incredible opportunity for image processing, because it offers an image processing system that is universally available, handheld, inexpensive, easy to program, networked, and provides processing power equivalent to a low-end personal computer. This chapter shows you how to begin to make use of this remarkable platform by focusing on image processing that happens immediately after capturing the image.

USING THE CAMERA ACTIVITY

If all you want to do is capture an image, things could not be much easier. All you have to do is create an `Intent` with the action `MediaStore.ACTION_IMAGE_CAPTURE`, passing it a filename as extended data with the name `MediaStore.EXTRA_OUTPUT`. Then call `startActivityForResult()`, passing your `Intent` and an identifier identifying this `Intent` to your `onActivityResult()` method.

What this does is fire up the camera application, giving the user the opportunity to control the camera parameters themselves and take a picture. The picture is stored into your chosen file, and your `onActivityResult()` method is called when it is done.

Listing 12-1 shows the key steps, and `SimpleCaptureActivity` in the provided code gives you the complete application.

LISTING 12-1: Taking a photo

```java
private final int PICTURE_ACTIVITY_CODE = 1;
private final String FILENAME = "sdcard/photo.jpg";
private void launchTakePhoto()
{
    Intent intent = new Intent(MediaStore.ACTION_IMAGE_CAPTURE);
    mFile = new File(FILENAME);
    Uri outputFileUri = Uri.fromFile(mFile);
    intent.putExtra(MediaStore.EXTRA_OUTPUT, outputFileUri);
    startActivityForResult(intent, PICTURE_ACTIVITY_CODE);
}
protected void onActivityResult(int requestCode, int resultCode,
                                Intent data)
{
    if (requestCode == PICTURE_ACTIVITY_CODE)
    {
        if (resultCode == RESULT_OK)
        {
            ImageView imageView =
                (ImageView) findViewById(R.id.imageView1);
            Uri inputFileUri = Uri.fromFile(mFile);
            imageView.setImageURI(inputFileUri);
        }
    }
}
```

If a picture is all you need, that's all you need to do. But you probably want to do more, and that's what the rest of this chapter is about. In reading it, you'll learn how to write an Activity that controls every aspect of the camera — focus, flash, white balance, and so on — and provides the user with a live preview for feedback. You then learn how to capture and use the preview image, eventually understanding how a complete image processing program, for barcode capture, works.

Controlling the Camera with Your Own Activity

Writing your own camera Activity gives you the opportunity to control everything there is to control about the camera. The developers of Android have provided a useful starting point in the CameraPreview Activity that is included in the API Demos sample code (http://developer .android.com/resources/samples/ApiDemos/src/com/example/android/apis/graphics/ index.html), which is the basis for this chapter's first program that controls the camera, called LiveCapture. This section shows how this Activity is constructed and then extends it to control more of the camera functions.

Android gives hardware developers maximum freedom in implementation, and nowhere is this truer than in the camera. Different Android platforms have zero, one, or more cameras, and each camera can have different capabilities. It is therefore essential that you write your Activity in such a way that it adapts to the cameras available to it. If you don't do that, at best you'll be limiting what your Activity can do — and, more likely, your Activity will crash when it encounters something it doesn't expect.

Claiming and Releasing a Camera

The first thing `LiveCaptureActivity` has to do is to determine which camera it will capture with — remember, there can be more than one! The basic process is shown in Listing 12-2.

LISTING 12-2: Choosing a camera

```
mNumberOfCameras = Camera.getNumberOfCameras();
CameraInfo cameraInfo = new CameraInfo();
for (int i = 0; i < mNumberOfCameras; i++)
{
    Camera.getCameraInfo(i, cameraInfo);
    if (cameraInfo.facing == CameraInfo.CAMERA_FACING_BACK)
    {
        mDefaultCameraId = i;
    }
}
if (mDefaultCameraId == -1)
{
    // test for no cameras
    if (nCameras > 0)
    {
        mDefaultCameraId = 0;
    } else
    {
        // nothing can be done; tell the user then exit
        Toast toast = Toast.makeText(getApplicationContext(),
                R.string.no_cameras, Toast.LENGTH_LONG);
        toast.show();
        finish();
    }
}
```

As Listing 12-2 shows, you start by determining the number of cameras using `getNumberOfCameras()`. Then you test each camera, reading its characteristics into a `CameraInfo` object instance created for this purpose. If at least one is facing away from the user (that is, facing toward the back of the Android device), `LiveCapture` chooses it.

The `if` statement following the camera-testing loop handles the case where no suitable camera is found. If this is because no camera is backward-facing, you use the first camera, if there is one. If the device has no camera at all, you give up.

Before looking into the internals of how the preview is shown to the user, there is one additional part of the setup. Camera programs must be well behaved, because many programs may want to use the camera, and only one can use it at a time. As an Android programmer, you know that your `Activity` can be stopped permanently whenever it has been paused. That is why it is essential to release the camera when your `Activity` is paused, as shown in Listing 12-3.

LISTING 12-3: Releasing the camera

```
protected void onPause() {
    super.onPause();
    if (mCamera != null) {
        mPreview.setCamera(null);
        mCamera.release();
        mCamera = null;
    }
}
```

If you don't release the camera, it is possible that your `Activity` could be terminated while still owning the camera — not a good situation, and very likely to result in a `RuntimeException` that will be hard to interpret (because it will happen when your program is no longer running).

Likewise, when your `Activity` starts, you'll want to resume camera ownership, as shown in Listing 12-4.

LISTING 12-4: Opening the camera

```
protected void onResume()
{
    super.onResume();
    mCamera = Camera.open(mDefaultCameraId);
    mPreview.setCamera(mCamera);
}
```

This is all you have to do to manage the selection and ownership of the camera. The next section discusses how the camera preview display works.

The Preview View

`Preview` is a `View` that shows a live preview of the camera image. The full code is in Listing 12-11 at the end of this chapter. You can use it like any other `View`, inserting it into a `Layout` by including it an XML layout description file, as `LiveCapture` does in its `main.XML`:

```
<jjil.android.Preview
    android:id="@+id/preview1"
    android:layout_width="match_parent"
    android:layout_height="match_parent">
</jjil.android.Preview>
```

The key thing to understand about `Preview` (and showing camera previews in Android in general) is that it shows the camera preview in a `SurfaceView` field. `SurfaceView` is the one class in Android that can show a camera preview. You must have a `SurfaceView` if you are going to use camera preview.

`Preview` creates its `SurfaceView` in its constructor, as shown in Listing 12-5.

LISTING 12-5: Creating the SurfaceView

```
public class Preview extends ViewGroup implements SurfaceHolder.Callback {
    private SurfaceHolder mHolder;
    private SurfaceView mSurfaceView;

    public Preview(Context context, AttributeSet attributeSet) {
        super(context, attributeSet);
        mSurfaceView = new SurfaceView(context, attributeSet);
        addView(mSurfaceView);
        // Install a SurfaceHolder.Callback so we get notified when the
        // underlying surface is created and destroyed.
        mHolder = mSurfaceView.getHolder();
        mHolder.addCallback(this);
        mHolder.setType(SurfaceHolder.SURFACE_TYPE_PUSH_BUFFERS);
    }
}
```

The other thing you'll notice about Preview's constructor is that it creates a SurfaceHolder (*mHolder*) to manage the SurfaceView. *mHolder* is the object that is used to communicate with the camera (through a callback in Preview) and connect it to the SurfaceView. Note that *mHolder*'s type is set to SurfaceHolder.SURFACE_TYPE_PUSH_BUFFERS. In some releases of Android, this was required for a SurfaceView used to show a camera preview (in later releases it is ignored).

Look next at the surfaceCreated() and surfaceDestroyed() methods in Preview, shown in Listing 12-6. These are the callback methods the SurfaceHolder uses to communicate with the Preview class. You told the SurfaceHolder about them when you invoked *mHolder*'s addCallback() method in Listing 12-5. The camera can't start using the SurfaceView until it has been created, which doesn't happen immediately. So the surfaceCreated() callback connects the camera to the SurfaceView through its SurfaceHolder, and surfaceDestroyed() terminates any camera preview that is going on.

LISTING 12-6: SurfaceHolder callback methods

```
public void surfaceCreated(SurfaceHolder holder) {
    try {
        if (mCamera != null) {
            mCamera.setPreviewDisplay(holder);
        }
    } catch (IOException exception) {
        Log.e(TAG, "IOException caused by setPreviewDisplay()", exception);
    }
}


public void surfaceDestroyed(SurfaceHolder holder) {
    if (mCamera != null) {
        mCamera.stopPreview();
    }
}
```

The rest of the `Preview` class deals with connecting to a particular camera, and, especially, choosing an appropriate preview size. It is important to realize that when you use camera preview you're ceding control of part of the Android display to the camera. That is the reason for the use of the `SurfaceHolder` and the callbacks that allow it to tell `Preview` when the `SurfaceView` is ready. `SurfaceHolder` mediates between the application, embodied in the `Preview` class, and the camera.

The image the camera gives to `SurfaceHolder` for display (and, as you'll see later, for image processing) is supplied by the camera in one of a few fixed sizes, called preview sizes. Cameras support different preview sizes because an image's use determines its shape and size (for example, a standard TV image has a small size and a 4:3 aspect ratio, whereas an HDTV image has a large size and a 16:9 aspect ratio). Android's graphics hardware can stretch the preview image to fit in whatever `View` you supply — but you don't want to change its aspect ratio (that would distort the image) and you do want to exactly fill the space you have for `Preview`, if possible. In other words, the aspect ratio of the camera image should match the aspect ratio of `Preview`.

Getting the aspect ratios to match is tricky because the camera that is being shown in the preview can change as the result of calls to the `setCamera()` method, and each camera supports different preview sizes. At the same time, the size of the `SurfaceView` object can change as the display is rotated and Android rebuilds the user interface.

`Preview` makes `setCamera()` available to choose a particular camera to preview, as shown in Listing 12-7. All `setCamera()` does is read the supported preview sizes from the camera and then call `requestLayout()`. `Preview`'s overrides of `onLayout()` and `onMeasure()` do the actual work of choosing an appropriate preview size and starting the camera using it based on `mSupportedPreviewSizes`.

LISTING 12-7: setCamera

```
public void setCamera(Camera camera) {
    mCamera = camera;
    if (mCamera != null) {
        mSupportedPreviewSizes =
            mCamera.getParameters().getSupportedPreviewSizes();
        requestLayout();
    }
}
```

The computation needed to choose the best preview size from the ones supported by the camera is done in `getOptimalPreviewSize()`, which chooses the preview size that matches the aspect ratio (if possible) or, failing that, the one that is closest to the desired height (which will at least give a preview image about the same resolution as your display area). You call `getOptimalPreviewSize()` from `switchCamera()` whenever the camera changes and you use the computed size to override `onLayout()` and `onMeasure()`. `onLayout()` stretches the camera preview image to fill `Preview`'s area as much as possible, centering the image if it doesn't completely fill the space. Finally, `surfaceChanged()` sets the camera parameters to this size, and starts preview.

 Never try to change the preview size while camera preview is running. If you do, you'll get a `RuntimeException`.

Note that you don't actually interact with the camera drawing code in any way, for example by overriding `onDraw()`. This is inaccessible, and under the control of the `SurfaceHolder`. The only way you can alter the display in the preview image area is by putting another (transparent) view in front of it in the z-order and drawing on that. You are also not allowed to modify the camera preview image in other ways common in Android, for example by making it partially transparent.

Controlling the Camera

`LiveCapture` controls just one camera parameter, the preview size, but you might want to control many camera parameters. Each camera allows you to control some or none of these parameters. The method of controlling them is similar to the technique used in `LiveCapture`:

1. Take control of the camera and use `getParameters()` to get a `Camera.Parameters` object for it.

2. Interrogate the `Camera.Parameters` object using get methods to determine what the camera supports.

3. Choose appropriate settings based on the requirements of the application and user.

4. Assign the chosen values by modifying the `Camera.Parameters` object using set methods and then call `setParameters()`.

Most camera parameters can be changed while camera preview is running without causing problems, but you have to stop and start camera preview whenever you switch cameras — otherwise you'll get the dreaded `RuntimeException`.

The next section examines how `LiveCapturePlus` controls more of the camera parameters. To keep things simple, you give the user a button for each different parameter; pressing the button advances the parameter to the next legal value.

Orientation

If you play with `LiveCapture` on an Android device you'll notice some disconcerting behavior: in some orientations, the preview image is sideways. This is because Android automatically rotates everything on the screen — text and so on — but it doesn't automatically do this for the camera preview. That is left for the application to control. You'll do this in an improved version of `LiveCapture`, called `LiveCapturePlus`, which will also allow you to control more of the camera hardware.

The relationship between the display orientation and the camera orientation is difficult to understand because it involves rotation around two different axes, of the camera and the display. Android gives you two measurements to determine how to orient the image:

➤ The current orientation of the display, from `getDefaultDisplay().getRotation()`. It is measured in a clockwise direction facing the display.

➤ The camera orientation, which is defined in the Android documentation as the "angle that the camera image needs to be rotated clockwise so it shows correctly on the display in its natural orientation." It is a field in the `CameraInfo` object, which is intrinsic to the camera — it doesn't change as the Android device is rotated.

Camera orientation needs more explanation. Digital cameras use an image sensor, which captures the image and supplies it as an array of pixels, and in which you may think of coordinate (0, 0) as the top-left corner, as shown in Figure 12-1. However, the pixel at (0, 0) could have come from any corner of the image sensor, depending on the camera design — Figure 12-1 shows an image sensor in which the pixel at (0, 0) comes from the top-*right* corner of the sensor. So you need to know how much the pixel array must be rotated so that it lines up again with the image sensor. This is the camera orientation.

You might think that the camera orientation in Figure 12-1 is 90°, but this actually depends on whether the camera is on the front or the back of the Android device. If the camera is on the back of the device, rotating the image 90° clockwise around the camera axis is correct. But if the camera is on the front of the device, the camera axis points the other way, so a 90° clockwise rotation will cause the image to be displayed upside down. You actually need to make a 90° *counter-clockwise* rotation, which is the same thing as a 270° rotation clockwise.

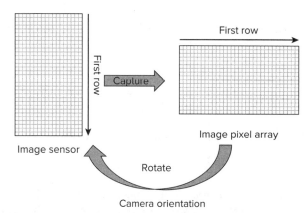

FIGURE 12-1: Camera orientation

The calculations for this are done in setCameraDisplayOrientation(), from ManagedCamera Activity (this is a simplified version of http://developer.android.com/reference/android/ hardware/Camera.html#setDisplayOrientation(int)), shown in Listing 12-8. (LiveCapturePlus and the rest of the samples in this chapter use this Activity by deriving their own activities from it.) You start by converting the current display orientation from an enumerated to a numeric value. Now, think of the display orientation as doing some of the work required to get the camera image oriented correctly — after all, the user has rotated the display (and image) for you! You have to compute what additional rotation you need. In the case of a backward-facing camera, all you have to do is take the difference between the rotation you want (that is, the camera orientation), and the display orientation. The calculation is the same for a frontward-facing camera, but you start with a counter-clockwise rotation by the camera orientation (that is, 360 minus the camera orientation). You then call setDisplayOrientation() to apply the calculated rotation to the camera image.

LISTING 12-8: setCameraDisplayOrientation

```
public void setCameraDisplayOrientation() {
    CameraInfo cameraInfo = new CameraInfo();
    Camera.getCameraInfo(mCameraCurrentlyLocked, cameraInfo);
```

```
int rotation = getWindowManager().getDefaultDisplay()
        .getRotation();
int degrees = 0;
switch (rotation) {
    case Surface.ROTATION_0: degrees = 0; break;
    case Surface.ROTATION_90: degrees = 90; break;
    case Surface.ROTATION_180: degrees = 180; break;
    case Surface.ROTATION_270: degrees = 270; break;
}

int desiredRotation =
    (cameraInfo.facing == Camera.CameraInfo.CAMERA_FACING_FRONT) ?
        (360 - cameraInfo.orientation) : cameraInfo.orientation;
int result = (desiredRotation - degrees + 360) % 360;
mCamera.setDisplayOrientation(result);
}
```

Zoom

LiveCapturePlus determines whether it should enable the camera zoom button with a simple test in switchCamera():

```
mButtonZoom.setEnabled(cameraParameters.isZoomSupported()
        && cameraParameters.getMaxZoom() > 0);
```

The value returned by getMaxZoom() can vary depending on the preview size, which is why LiveCapturePlus calls it after determining how it's going to show the preview, and the preview size, in setCameraDisplayOrientation().

 You should never call getMaxZoom() *without calling* isZoomSupported() *first to make sure it is allowed. Some cameras do not support zoom at all when using certain camera preview sizes, so always test* isZoomSupported() *after setting the preview size. Also, some cameras return 0 for* getMaxZoom() *to indicate that zoom is not supported, rather than returning false for* isZoomSupported().

In this example, the actual control of zoom is done in the onClickListener for the zoom button:

```
Camera.Parameters cameraParameters = mCamera.getParameters();
cameraParameters.setZoom((cameraParameters.getZoom() + 1)
                % cameraParameters.getMaxZoom() + 1);
mCamera.setParameters(cameraParameters);
```

All that's going on here is you are advancing zoom to the next level every time the user presses the zoom button. The zoom value is an arbitrary integer value. The actual magnification ratios from zoom are available in getZoomRatios().

Focus

Focus is defined as the distance at which an image of an object will be as sharp as possible. On Android devices focus is controlled by a string, which makes it possible to describe lots of different options for setting focus. You can set it at infinity, at a fixed value, or for close-up use with a macro lens (you see how to use autofocus later in this chapter).

First, a word on the importance of the macro lens. In many things you'll want to do with image processing on Android, you'll want to look at things close to the camera — barcodes, text, and so on. Doing this with a normal lens is next to impossible, because when you move the camera close to the object, it goes out of focus. You either have to move the camera far enough away so things are focused (but then the image is tiny) or move it up close to get a big enough image (but then it is out of focus.) That is why it is so wonderful that Android devices often have a macro lens, which is designed to focus well at close range, and provide good magnification.

The process for using focus is similar to that for zoom. When you switch to a new camera, you enable focus if any supported focus modes exist:

```
mlszFocusModes = cameraParameters.getSupportedFocusModes();
mButtonFocus.setEnabled(mlszFocusModes.size() > 0);
```

You then sequence through the various focus modes supported on the camera in the onClick() handler for *mButtonFocus*:

```
Camera.Parameters cameraParameters = mCamera.getParameters();
mnFocusMode = (mnFocusMode + 1) % mlszFocusModes.size();
cameraParameters.setFocusMode(mlszFocusModes.get(mnFocusMode));
mCamera.setParameters(cameraParameters);
```

Switching Cameras

The onClick() code for *mButtonSwitch* uses the switchCamera() method in the Preview class to switch from one camera to the next. It also manages its internal state (which buttons are enabled and so on). The important thing here is to stop camera preview before switching cameras, and to release the previous camera before you open the next.

You should start the camera preview again only after setting the camera preview size and display orientation. onClick() calls the advanceCamera() method in ManageCameraActivity to do this:

```
protected void advanceCamera()
{
    mCamera.stopPreview();
    mCamera.release();
    mDefaultCameraId = (mDefaultCameraId + 1) % mNumberOfCameras;
    mCamera = Camera.open(mDefaultCameraId);
    setCameraDisplayOrientation();
}
```

Flash

The flash modes that may be available on an Android camera are shown in Table 12-1. Flash is usually not available in live capture so the code for controlling it in LiveCapturePlus, generally, does not have any effect, but the process for controlling the flash is illustrated.

RuntimeExceptions WHEN SETTING CAMERA PARAMETERS

One quirk of flash — and some of the other camera parameters, such as white balance — is that setting them may generate a RuntimeException, *even though you are using a "legal" mode. This is apparently because the camera is in a state that is inconsistent with the requested parameter. This use of* RuntimeException *seems to be largely undocumented. The decision to generate* RuntimeExceptions *may be up to the camera manufacturer. This is the reason for catching (and ignoring) the* RuntimeException *in the* onClick *listener. The application could also report the failure to set the camera parameter to the user, or record that this camera does not support the requested parameter and avoid its use in the future.*

TABLE 12-1: Android Flash Modes

FLASH MODE	DESCRIPTION
FLASH_MODE_AUTO	Flash is used if required
FLASH_MODE_OFF	Flash will never be used
FLASH_MODE_ON	Flash will be fired during snapshot
FLASH_MODE_RED_EYE	If required, flash will be pre-fired before capture to reduce red-eye, then fired during snapshot
FLASH_MODE_TORCH	Flash is on continuously

Other Camera Parameters

Cameras support many other controllable parameters, which are also controlled in LiveCapturePlus.

White Balance

The effect of ambient light on the colors of a captured image is striking — without white balance compensation, an indoor scene illuminated with incandescent light looks orange — and one way to compensate for that is by using the camera's white balance function.

The settings supported in the CameraParameters class for white balance are shown in the following list. LiveCapturePlus controls white balance in the same way as focus, flash, and zoom.

➤ WHITE_BALANCE_AUTO

➤ WHITE_BALANCE_CLOUDY_DAYLIGHT

➤ WHITE_BALANCE_DAYLIGHT

➤ WHITE_BALANCE_FLUORESCENT

➤ WHITE_BALANCE_INCANDESCENT

➤ WHITE_BALANCE_SHADE

➤ WHITE_BALANCE_TWILIGHT

➤ WHITE_BALANCE_WARM_FLUOURESCENT

Except in specific situations where you know a lot about the scene, it is best to leave the default white balance setting (WHITE_BALANCE_AUTO, if supported) because you usually don't know what the ambient light is. If you are really concerned about color you should use algorithmic white balance to try to compensate for lighting changes that may not be detectable with the camera's automatic settings. Without compensation, colors can be skewed toward the color of the light, and, therefore, difficult to recognize. Some such techniques are discussed later.

Advanced Focus and Metering Settings

More advanced cameras allow the definition of specific areas in the image to control focus and exposure, in order to get the best possible image of an area of interest.

We will leave the choice of these settings to professional photographers, who make use of similar settings when getting the best possible image of a scene. Your program will probably not have access to the information needed to choose appropriate settings.

Scene Mode

Some cameras allow you to use "scene mode" to choose collections of preset values such as white balance, focus, metering, and flash. This allows you to take the best possible pictures whether you are taking a portrait, in a dark theater, or at a party. The scene modes available in Android are as follows:

➤ SCENE_MODE_ACTION

➤ SCENE_MODE_AUTO

➤ SCENE_MODE_BARCODE

➤ SCENE_MODE_BEACH

➤ SCENE_MODE_CANDLELIGHT

➤ SCENE_MODE_FIREWORKS

➤ SCENE_MODE_LANDSCAPE

➤ SCENE_MODE_NIGHT

➤ SCENE_MODE_NIGHT_PORTRAIT

➤ SCENE_MODE_PARTY

➤ SCENE_MODE_PORTRAIT

➤ SCENE_MODE_SNOW

➤ SCENE_MODE_SPORTS

➤ SCENE_MODE_STEADYPHOTO

➤ SCENE_MODE_SUNSET

➤ SCENE_MODE_THEATRE

You see how to use scene mode later in the barcode example program. It is best to use an appropriate scene mode, when available, for the type of image being captured if that is known, because you can expect that the camera manufacturer made reasonable choices for the scene type. For example, SCENE_MODE_FIREWORKS would turn off the flash and set for maximum exposure time. SCENE_MODE_PARTY would turn flash to FLASH_MODE_RED_EYE and set focus settings to take portraits and group shots.

GPS

Images captured and stored in files in Android have embedded GPS coordinates, which is useful for integration with map applications on the web. The setGps* calls enable you to control the GPS values written to the images.

Color Effects

For entertainment purposes, some cameras allow the color values in the image to be manipulated in various ways, such as giving everything a sepia tone, or making it look like a photographic negative. These modes are of little use for the purposes of this chapter.

CREATING A SIMPLE BARCODE READER

Now it's time to have some fun and build an interesting image processing application. Image processing is much easier when your application is trying to interpret something that "wants" to be interpreted, and the most common thing that is designed to be interpreted with image processing techniques is a barcode. BarcodeReaderActivity is a complete application that captures a camera preview image, decodes it, and attempts to read an EAN-13 barcode (the most common kind of barcode) from it.

BarcodeReaderActivity includes four interesting features not previously discussed:

➤ Decoding the barcode

➤ Autofocus

➤ Processing — not just displaying — the camera preview image

➤ Detecting the barcode and extracting it for decoding

The following sections explore each of these features in turn.

Understanding Barcodes

You've seen barcodes on many products. The most common kind of barcode, the one-dimensional barcode, consists of a number of vertical black and white stripes. EAN-13 barcodes, which are officially called International Article Numbers (originally "International" was "European"), encode 13 decimal digits. They are a superset of the Universal Product Code (UPC) barcodes used in the United States, so the example barcode reader will work for UPC codes, too. Such barcodes are typically used to identify a product by number.

In EAN-13 barcodes, each of the 13 digits, except the first (discussed later), is encoded with seven vertical bars (referred to here and in code comments as *elementary bars*), each of which can be white or black. There's no spacing between bars, so two adjacent bars of the same color look like one wide bar. Each digit has two different encodings, one with even parity (that is, an even number of black stripes) and one with odd parity.

For example, the digit 0, in odd parity, is encoded with the pattern 0001101, where 0 stands for a white bar and 1 stands for a black bar. It is shown in Figure 12-2.

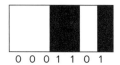

0 0 0 1 1 0 1

FIGURE 12-2: Odd parity barcode for zero

`BarcodeReader` keeps all the information describing EAN-13 barcodes in the `Ean13Barcode1D` class. The digit codes for the different odd parity digits are stored in a `HashMap`, as shown in Listing 12-9.

LISTING 12-9: Odd parity digit codes

```
/*  The odd parity left (character set A) barcodes for the ten
       digits are:
    0 = 3-2-1-1 = 0001101 = 0x0d
    1 = 2-2-2-1 = 0011001 = 0x19
    2 = 2-1-2-2 = 0010011 = 0x13
    3 = 1-4-1-1 = 0111101 = 0x3d
    4 = 1-1-3-2 = 0100011 = 0x23
    5 = 1-2-3-1 = 0110001 = 0x31
    6 = 1-1-1-4 = 0101111 = 0x2f
    7 = 1-3-1-2 = 0111011 = 0x3b
    8 = 1-2-1-3 = 0110111 = 0x37
    9 = 3-1-1-2 = 0001011 = 0x0b
*/
mhOddLeft = new HashMap<Integer, Character>();
mhOddLeft.put(0x0d, '0');
mhOddLeft.put(0x19, '1');
mhOddLeft.put(0x13, '2');
mhOddLeft.put(0x23, '4');
mhOddLeft.put(0x31, '5');
mhOddLeft.put(0x2f, '6');
mhOddLeft.put(0x3b, '7');
mhOddLeft.put(0x37, '8');
mhOddLeft.put(0x0b, '9');
```

VARIABLE NAMING CONVENTION

A brief note on the variable naming conventions used in this and later code: the initial prefix m *means the variable is a member variable or field, and the following lowercase characters indicate the type of the variable, using* n *for* int, sz *for* string, b *for* byte, h *for* HashMap, *and so on.*

An EAN-13 barcode consists of two groups of six individual digit barcodes, one after the other, with some additional decoration marking the beginning, middle, and end of the barcode. `Ean13Barcode1D` describes the overall structure of the barcode in public static final variables:

A three-bar pattern at the beginning and end, consisting of a black bar, a white bar, and a black bar:

```
public static final int LEFT_WIDTH = 3; // number of elementary bars in the
                                         // left-side pattern
public static final int RIGHT_WIDTH = 3; // number of elementary bars in
                                         // the right-side pattern
```

A five-bar pattern in the middle, consisting of alternating white and black bars, and beginning and ending with black bars, that separates the two groups of six digits:

```
public static final int MID_WIDTH = 5; // number of elementary bars in the
                                        // middle pattern
```

The entire barcode is guaranteed to have some white space surrounding it. That is why, when you are searching for the barcode in the image, you can look for some white space followed by the black-white-black pattern at the beginning and end.

The following are three complications in EAN-13 barcodes:

➤ An implied first digit, which is encoded in the parity of the digits in the left half of the pattern (but the first digit in the left half is always guaranteed to have odd parity).

➤ The last digit in the barcode is a check digit whose value is determined by a simple computation based on the other digits.

➤ The right half of the pattern is encoded exclusively with odd parity, and the white and black bars are reversed.

The following sections look at how `Ean13Barcode1D` handles each of these complications.

Parity and Implied First Digit

When you are decoding the left half of the barcode, you detect and record the parity of each digit in the `decodeBarcode()` method. At this point, *bStripes* is a binary encoding of the image (0 = black, 1 = white) and *nCurr* is an index into *bStripes* for the position of the current stripe you are interpreting:

```
for (int nDigit = 0; nDigit < LEFT_DIGITS; nDigit++) {
    int nSum = 0;
    // build an index into digitCodes for this pattern
    for (int l = 0; l < DIGIT_WIDTH; l++) {
        nSum = nSum * 2 + bCompressed[nCurr++];
    }
    if (nDigit == 0) {
        // in EAN-13 the first digit always has odd parity
        if (mhOddLeft.containsKey(nSum)) {
            sbBarcode.append(mhOddLeft.get(nSum));
            nLeftParity = 1;
        } else {
```

```
                            // the first digit didn't match any of the codes
                            return null;
                        }
                    } else {
                        // determine the parity of the digit
                        if (mhOddLeft.containsKey(nSum)) {
                            sbBarcode.append(mhOddLeft.get(nSum));
                            nLeftParity = (nLeftParity * 2) + 1;
                        } else if (mhEvenLeft.containsKey(nSum)) {
                            sbBarcode.append(mhEvenLeft.get(nSum));
                            nLeftParity = nLeftParity * 2;
                        } else {
                            return sbBarcode.toString();
                        }
                    }
                }
```

decodeBarcode() works by first building an index in the *nSum* integer that encodes the bit pattern from the image, using 1 for a black stripe and 0 for a white stripe. The digit 0, encoded in odd parity, will have the bit pattern 0001101, as shown in Figure 12-2, and will be encoded in *nSum* as the hex value 0x0d. decodeBarcode() then looks up the encoded value in *mhOddLeft* (the odd parity encoded digits) and *mhEvenLeft* (the even parity encoded digits). If the encoded value can't be found in either HashMap, it returns what it did find.

When decodeBarcode() finds the encoded value it records the parity in the *nLeftParity* integer value. After all the digits in the left pattern are read, *nLeftPattern* is used to find the encoded implied digit, which decodeBarcode() appends to the beginning of the barcode:

```
                if (mhFirstDigit.containsKey(nLeftParity)) {
                    sbBarcode.insert(0, mhFirstDigit.get(nLeftParity));
                } else {
                    return sbBarcode.toString();
                }
```

Once again, if decodeBarcode() can't find the encoded parity it returns what barcode it did find. The philosophy behind Ean13Barcode1D, as a demonstration program, is to return whatever portion of the barcode that has been read, in order to give the user feedback on what is being read. This makes for a better demonstration of barcode reading since the user can see some of the process of barcode reading. In a "real" barcode reading program you would return the complete barcode only after it has been read and the check digit verified.

The Check Digit

The check digit is computed in the verifyCheckDigit() method, which is called from decodeBarcode(), as shown in Listing 12-10.

LISTING 12-10: verifyCheckDigit

```
private static boolean verifyCheckDigit(String digits) {
    // compute check digit
    // add odd digits
```

```
            int nOddSum = 0;
            for (int i=1; i<digits.length()-1; i+=2) {
                nOddSum += Character.digit(digits.charAt(i), 10);
            }
            // add even digits
            int nEvenSum = 0;
            for (int i=0;i<digits.length()-1; i+=2) {
                nEvenSum += Character.digit(digits.charAt(i), 10);
            }
            // compute odd digit sum * 3 + even digit sum;
        int nTotal = nOddSum*3 + nEvenSum;
            // check digit is this sum subtracted from the next higher
            // multiple of 10
            int checkDigit = (nTotal/10 + 1) * 10 - nTotal;
        return Character.digit(
                    digits.charAt(digits.length()-1), 10) == checkDigit;
        }
```

The computation is specified by the design of EAN-13 barcodes. Sums of the odd and even digits are formed, and then the odd sum is multiplied by three and added to the even sum. The difference between the next higher multiple of 10 and this total is then computed. This will be a digit from 0–9. This should match the last digit in the barcode. If it does, ReadBarcode sets a checkmark in the barcode display:

```
        mTextViewResult.setText(szBarcode);
        mbFoundBarcode = Ean13Barcode1D.verifyCheckDigit(szBarcode);
        mCheckBoxResult.setChecked(mbFoundBarcode);
```

Right Half of the Barcode

The right half of the barcode is decoded similarly to the left half, with two differences: 1) In the right half white and black bars are reversed; 2) The right half uses odd parity exclusively. This simplifies the code quite a bit; all you have to do is encode the white bars as 1 and the black bars as 0, and then use the odd parity lookup table:

```
            // nCurr points to the end of the left digits
            nCurr += MID_WIDTH;
            for (int nDigit = 0; nDigit < RIGHT_DIGITS; nDigit++) {
                int nSum = 0;
                // build an index into digitCodes for this pattern
                for (int n = 0; n < DIGIT_WIDTH; n++) {
                    nSum = nSum * 2 + (1 - bCompressed[nCurr++]);
        }
                if (mhOddLeft.containsKey(nSum)) {
                    sbBarcode.append(mhOddLeft.get(nSum));
                } else {
                    // the first digit didn't match any of the codes
                    return sbBarcode.toString();
                }
            }
```

Once again, if decodeBarcode() doesn't find a match, it just returns the partial match for display.

Now it's time to take a step back to look at controlling the camera again, and discuss autofocus, which is crucial to processing a barcode.

Autofocus

To capture a good image of a barcode for processing, you must ensure it is in focus. Unlike camera properties like preview size or flash, autofocus is not a property you simply set and forget, putting the camera in autofocus mode indefinitely. It is, instead, a command you send to the camera, which eventually completes. What is actually happening during autofocus is the camera is physically moving the lens in and out and measuring the sharpness of the image it captures in certain defined areas (these areas can be controlled, on some cameras, by setting the focus areas using `setFocusAreas()`). This goes on for a while, after which the camera reports whether its measurements indicate it achieved good focus.

`BarcodeReaderActivity` initiates autofocus in its `onResume()` method, passing it *mReadBarcode*, which implements `Camera.AutoFocusCallback`:

```
mCamera.autoFocus(mReadBarcode);
```

`ReadBarcode`'s implementation of the callback is very simple:

```
@Override
public void onAutoFocus(boolean success, Camera camera) {
    if (!success) {
        // try again
        camera.autoFocus(this);
    } else {
        mnFocused = 5;
    }
}
```

When the camera calls the callback, it has focused the camera or not, as shown in the state of the *success* variable. The autofocus callback restarts autofocus if it failed. If it succeeded, it sets a variable (*mnFocused*) that will count down the number of attempts it makes to read a barcode. The assumption is that as the user moves the camera around, the barcode will stay in focus for a while, so you make several attempts to read it, giving the user time to position the barcode reader just right.

`onPreviewCallback()` is discussed in more detail soon. But just to complete the discussion of autofocus, the last thing `onPreviewCallback()` does is to start autofocus again:

```
} finally {
    if (--mnFocused == 0) {
        camera.autoFocus(this);
    }
}
```

mnFocused is decremented so it tries recognize the barcode a few times before giving up and starting autofocus again. (The camera will keep calling `onCameraPreview()` and you will keep processing images so long as *mnFocused* is non-zero.)

So, the overall process works like this:

1. Start autofocus.

2. When autofocus completes: if it failed, start it again, otherwise make several attempts to detect a barcode.

3. When it's done trying to detect the barcode, restart autofocus.

STOPPING CALLBACKS

Whenever you release the camera you should manually stop all callbacks — otherwise, it's possible that the callback will be called after the camera is released and you will get a hard-to-interpret RuntimeException. ManageCameraActivity *does this in its implementation of* onPause:

```
mCamera.autoFocus(null);
mCamera.setErrorCallback(null);
mCamera.setOneShotPreviewCallback(null);
mCamera.setPreviewCallback(null);
mCamera.setPreviewCallbackWithBuffer(null);
mCamera.setZoomChangeListener(null);
mCamera.release();
mCamera = null;
```

Note that it is safe to set the callbacks to null without first determining whether they have been set to anything else.

Using the Camera Preview Image and Detecting the Barcode

Android calls onPreviewFrame() when a camera preview image is ready for processing. This is set in the onResume() method of BarcodeReaderActivity:

```
mCamera.setPreviewCallback(mReadBarcode);
```

Please keep in mind two things about onPreviewFrame():

➤ The camera preview size, camera orientation, and even camera can vary from call to call, for example when the user changes the orientation of the device. So, it's important not to assume that the last preview image has anything in common with the current preview image.

➤ All preview image formats are very simple layouts of pixels without compression. The preview format is under control of the program that controls the camera, and it may be possible to choose a format to make your work easier. However, only the NV21 format is supported by all cameras, so unless you have a good reason to use a different format, you should use NV21, which is the default format.

Let's take a look at the NV21 format, because it is so important. It is based on the YUV color space, which is a relic of the conversion from black and white to color television — the Y in YUV is the original black and white television brightness value. U and V were added to the black and white signal so that color could be encoded. To be compatible with black and white televisions, the Y signal was sent first, and then the U and V signals were sent, the signal being structured so existing black and white televisions would ignore the U and V signals and just show Y. Color televisions could decode the U and V signals and use them, together with Y, to create a red, green, and blue (RGB) color value, which they would then show.

NV21 is structured much like those early color television signals. Y comes first, then U and V, at reduced resolution. (The resolution for U and V doesn't have to be as high as for Y because the human eye is less sensitive to changes in color than changes in brightness. By providing U and V at reduced resolution, NV21 saves space with little to no observable loss in image quality.)

Figure 12-3 shows NV21 layout in detail. The format consists of an array of N×N U pixels, followed by an N/2×N/2 array of pairs of V and U pixels, V coming first in each pair. All pixels are stored as 8-bit unsigned bytes with minimum value 0x00 and maximum value 0xff.

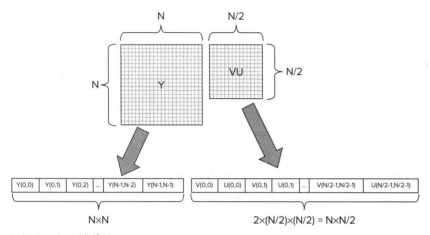

FIGURE 12-3: NV21 layout

In barcode reading you are not interested in color (using the color values from the camera preview image is discussed in the next chapter), so you can ignore the VU matrix and treat the camera preview image as an N×N unsigned byte array.

Take a look at the code in ReadBarcode's implementation of onPreviewFrame() that makes use of the input camera preview image. It begins by using the camera parameters to determine the dimensions of the preview image:

```
Parameters cameraParameters = camera.getParameters();
int imageFormat = cameraParameters.getPreviewFormat();
if (imageFormat == ImageFormat.NV21) {
    Size size = camera.getParameters().getPreviewSize();
```

In the barcode reading program you try to be as flexible as possible, allowing the user to read the barcode horizontally or vertically. This means you have to read the barcode either as a series of columns or as a series of rows from the image. The code to read the image values horizontally (column-wise) is straightforward:

```
int i = 0;
for (nCol = nStartCol; nCol < nEndCol; nCol++) {
    int nValue = 0xff & (int) data[nRowOffset + nCol];
    nValues[i++] = nValue;
}
```

The only interesting thing about this code is the transformation of the input byte value into an integer by a bitwise AND with the mask 0xff. The reason for this is that an image byte value runs from 0 (hex 0x00) (black) to 255 (hex 0xff) (white). Byte values in Java are signed, so if you were to use this value as a byte value directly, any value greater than 128 (0x80) would be sign-extended into a negative number — in other words, brightness values greater than 128 would be misinterpreted. By performing a bitwise AND with 0xff you remove the sign extension bits and convert the image byte into an unsigned integer value. For example, if the image value was 0xff this would be interpreted in Java as the signed byte value –1, and converted to the integer value –1, or 0xffffffff. Applying a bitwise AND of this with 0xff gives the integer value 0x000000ff, or 255, which is the value you want for computation.

You'll get to the actual search for the barcode shortly. If the barcode is not found horizontally, you repeat the search vertically, taking the image values by rows:

```
i = 0;
for (nRow = nStartRow; nRow < nEndRow; nRow++) {
    int nValue = 0xff & (int) data[nColOffset + nRow
            * width];
    nValues[i++] = nValue;
}
```

You may have noticed the odd (unusable) calls to DebugImage in this method. Those are discussed next.

Debugging Image Processing Programs on Android

For the most part, Android's excellent debugging tools — the emulator and the ability to step into programs running on Android devices, examine variables, and so on — work very well for image processing. However, it is almost impossible to debug an image processing program without controlling the images that are being processed. If you try to use the live images captured from a camera as input to the program, it is just too hard to ensure reliable, consistent input data. Also, sometimes it is necessary to input artificial images into image processing programs for testing. It is also very hard to debug image processing programs using the emulator because no live camera is available.

To do this, you need a method to capture good test images and then substitute them during test runs. onPreviewFrame() does this by using DebugImage. The methods in DebugImage enable you to capture the camera preview image and reuse it, or even substitute an artificial camera preview image for the one the camera would provide.

onPreviewFrame() uses two calls to DebugImage methods:

```
boolean bWrite = false, bRead = false;
if (bWrite) {
    DebugImage.writeGrayImage(data, width, height,
            "barcode.png");
}
if (bRead) {
    data = DebugImage.readGrayImage(width, height,
            "barcode.png");
}
```

The two methods from DebugImage (both static, making them easy to drop into a program) are:

```
boolean writeGrayImage(byte[] bData, int nWidth,
                    int nHeight, String szFilename)
```

and

```
byte[] readGrayImage(Integer nWidth, Integer nHeight, String szFilename)
```

You can use the `writeGrayImage()` method to write a gray image of your choice to the Android filesystem. All you have to do is set a breakpoint before the conditional test of *bWrite* and set the value to true, using the debugger, when you have a good test image (you could also do this by setting the value to true in the application source, or through a debug button, of course). Once the image is in the Android filesystem, you can upload it to a PC and examine it in detail, or even modify it to produce optimal test data. You can substitute this image for the camera preview image simply by setting the *bRead* value to true, either in the debugger or by editing the code.

It should be noted that these routines are anything but fast. They are intended to be used only for debugging purposes. Reading and writing images using these routines is much slower than capturing and displaying much higher-resolution images on a device, or writing them to the SD card. This is because the Android routines for writing compressed images to the SD card have been optimized, with hardware support.

Note that `writeGrayImage()` and `readGrayImage()` read and write only the gray component of the NV21 camera preview image. The next chapter discusses dealing with the color components.

Now let's return to discussing the detection and decoding of the barcode.

Detecting the Barcode

The `EAN13Barcode1D` class provides a method, `searchForBarcode()`, which searches for the barcode in a one-dimensional array of image values. `searchForBarcode()` makes use of some important image processing concepts to find the barcode:

➤ Local thresholding

➤ Image processing at multiple resolutions

Look at how these concepts are applied in `searchForBarcode()`.

The human eye does a remarkable job of compensating for variations in illumination, so that you can look at a scene that is brightly lit, say, by the sun, yet still make out objects in shadow — even though orders of magnitude more light is reaching the eye from an object in the sun than from an object in shadow. It does such a good job, in fact, that you are unaware of how much variation there is in a scene. But when you try to teach a computer to do image processing it becomes obvious what an incredible job our eyes are doing. A camera captures images with a very narrow range of image values (0 to 255), which are linearly distributed. When you look at an image captured by a camera, even an image of a white sheet of paper, you will see remarkable variation in brightness as the result of changes in illumination, even though the paper looks perfectly white to your eyes. You'll need to find ways to ignore these unimportant variations in brightness in order to find the things you're looking for.

Cameras like the ones used in Android devices compensate for brightness changes in a scene by changing the exposure time of the sensor capturing the image — longer exposure gives more light sensitivity. You may have noticed the camera taking a second or so to adjust this when changing from photographing a brightly lit scene to a darker one. But this just affects the overall scene brightness; you need to do more to deal with variations in brightness within the scene. For example, one side of a barcode can be quite a bit brighter than the other side. If you were to use a constant definition of "white" and "black" across the barcode, you might well be unable to distinguish the bars on one side or the other, because they would appear all white or all black.

searchForBarcode() uses a simple local averaging technique for comparing each pixel's brightness with the average brightness of the pixels around it to determine whether it is a white or black bar. If the brightness is greater than the local average, it is white; if not, it is black. The local average is computed efficiently by first computing the cumulative sum of the pixels in a row:

```
int[] nCumulativeSum = new int[nValues.length];
nCumulativeSum[0] = nValues[0];
for (int i = 1; i < nValues.length; i++) {
    nCumulativeSum[i] = nCumulativeSum[i - 1] + nValues[i];
}
```

nCumulativeSum[i] then contains the sum of pixels 0, 1, ..., i. To compute the sum of any series of pixels, say from *i+1* to *j*, all you need to do is to compute the difference between *nCumulativeSum[j]* and *nCumulativeSum[i]*. So to compute the average value of the pixels around a given pixel *i*, all you have to do is take the difference between appropriate values in *nCumulativeSum* and divide by the number of pixels in the average. This gives a simple, fast way to compute the local threshold:

```
int nPixelValue = nPixelSum / nPixCount;
int nLocalAverage = (nCumulativeSum[nEnd] - nCumulativeSum[nStart])
        / (nEnd - nStart);
if (nPixelValue > nLocalAverage) {   .
    bCompressed[j++] = 0;
} else {
    bCompressed[j++] = 1;
}
```

The other image processing concept that is being used in searchForBarcode() is processing the data at multiple resolutions. You do not know how close the barcode is to the camera. To adjust for this, you compress the image row into a series of white or black elementary bars (0 or 1 values), using local thresholding, taking first one pixel per elementary bar, then two pixels per elementary bar, and so on. This is done in a straightforward fashion:

```
// this is the number of pixels we look left and right to determine
// the local average.
final int LOCAL_THRESH = 32;
for (int nPixelsPerBar = 1;
    nPixelsPerBar < nValues.length / TotalWidth;
    nPixelsPerBar++) {
    int nPixVal = 0, nPixCount = 0, j = 0;
    byte[] bCompressed = new byte[nValues.length];
    for (int i = 0; i < nValues.length; i++) {
        nPixVal += nValues[i];
        nPixCount++;
        if (nPixCount == nPixelsPerBar) {
            int nEnd = Math.min(nValues.length - 1,
```

```
                                              i + LOCAL_THRESH);
                    int nStart = Math.max(0, i - LOCAL_THRESH);
                    … the code for computing bCompressed goes here …
                    nPixVal = 0;
                    nPixCount = 0;
                }
            }
```

The scan for the barcode start is very simple — you simply look for the pattern "00101" in the *bCompressed* array (the black-white-black bar pattern at the beginning of the barcode will always be preceded by some white space). On finding it, you look for the corresponding pattern ("10100") at the position corresponding to the barcode end. If you find both patterns, you attempt to decode the barcode.

Using all this code you can scan a barcode like the one in Figure 12-4.

9 771473 968012 >

FIGURE 12-4: Sample barcode

TRY THIS

Select the Barcode button and point the camera at the barcode in Figure 12-4.

Although this method shows some basic image processing concepts, is very fast, and works for well-behaved barcode images, it is far from perfect. The barcode is assumed to be positioned so that its white and dark elementary bars are all exactly the same integral width, and start, approximately, at an integral position in the image. Neither of these assumptions may be true — especially the assumption that the elementary bars are all the same width. When the paper the barcode pattern is printed on is not perpendicular to the line of sight from the camera, the elementary bars at one end of the barcode will be wider than the other. This is especially true because you expect the camera to be quite close to the barcode when scanning. In other words, you need to take into account perspective distortion of the barcode.

The best place to go for further understanding of how to process barcodes is the Zxing Google code site (http://code.google.com/p/zxing/). The code there not only handles perspective distortion and other image processing issues correctly and efficiently, but it also handles a very wide variety of barcodes, including both one-dimensional and two-dimensional codes. And it has implementations of barcode scanning for Android, J2ME, and many other platforms. This code has become the open source standard for barcode scanning — you've probably already used it on your Android device.

SUMMARY

In this chapter you learned how to build an `Activity` that controls the camera, including camera selection, zoom, focus, and other hardware camera parameters. The `Activity` used the camera preview to show the camera image, and you saw how to control the camera's autofocus and how to capture the preview image and use it in a simple barcode recognition program. You also learned about the structure of the NV21 format, which is Android's default preview image format, and the design of EAN-13 barcodes.

The next chapter delves further into image processing, describing how image processing programs are structured, and introduces JJIL, a library designed for image processing on mobile devices. You'll learn how to use JJIL to build image processing programs. The chapter concludes with an Android logo recognition program, which shows how to start with the color preview image, turn it into a form useful for processing, detect pixels of a certain color, extract regions of those pixels, pick out the most likely Android logo by size and color, and display its position — all quickly enough to track the logo as the user moves the device.

13

Image-Processing Techniques

WHAT'S IN THIS CHAPTER?

➤ Explaining how image-processing programs work

➤ Using JJIL to do image processing

➤ Example image-processing pipelines

In Chapter 12 you learned how to access and control Android's camera and to capture and process images. But there is much more to image processing than merely knowing how to capture images. Techniques have been developed over decades for dealing with a wide variety of problems in image processing, and these techniques can be applied directly to image processing in Android, with some care. This chapter shows you how to employ these techniques, first by describing the structure of image-processing programs in general, and then by illustrating image-processing program development with example programs.

THE STRUCTURE OF IMAGE-PROCESSING PROGRAMS

Image-processing programs have a characteristic structure that is driven by the need to transform large input images into a much smaller collection of meaningful results. The designers of image-processing programs take advantage of this characteristic structure in two ways: first, by designing data and control structures that match this characteristic structure, and, second, by developing algorithms that can be used again and again in different image-processing programs.

The Image-Processing Pipeline

Image-processing programs are generally structured as an image-processing pipeline: that is, they operate as a series of steps on images, starting with the input image, and at each stage transforming the image into a more useful — and often, smaller — image, or possibly into a different data structure. For example, in an Android image-processing program you may start with an input image in the NV21 color image format, transform that image into an RGB image, make some measurement (for example, of white balance) on that image, apply that measurement to the RGB image to produce a new RGB image (for example, using the white-balance measurement to do color correction), and then do further processing to extract some object of interest.

With the image-processing pipeline it is possible to consider each step as a separate unit, to make sure it is doing the right thing, and to swap in other steps to improve performance. In the color correction example just mentioned, one white-balance measurement can be substituted for another with little to no impact on the other stages except for, possibly, improved performance.

Common Image-Processing Operations

Broadly speaking, two different types of image-processing operations exist: those that take an image as input and produce a new image, and those that take an image and produce a different type of data structure. This section looks at the different kinds of each of these operations, taking them roughly in the order from the simplest computations to the most complex. You will often see them applied in this order in image pipelines because you want to apply the simplest operations early, when the image is large, reserving the more complex operations for later, when the amount of data has been reduced.

Image-to-Image Operations

Point operations apply a mathematical operation to the individual image pixels. Examples are:

➤ **Thresholding:** A simple threshold operation assigns 0 to values less than a certain value, called the threshold, and 1 to values greater than the threshold. You used thresholding in Chapter 12 to change the input image values (which ranged in value from 0 to 255) to binary values for recognizing the barcode. Figure 13-1 shows a thresholding operation.

FIGURE 13-1: Thresholding an image

➤ **Histogram equalization:** Histogram equalization is a way of improving image contrast. A *histogram* is a frequency count of pixel values. Images with poor contrast tend to have histograms that are "bunched up" in a small portion of the potential image values. An example is shown in Figure 13-2. In the original image the strawberry has low contrast, with pixel values only in the midrange, as the histogram shows. Histogram equalization reassigns pixel values so the histogram is stretched out over the full range of pixel values. The resulting image has much higher contrast, and it is easier to pick out features that may be of interest, such as the seeds.

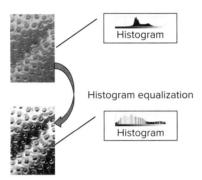

FIGURE 13-2: Histogram equalization

➤ **Conversion:** *Conversion* operations are point operations of a special kind: you take an image of one type and convert it to another type without interpreting the contents of the image pixels in any other way. For example, you might convert an Android NV21 color image into an RGB color image, or convert an RGB color image into a gray image. Conversion operations are usually quite fast and can be implemented with table lookup or heavily optimized calculation. For example, the calculation used to convert the NV21 image, which represents colors with YUV (input integer values nY, nU, and nV), to the RGB color space (output integer values nR, nG, and nB), used in calculation, is:

```
int nC = nY - 16;
 int nD = nU - 128;
 int nE = nV - 128;
 int nR = Math.max(0, Math.min(255, (( 298 * nC             + 409 * nE + 128) >> 8)));
 int nG = Math.max(0, Math.min(255, (( 298 * nC - 100 * nD - 208 * nE + 128) >> 8)));
 int nB = Math.max(0, Math.min(255, (( 298 * nC + 516 * nD           + 128) >> 8)));
```

You learn more about the NV21 image later in this chapter.

➤ **Reduction:** I *reduction* operations you reduce the size of the image by a constant factor, for example by averaging 2×2 square pixel areas to halve the image width and height. These operations are frequently optimized with mathematical tricks like the one used to compute the local threshold in barcode detection in Chapter 12. The cumulative sum of pixels was calculated so you could calculate the sum of pixels from $i+1$ to j just by subtracting `nCumulativeSum[i]` from `nCumulativeSum[j]`.

➤ **Spatial transformation:** *Spatial transformation* operations rearrange the positions of the pixels without changing their values, for example by rotating or stretching them. You can implement these operations efficiently using table lookups.

➤ **Filtering:** *Filtering* operations apply a two-dimensional mathematical filter to enhance some feature of interest, or to filter out some unwanted artifact. These operations include edge detection, smoothing, noise reduction, contrast enhancement, and so on. There is a vast literature on these operations, which lend themselves to mathematical as well as computational analysis and optimization.

➤ **Grouping:** *Grouping* operations are an important step toward reducing the image into a small collection of features, but they still produce an image as output. An example is connected components, which labels an input binary image so that two pixels have the same value only if there is a connected path between them in the input. These operations tend to be relatively expensive, and are applied only after other, less expensive, operations have been applied to reduce the image size.

Next you look at operations that transform an image into another type of data structure. This is a key step in extracting useful information from an image. These operations do not naturally fall into groups, so you will simply see some important examples.

Image-to-Object Operations

Perhaps the most important image-to-object operation is computing a *histogram*. A histogram is a frequency count of pixel values. For gray byte images it is just an array of 256 integer values, with value i equal to the number of occurrences of pixel value i. Histograms are used to enhance the contrast of an image and to choose appropriate values for thresholding.

An important operation for finding objects in an image is *Hough transform*. This operation performs a spatial transformation of an image of a special kind, which is designed to locate objects of a specific shape. The simplest, and original, Hough transform was designed to find lines in photographs from cloud chambers. Lines were parameterized in a two-dimensional array by slope and y-intercept. Each pixel that passed a threshold test was mapped to all possible lines that could pass through that point, and array elements corresponding to those lines were incremented. The peaks in the array corresponded to the lines in the image. Hough transforms have been developed to detect all sorts of shapes.

After labeling an image with connected components, the next step is usually to extract descriptions of the connected regions with *feature extraction*. This algorithm produces a list of the connected regions in the image and measures their area, center, perimeter, and possibly other useful features. You can use these features to determine where a particular object you are looking for is located.

Because these image-processing operations are so important and do the same kinds of processing, it makes sense to organize them with data and control structures that make them easy to use and develop. I have built such a library, called Jon's Java Imaging Library (JJIL), which is the subject of the next section.

Jon's Java Imaging Library (JJIL)

JJIL has been optimized specifically for image processing on devices where computation and memory are in limited supply, such as Android devices. JJIL is open source and available at `http://code.google.com/p/jjil/` and includes all the image-processing operations described in the preceding sections. This section explores the structure of JJIL.

Image

Two core concepts in JJIL are defined in `jjil.core`: `Image` and `PipelineStage`. An `Image` is an object that stores image data and has a definite width and height. `Image`s also support access to their data as an array. A number of different types of images exist: gray (8-bit, 16-bit, and 32-bit pixel); color (8-bit pixel); and complex (32-bit pixel). More specialized images also exist, such as a sub-image type for taking a portion of an input image and keeping track of the location of that portion.

All Image types support these methods:

➤ The constructor `Image(int cWidth, int cHeight)` creates a new image of the given width and height.

➤ `Image clone()` returns a "deep" copy of the image, that is, one that actually creates a copy of the image pixels. Note that images processed in pipeline stages are usually passed using a "shallow" copy, allowing reuse of their pixels, for efficiency in space.

➤ `int getHeight()` returns the image height.

➤ `int getWidth()` returns the image width.

Image types also support a method for accessing their pixels. To make this as efficient as possible, the image data can be accessed directly as a one-dimensional array. This method is called `get-Data()`. For example, `Gray8Image` (an image supporting signed 8-bit image pixels) implements this method:

```
byte[] getData()
```

PipelineStage

A `PipelineStage` is an image-to-image operation. It takes a single image as a parameter and produces another image as output. Other parameters must be supplied through the constructor or auxiliary methods. The input and output types of `PipelineStage` are both `Image`; this makes it easier to compose multiple stages into a sequence (especially in the absence of generic types), but makes it necessary to check parameter types at run time.

A `PipelineStage` must implement this method:

```
void push(Image imageIn)
```

It may also implement these methods, or it can use the default implementations:

```
boolean isEmpty()
Image getFront()
```

The semantics of these methods are:

➤ `push(Image)`: Takes an `Image` as input. After verifying that it is of the right type (for example, `Gray8Image` or `RgbImage`), do whatever processing is required for this input. The output, if any, is saved so it can be retrieved using `getFront()` and the presence of an output, if there is one, is set so it can be retrieved using `isEmpty()`.

➤ `isEmpty()`: Returns a boolean value indicating whether or not an output is available from the `PipelineStage`. Each pipeline stage is allowed to return zero, one, or any other number of outputs given an input. The user of the `PipelineStage` must test for the presence of an output using `isEmpty()` before attempting to retrieve it — otherwise, an exception is generated when `getFront()` is called.

➤ `getFront()`: Returns the next `Image` resulting from processing an input using `push()`. When `getFront()` is called, the current image is "popped" from the `PipelineStage`'s internal storage; calling `getFront()` again returns a new image, if there is one (which can be determined using `isEmpty()`). If there is no image, `IllegalStateException` is thrown. When more than one image is provided by a pipeline stage, each new image is retrieved with a new call to `getFront()`, after using `isEmpty()` to detect the image's presence.

In addition to these public methods, `PipelineStage` implements a protected method to help the implementer of `PipelineStage`-derived classes. This is:

```
setOutput(Image imageResult)
```

This method is used in the common case where a `push()` operation returns a single `Image`. The implementer of `push()` calls `setOutput(Image imageResult)` to set the output of the `push()` operation to *imageResult*, and then the default implementations of `isEmpty()` and `getFront()` will correctly provide the image to the caller.

A complete example (from `jjil.algorithm`) of a simple `PipelineStage` is shown in the following code. It implements a conversion operation, converting a signed byte image (a `Gray8Image`) into a 32-bit image (a `Gray32Image`):

```
        public class Gray82Gray32 extends PipelineStage {
            /** Creates a new instance of Gray82Gray32 */
            public Gray82Gray32() {
            }
    /** Converts an 8-bit gray image into a 32-bit image by replicating,
         * changing the data range of the bytes from -128->127 to 0->255.
         *
         * @param image the input image.
         * @throws IllegalArgumentException if the input is not a
         * Gray8Image
         */
        public void push(Image image) throws IllegalArgumentException {
            if (!(image instanceof Gray8Image)) {
                throw new IllegalArgumentException(image.toString() + "" +
                    " should be a Gray8Image, but isn't");
            }
            Gray8Image gray = (Gray8Image) image;
            byte[] grayData = gray.getData();
            Gray32Image gray32 = new Gray32Image(image.getWidth(), image.getHeight());
            int[] gray32Data = gray32.getData();
            for (int i=0; i<gray.getWidth() * gray.getHeight(); i++) {
                /* Convert from signed byte value to unsigned byte for
                 * storage in the 32-bit image.
                 */
```

```
            int grayUnsigned = ((int)grayData[i]) - Byte.MIN_VALUE;
            /* Assign 32-bit output */
            gray32Data[i] = grayUnsigned;
        }
        super.setOutput(gray32);
    }
}
```

This `PipelineStage` implements only the `push()` method. It relies on the default implementations of `isEmpty()` and `getFront()`.

The first step in `push()` is to verify that the argument is of the right type. You must do this test at run time because all `PipelineStages` take `Image` parameters:

```
if (!(image instanceof Gray8Image)) {
    throw new IllegalArgumentException(image.toString() + "" +
        " should be a Gray8Image, but isn't");
}
```

After this test you can safely get a reference to the input parameter as a `Gray8Image`:

```
Gray8Image gray = (Gray8Image) image;
```

Having the `Gray8Image` reference enables you to access the data (pixels) in the image:

```
byte[] grayData = gray.getData();
```

You will need an output image to store the result. If the output was also a `Gray8Image`, the normal thing to do would be to reuse the input. (To save on memory, `PipelineStages` are allowed to modify their input. Callers should not assume the input will not be modified and must use `clone()` to make a copy of the input if they need to keep the original data.) But this output is a `Gray32Image`, not a `Gray8Image`. So, you must create a new image to hold the result:

```
Gray32Image gray32 = new Gray32Image(image.getWidth(), image.getHeight());
```

You can get a pointer to the output data just as you did with the input image:

```
int[] gray32Data = gray32.getData();
```

Now you will set the output pixels. The loop iterates over all pixels by treating them as one large array (note that, because the input and output images are the same size, there is no possibility of out-of-bounds access). You don't need to do the arithmetic needed to treat the image as a two-dimensional array because this is a point operation:

```
for (int i=0; i<gray.getWidth() * gray.getHeight(); i++) {
```

The actual conversion of an 8-bit signed value to a 32-bit integer adds an offset, so the minimum value in the signed pixel (that is, –128) maps to 0. As a convention, image-processing algorithms manipulate image data as unsigned integer values, with 0 representing black and 255 (in 8-bit image data) representing white. It simplifies some algorithms to map that special value to and from the minimum byte value:

```
int grayUnsigned = ((int)grayData[i]) - Byte.MIN_VALUE;
/* Assign 32-bit output */
gray32Data[i] = grayUnsigned;
```

Note that `Byte.MIN_VALUE = -128`, so the subtraction in the first statement actually adds 128 to the signed byte value after it is converted to integer.

The final step in the algorithm is to provide the output to the caller. You do this using the protected `setOutput()` method of `PipelineStage`:

```
super.setOutput(gray32);
```

You use the class as follows:

```
Gray8Image imGray8 = new Gray8Image(cWidth, cHeight);
/* ... initialize imGray8... */
Gray82Gray32 g8232 = new Gray82Gray32();
g8232.push(imGray8);
if (g8232.isEmpty()) {
    /* error, this should never happen */
}
Image imResult = g8232.getFront();
if (!(imResult instanceof Gray32Image)) {
    /* error, Gray82Gray32 returned wrong type */
}
Image imGray32 = (Gray32Image) imResult;
/* ... use imGray32 ... */
```

Now that you understand how to build image-to-image operations in JJIL, take a look at how they are assembled into image-processing pipelines using two JJIL control structures, `Sequence` and `Ladder`.

Sequence

A `Sequence` is just what its name implies, a sequence of image-to-image operations, in other words, a sequence of `PipelineStage` operations. `Sequence` is itself a `PipelineStage`, so `Images` can be passed through a series of image-processing algorithms simply by constructing the `Sequence`, and then using `push()` on the `Sequence`.

An example is shown in the following code. This sequence (from a barcode-reading system) converts a color image to gray by selecting the green component, crops the gray image, and then applies a horizontal Canny edge-detection operation to the result:

```
Sequence seq = new Sequence();
seq.add(new RgbSelect2Gray(RgbSelect2Gray.GREEN));
seq.add(new GrayCrop(dTopLeftX, dTopLeftY, cWidth, cHeight));
seq.add(new CannyHoriz(cCannyWidth));
seq.push(imageInput.clone());
if (seq.isEmpty()) {
    /* error -- no output from Canny */
}
Image imageResult = seq.getFront();
```

Once a `Sequence` is constructed, it can be used over and over to process images. The logic in the `Sequence` class's implementation of `push()` handles `isEmpty()` and `getFront()` properly so that if a `PipelineStage` produces more than one output, each output will be passed to later stages in the `Sequence`, so that a `Sequence` can produce as many outputs as are provided by the `PipelineStages` it is made from.

Ladder

Some image-processing pipelines are more complex than a simple linear order: they combine multiple images to produce a result. `Ladder` provides a simple mechanism for combining two `PipelineStages` (which may, of course, be `Sequences`) into a new `PipelineStage`. It takes the two `PipelineStage` objects as well as a special class derived from the abstract class `Ladder.Join`. It is constructed as follows:

```
Ladder(PipelineStage pipeFirst, PipelineStage pipeSecond, Ladder.Join join)
```

The class inheriting from `Ladder.join` must implement this method:

```
Image doJoin(Image imageFirst, Image imageSecond)
```

This method takes two images as parameters and combines them to produce a single image as an output.

`Ladder` is itself a `PipelineStage`. Its `push()`, method works as shown in Figure 13-3.

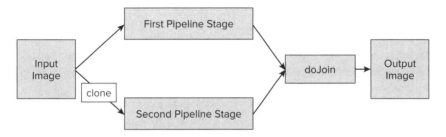

FIGURE 13-3: Ladder

As Figure 13-3 illustrates, `Ladder`'s implementation of `push()`, first copies the input image (using `clone()`) so that each `PipelineStage` gets its own copy. This way, one `PipelineStage` can freely alter the image data without affecting the other. After processing, the resulting `Image` objects are combined using the `doJoin()` operation.

The two `Sequences` do not need to have the same number of steps. One can do a series of operations on its input, while the other might do something much simpler. `Ladder` handles `isEmpty()` and `push()` properly in manipulating the outputs of its `PipelineStages`, but it does require that an output `Image` be available from one `PipelineStage` whenever one is available from the other `PipelineStage`, so the number of images resulting from a `push()`, operation on each pipeline must be the same. Otherwise it could not call `doJoin()` at the appropriate time.

As a simple example of the use of `Ladder`, suppose you want to detect barcodes in an image but have to do this on a device that does not have an autofocusing camera, like Android devices do. Somehow you have to sharpen the blurry image for better recognition. You might begin by requiring the user to scan the barcode horizontally, so the barcode edges are vertical, and then try to sharpen the vertical edges in the image. One way to do this is to use Gaussian blurring. The idea behind this technique is to blur the image horizontally, and then subtract the blurred image from the original image. The result is shown in Figure 13-4.

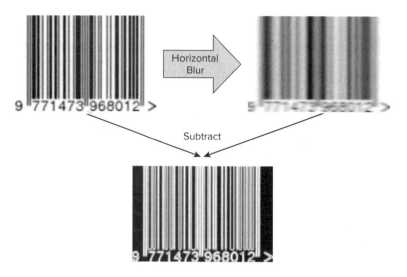

FIGURE 13-4: Enhancing an out-of-focus barcode

The code for this Ladder uses the GraySub class from jjil.algorithm, which implements doJoin() by taking the difference of its two Gray8Image inputs. It also makes use of GaussHoriz, which performs a horizontal blur operation on its Gray8Image, and copy(), a method which does a shallow copy (that is, not creating new pixels; it is not necessary to replicate the pixels because Ladder's push operation does that) of the input to the output. It also uses Copy, a null PipelineStage (note the case — this is different from the copy method mentioned previously), which just copies its input to its output, so that the blurred image can be subtracted from the original:

```
/* Create Copy PipelineStage */
        Copy c = new Copy();
        /* Create Gauss blur PipelineStage */
        GaussHoriz gh = new GaussHoriz(10);
        /* Create Join object */
        GraySub gs = new Gray8Sub();
        /* Create Ladder */
        Ladder lad = new Ladder(c, gh, gs);
```

Images can be deblurred using this Ladder simply by:

```
lad.push(imageIn);
if (lad.isEmpty()) {
/* error, no output */
}
Image imageOut = lad.getFront();
```

After using this Ladder for a while, you might notice that the output tends to be pretty dark. This is because you are subtracting two images with nearly the same value, giving a result close to 0 (black). A simple way to fix this is to perform histogram equalization, using GrayHistEq from jjil.algorithm. You just create a new Sequence, putting the Ladder first, and then adding a histogram equalization stage. The resulting code can be written as simply as:

```
/* Create Ladder */
Ladder lad = new Ladder(
```

```
      new Copy(),
      new GaussHoriz(10),
      new GraySub());
/* Create Sequence */
Sequence seq = new Sequence(lad);
seq.add(new GrayHistEq());
```

The entire sequence can be executed simply by:

```
seq.push(imageIn);
if (seq.isEmpty()) {
    // error, no output
}
Image imageOut = seq.getFront();
```

Of course, once a `Ladder` like this is constructed, it can be used over and over to process images, just as a `Sequence` can be.

Now that you understand the structure of JJIL, take a step back and see how you can integrate image processing using JJIL into an Android application designed to detect the Android logo.

JJIL and Detecting the Android Logo

As a simple example, write a program to detect the Android logo in an image, keying off the color of the logo and its compactness. Start with the simple `ReadBarcode` program you developed in Chapter 12 and show how JJIL can be integrated into the `onPreviewFrame()` method to show the position of the logo.

Start with a simple approach — too simple to work well, but it's a start:

1. Take a color image.

2. Look for pixels that are close to green.

3. Find the largest connected region of these pixels.

4. You've found the logo. Draw a green rectangle around it.

I've built a simple framework for developing this image-processing program in `DetectLogo`, shown in Figure 13-5. You'll use it as the basis for other image-processing programs you develop. It shows the camera preview image in the top window and provides another screen area for showing the processed image and any results. You use a class derived from `ImageView` (called `LogoView`) to show the image bitmap and any processed results — in this case, a green rectangle showing where you think the logo is.

Take a quick look at some of the tools for debugging image-processing programs. Just as, in the previous chapter, you provided a way to read and write gray images for debugging, here you provide a way to read and write color images in `DebugImages.writeNv21Image` and `DebugImages.readImage2Nv21`. They do the conversion necessary between the YUV color space used in Android and the RGB color space in which you do your processing. The actual code for converting between RGB and Android's YUV is given in `jjil.android.AndroidColors`.

FIGURE 13-5: DetectLogo

Look at the image-processing pipeline in DetectLogo and see how each of the preceding steps are implemented. The primary image processing is done in a pipeline you set up in the constructor:

```
RgbAbsDiffGray radg = new RgbAbsDiffGray(Color.GREEN);
Gray8Threshold g8t = new Gray8Threshold(-48, true);
mSeqThreshold = new Sequence(radg);
mSeqThreshold.add(g8t);
```

mSeqThreshold has two steps: use RgbAbsDiffGray to calculate the difference between the RGB pixel color and a target color, in this case green (because the Android logo is green). This is output as a Gray8Image where Byte.MIN_VALUE (that is, –128) represents zero difference, and Byte.MAX_ VALUE is the maximum difference. The next stage in the pipeline uses Gray8Threshold to threshold this image at –48, passing (that is, setting to 255) all pixels less than the threshold and setting pixels greater than the threshold to 0 (black). (The value –48 was chosen experimentally — it isolated the green portions of the image.) The result is similar to that shown in the bottom half of Figure 13-5: notice how the green parts of the Android logo as well as the green apples show up as blobs.

You process the input image just by pushing it into the pipeline:

```
mSeqThreshold.push(rgb);
Image imThresholded = mSeqThreshold.getFront();
```

Then you pass the resulting thresholded image to *mG8cc*, an object of type Gray8ConnComp, to compute the connected components of the image:

```
mG8cc.push(imThresholded);
```

Connected components is a key step in finding the logo (as it is in many image-processing programs) because it turns the image into a small collection of regions. Each blob of connected pixels in the input image ends up as a distinct item in the output of `Gray8ConnComp`. The outputs are also sorted in size (number of connected pixels) so you can choose the largest connected region and get its bounding rectangle very simply:

```
if (mG8cc.getComponentCount() > 0)
{
    Rect r = mG8cc.getComponent(0);
```

This bounding rectangle is passed to the `LogoView` object for display.

Before you get too far into the algorithm, try running the program as. You can run it in the book app by clicking the Detect Logo button. You may notice two things: 1) It's slow as molasses; 2) It doesn't work too well.

The fundamental problem with the speed of the program is that it is processing large images on a computer with limited processing power. Smartphones are nowhere near a modern desktop computer in terms of performance — nor should you expect them to be, given all the limitations the designers had to deal with. But, in fact, they do have enough processing power for image processing. If you look at the history of image processing, it was in the early 1980s that desktop PCs started taking a major role in image processing for real-time systems — and smartphones do have processing power comparable to, and in many cases greater than, what was available on a desktop PC in the early 1980s. What's the problem?

The problem, simply, is that the images you are processing are far too large for the task at hand. When image processing was taken over by desktop PCs in the 1980s they were processing images of size 512×512 or even 256×256 (which was all the electronic cameras then in use could produce). The Android camera produces images many times larger than that. You have to limit the image size to achieve the speed you need in an Android application.

Choose the Right Image Size

To detect the Android logo with a simple-minded approach, you do not need a high-resolution image. In fact, because you aren't looking at the internal structure of the logo, it does not matter if the image is a bit blurry — and a high-resolution image actually slows you down. So you need to reduce the image size as much as possible to process the image quickly.

You have a number of ways to do this. The most obvious, because you are using the image preview function of the camera, is to set an appropriate preview size. Change the `switchCamera()` method of `DetectLogoActivity` to the version used in `ManageCameraFasterActivity`:

```
Camera.Parameters cameraParameters = mCamera.getParameters();
List<Size> sizes = cameraParameters.getSupportedPreviewSizes();
int width = Integer.MAX_VALUE, height = Integer.MAX_VALUE;
for (int i=0; i<sizes.size(); i++) {
    Size s = sizes.get(i);
    if (s.width < width) {
        width = s.width;
        height = s.height;
    }
}
cameraParameters.setPreviewSize(width, height);
mCamera.setParameters(cameraParameters);
```

This code reads the preview sizes available for the camera and chooses the one with the smallest width, which generally gives you the smallest image size available.

Now `DetectLogoFaster` sets the camera preview size as small as possible, but it's still too big. Why? Well, with the device I'm using to test this code, the camera preview sizes available are 1280 × 720, 960 × 544, 800 × 400, 640 × 480, and 480 × 320. Even a 480 × 320 image has 153,600 pixels. That is a lot of pixels to process!

Another way to reduce the image size is with an image-processing operation, such as averaging. You'll do this in `DetectLogoFaster`. Take a look at the image-processing pipeline used there:

```
RgbAbsDiffGray radg = new RgbAbsDiffGray(Color.GREEN);
Gray8Reduce g8r;
try {
    g8r = new Gray8Reduce(2,2);
} catch (Error e) {
    return;
}
// then pass all pixels less than -84
Gray8Threshold g8t = new Gray8Threshold(-84, true);
// Now build the pipeline
mSeqThreshold = new Sequence(radg);
mSeqThreshold.add(g8r);
mSeqThreshold.add(g8t);
```

You saw how image-processing pipelines are built using JJIL previously, so, briefly, this pipeline first compares the color of each color pixel to green (of course, it's green because you're looking for the Android logo, which is green) using `RgbAbsDiffGray`, which computes the absolute value of the difference in color space between a specified color and each pixel. This is returned as a signed byte value, offset by –128. You then average this byte image, reducing its size by a factor of two horizontally and vertically, using `Gray8Reduce`. You then threshold the image with a fixed threshold (–84) with `Gray8Threshold`. This turns the green pixels to white, making them easy to detect, and sets everything else black, making it easy to ignore.

Now `DetectLogoFaster` is applying two techniques for increasing speed — selecting the closest image size appropriate to the task, and reducing the image size computationally. But it is still not fast enough. What else can you do?

It would be nice if the Android operating system gave us a good way to change the image size using hardware acceleration — but it doesn't, at least not now (hint, hint). You are left to your own devices.

Start by modifying the NV21 to the `RgbImage` conversion routine in `Nv212RgbImage` so that it doesn't create an `RgbImage` that is too big in the first place. Remember that the NV21 image subsamples the V and U color planes at half the resolution of the Y luminance plane. Change `getRgbImage()` to return an image that is sampled at the resolution of the color planes, instead of the luminance plane. `getRgbImageReduced()` does this:

```
public static RgbImage getRgbImageReduced(byte[] data, int width, int height) {
    RgbImage rgb = new RgbImage(width / 2, height / 2);
    int nVuOffset = width * height;
    for (int i = 0; i < height; i += 2) {
        for (int j = 0; j < width; j += 2) {
            int nY = 0xff & data[i * width + j];
            nY += 0xff & data[i * width + j + 1];
```

```
                nY += 0xff & data[(i + 1) * width + j];
                nY += 0xff & data[(i + 1) * width + j + 1];
                nY /= 4;
                int nV = 0xff & data[nVuOffset + (i / 2) * width + j];
                int nU = 0xff & data[nVuOffset + (i / 2) * width + j + 1];
                rgb.getData()[i / 2 * width / 2 + j / 2] = AndroidColors.yuv2Color(
                    nY, nU, nV);
            }
        }
        return rgb;
    }
```

The inner loop starts by taking the four luminance pixels that it will average to produce one output pixel and summing them in the variable `nY`. Dividing `nY` by four gives the average luminance value. It then accesses the color planes to set `nV` and `nU` to the color values. It then calls `yuv2Color()` to compute the RGB color value. By averaging the luminance value before calling `yuv2Color()`, the code avoids three relatively expensive color calculations — in other words, by moving the image reduction to the earliest stage possible, the total computation is reduced significantly.

With these changes, `DetectLogoFaster` works with reasonable speed — the update time is a second or less. However, if it was not fast enough, here are some other techniques to reduce the image size and increase processing speed:

➤ **Subsample without averaging:** In `getRgbImageReduced()` you take the time to average the four luminance pixels in each 2 × 2 block. You could simply use one of the four pixels without averaging. This may work in some situations, but the technique must be used with care because you may introduce *aliasing* into the subsampled image.

Figure 13-6 shows how aliasing can lead to incorrect results when you reduce the size of an image. The input image has a diagonal stripe pattern, with the stripes running from the bottom left to the top right. When you reduce the image size by properly averaging the input pixels, you get an image like that on the top right. The diagonal stripe pattern is still present. When you don't average the input pixels, you get an image like that on the bottom right. Here, the diagonal stripe pattern has been replaced by a cross-hatch pattern. The original image content has been replaced with something entirely different — some of the stripes run in the opposite direction.

You don't have to worry about this effect in the Android logo recognition program because you are not worried about the internal structure of the logo, so any feature introduced by subsampling won't affect your program. But if you were looking in detail at an image feature, for example to recognize text, aliasing would play an important role.

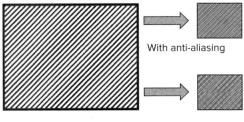

With anti-aliasing

Without anti-aliasing

FIGURE 13-6: Aliasing

➤ **Crop:** You can crop the image to a region of interest. This technique doesn't apply to the search for an Android logo in the image because you don't know where it is, but it is a key step in image processing where you can give direct feedback to the user on how to position the camera, as you can in Android. In effect, the barcode scanning program works this way — the user knows to position the camera so the barcode is in the middle of the image, keeping you from searching all over the image for it.

A simple way to give the user this feedback is to add a partially transparent layer in front of the camera preview image (that is, in front of the `Preview` object). (Remember, you can't actually draw on the camera preview image. You must add a layer in front of it to modify how it looks on the Android screen.) You could obscure the parts of the image you didn't want to process and outline the area of interest.

Of course, if you do this, you'll want to convert just the image pixels in the region of interest, which means you need a different version of `getRgbImage()`.

Now that `DetectLogoFaster` is fast enough, see what you can do to improve its importance, working in a new program called `DetectLogoBetter`.

Improving Reliability in Image Processing

The single most important thing image-processing engineers do to improve the reliability of their programs is to *control the environment*. That is, they set up cameras, illumination, and the objects they are taking pictures of so that the images vary as little as possible. Then, once the image-processing program is optimized for this situation, the same optimization will apply to all images in the future. Barcode detection uses this technique — the barcode symbol has been designed to make image processing of the barcode as easy as possible.

Unfortunately, with Android, you don't have much control over the imaging environment. Any Android image-processing program has to deal as best it can with variations in:

➤ Positioning of the camera

➤ The camera device itself

➤ Luminance

➤ Color balance

You're already allowing the users to position the camera as they like, and supporting different cameras, so take a look at some ways to handle luminance and color balance. You'll do this in a new version of `DetectLogoFaster` called `DetectLogoBetter`.

To deal with variations in luminance, you normalize the gray image so that the same threshold will apply regardless of the input illumination. In this way a dark and a bright image of the same scene will be recognized in the same way. You do this by adding a histogram equalization step to the code, using `Gray8HistEq`:

```
mSeqThreshold = new Sequence(radg);
mSeqThreshold.add(g8r);
mSeqThreshold.add(new Gray8HistEq());
mSeqThreshold.add(g8t);
```

This enables you to set the threshold to a fixed value and be reasonably confident that it will work.

The second thing you can do is to compensate for the color of the light in the scene. As you saw in Chapter 12, you can set the camera's white balance to automatically compensate for different kinds of light sources — incandescent, fluorescent, daylight, and so on. But, generally speaking, you do not want to burden the user with choosing the right setting to make your program work — and anyway, not all Android cameras support white balance. What can you do algorithmically?

Many techniques for automatic white balance exist, but, generally speaking, they come down to two steps:

1. Examine the scene and make a guess at the luminance color by looking at the light areas of the image. In most situations the brightest areas in the image are of something that is white, so if it appears to have a color that must be due to the color of the light.

2. Modify the color values to compensate.

You'll try a very simple approach to this in `DetectLogoBetter`. First, you find the brightest pixel in the image. Next, you adjust the color values before searching for the green pixels.

You use `FindBrightestPoint` to search for the brightest pixel. You compute the pixel brightness simply by summing the red, green, and blue values for the pixel. You then find the largest sum, saving the color of that pixel:

```
int nLuminance = Integer.MIN_VALUE;
for (int i = 0; i < rgb.getHeight(); i += mnSkipVert)
{
    for (int j = 0; j < rgb.getWidth(); j += mnSkipHoriz)
    {
        int cColor = rgb.getData()[i * rgb.getHeight() + j];
        int nThisLuminance = RgbVal.getR(cColor) + RgbVal.getG(cColor)
                + RgbVal.getB(cColor);
        if (nThisLuminance > nLuminance)
        {
            nLuminance = nThisLuminance;
            mcBrightestColor = cColor;
        }
    }
}
```

Note that `FindBrightestPoint` doesn't actually test every pixel in the image — you skip a number of pixels horizontally (*mnSkipHoriz*) and vertically (*mnSkipVert*). Scene illumination varies gradually from point to point so you will probably find the brightest pixel — or one near enough — this way, and you save a lot in computation. Typical values for *mnSkipHoriz* and *mnSkipVert* are 8, which means one in every 64 pixels (a little more than one percent) is sampled. The law of large numbers from statistics gives you a very good chance at making a reasonable guess even with such a small sample.

Next, you change `RgbAbsDiffGray` to take an additional parameter, which you can set after the pipeline is created, so you can set the white balance. The new `PipelineState` is

`RgbAbsDiffGrayWb`. When you build the image-processing pipeline you'll retain a reference to the `RgbAbsDiffGrayWb` so you can set the white balance value before processing:

```
mRadg = new RgbAbsDiffGrayWb(Color.GREEN);
g8r = new Gray8Reduce(2, 2);
Gray8Threshold g8t = new Gray8Threshold(-96, true);
mSeqThreshold = new Sequence(mRadg);
mSeqThreshold.add(g8r);
mSeqThreshold.add(new Gray8HistEq());
mSeqThreshold.add(g8t);
```

You push the input `RgbImage` to *mFbp*, an object of type `FindBrightestPoint`, to get the white-balance color. Then you set the white-balance color before processing by calling the `setWhiteBalance()` method of *mRadg*:

```
mFbp.push(rgb);
int nBrightestColor = mFbp.getBrightestColor();
mRadg.setWhiteBalance(nBrightestColor);
...
mSeqThreshold.push(rgb);
```

To use the white-balance color you'll compensate for the color of the illumination by modifying the color of each RGB pixel so it has the color it would have if the illumination were white. Figure 13-7 shows an example. Suppose the illumination was tinted orange, the way it would be under incandescent light. Then the white balance RGB color might be, for example (255, 228, 190). Under this light, a green object the color of the Android logo, which has the official RGB color (164, 198, 57), would tend to have its green, and especially its blue, color muted. The effect of light color on a surface is multiplicative. So, the Android logo might have the RGB color (165, 146, 42), as shown in Figure 13-7. The Android logo is no longer green, but more of an olive brown.

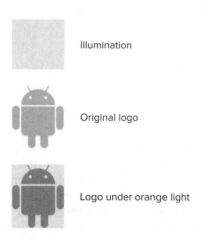

Illumination

Original logo

Logo under orange light

FIGURE 13-7: Effect of light on the Android logo

You compensate for this in `RgbAbsDiffGrayWb` by undoing the multiplicative effect of the light — you divide by the color the light has, and multiply by the value it should have (that is, white):

```
int nR = (r * Byte.MAX_VALUE) / mBrightestR;
int nG = (g * Byte.MAX_VALUE) / mBrightestG;
int nB = (b * Byte.MAX_VALUE) / mBrightestB;
```

The last step in improving the performance of `DetectLogoBetter` is to take into account the approximate shape of the Android logo — it is approximately rectangular. You check for this by using an easy-to-compute number, namely the perimeter squared divided by the area. This dimensionless number, which is commonly used in image processing for just this purpose, is a measure of the compactness of a shape. A longer, thinner region will have a long perimeter compared to its area and so will have a high value.

The implementation of this is straightforward, given the perimeter and pixel count measures from `Gray8ConnComp`:

```
int perimeter = mG8cc.getPerimeter(i);
int area = mG8cc.getPixelCount(i);
int compactness = perimeter * perimeter / area;
if (compactness < nBestCompactness) {
    nBestCompactness = compactness;
    nBestComponent = i;
}
```

The result looks for a greenish blob that is more or less rectangular and larger than a certain minimum size. This is a pretty fair description of the Android logo, from an image-processing point of view.

This is as far as you will go in improving the performance of `DetectLogoBetter`. If you wanted to go further you would change the code to use the actual target color of the Android logo, rather than the system `Color.GREEN`, and do a more careful job on white balance, rather than just taking the brightest pixel as a guide to the luminance color. You could also take into account the detailed shape of the Android logo by looking at each suspiciously green blob in the image — for example, you could refer back to the original color image to examine the corresponding full-resolution image, and look for the details you would expect to find in the Android logo — the shape outline, the eyes, and the arms.

DETECTING FACES

This chapter has focused on writing image processing programs starting with simple, general operations. But Android also includes some sophisticated image processing routines for face detection, and you should also know about these.

Incidentally, please do not confuse face detection with face recognition. Android introduced some proprietary code for face recognition in the Ice Cream Sandwich release of the operating system by providing a *Face Unlock* program. You can train your device to recognize your face and unlock when it sees you. This is not the same thing as face detection, and in any case there is, at this writing, no public

API for face recognition — you can't train it to recognize more than one face, or make it do anything other than unlock your device. These capabilities will undoubtedly come in future releases of Android.

In face detection you are simply determining whether there is a face somewhere in the image, and, if so, where it is. The basic process for detecting faces uses the `android.media.FaceDetector` class. To use this, you must first create a `FaceDetector` object:

```
FaceDetector fd = new FaceDetector(nWidth, nHeight, nFaces);
```

Here *nWidth* and *nHeight* are the size of the image to be processed, and *nFaces* gives the number of faces that will be searched for. You can use the same `FaceDetector` object over and over so long as the image size does not change.

To detect the faces you just call the `findFaces()` method in `FaceDetector`:

```
int nFaces = fd.findFaces(bmp, faces);
```

Here *bmp* is the `Bitmap` image where you want to find faces, and *faces* is an array of `FaceDetect.Face` objects which will be set to the detected faces. *nFaces* is set to the number of faces detected.

The `FaceDetect.Face` object includes this useful information on detected faces:

➤ The confidence of the detection, returned as a floating-point value. Any value above 0.3 is considered "good."

➤ The position of the midpoint of the eyes.

➤ The distance between the eyes.

➤ The orientation of the face.

Note that the actual size of the face is not returned — you have to estimate this from the distance between the eyes. And the orientation of the face is returned in three dimensions, measured in terms of the angles around the x, y, and z axes.

IMAGE-PROCESSING RESOURCES

Image processing is an engineering field in itself, and Chapters 12 and 13 have served only as a brief introduction, concentrating on techniques that may be most useful on a mobile platform. Fortunately, many resources are available for free on the web:

➤ OpenCV (http://tech.groups.yahoo.com/group/OpenCV/) is the preeminent Internet discussion group on image processing and computer vision. It includes an active mailing list and a large (more than 500 algorithms) library of image-processing programs, as well as image resources useful for testing, and a book (*Learning OpenCV: Computer Vision with the OpenCV Library*) introducing computer vision with the library. OpenCV's image-processing library is written in C++, but it is still a useful starting point for Android programmers.

➤ Many online tutorials on image processing are available; for example, Alan Peters of Vanderbilt University provides an 18-part lecture series at www.archive.org/details/ Lectures_on_Image_Processing, and Srinivasa Narasimhan and Tai-sing Lee of Carnegie Mellon University provide their lecture notes at www.cs.cmu.edu/afs/cs.cmu.edu/ academic/class/15385-s06/lectures/ppts/.

➤ Many image-processing journals are available online, for example *Image Processing On Line* (`www.ipol.im/`).

Many good textbooks are also available that introduce the field of image processing. These include:

➤ *Digital Image Processing* (3rd edition) by Rafael C. Gonzalez and Robert E. Woods.

➤ *Fundamentals of Digital Image Processing* by Anil K. Jain.

➤ *Digital Image Processing* by William K. Pratt.

SUMMARY

This chapter took you from a familiarity with the Android camera and Android programming to a basic understanding of image processing using Android. The chapter introduced the image-processing pipeline, which is the fundamental way image-processing programs are structured, and described some important image-processing algorithms. Next, you saw how to capture and use the Android color image. You saw how a simple program for detecting the Android logo was structured, and learned how to improve the program's speed by limiting the size of the image to be processed. Then you saw how to improve the program's reliability by taking into account variations in illumination and white balance, eventually using the shape of the logo to help guide detection. You also learned about Android's face detection feature. Finally, you were given a starting point to find out more about image processing, including the many free resources available on the web.

Images are not the only external data an Android device can sense. Devices can also use the microphone to sense audio data. The next chapter shows you how to detect patterns in audio recordings, just as this chapter showed you detect patterns in captured images.

14

Using the Microphone

WHAT'S IN THIS CHAPTER?

➤ Recording maximum amplitude and raw audio data

➤ Processing asynchronously

➤ Implementing a clapper

➤ Signal processing to determine volume and frequency

Many Android devices are also phones, and hence provide a microphone to the user. Apps can use the microphone as a sensor to record audio and then analyze the resulting recording.

Many apps might benefit from analyzing the audio recording. For example, an app could detect a clap or a certain sound to help the user communicate a command. Instrument tuners and other utilities are also possible.

This chapter describes how to use the `MediaRecorder` and `AudioRecord` APIs to record and analyze audio to detect patterns. It describes some utility classes to help you use the APIs. To demonstrate, this chapter shows how to create several versions of a clapper.

INTRODUCING THE ANDROID CLAPPER

The clapper, shown in Figure 14-1, is a device invented in 1986 that attaches to an electrical socket and turns it on and off in response to a person's claps. You can implement something similar on Android that improves upon the features of the original clapper. Instead of activating an electrical outlet, though, your app may take another action instead.

Table 14-1 shows the different implementations of a clapper in this chapter. The clapper and loud noise clappers perform in a similar way to the original clapper: the user triggers them by making a loud sound. The singing clapper improves the loud noise clapper by triggering only if it hears a consistent frequency, such as one that a user might make while singing. By responding only to a consistent frequency, the improved clapper ignores unwanted triggering from sounds such as dogs barking, fireworks going off, and other loud noises.

The clapper implementations show how to use `MediaRecorder` and `AudioRecord` and describe signal processing techniques to estimate a signal's volume and frequency.

FIGURE 14-1: A clapper plugs into the wall and controls turning on and off an electrical socket.

TABLE 14-1: Different Implementations of a Clapper

NAME	HOW	TRIGGER	DETECT WHEN
Clapper	`MediaRecorder`	Clap hands	High maximum amplitude
Loud Noise	`AudioRecord`	Clap hands	Sustained high amplitude
Singing	`AudioRecord`	Singing "oooooo"	Consistent frequency such as what a person might produce by singing the same tone. Won't be triggered by claps, door slams, dogs barking, or people talking.

TRY THIS

You can try the three clappers by accessing the "Clapper" button within the book's app. The app enables you to try each clapper, view logging output, and use some provided sound samples to experiment.

USING MEDIARECORDER TO ANALYZE MAXIMUM AMPLITUDE

Of the two ways to collect audio information from Android, `MediaRecorder` is the most limited and the simplest, yet it is also quite robust. The `MediaRecorder` handles many of the recording details, such as acquiring audio data and calculating maximum amplitude, and hence makes it easy to use.

Maximum amplitude is quite useful for detecting patterns within an audio recording. To access it, an app calls `MediaRecorder.getMaxAmplitude()`, which returns its value since the last call to it.

The value ranges from 0 to 32767 (the maximum value that can fit in a `short`) and does not represent a specific unit. An app can use periodic calls to the method to record maximum amplitude values over time. Also, an app needs to monitor maximum amplitude asynchronously so it can do other tasks while recording and remain responsive to the user.

You can use the following set of three classes and interfaces to collect and analyze maximum amplitude:

➤ `MaxAmplitudeRecorder`: Executes `MediaRecorder`, collects maximum amplitude, and passes it to an `AmplitudeClipListener`.

➤ `AmplitudeClipListener`: Listens for new maximum amplitude and possibly stops recording.

➤ `RecordAmplitudeTask`: An `AsyncTask` that executes `MaxAmplitudeRecorder` asynchronously and updates the user interface before and after execution.

Recording Maximum Amplitude

First, an app needs the right permissions and hardware. Then, it can prepare the `MediaRecorder` for use and start recording.

To record audio, an app needs following permission:

```
<uses-permission android:name="android.permission.RECORD_AUDIO" />
```

Optionally, an app can check if the device has a microphone by using the code in Listing 14-1.

LISTING 14-1: Checks if a device has a microphone

```
public static boolean hasMicrophone(Context context)
{
    return context.getPackageManager().hasSystemFeature(
            PackageManager.FEATURE_MICROPHONE);
}
```

With the correct permissions and the presence of a microphone, an app can safely create and prepare a `MediaRecorder` for use. Creating the `MediaRecorder` requires several steps in a particular order. Listing 14-2 shows a utility method that creates it with the typical parameters.

LISTING 14-2: Creates and prepares a MediaRecorder for use

```
public static MediaRecorder prepareRecorder(String sdCardPath)
        throws IOException
{
    if (!isStorageReady())
    {
        throw new IOException("SD card is not available");
    }
```

continues

LISTING 14-2 *(continued)*

```
MediaRecorder recorder = new MediaRecorder();
//set a custom listener that just logs any messages
RecorderErrorLoggerListener recorderListener =
        new RecorderErrorLoggerListener();
recorder.setOnErrorListener(recorderListener);
recorder.setOnInfoListener(recorderListener);

recorder.setAudioSource(MediaRecorder.AudioSource.MIC);
recorder.setOutputFormat(MediaRecorder.OutputFormat.THREE_GPP);
Log.d(TAG, "recording to: " + sdCardPath);
recorder.setOutputFile(sdCardPath);
recorder.setAudioEncoder(MediaRecorder.AudioEncoder.AMR_NB);
recorder.prepare();
return recorder;
}
```

Preparing a `MediaRecorder` proceeds through the following steps:

1. Check if an SD card is available. Because `MediaRecorder` requires a file to record audio data and the path is on the SD card, the device must have its SD card available. If it is not available, throw an `IOException`.

2. Create the `MediaRecorder` object.

3. Set the default `OnError` and `OnInfo` listeners that log output.

4. Set the audio source to `MediaRecorder.AudioSource.MIC`.

5. Set the output format to `MediaRecorder.OutputFormat.THREE_GPP`. The Android documentation recommends this format, but others are possible.

6. Set the output file. The `MediaRecorder` uses this file to store all recorded output. Even if your app is not using the recorded file, `MediaRecorder` still needs this to hold temporary data.

7. Set the audio encoder to `MediaRecorder.AudioEncoder.AMR_NB`. The output format of the audio.

8. Call `prepare()`. After this call, the recorder is ready to start.

You can find additional information about the audio formats at `http://developer.android.com/guide/appendix/media-formats.html#core`.

While preparing a `MediaRecorder`, the code may generate several `Exceptions`. An `IllegalStateException` may occur if the code executes the setup in the incorrect order. The exception should never occur unless calling code misuses the setup routine. An `IOException` is also possible if the SD card is not available.

Once an app obtains a properly initialized `MediaRecorder` it can start recording, check maximum amplitude in a loop, and analyze the resulting amplitude. You can implement this process using `MaxAmplitudeRecorder`, shown in Listing 14-3, and `AmplitudeClipListener`, shown in Listing 14-4.

MaxAmplitudeRecorder has a startRecording() which contains the recording loop. Before running the loop, the code calls getMaxAmplitude(). The code does this because the first getMax-Amplitude() call returns zero and subsequent calls report its value since it was last called. Thus, by calling getMaxAmplitude() once before the loop starts, the code ensures the first value returned is a useful one. The loop waits for a time (and possibly stops if external code indicated so while it was waiting), records the getMaxAmplitude() value, passes it to an AmplitudeClipListener for analysis, and stops recording if the AmplitudeClipListener returns true. Using this procedure the loop periodically collects and analyzes maximum amplitude and ends if one of three conditions occur:

➤ The AmplitudeClipListener returns true.

➤ External code calls stopRecording(), which sets *continueRecording* to false.

➤ External code cancels the AsyncTask.

LISTING 14-3: Records the maximum amplitude periodically

Available for download on Wrox.com

```java
public class MaxAmplitudeRecorder
{
    private static final String TAG = "MaxAmplitudeRecorder";

    private static final long DEFAULT_CLIP_TIME = 1000;
    private long clipTime = DEFAULT_CLIP_TIME;

    private AmplitudeClipListener clipListener;

    private boolean continueRecording;

    private MediaRecorder recorder;

    private String tmpAudioFile;

    private AsyncTask task;

    /**
     *
     * @param clipTime
     *             time to wait in between maxAmplitude checks
     * @param tmpAudioFile
     *             should be a file where the MediaRecorder can write
     *             temporary audio data
     *
     * @param clipListener
     *             called periodically to analyze the max amplitude
     * @param task
     *             stop recording if the task is canceled
     */
    public MaxAmplitudeRecorder(long clipTime, String tmpAudioFile,
            AmplitudeClipListener clipListener, AsyncTask task)
    {
        this.clipTime = clipTime;
        this.clipListener = clipListener;
```

continues

LISTING 14-3 *(continued)*

```java
        this.tmpAudioFile = tmpAudioFile;
        this.task = task;
    }

    /**
     * start recording maximum amplitude and passing it to the
     * {@link #clipListener} <br>
     * @throws {@link IllegalStateException} if there is trouble creating
     * the recorder
     * @throws {@link IOException} if the SD card is not available
     * @throws {@link RuntimeException} if audio recording channel is occupied
     * @return true if {@link #clipListener} succeeded in detecting something
     * false if it failed or the recording stopped for some other reason
     */
    public boolean startRecording() throws IOException
    {
        Log.d(TAG, "recording maxAmplitude");

        recorder = AudioUtil.prepareRecorder(tmpAudioFile);

        // when an error occurs just stop recording
        recorder.setOnErrorListener(new MediaRecorder.OnErrorListener()
        {
            @Override
            public void onError(MediaRecorder mr, int what, int extra)
            {
                // log it
                new RecorderErrorLoggerListener().onError(mr, what, extra);
                // stop recording
                stopRecording();
            }
        });

        //possible RuntimeException if Audio recording channel is occupied
        recorder.start();
        continueRecording = true;
        boolean heard = false;
        recorder.getMaxAmplitude();
        while (continueRecording)
        {
            Log.d(TAG, "waiting while recording...");
            waitClipTime();
            //in case external code stopped this while read was happening
            if ((!continueRecording) || ((task != null) && task.isCancelled()))
            {
                break;
            }

            int maxAmplitude = recorder.getMaxAmplitude();
            Log.d(TAG, "current max amplitude: " + maxAmplitude);

            heard = clipListener.heard(maxAmplitude);
```

```
            if (heard)
            {
                stopRecording();
            }

        Log.d(TAG, "stopped recording max amplitude");
        done();

        return heard;
    }

    private void waitClipTime()
    {
        try
        {
            Thread.sleep(clipTime);
        } catch (InterruptedException e)
        {
            Log.d(TAG, "interrupted");
        }
    }

    /**
     * stop recorder and clean up resources
     */
    public void done()
    {
        Log.d(TAG, "stop recording on done");
        if (recorder != null)
        {
            try
            {
                recorder.stop();
            } catch (Exception e)
            {
                Log.d(TAG, "failed to stop");
                return;
            }
            recorder.release();
        }
    }

    public boolean isRecording()
    {
        return continueRecording;
    }

    public void stopRecording()
    {
        continueRecording = false;
    }
}
```

LISTING 14-4: Listens for maximum amplitude

```
public interface AmplitudeClipListener
{
    /**
     * return true if recording should stop
     */
    public boolean heard(int maxAmplitude);
}
```

You can use `MaxAmplitudeRecorder` and `AmplitudeClipListener` to analyze maximum amplitude over time. One important implementation detail is that the recording loop in `MaxAmplitudeRecorder` should be run asynchronously, otherwise an app would be unresponsive while it was waiting to record another maximum amplitude value. The next section describes how to run `MaxAmplitudeRecorder` asynchronously using an `AsyncTask`.

Asynchronous Audio Recording

Most likely, an app needs to do something else while recording audio. For example, it may need to keep the UI responsive. To implement this, an app needs to record audio asynchronously. Additionally, an app needs to process the results of the recording when it is done. For both these features, an app can use an `AsyncTask` such as `RecordAmplitudeTask`.

Listing 14-5 shows the code for `RecordAmplitudeTask`. When external code calls `execute()`, Android calls `doInBackground()`. In that method, `RecordAmplitudeTask` creates a `MaxAmplitudeRecorder` and runs it until the `startRecording()` method returns. Its `onPostExecute()` method receives the recording result and updates the UI by setting the text of status and log `TextViews`

Available for
download on
Wrox.com

LISTING 14-5: Executes MaxAmplitudeRecorder, passes results to a AmplitudeClipListener, and updates user interface before and after recording

```
public class RecordAmplitudeTask extends
        AsyncTask<AmplitudeClipListener, Void, Boolean>
{
    private static final String TAG = "RecordAmplitudeTask";

    private TextView status;
    private TextView log;
    private Context context;
    private String taskName;

    private static final String TEMP_AUDIO_DIR_NAME = "temp_audio";

    /**
     * time between amplitude checks
     */
    private static final int CLIP_TIME = 1000;

    public RecordAmplitudeTask(Context context, TextView status, TextView log,
            String taskName)
```

```
{
    this.context = context;
    this.status = status;
    this.log = log;
    this.taskName = taskName;
}

@Override
protected void onPreExecute()
{
    // tell UI recording is starting
    status.setText(context.getResources().getString(
            R.string.audio_status_recording)
            + " for " + taskName);
    AudioTaskUtil.appendToStartOfLog(log, "started " + taskName);
    super.onPreExecute();
}

/**
 * note: only uses the first listener passed in
 */
@Override
protected Boolean doInBackground(AmplitudeClipListener... listeners)
{
    if (listeners.length == 0)
    {
        return false;
    }

    Log.d(TAG, "recording amplitude");
    // construct recorder, using only the first listener passed in
    AmplitudeClipListener listener = listeners[0];
    String appStorageLocation =
        context.getExternalFilesDir(TEMP_AUDIO_DIR_NAME).getAbsolutePath()
                + File.separator + "audio.3gp";
    MaxAmplitudeRecorder recorder =
            new MaxAmplitudeRecorder(CLIP_TIME, appStorageLocation,
                    listener, this);

    //set to true if the recorder successfully detected something
    //false if it was canceled or otherwise stopped
    boolean heard = false;
    try
    {
        // start recording
        heard = recorder.startRecording();
    } catch (IOException io)
    {
        Log.e(TAG, "failed to record", io);
        heard = false;
    } catch (IllegalStateException se)
    {
        Log.e(TAG, "failed to record, recorder not setup properly", se);
        heard = false;
    } catch (RuntimeException se)
```

continues

LISTING 14-5 *(continued)*

```
            {
                Log.e(TAG, "failed to record, recorder already being used", se);
                heard = false;
            }

            return heard;
        }

        @Override
        protected void onPostExecute(Boolean result)
        {
            // update UI
            if (result)
            {
                AudioTaskUtil.appendToStartOfLog(log, "heard clap at "
                        + AudioTaskUtil.getNow());
            }
            else
            {
                AudioTaskUtil.appendToStartOfLog(log, "heard no claps");
            }
            setDoneMessage();
            super.onPostExecute(result);
        }

        @Override
        protected void onCancelled()
        {
            AudioTaskUtil.appendToStartOfLog(log, "cancelled " + taskName);
            setDoneMessage();
            super.onCancelled();
        }

        private void setDoneMessage()
        {
            status.setText(context.getResources().getString(
                    R.string.audio_status_stopped));
        }
    }
```

code snippet RecordAmplitudeTask.java

Now that you know how to record maximum amplitude, the next section shows you how to analyze the maximum amplitude to implement a clapper.

IMPLEMENTING A CLAPPER

The previous sections described how to record maximum amplitude. To use the described code, an app needs to provide an AmplitudeClipListener. Listing 14-6 shows the implementation of one that listens for a single clap. The heard() method checks *maxAmplitude* value against a threshold to determine if it heard a clap.

Choosing a threshold is dependent on several factors. A low value makes an app very sensitive. It makes it easy for the user to trigger but also increases accidental triggering. A high value makes the app less sensitive, but might require the user to make a very loud sound to activate it.

The environment also can help determine what threshold is appropriate. If the user is in a noisy place, the threshold should be high to minimize false triggering. On the other hand, if the user is in a quiet place where he can't make too much noise, a low value might be the only way to allow the user to politely trigger it. Knowledgeable users may adjust the sensitivity depending on their circumstances. In my experience a value of 18000, which is slightly more than 50% of the maximum value, is a good compromise between being too sensitive and making it easy for users to trigger the clap.

LISTING 14-6: Reports if maximum amplitude is above a certain threshold

```
public class SingleClapDetector implements AmplitudeClipListener
{
    private static final String TAG = "SingleClapDetector";

    /**
     * required loudness to determine it is a clap
     */
    private int amplitudeThreshold;

    /**
     * requires a little of noise by the user to trigger, background noise may
     * trigger it
     */
    public static final int AMPLITUDE_DIFF_LOW = 10000;
    public static final int AMPLITUDE_DIFF_MED = 18000;
    /**
     * requires a lot of noise by the user to trigger. background noise isn't
     * likely to be this loud
     */
    public static final int AMPLITUDE_DIFF_HIGH = 25000;

    private static final int DEFAULT_AMPLITUDE_DIFF = AMPLITUDE_DIFF_MED;

    public SingleClapDetector()
    {
        this(DEFAULT_AMPLITUDE_DIFF);
    }

    public SingleClapDetector(int amplitudeThreshold)
    {
        this.amplitudeThreshold = amplitudeThreshold;
    }

    @Override
    public boolean heard(int maxAmplitude)
    {
        boolean clapDetected = false;

        if (maxAmplitude >= amplitudeThreshold)
```

continues

LISTING 14-6 *(continued)*

```
            {
                Log.d(TAG, "heard a clap");
                clapDetected = true;
            }

            return clapDetected;
        }
    }
```

An app can use `MediaRecorder` to collect maximum amplitude values over time. This value is quite useful and easy to acquire. However, for more advanced audio analysis where an app needs access to the raw audio signal and greater control over the recording process, an app must use `AudioRecord`, which the next section describes.

ANALYZING RAW AUDIO

Sometimes the maximum amplitude value from the `MediaRecorder` is not enough for certain tasks. First, `MediaRecorder` doesn't have methods to directly retrieve the raw audio data, which makes it inconvenient for immediate analysis. Second, `MediaRecorder` compresses the audio. This is not a problem if an app is analyzing maximum amplitude. However, if an app is analyzing the raw audio signal it might introduce some unwanted distortion. Thus, for analyzing audio data for information beyond maximum amplitude, an app should use the data from `AudioRecord` instead of `MediaRecorder`.

Using `AudioRecord` allows an app to collect the raw, uncompressed audio bytes. The bytes contain recorded samples of the signal's amplitude over time. You can apply many kinds of signal processing algorithms to this data. This section shows how to implement two kinds of clappers that perform two kinds of signal processing: one to determine volume and another to estimate frequency. Also, this section utilizes several classes to help you utilize `AudioRecord`:

➤   `AudioClipRecorder`: Executes `AudioRecord` to record audio clips and pass resulting audio data to an `AudioClipListener`.

➤   `AudioClipListener`: Listens for audio data and possibly stops recording.

➤   `RecordAudioTask`: An `AsyncTask` that executes `AudioClipRecorder` asynchronously and updates the user interface before and after execution. Similar to code in Listing 14-5.

Listing 14-7 shows the complete `AudioClipRecorder` and Listings 14-8 and 14-10 show implementations of `AudioClipListener` for two clappers.

To understand how these classes work, you need to understand how to set the input parameters, how the recording loop works, and how to analyze the resulting audio data.

Setting Audio Input Parameters

`AudioRecord` provides several parameters an app can set to achieve certain effects:

➤ Achieve a certain audio quality by setting sampling and encoding.

➤ Record for audio clips of a certain time length.

➤ Avoid buffer overflows.

Table 14-2 shows the various input parameters needed to create an `AudioRecord`.

TABLE 14-2: Input Parameters for AudioRecord

VALUE	POSSIBLE VALUES	DESCRIPTION
Encoding	`AudioFormat.ENCODING_PCM_16BIT` or `AudioFormat.ENCODING_PCM_8BIT`	Specifies the size of each audio data byte. 16 bit has a bigger range than 8 bit. One audio sample is called a "frame" by the Android documentation.
Sampling rate	According to the Android source code, any value between 4000 and 48000 is valid. Use 8000 for a low quality sound used in telephones. Use 44100 for CD recording quality. 44100 is the only value guaranteed to work on all devices.	Number of samples to record per second in Hz.
BufferSize	Greater than value returned from `AudioRecord.getMinBufferSize()`	Number of bytes in the recording buffer. If the buffer size is too small and an app doesn't read it fast enough, buffer overflow occurs and an app loses data. Apps usually set the buffer higher than needed by a factor of 3 or 10, depending on the application. Also, for 16-bit encoding, each sample utilizes two bytes so apps may want to increase the buffer size to hold enough samples.
Channel	`AudioFormat.CHANNEL_IN_MONO`, `AudioFormat.CHANNEL_IN_STEREO`, or other, more specific mono or stereo `CHANNEL` from `AudioFormat`.	The audio channels to record. Mono uses a single audio stream and stereo uses two. Using stereo doubles the data collected. Unless your audio analysis requires it, mono is sufficient for most uses.

To illustrate how you might set these parameters, consider how you would set them to record audio clips containing data for a certain amount of time. For example, if you want an app to collect audio clips containing approximately 2 seconds of audio data with a sample rate of 8000Hz, an encoding of `AudioFormat.ENCODING_PCM_16BIT`, and a single audio channel the parameter settings would be:

➤   **Encoding:** `AudioFormat.ENCODING_PCM_16BIT`

➤   **Sampling rate:** 8000

➤   **BufferSize:** Sample rate * 2 * 2 * 3 = 192000

>   ➤   Multiply sample rate by 2 because two seconds of samples would be 16000 samples.

>   ➤   Multiply by 2 again because each sample is 2 bytes big and the buffer size is specified in bytes.

>   ➤   Multiply by 3 to provide extra buffer space and avoid buffer overflow.

➤   **Channel:** `AudioFormat.CHANNEL_IN_MONO`

If an app needs to analyze the data as fast as possible it can use a minimum sized buffer. Some example parameters might be:

➤   **Encoding:** `AudioFormat.ENCODING_PCM_16BIT`

➤   **Sampling rate:** 8000

➤   **BufferSize:** `AudioRecord.getMinBufferSize()`* 3. Use the minimum buffer size, but increase it by 3 to prevent buffer overflows.

➤   **Channel:** `AudioFormat.CHANNEL_IN_MONO`

`AudioClipRecorder` has methods that help calculate the size of the recording buffer. In particular, `startRecordingForTime()` makes the calculation necessary to achieve recording clips that contain data for a certain amount of time.

Preparing AudioRecord

The two `startRecording()` methods in `AudioClipRecorder` determine the size of the recording and read buffers and then create an `AudioRecord` that is ready for use. The methods proceed through the following steps:

1.   Determine minimum recording buffer and read buffer sizes:

>   ➤   **Use the minimum:** `startRecording()` uses `AudioRecord.getMinBufferSize()` as the recording buffer size and also as the read buffer size.

>   ➤   **Calculated:** `startRecordingForTime()` calculates how many samples it needs to create a read buffer that holds enough samples for the desired time. It uses

`determineCalculatedBufferSize()` to adjust the recording buffer size so that it holds enough samples for a given encoding and is bigger than the minimum size.

2. Create `AudioRecord` within `doRecording()`:

➤ Check if the recording buffer size is an error value. If so, do not proceed.

➤ Increase the size of the recording buffer by a factor.

➤ Set sample rate, encoding, channels, recording buffer.

3. Create read audio buffer:

➤ Allocates the read buffer as a *short [readBufferSize]*.

Recording Audio

Once `AudioClipRecorder` properly creates an `AudioRecord` that is ready for use, `doRecording()` starts recording by setting the *continueRecording* state variable to true and executing `AudioRecord.startRecording()`. Then it begins the following recording loop:

1. Read audio data: Execute `AudioRecord.read()`, which blocks until there is enough data to fill the read buffer.

2. Possibly stop recording: Exit the loop if external code indicated that recording should stop while the code was blocked. External code can indicate this by calling `stopRecording()` or by cancelling the `AsyncTask` used to construct `AudioClipRecorder`.

3. Check for errors: Create a log if `read()` causes an error.

4. Do processing: The `AudioClipRecorder`, *clipListener*, does some processing based on the data it received. Meanwhile `AudioRecord` continues to add to the recording buffer. If *clipListener* takes too long, `AudioRecord` might fill the buffer and log a buffer overflow error so it should finish quickly

5. Possibly stop recording: Stop the loop if `AudioClipListener` returns true.

Using OnRecordPositionUpdateListener

As an alternative, an app may also use an `OnRecordPositionUpdateListener` to process the audio data. To use it, an app specifies a number of samples, which the Android documentation calls *frames*, to wait. When `AudioRecord` records that many samples, it calls the listener. The recording loop must still call `read()` but it does not need to process results.

For example, an app might specify that `AudioRecord` should update `OnRecordPositionUpdateListener` every 8000 samples by calling `setPositionNotification Period(8000)` If the sample rate is 8000, this causes `AudioRecord` to call the listener about once every second. Also, an app has to make sure that the recording buffer is big enough to hold 8000 samples. For this, `AudioClipRecorder.startRecordingForTime()` is useful.

Listing 14-7 contains a `setOnPositionUpdate()` method that shows how to create and set an `OnRecordPositionUpdateListener`. It also contains the complete source code for `AudioClipRecorder`.

Available for
download on
Wrox.com

LISTING 14-7: Records audio with AudioRecord

```
public class AudioClipRecorder
{
    private static final String TAG = "AudioClipRecorder";

    private AudioRecord recorder;
    private AudioClipListener clipListener;

    /**
     * state variable to control starting and stopping recording
     */
    private boolean continueRecording;

    public static final int RECORDER_SAMPLERATE_CD = 44100;
    public static final int RECORDER_SAMPLERATE_8000 = 8000;

    private static final int DEFAULT_BUFFER_INCREASE_FACTOR = 3;

    private AsyncTask task;

    private boolean heard;

    public AudioClipRecorder(AudioClipListener clipListener)
    {
        this.clipListener = clipListener;
        heard = false;
        task = null;
    }

    public AudioClipRecorder(AudioClipListener clipListener, AsyncTask task)
    {
        this(clipListener);
        this.task = task;
    }

    /**
     * records with some default parameters
     */
    public boolean startRecording()
    {
        return startRecording(RECORDER_SAMPLERATE_8000,
                AudioFormat.ENCODING_PCM_16BIT);
    }

    /**
     * start recording: set the parameters that correspond to a buffer that
     * contains millisecondsPerAudioClip milliseconds of samples
     */
```

```java
public boolean startRecordingForTime(int millisecondsPerAudioClip,
        int sampleRate, int encoding)
{
    float percentOfASecond = (float) millisecondsPerAudioClip / 1000.0f;
    int numSamplesRequired = (int) ((float) sampleRate * percentOfASecond);
    int bufferSize =
            determineCalculatedBufferSize(sampleRate, encoding,
                    numSamplesRequired);

    return doRecording(sampleRate, encoding, bufferSize,
            numSamplesRequired, DEFAULT_BUFFER_INCREASE_FACTOR);
}

/**
 * start recording: Use a minimum audio buffer and a read buffer of the same
 * size.
 */
public boolean startRecording(final int sampleRate, int encoding)
{
    int bufferSize = determineMinimumBufferSize(sampleRate, encoding);
    return doRecording(sampleRate, encoding, bufferSize, bufferSize,
            DEFAULT_BUFFER_INCREASE_FACTOR);
}

private int determineMinimumBufferSize(final int sampleRate, int encoding)
{
    int minBufferSize =
            AudioRecord.getMinBufferSize(sampleRate,
                    AudioFormat.CHANNEL_IN_MONO, encoding);
    return minBufferSize;
}

/**
 * Calculate audio buffer size such that it holds numSamplesInBuffer and is
 * bigger than the minimum size<br>
 *
 * @param numSamplesInBuffer
 *            Make the audio buffer size big enough to hold this many
 *            samples
 */
private int determineCalculatedBufferSize(final int sampleRate,
        int encoding, int numSamplesInBuffer)
{
    int minBufferSize = determineMinimumBufferSize(sampleRate, encoding);

    int bufferSize;
    // each sample takes two bytes, need a bigger buffer
    if (encoding == AudioFormat.ENCODING_PCM_16BIT)
    {
        bufferSize = numSamplesInBuffer * 2;
    }
    else
    {
        bufferSize = numSamplesInBuffer;
    }
```

continues

LISTING 14-7 *(continued)*

```java
        if (bufferSize < minBufferSize)
        {
            Log.w(TAG, "Increasing buffer to hold enough samples "
                    + minBufferSize + " was: " + bufferSize);
            bufferSize = minBufferSize;
        }

        return bufferSize;
    }

    /**
     * Records audio until stopped the {@link #task} is canceled,
     * {@link #continueRecording} is false, or {@link #clipListener} returns
     * true <br>
     * records audio to a short [readBufferSize] and passes it to
     * {@link #clipListener} <br>
     * uses an audio buffer of size bufferSize * bufferIncreaseFactor
     *
     * @param recordingBufferSize
     *            minimum audio buffer size
     * @param readBufferSize
     *            reads a buffer of this size
     * @param bufferIncreaseFactor
     *            to increase recording buffer size beyond the minimum needed
     */
    private boolean doRecording(final int sampleRate, int encoding,
            int recordingBufferSize, int readBufferSize,
            int bufferIncreaseFactor)
    {
        if (recordingBufferSize == AudioRecord.ERROR_BAD_VALUE)
        {
            Log.e(TAG, "Bad encoding value, see logcat");
            return false;
        }
        else if (recordingBufferSize == AudioRecord.ERROR)
        {
            Log.e(TAG, "Error creating buffer size");
            return false;
        }

        // give it extra space to prevent overflow
        int increasedRecordingBufferSize =
            recordingBufferSize * bufferIncreaseFactor;

        recorder =
                new AudioRecord(AudioSource.MIC, sampleRate,
                        AudioFormat.CHANNEL_IN_MONO, encoding,
                        increasedRecordingBufferSize);
```

```
        final short[] readBuffer = new short[readBufferSize];

        continueRecording = true;
        Log.d(TAG, "start recording, " + "recording bufferSize: "
                + increasedRecordingBufferSize
                + " read buffer size: " + readBufferSize);

        //Note: possible IllegalStateException
        //if audio recording is already recording or otherwise not available
        //AudioRecord.getState() will be AudioRecord.STATE_UNINITIALIZED
        recorder.startRecording();

        while (continueRecording)
        {
            int bufferResult = recorder.read(readBuffer, 0, readBufferSize);
            //in case external code stopped this while read was happening
            if ((!continueRecording) || ((task != null) && task.isCancelled()))
            {
                break;
            }
            // check for error conditions
            if (bufferResult == AudioRecord.ERROR_INVALID_OPERATION)
            {
                Log.e(TAG, "error reading: ERROR_INVALID_OPERATION");
            }
            else if (bufferResult == AudioRecord.ERROR_BAD_VALUE)
            {
                Log.e(TAG, "error reading: ERROR_BAD_VALUE");
            }
            else
            // no errors, do processing
            {
                heard = clipListener.heard(readBuffer, sampleRate);

                if (heard)
                {
                    stopRecording();
                }
            }
        }
        done();

        return heard;
    }

    public boolean isRecording()
    {
        return continueRecording;
    }
```

continues

LISTING 14-7 *(continued)*

```java
public void stopRecording()
{
    continueRecording = false;
}

/**
 * need to call this when completely done with recording
 */
public void done()
{
    Log.d(TAG, "shut down recorder");
    if (recorder != null)
    {
        recorder.stop();
        recorder.release();
        recorder = null;
    }
}

/**
 * @param audioData
 *               will be filled when reading the audio data
 */
private void setOnPositionUpdate(final short[] audioData,
        final int sampleRate, int numSamplesInBuffer)
{

    OnRecordPositionUpdateListener positionUpdater =
            new OnRecordPositionUpdateListener()
            {
                @Override
                public void onPeriodicNotification(AudioRecord recorder)
                {
                    // no need to read the audioData again since it was just
                    // read
                    heard = clipListener.heard(audioData, sampleRate);
                    if (heard)
                    {
                        Log.d(TAG, "heard audio");
                        stopRecording();
                    }
                }

                @Override
                public void onMarkerReached(AudioRecord recorder)
                {
                    Log.d(TAG, "marker reached");
                }
            };
    // get notified after so many samples collected
    recorder.setPositionNotificationPeriod(numSamplesInBuffer);
    recorder.setRecordPositionUpdateListener(positionUpdater);
```

```
      }
   }
```

code snippet AudioClipRecorder.java

Now that you know how to record some raw audio data, the next two sections show how to analyze the data to implement different versions of the clapper.

USING LOUD NOISE DETECTION

One way to implement a clapper is to determine if the app heard a loud noise. `LoudNoiseDetector` is an `AudioClipRecorder` that implements the required processing. Listing 14-8 shows its implementation.

Specifically, `LoudNoiseDetector` performs two tasks:

➤ **Calculate the current volume:** `LoudNoiseDetector` calculates the root mean squared of the recorded signal. Root mean squared computes a "quadratic mean" value. The advantage of using root mean squared over finding the maximum value is that root mean squared takes into account all data points. This makes the calculation robust against single or short-lived time periods of high amplitude and allows only meaningful high amplitude signals to have an effect.

➤ **Determine if the recorded sound is loud is enough:** `LoudNoiseDetector` compares the current volume with a fixed threshold such as 2000. The volume may range from 0 to 32767. It is considerably harder, however, to reach the maximum range since all values within a recording are taken into account. Therefore, in my experience, a value of 2000 seems to work well.

LISTING 14-8: Determines if audio data contains a loud noise

```java
public class LoudNoiseDetector implements AudioClipListener
{
    private static final String TAG = "LoudNoiseDetector";

    private double volumeThreshold;

    public static final int DEFAULT_LOUDNESS_THRESHOLD = 2000;

    public LoudNoiseDetector()
    {
        volumeThreshold = DEFAULT_LOUDNESS_THRESHOLD;
    }

    public LoudNoiseDetector(double volumeThreshold)
    {
        this.volumeThreshold = volumeThreshold;
    }
```

continues

LISTING 14-8 *(continued)*

```
@Override
    public boolean heard(short[] data, int sampleRate)
    {
        boolean heard = false;
        // use rms to take the entire audio signal into account
        // and discount any one single high amplitude
        double currentVolume = rootMeanSquared(data);

        if (currentVolume > volumeThreshold)
        {
            Log.d(TAG, "heard");
            heard = true;
        }

        return heard;
    }

    private double rootMeanSquared(short[] nums)
    {
        double ms = 0;
        for (int i = 0; i < nums.length; i++)
        {
            ms += nums[i] * nums[i];
        }
        ms /= nums.length;
        return Math.sqrt(ms);
    }
}
```

The loud noise clapper, presented in this section, is slightly more robust than the clapper presented earlier because it uses the entire recorded signal to determine volume. Despite this, it still uses volume to detect claps and any method that does so can lead to accidental triggering from extraneous loud noises. The next section describes a more sophisticated signal-processing algorithm that makes the clapper more robust.

USING CONSISTENT FREQUENCY DETECTION

Sounds other than a person's clap could accidentally trigger the original clapper. For example, a dog barking or fireworks going off could accidentally activate it, which could result in the lights going on in the middle of the night. This section describes ConsistentFrequencyDetector, which is an AudioClipListener. ConsistentFrequencyDetector implements a method that creates a clapper that triggers only if it hears an intentional sound and does not easily trigger if it hears other loud noises.

Instead of a loud noise, ConsistentFrequencyDetector detects a period of time that has a consistent frequency. By doing so, ConsistentFrequencyDetector ignores talking, loud noises, and triggers only if it hears a sustained tone that a person can easily create by singing.

To implement this approach, ConsistentFrequencyDetector analyzes the audio to estimate frequency and records a history of previous frequencies so it can detect if it hears a consistent one.

Estimating Frequency

A simple way to analyze for frequency is the zero-crossing method. Listing 14-9 shows the code for calculating frequency using this method. More accurate algorithms exist, such as autocorrelation and Fast Fourier Transform, however ConsistentFrequencyDetector uses the zero-crossing method because it does not need an exact frequency and the method is simple to implement.

The zero-crossing method counts how many times the audio signal crosses from positive to negative or from negative to positive. Two zero crossings indicate one cycle in the signal. Hence, the frequency in Hz is how many pairs of zero crossings occur per second.

The algorithm for calculating zero crossing is as follows:

1. Calculate number of zero crossings.

2. Determine how many seconds of data the samples represent.

3. Determine the number of cycles.

4. Calculate frequency as number of cycles divided by seconds of data.

For example, if the sample size is 8000 and there are 16000 samples, the number of seconds recorded is 2. If the number of crossings in the data is 2204, the number of cycles is 1102 and the detected frequency is 551.

LISTING 14-9: Estimates frequency by using the zero-crossing method

```java
public class ZeroCrossing
{
    public static int calculate(int sampleRate, short [] audioData)
    {
        int numSamples = audioData.length;
        int numCrossing = 0;
        for (int p = 0; p < numSamples-1; p++)
        {
            if ((audioData[p] > 0 && audioData[p + 1] <= 0) ||
                (audioData[p] < 0 && audioData[p + 1] >= 0))
            {
                numCrossing++;
            }
        }

        float numSecondsRecorded = (float)numSamples/(float)sampleRate;
        float numCycles = numCrossing/2;
        float frequency = numCycles/numSecondsRecorded;

        return (int)frequency;
    }
}
```

The zero-crossing method works well for sound waves that have very little noise. To highlight this point, consider the sound wave in Figure 14-2. It shows a 440Hz sine wave, generated by a tone generator and recorded on an Android device. Because a tone generator created the sound, it has very little noise.

It is possible to accurately determine the frequency of this signal with some additional information. First, by looking at Figure 14-2 you can see that the signal repeats about every 100 samples. Second, the app sampled at a rate of 44100Hz. With this information you can determine that 100 data points represents 0.0023 seconds. Then to determine how many times the signal repeats in 1 second, compute 1/0.0023. The result is equal to 435Hz, which is close to the recorded frequency of 440Hz.

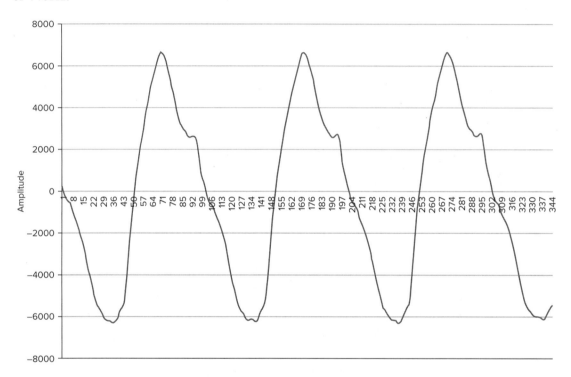

FIGURE 14-2: 440Hz sine wave tone recorded on an Android phone

Real audio signals are rarely as clean as those generated from a tone generator. Figure 14-3 shows the audio data for a person singing a 440Hz tone. Even though the person is singing the same tone as the tone generator, the signal is much more complex and does not vary as regularly. It has too many zero-crossings for the zero-crossing method to determine the precise frequency.

However, the frequency value from the zero-crossing method stays within the same, small range while a person is singing the same tone. When a person is talking, the frequency varies greatly. When a loud noise occurs, the frequency changes only briefly. Thus, even though the zero-crossing method cannot produce a precise measurement of frequency, it can still determine if the sound is singing, which is what you need to implement the singing clapper.

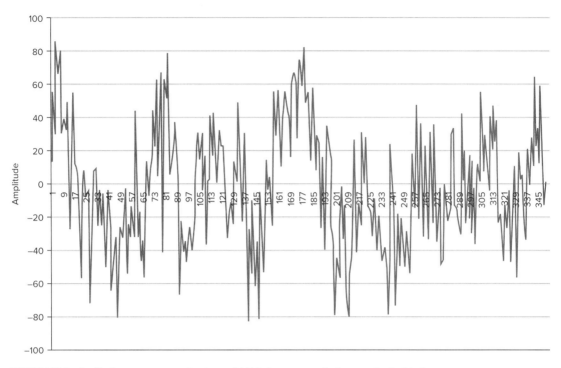

FIGURE 14-3: Audio from a person singing a 440Hz tone recorded on an Android phone

Implementing the Singing Clapper

As the previous section explained, the zero-crossing method is the audio processing technique you need to implement the singing clapper, but several other steps are required to create a clapper that triggers when the user sings a loud, consistent tone. Listing 14-10 shows the implementation of the singing clapper by the `ConsistentFrequencyDetector` class. `ConsistentFrequencyDetector` performs several steps:

➤ Keeps a history of previous frequencies.

➤ Calculates frequency for a given audio recording using the zero-crossings method.

➤ Detects when the history contains frequencies within a range threshold, such as 100.

➤ Ignores any recordings that are silence, because silence can have a consistent frequency itself. Silence is any recording that has a root mean squared value below a threshold such as 2000.

Beyond the code in `ConsistentFrequencyDetector`, it is also useful for an app to configure `AudioClipRecorder` to record audio for a specific amount of time. By doing so, the app can define the length of time it must hear a consistent frequency before triggering.

To set up `AudioClipRecorder` in this way, `AudioClipRecorder` has a `startRecordingForTime()` method. Calling it with *millisecondsPerAudioClip* equal to 1000 sets up `AudioRecord` to pass about 1 second of data to `ConsistentFrequencyDetector` every time `AudioClipRecorder` calls it. If `ConsistentFrequencyDetector` has a history size of 3, it means that the user must make a singing tone for 3 seconds in order to trigger the clapper.

LISTING 14-10: Analyzes audio data to detect a consistent frequency

Available for
download on
Wrox.com

```java
public class ConsistentFrequencyDetector implements AudioClipListener
{
    private static final String TAG = "ConsistentFrequencyDetector";

    private LinkedList<Integer> frequencyHistory;

    private int rangeThreshold;
    private int silenceThreshold;

    public static final int DEFAULT_SILENCE_THRESHOLD = 2000;

    public ConsistentFrequencyDetector(int historySize, int rangeThreshold,
            int silenceThreshold)
    {
        frequencyHistory = new LinkedList<Integer>();
        // pre-fill so modification is easy
        for (int i = 0; i < historySize; i++)
        {
            frequencyHistory.add(Integer.MAX_VALUE);
        }
        this.rangeThreshold = rangeThreshold;
        this.silenceThreshold = silenceThreshold;
    }

    @Override
    public boolean heard(short[] audioData, int sampleRate)
    {
        int frequency = ZeroCrossing.calculate(sampleRate, audioData);
        frequencyHistory.addFirst(frequency);
        // since history is always full, just remove the last
        frequencyHistory.removeLast();
        int range = calculateRange();

        boolean heard = false;
        if (range < rangeThreshold)
        {
            // only trigger it isn't silence
            if (AudioUtil.rootMeanSquared(audioData) > silenceThreshold)
            {
                Log.d(TAG, "heard");
                heard = true;
            }
            else
            {
                Log.d(TAG, "not loud enough");
            }
        }
```

```
        return heard;
    }

    private int calculateRange()
    {
        int min = Integer.MAX_VALUE;
        int max = Integer.MIN_VALUE;
        for (Integer val : frequencyHistory)
        {
            if (val >= max)
            {
                max = val;
            }

            if (val < min)
            {
                min = val;
            }
        }

        return max - min;
    }
}
```

code snippet ConsistentFrequencyDetector.java

This section showed how to use `AudioRecord` to record raw audio data and some signal processing algorithms you can use to create improved versions of the clapper. The algorithms discussed were just a few of the available algorithms you can use to analyze recorded audio. With an understanding of how `AudioRecord` works, you can reuse the recording code discussed in this chapter to collect the audio data you need to implement other signal processing algorithms and detect other features within recorded audio.

SUMMARY

This chapter described how to use the microphone as an audio sensor. It showed how to record audio using `MediaRecorder` and `AudioRecord` and described some utility classes. Using `MediaRecorder`, an app can analyze the maximum amplitude of recorded audio during a period of time. Using `AudioRecord`, an app can analyze the raw audio data and perform signal processing on it.

This chapter contained one potential application for audio processing: a clapper. It presented three different implementations: one that used `MediaRecorder` to detect high maximum amplitudes, one that used `AudioRecord` to detect sustained high amplitudes, and one that used `AudioRecord` to detect a consistent singing tone. These examples highlight how to use the APIs, utility classes, and some simple signal processing techniques.

Utilizing the microphone ends this part's discussion of how to sense augmented and non-augmented objects using the NFC scanner, camera, and microphone. With the right algorithms and API usage techniques, Android devices can readily detect objects that are meant to be detected, such as NFC tags and bar codes. Also, Android devices are powerful enough to recognize some visual and audio patterns, like an image of an Android logo or a singing tone, without the need to augment objects in the world with clues. Being able to detect these things is a powerful feature of Android!

The next, and final, part of this book tackles speech recognition. Like the sensors described in this part, speech recognition enhances the awareness of an app. It allows an app to discern a specific kind of information from audio recordings: spoken words.

PART IV
Speaking to Android

15

Designing a Speech-enabled App

WHAT'S IN THIS CHAPTER?

- ➤ Understanding Android's speech capabilities
- ➤ Introducing the user interface screen flow
- ➤ Designing a voice user interface
- ➤ Soliciting feedback from users

People love using speech to command their phones for many reasons. One reason is that they sometimes prefer dictation rather than awkwardly typing text into a small keyboard. Another reason is that they need access to their devices while they are in the world. For example, they are pleased when they can be driving and still compose messages to send to their friends.

These reasons may seem anecdotal, but the proof is in the downloads. Some apps that use speech are popular. Google Voice Actions, for example, is an app that enables users to perform a wide variety of tasks from a single voice prompt. It has more than one million downloads.

The downloads do not come easy, however. Allowing users to speak to their devices is challenging to design and implement. Android supports speech input and output with APIs for speech recognition and Text-to-Speech (TTS). Using the APIs effectively is only part of the task. The other part is designing and implementing a complete voice user interface (VUI) with all its supporting components.

A VUI is a user interface that utilizes a user's speech as input, pre-recorded or synthesized speech for output, or both. A VUI consists of a set of voice actions, where each voice action allows the user to perform a certain task.

A well-designed and -implemented VUI minimizes the chance of speech recognition errors, has intuitive commands, and enables all users to gracefully command their devices even if errors occur. A poorly designed one contains obscure, hard-to-remember, and hard-to-recognize commands that cause numerous errors.

The ultimate goal of designing a VUI is to prevent users from becoming frustrated and helping them become expert users. This chapter shows you how.

Android provides APIs and user interface components to give you the building blocks you need to construct VUIs. Your design task is to assemble them into a VUI that helps the users accomplish certain tasks. First, you must decide what types of voice actions to include. You may decide to create one-way commands or more complicated back-and-forth conversations between the app and user, depending on how complex the task is. After you have chosen the voice actions, your next task is to design the spoken dialogue. This entails deciding what the user can say and how the device responds. Your design should consider how humans and machines process language. For humans, the design should take care to provide the right spoken cues, and for machines, the design should make sure that the app can easily understand what the human says. Finally, you can test your design using various techniques that help you refine your VUI based on how users react to it. Overall, you can use the suggestions in this chapter to design a tested, well-designed VUI that you can implement using the techniques in Chapters 17–19.

KNOW YOUR TOOLS

Android has built-in APIs for speech recognition and TTS. The speech recognition API allows devices to collect audio from users and convert it to text. TTS allows the device to go in the reverse direction, converting text into audio. Speech recognition and TTS are available on most devices. Devices with limited functionality, like the Nook, or devices without Internet connectivity do not support one or both. In addition, the necessary language data is not pre-installed on all devices, and some could require configuring. Still, a developer can assume that a majority of devices support these APIs. To get speech recognition and TTS working on unsupported devices, developers must use third-party providers such as iSpeech (www.ispeech.org/) or Nuance (www.nuance.com/for-partners/by-solution/mobile-developer-program/index.htm).

FIGURE 15-1: Speech input dialog shown to the user while collecting speech

Following is a list of speech recognition features:

➤ It utilizes a remote server to process audio recorded by the device. This creates a small delay in the recognition and makes it require Internet access to function.

➤ Android's speech input dialog, shown in Figure 15-1, is the standard interface for collecting speech, but it is possible to customize the speech collection process.

➤ Android packages the recognition result into a List<String> of potential speech-to-text conversions with a confidence score attached to each. Chapter 17 describes how to interpret these conversions.

Following is a list of TTS features:

➤ Supports a limited set of languages.

➤ Each language has only one voice.

➤ Runs on the device without an Internet connection.

➤ Sometimes mispronounces words, but there is no way to change pronunciation. For example, currently it speaks "environment" with an emphasis on the "ron" part of the word. Fortunately, sometimes new releases of Android contain updates to the TTS functionality that improve pronunciation.

TRY THIS

Try the Say the Magic Word button. Click the Speak button and attempt to say the magic word "tree."

Say the Magic Word shows you how speech recognition and TTS can work together to create a simple app. It also highlights one limit of speech recognition: it is sometimes inaccurate.

In the Say the Magic Word screen, the user has to say the magic word "tree." Figure 15-2 shows a successful attempt on the left and a failed attempt on the right. If the app fails to recognize the word, it will report what it thought the user said. In the failed attempt from Figure 15-2, the app thought the user said "three." Does the magic word screen always understand you?

Figure 15-2: The Say the Magic Word screens make the user say "tree."

In summary, Android devices can understand what users say and reply back. Most devices have these capabilities. Chapter 16 describes the mechanics of using the APIs. The remainder of this chapter describes how to design VUIs, while taking these capabilities into account.

USER INTERFACE SCREEN FLOW

Android provides speech recognition and TTS, but an app needs other user interface elements to implement a complete VUI. A VUI can have one or more voice actions. Each voice action requires one or more turns to accomplish a task. A turn consists of a user action or utterance followed by a system action and/or utterance. Figure 15-3 shows the screens the user sees when completing one turn on an Android device.

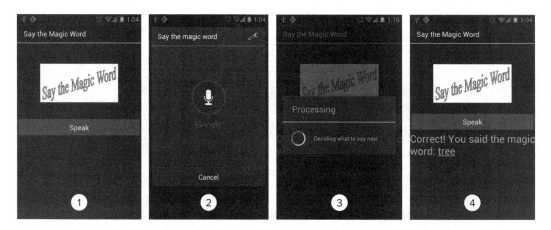

FIGURE 15-3: Sequence of screens to complete one turn of user utterance and app response

During the turn, the user activates speech, speaks, waits, and then hears and sees the response. Not all turns have these steps. (Some have only speech output, for example).

Figure 15-3, Screen 1, Activation: The app provides a way for the user to activate speech recognition. In this case, it is a button, but other options are available that may work when the user wants to operate the device eyes-free or hands-free.

Figure 15-3, Screen 2, Prompt: After the user clicks the button, the app indicates that it is waiting for speech input by showing a Say the Magic Word dialog. The user then speaks. The dialog is Android's default speech recognition dialog that should look familiar to users. There is customizable text within the dialog that the app can use as a prompt to remind the users what they can say. Your design should contain the words for the prompt as well as the words the user can say when presented with the dialog.

Figure 15-3, Screen 3, Processing: The speech API controls converting audio to text while the user waits. To do this, the API records audio, sends it to Google servers, and returns with a list of possible text recognitions. The app processes these possible recognitions to determine which one the user actually said.

Figure 15-3, Screen 4, Take action: The app decides what it should do in response. For the app in Figure 15-3, the app displays "Correct! You said the magic word: tree" and speaks it using TTS. Part of your design involves crafting these responses.

As you can see, the user goes through a four-step process to complete a turn. Your voice actions may have one or more of these turns. The next section describes some factors to consider when deciding.

VOICE ACTION TYPES

Using speech recognition and TTS, developers can build various types of voice actions for VUIs within their apps. Table 15-1 lists four types. Reader actions read text aloud, Listener actions only record what the user says Commands are single turn actions, and multi-turn Commands can last multiple turns. An app may have a mixture of these voice actions.

TABLE 15-1: Types of Voice Actions with Different Degrees of Complexity

ACTION TYPE	TTS	SPEECH	STATELESS	DESCRIPTION	EXAMPLE TASK TYPES AND COMMAND WORDS
Reader	Yes	No	Yes	Reads text.	E-mail reader, GPS navigator
Listener	No	Yes	Yes	Transcribes everything the user says as text.	E-mail writer
Command	Maybe	Yes	Yes	The user issues a command to the app via speech using a single turn. If the command fails, the user must retry. The app may speak text in reply, but does not ask follow-up questions.	Recipe reader: "Next step" E-mail reader: "Read first"
Multi-turn Command	Yes	Yes	No	The user issues a speech command to the app and the app may reply with additional requests for information. Because the conversation between the user and the app could have multiple turns, the app must maintain state.	To-do List management "User: Add bread" "App: which list?" "User: grocery"

The main trade off between Reader, Listener, Command, and Multi-turn Command actions is *naturalness* and *power* versus *accuracy*. The more words and phrases a user can use to accomplish a goal, the more natural the action is. The more that the actions accomplish, the more powerful the action is. The more accurate an action is, the easier it is for the app to understand the user. When an app restricts the vocabulary and complexity of the speech input, it becomes more accurate at the cost of naturalness and power.

The four action types cover various degrees of the trade off. A Reader action is always accurate, because the user is using traditional input methods. A Listener is less accurate because speech recognition may not understand the user and transcribe the wrong text. However, a Listener is always accurate in performing the correct function of transcribing everything the user says. A Command action is less accurate, because, like a `Listener` action, speech recognition may not understand the spoken input. However, a `Command` action can also cause the app to perform the wrong task or fail outright if the user does not say the correct command words. Despite this possibility of failure, spoken words can be more natural than clicking a button, and a speech action may accomplish a lot in just a few words. A `Multi-turn Command` action is even less accurate because it may take multiple turns between user and app to accomplish a task. The more turns there are, the higher the chance of a recognition error and task failure. However, a `Multi-turn Command` action can support complex tasks that take multiple inputs to fully complete. Additionally, `Multi-turn Command` actions can be more efficient in some cases because they can ask follow-up questions if needed. Using a `Command` would require the user to try again without any memory of previous attempts.

Beyond these are open-ended dialogue systems. Such systems are designed to be completely natural, and hence can accept any customary speech input within a domain. They are powerful because they are designed to allow the user to complete complex tasks using a variety of language. For example, an airline scheduling system might start by asking, "How can I help you?" From there, users specify the various constraints and desires for their travel in any order they please. The users use the same language they would if they were speaking to a human. The system understands all user utterances and tracks the parts of the travel the user has specified. If any gaps exist, the system queries the user for additional information. The resulting conversation could take many different paths, have a variety of vocabulary, and potentially be long. The design process is hence more involved than what is described here.

 For more information on the design of open-ended dialogue systems, consult Randy Harris's book Voice Interaction Design.

You can build many useful apps with `Reader`, `Listener`, `Command`, and `Multi-turn Command` actions alone.

VOICE USER INTERFACE (VUI) DESIGN

Developing voice interfaces that are natural and powerful requires a well thought out and tested design. This section focuses on the design techniques you need to design a VUI. After using these techniques, your design will include a set of voice actions that have been tested on real users. Your only remaining task will be to implement that design so that Android's speech recognition is accurate.

Apps enable users to perform various tasks traditionally using a graphical user interface (GUI) that allows them to tap and view a screen. Any of these tasks could be potentially enhanced or replaced by adding a VUI. In a VUI, the user is speaking, listening, and potentially not looking at a screen.

These two interaction methods are appropriate for different tasks and should be designed using different techniques. This section explores what methods work best for VUIs and contrasts them with some methods that are better suited for GUIs. First, it examines whether or not to add voice actions in the first place.

Deciding Appropriate Tasks for Voice Actions

You have several considerations for determining if your task is appropriate for a voice action. The decision partially depends on the properties of speech input and output.

Using speech input incurs several potentially tedious tasks for the user. It takes extra time to proceed through the process of activating speech recognition, speaking, and waiting for response. The speech recognition can also fail and require the user to retry. However, in certain scenarios, the benefits of speech input outweigh the burdens of using it.

Speech output is transient and easily forgotten. If a display is not available, users must remember everything that the app says. Therefore, it is possible the users will forget what the app just said a moment ago.

Given these properties, this section contains some recommendations about what tasks are suitable for voice actions. For more recommendations, see `http://java.sun.com/products/java-media/speech/forDevelopers/jsapi-guide/UserInterface.html`. First, you should consider a voice action if your app addresses one of these two concerns:

➤ *There is no other way to collect input or look at output:* When the user's hands or eyes are busy, the only way to safely use the app may be speech input and output. These conditions can happen when a user is performing certain activities such as driving, cooking, or fighting a war.

➤ *The user gains a large productivity increase compared to using a GUI:* Voice actions can be very powerful and let the user accomplish a lot with a single speech input. If the voice action does not provide such a benefit, the user will prefer to use the reliable and faster GUI alternative. For example, a powerful voice action might allow a user to say one utterance instead of selecting items from five different selection boxes, or to say one word to select an action instead of scrolling down a long 100-item list.

If your app has a task that satisfies one of these concerns, a VUI may be appropriate. However, your app's task may have additional requirements that make a VUI infeasible. Hence, you should consider the following:

➤ *Use speech input only if the user can tolerate occasional errors:* Any speech input could result in occasional errors. For some tasks, such as reading e-mail, errors are acceptable. If a read e-mail command fails once in a while, the user can retry without too much distress. For other tasks, such as an app for emergency rescue, errors are unacceptable. In a time-critical app for emergency rescue, delaying an action by even a second could be life threatening.

➤ *Use speech output for small amounts of information:* Keep speech output short and do not use it to convey large amounts of information. Speech output is not good at communicating large amounts of information because users easily forget it. For example, to make certain conclusions about a table of data, a user would need to analyze it. To communicate a table of data, a VUI would need to speak every single data item. By the time the app speaks the last data item, the user has likely forgotten it all, leaving the user unable to really do any analysis. In contrast, a user would have no problem thinking about the spatially organized data in a GUI all at once.

➤ *Consider the environment:* Speech input and output may not be appropriate for the environment. The expected environment for the app could cause speech input or output to function poorly. In particular, a noisy environment could be problematic. It may not allow the user to hear speech output. A noisy environment could also cause speech input to fail by allowing any extraneous sounds to enter any speech recordings. Quiet environments could also be a problem because they are not conducive to listening or speaking out loud.

Designing What the App and Users Will Say

After you have decided which tasks need voice actions, you must then decide what your users and your app will say. The techniques described here give you some ideas about how to design the commands and conversations.

Constrain Speech Input to Increase Accuracy

Apps cannot easily understand unconstrained speech. Human speech is highly variable and entails a large vocabulary. Although this breadth makes speech extremely expressive, it also makes it difficult for an app understand, and hence unable to take full advantage of humans' ability to communicate. Even with the best natural language processing technology, apps are unable to understand unbounded speech.

Developers should consider the complexity of allowed speech input when designing a VUI. Constraining speech input will increase recognition accuracy at the cost of expressiveness. For example, many ways exist to indicate an affirmative response — yes, right, OK, sure, fine, sure thing, you got it, and so on — but if you limit your app to "yes" it will be easier for the app to recognize. However, as a consequence, users will have to learn to only say "yes" and not the other words.

Train Users to Know What They Can Say

In a VUI, users don't know what they can say nor what the app can understand. This is especially true when an app constrains the speech input to a few command words. Some users will expect an app to understand anything they say, and others will be dumbfounded by a speech prompt. These problems do not exist in a GUI, which has visual elements such as buttons and menus that allow users to discover easily what they can do.

Therefore, a VUI must train the users to understand the boundaries of what it can and cannot understand, especially if the app is hands-free and eyes-free. Existing apps accomplish this goal in several ways.

One is to have different kinds of help screens that show you what the commands are or what you might say. Figure 15-4 shows examples from three different speech apps: Google Voice Search, Vlingo, and Edwin. Each has a different help screen. Google Voice Search shows users one command at a time, highlighting in bold what the command words are. Vlingo provides a list and highlights command words in blue, and Edwin provides sample phrases.

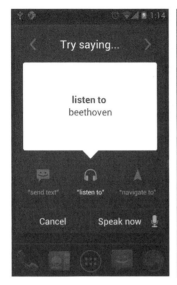
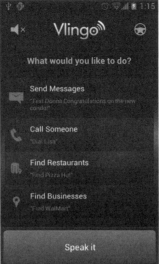
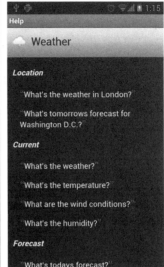

FIGURE 15-4: Three help screens from Google Voice Search, Vlingo, and Edwin show different ways to explain to users what they can say.

Another way to train users is to include suggestions within the speech. For example, the Voice Commands app from Nuance leads the user through a series of short commands and then teaches the user shortcuts after the command is done. For example, the user can say "check" and then say "missed calls" to hear any missed calls. After hearing some results, the app says, "Next time just say check missed calls."

Another kind of training involves encouraging your users to use certain words or to speak in a certain way. This is called "stealth training" and here is how it works. Say you have a VUI that allows users to "check" or "uncheck" a box, but you prefer them to say "mark" and "clear" because those words are more easily recognized. To accomplish this, the app still recognizes "uncheck." However, when the app responds it includes "clear" in the response by saying something like this: "cleared item 1." After hearing "cleared" several times, the user may start using "clear" instead of "uncheck," which is desirable because the app will recognize "clear" more times than it will recognize "uncheck."

Beyond training, an app can use prompts to let users know what they can say.

Prompt the Users so They Know What to Say

A prompt is text spoken or displayed to users. Several different kinds of prompts exist:

➤ *Explicit prompts:* If the possible input is highly constrained, an app can tell the users what they can say directly and accept only those inputs. For example, the prompt "Say yes or no" would accept only "yes" or "no."

➤ *Implicit prompts:* Prompts can use the conventions of speech to suggest what the user should say in a reply. For example, a prompt such as "Would you like e-mail or voicemail?" would encourage the user to say "e-mail" or "voicemail" in response.

➤ *Tapered prompts:* Sometimes users do not need prompting to determine what they can say. Excessive prompting can make a VUI tedious and repetitive to use. To avoid this, an app can use tapered prompts. For example, if the app has a series of questions it needs to ask the user, the resulting dialogue could easily become repetitive. In tapered prompts, the app would remove the repetitive parts as the conversation progresses and the user will still know what to say. For example, if an app is prompting for an address, it might sound like this:

App: Please say your street.

User: 1 Main St.

App: Please say your state.

User: Massachusetts

App: Please say your zip code.

User: 01808

The conversation continuously says "Please say your X," which is unnecessary the second and third time. The following tapered prompts work as well and are shorter:

App: Please say your street.

User: 1 Main St.

App: Your state?

User: Massachusetts

App: Zip code?

User: 01808

Once users have learned what they can say, they must learn to trust that the app produces the correct outcomes in response. The next section describes how to build this trust by properly confirming actions and dealing with errors.

Confirm Success and Help Users Recover from Errors

Speaking a voice command is risky because it could fail for many reasons. Errors are possible in a VUI that almost never occur in GUIs. In a GUI, if the users want to hit a button, they almost always are successful. For example, it is relatively rare to accidentally hit the OK button when you are trying to hit the Cancel button on a typical GUI dialog. With a VUI, however, the number of possible selections in a single dialog could be large. Given that and the uncertainty of the recognition accuracy, it can be far more common to accidentally select the wrong button.

Additionally, after something fails or is successful in a GUI, the screen can visually display the result of the action. With an eyes-free VUI, users need another way to determine if their command was successful.

For these two reasons, you need to provide a way for users to recover from any mistakes they or the app make. At the same time, you don't want to overwhelm users with too many confirmations, which can be arduous. You also need to allow users to confirm that their voice command was successful. Here are several suggestions:

- ➤ *Confirm visually*: If available, display the result of the action on the screen.

- ➤ *Use implicit confirmation*: For non-critical actions, the app should assume that the recognition was successful. It should implicitly confirm the result of the action in its response. For example, in response to "Add apple," the app should respond "Added apple" so the user knows that the app properly recognized "apple." If the app says "Added pumpkin," the user will know it misrecognized "apple." If the app just says "OK," the user has no idea if the app succeeded or failed.

- ➤ Explicit confirmation isn't always necessary. For example, if the system responded, "Would you like to add Apple?" and then required the user to say yes or no, explicit confirmation would be burdensome and time consuming.

- ➤ By assuming that the users were successful, and implicitly confirming, users can work efficiently in full knowledge of the results of their actions, without any needless confirmations.

- ➤ *Use explicit confirmation when necessary*: For actions that can't be undone, explicitly ask the user to confirm. For example, "Are you sure you want to delete X?"

- ➤ *Allow for undo*: When the app performs the wrong action, allow the user to undo it with another command. This allows your app to continue most of the time and gives the user a way to correct the app when it fails.

- ➤ *Give the user a non-speech method for accomplishing the same task*: It might be that the user is getting frustrated or simply doesn't have the time to figure out how to use speech. In such cases, it is nice to have a method for manually operating the user interface even if it requires a lot of work for the user. Users will be happy to know they can use a 100 percent effective method if they need to.

- ➤ *Use progressive assistance to help*: Provide additional help the more times the system fails. For example, on the first failure an app can say "What?" then on the second say, "I don't understand" and on the third be explicit and say "Sorry, you can say, 'send e-mail or cancel to exit.'"

- ➤ *Fall back to easier to recognize commands*: If a user fails to execute a command, an app could fall back to another speech command that is easy to recognize. For example, if a user says "check voicemail" several times without success, the app could offer a list selection voice action like "Would you like to check voicemail or e-mail?" Although the list may be more cumbersome, the possible responses are fewer and hence will more likely lead to success.

Help Users Recover from Accidental Speech Activation

Recognition errors occur when an app doesn't understand the user, but the app can also fail if the user accidentally activates speech recognition. Accidental triggering can occur, especially if the speech trigger is based on incoming sound. In such activation, the app starts speech input whenever it hears a certain sound. The user could also accidentally hit a "Speak now" button.

When an accidental speech activation occurs, it puts the user in an awkward situation where the app prompts the user for an input, but the user has nothing to say. To compensate, the VUI should provide a spoken word, such as "cancel," that allows the user to exit from the speech prompt in case such an error occurs.

In some cases it is possible to prevent recognition errors in the first place by instructing the user on how to properly speak to the speech recognizer.

Teach Users Proper Speech Hygiene

Any behavior that causes people to speak differently than they normally would causes the speech recognizer to be less accurate. Unfortunately, these behaviors usually get worse when more errors occur. However, some ways of speaking, though awkward, improve speech recognition and can be useful when a user is having trouble. To help make users become experts at speaking to their devices, they should learn the following techniques:

➤ *Try to speak normally*: When people get frustrated, they start over-pronouncing words. They may over-emphasize one word like: "what's NEXT?" and say "next" much louder than normal. They might stretch out a particular vowel like "what's neeeext?" They may just yell the words. These distortions make it more difficult for the speech recognizer because it is made to recognize normal speech. The unfortunate part of this is that the angrier users get, the more recognition problems occur. The more problems that occur, the more upset users get.

➤ *If having trouble, leave a short pause between words*: Leaving a short pause between words helps recognition. It relieves the recognizer from having to determine where one word ends and another begins, and it also lessens the distortion that occurs when you speak two words together. It takes longer and is awkward to speak that way, but it is useful for cases when a user is really having trouble.

TRY THIS

To see the effect of leaving short pauses between words, try using the keyboard voice input. To access the voice input, open any text soft keyboard (for example, in the mail program) and tap the microphone icon to the left of the space bar. Speak "It's not easy to wreck a nice beach" as you normally would. Then do it again, but leave a short pause between words. Which did the device recognize best without changing any words?

Use Menus Cautiously

Constraining speech input and handling and avoiding errors can help the user execute their voice action reliably. However, the required sequence of a voice action's turns can also affect the user's ability to execute it. When designing your app's voice action you should consider that VUIs are temporal, not spatial, which makes certain interaction patterns taxing. For example, navigating menus, a common GUI technique, is poorly suited for VUIs because menus are meant to be seen and allow the users to scan the sectioned contents to quickly find what they want. In a VUI, the users have no way to do so, and hence have to try to keep the menu hierarchy and sections all in their short-term memory to know where to go.

If the VUI forces the user to "go back" or "go to step 5," it is forcing the user to think spatially, which is difficult. Any sequence of list selections may cause this to happen.

Conversations are better structured around building a shared understanding than navigating a menu structure. The closer a VUI can get to that kind of interaction, the easier it will be to operate.

Hence, if possible, a VUI should not force the user into such hierarchies of list selections. However, to do so requires opening up prompts for many different possible inputs. This may not be possible because the more inputs a prompt can accept, the harder it will be to recognize.

For example, consider a pizza ordering VUI that sounds like this:

> App: First select a size. You can select small, medium, or large.
>
> User: Large
>
> App: Select a topping. You can select mushrooms or pepperoni.
>
> User: Mushrooms
>
> App: Select a crust. You can select deep dish or normal.
>
> User: Deep dish
>
> App: Is the order complete?
>
> User: Go back to start
>
> … redo the whole conversation.

In this VUI, the user specifies a certain part of his pizza order one step at a time. If the user gets to the end and wants to change the size, he would have to "go back" twice to get back to the size selection step or "go back to start" to start again. Hopefully, the user remembers where two steps back is. Another way to design this VUI is to sound like this:

> User: Size large
>
> App: OK, large.
>
> User: Topping mushrooms.
>
> App: OK, mushrooms.
>
> User: Crust, deep dish.
>
> App: OK, deep dish.
>
> User: Size small.
>
> App: OK, small.

In this other version, the app accepts any of the three pizza attributes from the prompt. Thus, the users can specify their attributes one at a time and, in a similar manner, change one at the end in a single step without having to "go back." The drawback of this approach is that it is harder for the app to recognize the user's speech because more possible inputs exist at the prompt.

After the Design

Using the recommendations in this section, you can design voice actions that users desire, are easy to learn, and can operate reliably. Before you release your app, you should consider testing your design first. Doing so can uncover unforeseen obstacles users encounter while trying to use your VUI. The next section describes some ways to accomplish that goal.

TESTING YOUR DESIGN

When designing a VUI, users can help you to identify standard vocabulary and interaction patterns and what users expect the app to understand. This section discusses three techniques that can help gather information from users: natural dialogue studies, Wizard of Oz studies, and beta tests.

Learning the words and interaction patterns requires you to observe users speaking about the topic and trying to interact with your app. For example, if you are adding a "compose" command to an e-mail app, you want to know all the different words people use to initiate sending an e-mail. You may discover that some people prefer to say "write" instead of "compose" and decide to include "write" as an alternate way to activate the "compose" command. Also, you may discover that it is easier for the speech recognizer to understand "write" instead of "compose" and decide to support only "write" as the command.

One method of observing users is called a natural dialogue study. In this study, you ask a group of people to carry on a dialogue about the subject you are interested in and record a transcript. You can also examine any existing corpora. In the case of an e-mail app, you could have one person try to ask another person to send an e-mail for them. For a cooking app, you might observe one person helping another person follow a recipe.

The advantage of a natural dialogue study is that you can observe a greater variety of words and interactions because the people involved are less influenced by any experimental environment.

Natural dialogue studies are helpful for learning generally about what people say, but don't allow you to test what people might say to the implemented app or how they will react to the app's responses. For this, you can use a Wizard of Oz study.

In a Wizard of Oz study, users interact with a realistic app, but any app responses are generated by a human, also known as the wizard. The users are unaware that the responses are coming from a human. They think the app is generating them.

Implementing this kind of study involves several details. First, the wizard should respond in such a way that the users cannot tell that they are talking to a human. For example, to make the app more realistic, the experiment may include a way for the wizard to deliver responses via machine-generated speech. Second, to get an accurate glimpse at how the real app would function, the wizard should try to behave like the machine would. The wizard should follow a script that best approximates what the app will be capable of. Also, the wizard should not give the app unreasonable understanding capabilities. For example, if the user says something to the app that it would have no way of understanding, such as a sarcastic statement, the wizard should respond with the app not understanding.

Wizard of Oz studies offer a way to test your VUI while it is being designed and implemented. You can gauge users' reactions to the app's utterances and you can discover additional desires the user may have. For example, while performing such a study for Digital Recipe Sidekick's voice-controlled recipe reader, I noticed that users wanted to navigate the recipe steps in random order instead of sequentially. Originally, I limited the user to hearing the steps one after another, but after the study I allowed the user to navigate by step number as well.

Besides performing experiments, you can also observe the app performance by collecting transcripts from beta tests or deployed app users. Such information allows you to fine-tune the VUI even further. In particular, it helps to expose how effective your design is when increased recognition errors exist due to live speech recognition occurring in various environments.

After completing some or all of these studies, you will have a good understanding of which commands people want and what words they want to use to activate them. From here, you can use the techniques discussed in the remaining chapters to implement them.

SUMMARY

This chapter outlined how to design a VUI that utilizes the speech recognition and TTS tools that Android provides. Your design should include the tasks that need voice actions and the spoken dialogue needed to accomplish them. If it takes into account the suggestions in this chapter, your VUI will use voice actions only for appropriate tasks and be easy for users to use.

Your remaining task is to implement the voice actions you designed. This may involve adjusting the design as you learn which words and interactions work best in practice. Specifically, you'll need to solve several challenges: implement code to operate the Android APIs (Chapter 16), implement code that recognizes the spoken words from the user (Chapter 17), execute voice actions in a modular and user-friendly way (Chapter 18), and select an appropriate speech activation method (Chapter 19).

REFERENCES

Harris, Randy Allen. 2005. *Voice Interaction Design*: *Crafting the New Conversational Speech Systems*. San Francisco: Elsevier Inc.

http://java.sun.com/products/java-media/speech/forDevelopers/jsapi-guide/UserInterface.html (accessed October 10, 2011).

16

Using Speech Recognition and Text-To-Speech APIs

Speech recognition enables users to speak to their Android device and Text-To-Speech (TTS) enables the device to speak back. This chapter explores how to use the speech recognition and TTS APIs and how to properly handle the details of initializing and executing their various functions. In addition, this chapter describes code you can reuse to handle common procedures.

TEXT-TO-SPEECH

To use TTS, apps must perform the following steps:

1. Initialize the `TextToSpeech` object. Verify that the device supports the desired language, download additional data if necessary, and wait for an asynchronous TTS engine initialization process to complete.

2. Operate the `TextToSpeech` API to play speech, sounds, and silence.

3. Implement an `Activity` that handles managing the `TextToSpeech` life cycle as well as any user interactions that are required during initialization or speaking.

This chapter presents an implementation of `TextToSpeech` that involves several classes. The classes implement two groups of functionality: initializing and using TTS. The design implements these with three classes and an interface between two of them. Specifically, here are the classes and their functions:

➤ `TextToSpeechStartupListener`: An interface containing methods for the possible outcomes of the initialization procedure.

➤ `TextToSpeechInitializer`: A class to execute the initialization procedure and call back to a `TextToSpeechStartupListener`.

➤ `LanguageDataInstallBroadcastReceiver`: Handles tracking when the user completes language data installation.

➤ `TextToSpeechDemo`: An `Activity` to implement a simple usage of `TextToSpeech` to read a short script. It manages the life cycle of the `TextToSpeech` object and implements any necessary interactions with the user.

These classes enable you to reuse `TextToSpeechInitializer` and `LanguageDataInstallBroadcastReceiver` within your own `Activity`, and possibly use `TextToSpeechDemo` as a template.

Beyond these classes, three demonstration activities help show all of the `TextToSpeech` features. They are located under the Text to Speech heading of the book's companion app. They are:

➤ **Demo:** The `TextToSpeechDemo Activity`. As described in the previous list, it shows a simple usage of TTS.

➤ **Try Text to Speech:** A playground where you can set all the different parameters of the `TextToSpeech` object and observe how they affect the output.

➤ **Diagnostics:** Has a few functions that show detailed information about the TTS engine for the particular device.

Initialization

Before an app can use TTS, it needs to create a `TextToSpeech` object. Preparing the object for use requires one of two partially asynchronous procedures. The difference between the two procedures involves how the app checks for language support. One procedure, implemented with `TextToSpeechInitializer`, uses on `Locales` and API calls to `TextToSpeech`. The other, implemented with `TextToSpeechInitializerByAction`, uses voice descriptions and an `Intent` with the `ACTION_CHECK_DATA` action. The procedure in `TextToSpeechInitializer` is simpler, but in some cases you may need the procedure in `TextToSpeechInitializerByAction`. Both procedures check for language support and use `TextToSpeechStartupListener` to return results.

`TextToSpeechStartupListener` contains methods that represent the various outcomes of the initialization process. Listing 16-1 shows its code. When the initializer is successful, it calls onSuccessfullInit() to deliver a fully initialized TextToSpeech object that is ready to be used. Along the way, the initializer may call any of the other methods to deal with contingences.

The code that uses TextToSpeech is a good place to implement TextToSpeechStartupListener. For example, SayMagicWordDemo shown in Listing 16-22 later in this chapter, contains an example implementation. SayMagicWordDemo is the main Activity and it uses TextToSpeech. By implementing TextToSpeechStartupListener it can receive the TextToSpeech object when it is ready. Also, SayMagicWordDemo can appropriately respond to any errors or initialization steps that require user intervention.

LISTING 16-1: Callback interface to handle various initialization outcomes

```
public interface TextToSpeechStartupListener
{
    /**
     * tts is initialized and ready for use
     *
     * @param tts
     *              the fully initialized object
     */
    public void onSuccessfulInit(TextToSpeech tts);

    /**
     * language data is required, to install call
     * {@link TextToSpeechInitializer#installLanguageData()}
     */
    public void onRequireLanguageData();

    /**
     * The app has already requested language data, and is waiting for it.
     */
    public void onWaitingForLanguageData();

    /**
     * initialization failed and can never complete.
     */
    public void onFailedToInit();
}
```

Initialization with Locale

Initializing TextToSpeech involves waiting for the asynchronous TTS engine startup to complete, and then setting the TextToSpeech settings. Setting the language setting is complicated by requiring a check first and a potential language data download.

Figure 16-1 describes the procedure from TextToSpeechInitializer. The circles are initialization steps and the squares represent four possible end states.

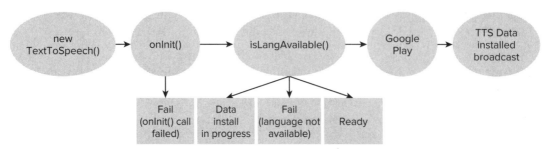

FIGURE 16-1: Asynchronous initialization procedure for creating and configuring TTS

First, the app creates a new `TextToSpeech` and passes in an `OnInitListener`. Android immediately returns control to the app and begins an asynchronous initialization process. Meanwhile, any calls to `TextToSpeech`, such as `setLanguage()`, will be ineffective. Therefore, to reliably initialize `TextToSpeech`, your app should disable TTS functions while initialization is occurring and wait to configure it until the initialization is complete.

Second, `TextToSpeech` finishes its asynchronous initialization and it calls `OnInitListener.onInit()`. The code needs to execute two tasks during `onInit()`.

The app must check the *success* variable passed in `onInit()`. If it is `TextToSpeech.FAILURE`, the initialization failed and TTS cannot initialize.

Then, the device must check if it supports the desired language. If the device supports the language, `TextToSpeech` is ready. If the device cannot ever support the language, it fails. If the device supports the language but is missing language data, the user must download it via Google Play. If the user has already begun downloading the language data, the app may end by reporting that data install is in progress. When the user finishes installing the language data, the installer broadcasts `android.speech.tts.engine.TTS_DATA_INSTALLED`.

Implementing TTS Initialization

`TextToSpeechInitializer` manages the initialization process just described. The initialization process begins in its `createTextToSpeech()`, shown in listing 16-2, and continues in its `setTextToSpeechSettings()` method, shown in Listing 16-3. These methods execute asynchronously. When complete, they make callbacks to one of the methods in `TextToSpeechStartupListener`.

If the external code determines language data is required, it may elect to install the data. If so, the code in listings 16-5 and 16-6 show how to activate the language install only once by starting an `Intent`, using a shared preference, and waiting for a broadcast result.

The following sections explore these steps in detail.

Starting TTS Initialization

First, the initialization code must create the `TextToSpeech` object. The `createTextToSpeech()` method handles this. It takes the `locale` of the desired language as input so the initialization can set it later within the `setTextToSpeechSettings()` method. It also creates an anonymous `OnInitListener` class as the `OnInitListener` to handle the `onInit()` callback from `TextToSpeech`.

LISTING 16-2: Creates a TextToSpeech object with an OnInitListener

```
private void createTextToSpeech(final Locale locale)
{
    tts = new TextToSpeech(context, new OnInitListener()
    {
        @Override
        public void onInit(int status)
        {
            if (status == TextToSpeech.SUCCESS)
            {
                setTextToSpeechSettings(locale);
            } else
            {
                Log.e(TAG, "error creating text to speech");
                callback.onFailedToInit();
            }
        }
    });
}
```

`setTextToSpeechSettings()` either succeeds at configuring `TextToSpeech` and reports success, or makes a callback depending on whether the device can support the desired language.

Checking for Language Support using a Locale

`setTextToSpeechSettings()`, shown in Listing 16-3, checks for language availability. It does this by checking the output from `TextToSpeech.isLanguageAvailable()`. Depending on the result, it makes different callbacks to `TextToSpeechInitializer`.

`TextToSpeech.isLanguageAvailable()` takes a `Locale` as input and returns five possible values. If your app is not changing the default language, it should pass in `Locale.getDefault()`. Following is a summary of the five possible return values and what they mean.

➤ `TextToSpeech.LANG_AVAILABLE`: TTS is ready, and supports the language.

➤ `TextToSpeech.LANG_COUNTRY_AVAILABLE`: TTS is ready, and supports the language and country.

➤ `TextToSpeech.LANG_COUNTRY_VAR_AVAILABLE`: TTS is ready, and supports language, country, and variant.

➤ `TextToSpeech.LANG_NOT_SUPPORTED`: TTS has failed. The app cannot support the language.

➤ `TextToSpeech.LANG_MISSING_DATA`: TTS is not ready yet. The app needs make the user download the language data first.

Available for
download on
Wrox.com

LISTING 16-3: Sets TextToSpeech settings or callback to handle contingencies based on language data availability

```java
private void setTextToSpeechSettings(final Locale locale)
{
    Locale defaultOrPassedIn = locale;
    if (locale == null)
    {
        defaultOrPassedIn = Locale.getDefault();
    }
    // check if language is available
    switch (tts.isLanguageAvailable(defaultOrPassedIn))
    {
        case TextToSpeech.LANG_AVAILABLE:
        case TextToSpeech.LANG_COUNTRY_AVAILABLE:
        case TextToSpeech.LANG_COUNTRY_VAR_AVAILABLE:
            Log.d(TAG, "SUPPORTED");
            tts.setLanguage(locale);
            callback.onSuccessfulInit(tts);
            break;
        case TextToSpeech.LANG_MISSING_DATA:
            Log.d(TAG, "MISSING_DATA");
            // check if waiting, by checking
            // a shared preference
            if (LanguageDataInstallBroadcastReceiver
                    .isWaiting(context))
            {
                Log.d(TAG, "waiting for data...");
                callback.onWaitingForLanguageData();
            } else
            {
                Log.d(TAG, "require data...");
                callback.onRequireLanguageData();
            }
            break;
        case TextToSpeech.LANG_NOT_SUPPORTED:
            Log.d(TAG, "NOT SUPPORTED");
            callback.onFailedToInit();
            break;
    }
}
```

code snippet TextToSpeechInitializer.java

Before continuing in this discussion, consider the possible reasons for requiring language data and what happens when a device downloads it. On any given device, an app can get different values from isLanguageAvailable() for each possible Locale. The values depend on how much, if any, language data is installed on the device.

Figure 16-2 shows some output from the code in Listing 16-4. It contains the language, country, and variant, separated by underscores for any Locale that the device supports partially or completely. The text output after the Locale description describes any lack of device support. If the text says

NOT_SUPPORTED it means that the device does not support the Locale at all. If it says MISSING_DATA the device can support the Locale, if it had the TTS data.

If the device partially supports the Locale, the output describes which parts it supports. For example, the output in Figure 16-2 shows that the device supports Spanish with an ES country, but not a AR country. If the device supported the AR country, it would have printed es_AR COUNTRY_AVAILBLE. Also, the output shows that the device does not support the POSIX variant of en_US_POSIX, but does support the language and country. In either case, the device supports some form of English and Spanish, if not exactly the one the Locale specifies.

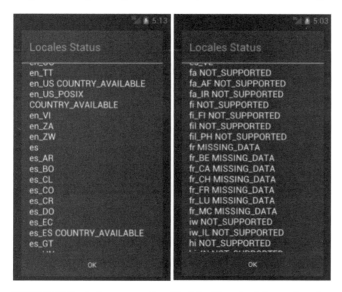

FIGURE 16-2: isLanguageAvailable() output for various Locales on a particular device

LISTING 16-4: Code required to describe which Locales a device supports

```java
public static String getLanguageAvailableDescription(TextToSpeech tts)
{
    StringBuilder sb = new StringBuilder();
    for (Locale loc : Locale.getAvailableLocales())
    {
        int availableCheck = tts.isLanguageAvailable(loc);
        sb.append(loc.toString()).append(" ");
        switch (availableCheck)
        {
            case TextToSpeech.LANG_AVAILABLE:
                break;
            case TextToSpeech.LANG_COUNTRY_AVAILABLE:
                sb.append("COUNTRY_AVAILABLE");
                break;
            case TextToSpeech.LANG_COUNTRY_VAR_AVAILABLE:
                sb.append("COUNTRY_VAR_AVAILABLE");
                break;
```

continues

LISTING 16-4 *(continued)*

```
                case TextToSpeech.LANG_MISSING_DATA:
                    sb.append("MISSING_DATA");
                    break;
                case TextToSpeech.LANG_NOT_SUPPORTED:
                    sb.append("NOT_SUPPORTED");
                    break;
            }
            sb.append("\n");
        }
        return sb.toString();
    }
```

Downloading the language data adds support only for some languages. In the example from Figure 16-2, the device returns NOT_SUPPORTED for the fi Locale. NOT_SUPPORTED means that a device will never support the given Locale, even if the user downloads the language data. The fr Locale has a MISSING_DATA value. MISSING_DATA means that the device needs to download the language data before saying "Bonjour" with the appropriate French accent.

TRY THIS

In the Diagnostics screen, click See Locales Status. The resulting dialog shows the output from the code in Listing 16-4.

Handling the Language Check Result and Installing Language Data

Now, after the call to isLanguageAvailable(), the initialization could have failed in two ways: via onInit()'s *success* integer or by isLanguageAvailable() returning LANG_NOT_SUPPORTED. This leaves one contingency: the device needs to install language data. Most devices will not require downloading the language data because it is pre-installed or because they have already run your app's initialization. However, you still must include code to download language data to handle the devices that have installed data for only some languages or none at all.

If the device needs language data, the app has to send the user to Google Play to download and install the SpeechSynthesis Data app. During installation, the app copies the necessary language data to the SD card. Meanwhile, if the user starts the app again it is useful to inform the user to wait until the installation is complete. Figure 16-3 shows the screens the user sees when needing to download language data using the implementation this section describes.

First, in screen 1, the app fails a language check and prompts the user with a dialog.

Second, the user clicks Yes on screen 1 and the app sends the user to Google Play to download the language data. Screen 2 shows Google Play page where the user has started the download.

Third, if the user returns to the app before the download is complete, the user sees screen 3. The user will continue to see screen 3 until the installation notifies the app. After completing the installation and restarting the app, the user will not see these three screens again and TextToSpeech will be available for the app to use.

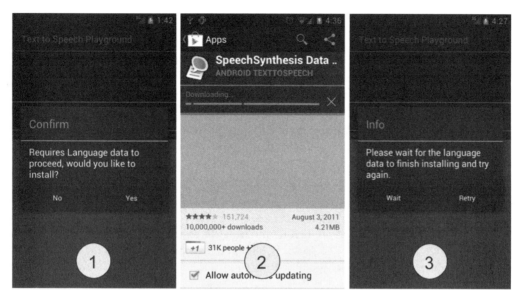

FIGURE 16-3 Screens a user could see while an app is initializing TextToSpeech

Android makes it easy for an app to move the user to Google Play via sending an `Intent` with a `TextToSpeech.Engine.ACTION_INSTALL_TTS_DATA` action. The action executes an `android.intent.action.VIEW` action for `market://search?q=pname:com.svox.langpack.installer`.

To use the `Intent` external code responds to the `onRequireLanguageData()` callback. In that callback, the external code can optionally prompt the user, and decide whether or not to proceed with installing the language data. If the app decides that it should install the language data it makes a call to the `TextToSpeechInitializer.installLanguage()` method. Listing 16-5 shows how the method sends an `Intent` with an `ACTION_INSTALL_TTS_DATA` action.

LISTING 16-5: Launch install language data

```
public void installLanguageData()
{
    // set waiting for the download
    LanguageDataInstallBroadcastReceiver.setWaiting(context, true);

    Intent installIntent = new Intent();
    installIntent.setAction(TextToSpeech.Engine.ACTION_INSTALL_TTS_DATA);
    context.startActivity(installIntent);
}
```

Once an app sends the `Intent`, Android should take the user to Google Play where they can start downloading the language data. However, your app should handle the case where the user restarts your app before the device completes the data installation. This situation will cause your app's language data check to fail, and potentially trigger sending the user to Google Play again.

Sending the user to the Google Play again will not help the download happen faster nor help the user start using your app. The result could be a loop that confuses and frustrates the user.

To handle this conundrum, the language installer broadcasts an `Intent` with `TextToSpeech.Engine.ACTION_TTS_DATA_INSTALLED` when it completes installation. Your app can listen for this `Intent` and notify the user to retry after the language is installed.

The code for this chapter handles this by using shared preferences. It sets a "waiting" shared preference before sending the user to the Google Play. Then a `BroadcastReceiver` switches the preference when the installation completes. When a user starts the data check, the app checks the "waiting" shared preference and informs the user appropriately before resending the user to the Google Play.

Implementing this plan involves setting and checking the shared preference, a new `LanguageDataInstallBroadcastReceiver` class, and code within two parts of `TextToSpeechInitializer`. First, the `installLanguageData()` method from Listing 16-5 sets the "waiting" preference before initiating the install. Second, the `LanguageDataInstallBroadcastReceiver` class, shown in Listing 16-6, clears the "waiting" preference when it receives the appropriate broadcast. It requires the manifest entry, shown in Listing 16-7, to receive the correct broadcast. Third, the `isLanguageAvailable()` method from Listing 16-3 checks the preference using `LanguageDataInstallBroadcastReceiver.isWaiting()` and reports the result to the `TextToSpeechStartupListener`.

Available for
download on
Wrox.com

LISTING 16-6: Broadcast listener to track when language data is installed

```java
public class LanguageDataInstallBroadcastReceiver extends BroadcastReceiver
{
    private static final String TAG = "LanguageDataInstallBroadcastReceiver";

    private static final String PREFERENCES_NAME = "installedLanguageData";

    private static final String WAITING_PREFERENCE_NAME =
            "WAITING_PREFERENCE_NAME";

    private static final Boolean WAITING_DEFAULT = false;

    public LanguageDataInstallBroadcastReceiver()
    {
    }

    @Override
    public void onReceive(Context context, Intent intent)
    {
        if (intent.getAction().equals(
                TextToSpeech.Engine.ACTION_TTS_DATA_INSTALLED))
        {
            Log.d(TAG, "language data preference: " + intent.getAction());
            // clear waiting state
            setWaiting(context, false);
        }
    }
```

```
/**
 * check if the receiver is waiting for a language data install
 */
public static boolean isWaiting(Context context)
{
    SharedPreferences preferences;
    preferences =
            context.getSharedPreferences(PREFERENCES_NAME,
                    Context.MODE_WORLD_READABLE);
    boolean waiting =
            preferences
                    .getBoolean(WAITING_PREFERENCE_NAME, WAITING_DEFAULT);
    return waiting;
}

/**
 * start waiting by setting a flag
 */
public static void setWaiting(Context context, boolean waitingStatus)
{
    SharedPreferences preferences;
    preferences =
            context.getSharedPreferences(PREFERENCES_NAME,
                    Context.MODE_WORLD_WRITEABLE);
    Editor editor = preferences.edit();
    editor.putBoolean(WAITING_PREFERENCE_NAME, waitingStatus);
    editor.commit();
}
}
```

code snippet LanguageDataInstallBroadcastReceiver.java

LISTING 16-7: AndroidManifest.xml entry to activate the BroadcastReceiver

```
<receiver
  android:name="root.gast.speech.tts.LanguageDataInstallBroadcastReceiver">
  <intent-filter>
        <action
          android:name="android.speech.tts.engine.TTS_DATA_INSTALLED"/>
  </intent-filter>
</receiver>
```

Setting TTS Listener

A final part of the setup is to optionally set an OnProgressUpdatedListener. TextToSpeech calls the OnProgressUpdatedListener when it starts speaking, is done speaking, or when there is an error. The methods contain an *utteranceId* parameter which is useful in various ways to help apps know when speaking a certain utterance has completed. Subsequent sections in this chapter and other chapters utilize it in various ways.

At the moment, setting the listener is somewhat awkward. First, it is an abstract class that an app must extend. This means your `Activity` cannot extend it. One way around this is to use an anonymous class. Second, setting the listener can also produce some error codes that an app may check. Third, an app needs to set the listener only after it is initialized. Fourth, `UtteranceProgressListener` is a new class in Android 4.0.3. To be backward compatible, an app needs insert a build version check. All this means it takes several lines of code to set the listener in a way that is convenient to use and backward compatible.

Listing 16-22 shows code that sets the listener after successful initialization in its `setTtsListener()` method. If the app's API level is greater or equal to than 15, version 4.0.3 or greater, the app uses `UtteranceProgressListener`. Otherwise, it uses an older `OnUtteranceCompletedListener` interface. In either case, the resulting listener call an `onDone()` method.

Summary of Initialization Procedure

In summary, the classes described thus far implement a procedure that initializes the `TextToSpeech` object using a `Locale` and callback to an interface implementation that decides how to process the possible outcomes. Using the procedure, an app can reliably obtain an initialized `TextToSpeech` object that is ready for use. The Testing TTS initialization note shows instructions for how to test the initialization process on an emulator.

The next section discusses an alternate initialization procedure that uses the same code as this one with a different method for checking language availability. The check uses the `TextToSpeech.Engine.ACTION_CHECK_TTS_DATA` action. The next section also describes other uses of the action besides initialization.

TESTING THE TTS INITIALIZATION

The initialization process is difficult to debug or test. It's likely that your device has the language data already installed. If so, your device will never need the initialization procedure. Even if your device does not have the language data, once you install it, there is no way to uninstall it via the Android user interface. Fortunately, you can still test using an emulator.

The language data files reside inside a protected area of the Android operating system. Therefore, you need to use an emulator to access it. Follow the procedure outlined here to use `adb` to accomplish it.

Manual language data uninstallation procedure:

1. Start an emulator with version greater than 2

2. Execute: `adb remount`

3. Execute: `adb shell rm -r /system/tts/lang_pico/*`

Next, the emulator requires some additional steps because it cannot run Google Play. Without Google Play the emulator must get the language data from somewhere else. You can simulate the install by performing a manual install of the data using the following procedure.

Manually installing language data procedure for an emulator:

1. Download `com.svox.langpack.installer_1.0.1.apk` from `http://code.google.com/p/eyes-free/downloads/list`

2. Execute: `adb install com.svox.langpack.installer_1.0.1.apk`

This install behaves identically to installing from Google Play and installs the language data to the SD card.

In summary, with some manual steps it is possible to test the TTS initialization procedure using an emulator.

Check TTS Data Action

The `TextToSpeech.Engine.ACTION_CHECK_TTS_DATA` has two uses. First, you can use it to check for supported languages. Second, you can use it to query for detailed information about the TTS engine. Hence, it can be used as part of an alternative initialization procedure or to gather information.

TRY THIS

Under Diagnostics, click data check to see the output from the `ACTION_CHECK_TTS_DATA` action.

Voices

The action works on "voices" instead of `Locales`. A voice is a three-part string formatted as *lang-COUNTRY-variant* where *COUNTRY* and *variant* are optional. For example, US English is `eng-USA`. Variant is a completely unspecified field, but may take on values such as `FEMALE`.

The format of a voice is not the same as what you get from `Locale.toString`, and there is no robust way to directly derive it from a `Locale`. Hence, either an app must do a best match between the `Locale`'s ISO3Country and ISO3Language fields and all available voice strings beforehand, or your app must know ahead of time which `Locales` will map easily.

Listing 16-8 performs a simple mapping from `Locale` to voice. However, it could result in a voice called `eng-AUS`, which will not pass the language check because the available voice is called `eng-USA` not `eng-AUS`.

LISTING 16-8: Converts Locale to a voice, only works for certain Locales

```
public static String convertLocaleToVoice(Locale loc)
{
    String country = loc.getISO3Country();
    String language = loc.getISO3Language();
    StringBuilder sb = new StringBuilder();
```

continues

LISTING 16-8 *(continued)*

```
        sb.append(language);
        if (country.length() > 0)
        {
            sb.append("-");
            sb.append(country);
        }
        return sb.toString();
    }
```

Using the ACTION_CHECK_TTS_DATA Action for Initialization

The ACTION_CHECK_TTS_DATA action differs from the Locale-based initialization in that it does not need a Locale and does not need to check isLanguageDataAvailable(). Instead, the app checks the result code from the action to determine whether or not the user needs to download the language data. This results in a different control flow that is summarized in Figure 16-4. TextToSpeechInitializerByAction implements the initialization procedure using the action.

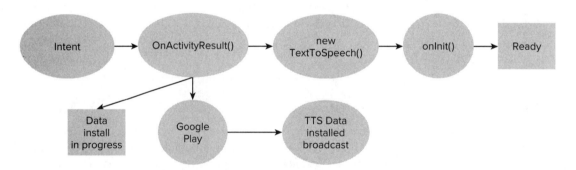

FIGURE 16-4: Initialization workflow using the ACTION_CHECK_TTS_DATA action

To start initialization, an app sends an Intent with the TextToSpeech.Engine.ACTION_CHECK_TTS_DATA action and processes the result within OnActivityResult(). From there, an app continues the same way it did during the Locale-based initialization. It either creates a new TextToSpeech object or if the app requires language data, it sends the user to Google Play. The only difference is that this procedure does not require checking for language data after onInit() because the procedure has already done that by checking the Intent results.

The *responseCode* describes the result of the check. If it returns `TextToSpeech.Engine.CHECK_VOICE_DATA_PASS`, the device has all the language data and it can continue to create a new `TextToSpeech` object.

If the `Intent` returns anything else, the device does not have adequate language data. For example, if a device has the eng-USA and spa-ESP voices but is missing the deu-DEU voice, the data check will return something other than `TextToSpeech.Engine.CHECK_VOICE_DATA_PASS` and fail.

If an app is interested in only specific voices, it may pass in an optional `ArrayList` of voice strings for `EXTRA_CHECK_VOICE_DATA_FOR` to check for particular voices. For example, an app might use this to check if the device supports only the eng-USA voice. Even if the app supports eng-USA but doesn't support deu-DEU, the data check will still succeed and return `CHECK_VOICE_DATA_PASS`.

`TextToSpeechInitializerByAction` implements the initialization procedure just described. It starts by sending the `TextToSpeech.Engine.ACTION_CHECK_TTS_DATA` Intent with a possible voice to check. Listing 16-9 shows `TextToSpeechInitializer` its `startDataCheck()` method. The method takes in an `Activity` because it has to call `startActivityForResult()`.

LISTING 16-9: Sends an Intent with **ACTION_CHECK_TTS_DATA** action with optional **EXTRA_ CHECK_VOICE_DATA_FOR** extra

```
public void startDataCheck(Activity activity, String voiceToCheck)
{
    Intent check = new Intent();
    check.setAction(TextToSpeech.Engine.ACTION_CHECK_TTS_DATA);
    Log.d(TAG, "launching speech check");
    if (voiceToCheck != null && voiceToCheck.length() > 0)
    {
        Log.d(TAG, "adding voice check for: " + voiceToCheck);
        // needs to be in an ArrayList
        ArrayList<String> voicesToCheck = new ArrayList<String>();
        voicesToCheck.add(voiceToCheck);
        check.putStringArrayListExtra(
                TextToSpeech.Engine.EXTRA_CHECK_VOICE_DATA_FOR,
                voicesToCheck);
    }
    activity.startActivityForResult(check,
            CommonTtsMethods.SPEECH_DATA_CHECK_CODE);
}
```

When the `Activity` returns a result, the calling `Activity` must execute the `handleOnActivityResult()` method to complete the initialization. Listing 16-10 shows the `handleOnActivityResult()` method. Notice that it sets the language without checking `isLanguageAvailable()`. It also assumes that the calling `Activity` passed in the right `Locale` for the particular voice. The calling `Activity` sets *targetLocale* in is the constructor for `TextToSpeechInitializerByAction`.

Available for
download on
Wrox.com

LISTING 16-10: Handles the result from **ACTION_CHECK_TTS_DATA**

```java
private Locale targetLocale;
public void handleOnActivityResult(Context launchFrom,
        int requestCode, int resultCode, Intent data)
{
    if (requestCode == CommonTtsMethods.SPEECH_DATA_CHECK_CODE)
    {
        switch (resultCode)
        {
            case TextToSpeech.Engine.CHECK_VOICE_DATA_PASS:
                // success, create the TTS instance
                Log.d(TAG, "has language data");
                tts = new TextToSpeech(launchFrom, new OnInitListener()
                {
                    @Override
                    public void onInit(int status)
                    {
                        if (targetLocale != null)
                        {
                            tts.setLanguage(targetLocale);
                        }
                        if (status == TextToSpeech.SUCCESS)
                        {
                            callback.onSuccessfulInit(tts);
                        } else
                        {
                            callback.onFailedToInit();
                        }
                    }
                });
                break;
            case TextToSpeech.Engine.CHECK_VOICE_DATA_MISSING_VOLUME:
            case TextToSpeech.Engine.CHECK_VOICE_DATA_FAIL:
            case TextToSpeech.Engine.CHECK_VOICE_DATA_BAD_DATA:
            case TextToSpeech.Engine.CHECK_VOICE_DATA_MISSING_DATA:
                Log.d(TAG, "no language data");
                callback.onRequireLanguageData();
        }
    }
}
```

code snippet TextToSpeechInitializerByAction.java

Either this `Intent`-based process or the `Locale`-based initialization may be more convenient for your app. The `Intent`-based process has the advantage that it allows your app to check language data without creating a `TextToSpeech` object. It also allows your app to easily query for what voices are available. An app could use the return values to propose with "which language would you like to speak?" to the user, for example.

This approach has some drawbacks, however. First, the `Intent`-based process involves two asynchronous processes. It must wait for the `Intent` to finish and then wait for the `TextToSpeech` to initialize. This increases the procedure's complexity. Second, it requires an `Activity` and handling an `onActivityResult()`, which makes it awkward to separate out the functionality into a separate class. Finally, the `Intent`-based process needs a `Locale` to set its language. Because it already needs a `Locale`, it might as well use the `Locale`-based initialization instead of dealing with voice strings.

Using the ACTION_CHECK_TTS_DATA Action to Gather TTS Engine Information

In addition to checking for language data, `ACTION_CHECK_TTS_DATA` returns additional information about the TTS engine via various extras. The information is useful for debugging a TTS engine and for learning what languages a device supports. The results may be different depending on the implementation. The Android documentation only specifies the format of `EXTRA_AVAILABLE_VOICES` and `EXTRA_UNAVAILABLE_VOICES`; the others are left for the TTS engine to decide.

Table 16-1 summarizes the output types and shows some possible results for the default TTS engine installed on Android.

TABLE 16-1: Extra information provided with ACTION_CHECK_DATA for the default TTS engine

RETURN	MEANING	EXAMPLE OUTPUT
EXTRA_AVAILABLE_VOICES	Voices installed on the device formatted as lang-country-variant where country and variant are optional.	eng-USA, spa-ESP, eng-USA-FEMALE
EXTRA_UNAVAILABLE_ VOICES	Voices not supported by the device.	deu-DEU, eng-GBR, fra-FRA, ita-ITA
EXTRA_VOICE_DATA_ ROOT_DIRECTORY	The voice data location.	/mnt/sdcard/svox
EXTRA_VOICE_DATA_FILES	Lists data file names.	de-DE_gl0_sg.bin, de-DE_ta.bin, en-GB_ kh0_sg.bin, en-GB_ta.bin, en-US_lh0_sg.bin
EXTRA_VOICE_DATA_ FILES_INFO	A list of voices, presumably correlated with the data files.	deu-DEU, deu-DEU, eng-GBR, eng-GBR, ….

Figure 16-5 shows the output from a device using the "data status" button in the book's app. The output shows that the device fails the "data status" check because it has only four of six languages installed and describes which voices are available and which are missing.

An app can use the ACTION_CHECK_TTS_DATA action to initialize TTS and also to gather TTS implementation details. As discussed previously, an app can also initialize TTS using just a Locale. The code described in the previous sections helps you to implement TTS initialization quickly so that you can focus on using TTS. The next section describes how.

Speaking

After the initialization process the app can readily utilize the TextToSpeech object to play speech, prerecorded audio, and silence. This section describes its various methods and demonstrates their usage within the TextToSpeechDemo Activity and the Try Text to Speech button in the book's app.

When speaking, the TextToSpeech object proceeds through the following steps:

1. App calls speak(), playSilence(), or playEarcon().

2. Speaking begins.

3. Interrupt speaking if app calls stop(), report true if app calls isSpeaking().

FIGURE 16-5: Output from the ACTION_CHECK_TTS_DATA

4. Speaking ends.

5. TextToSpeech possibly calls onDone() on its UtteranceProgressListener..

The first step involves playing one of four possible types of audio. You can use various "speak" or "play" methods. Table 16-2 describes the audio types TextToSpeech can play and the methods needed.

TABLE 16-2: Different Kinds of Audio TextToSpeech Can Play

WHAT	DESCRIPTION	HOW TO CONFIGURE	TTS API
Speech	Synthesized speech from arbitrary text input.	None	speak(text)
Prerecorded speech	Audio file to play when given certain text input.	addSpeech(key, audio file)	speak(key)
Earcons	A sound typically used at the start of an utterance to solicit attention. Does not trigger onDone() on versions of Android before 4.0.	addEarcon(name, audio file)	playEarcon(name)
Silence	A period of silence.	None	playSilence()

`TextToSpeech` may not play the audio immediately, however. It manages a play queue and plays each piece of audio one at a time as it receives it. The "speak" and "play" methods add to the queue. An app can control the queue behavior by passing in a *queueMode* parameter. If the app passes `QUEUE_ADD`, `TextToSpeech` adds the audio to its queue. If the app uses `QUEUE.FLUSH`, `TextToSpeech` stops anything that is currently playing and starts playing audio immediately.

Figure 16-6 shows the result of speaking an earcon, then two silences, and finally the text "Heart" in the book's companion app.

The speak and play methods also take a `Map<String,String>` as input. The values in the `Map` represent additional parameters for the audio playback. Android defines four possible keys for the parameters, but specific TTS engines may have additional parameters. The possible parameters are:

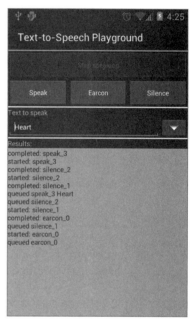

➤ `KEY_PARAM_STREAM`: Any of the `STREAM` constants from `AudioManager`. `TextToSpeech` will send any audio output to the specified stream.

➤ `KEY_PARAM_UTTERANCE_ID`: ID to be passed to `onDone()` when TTS finishes speaking it. If this key is not present, `TextToSpeech` does not call `onDone()`.

➤ `KEY_PARAM_VOLUME`: Value from 0 to 1 representing the relative volume of spoken text compared to the current stream.

➤ `KEY_PARAM_PAN`: Value from −1 to +1 representing how far left or right to send the spoken text.

FIGURE 16-6: Output from the book's app showing how TextToSpeech queued, started, and then completed playing various audio

One note about streams: you may also set the global volume stream for the `Activity` by executing an `Activity`'s `setVolumeControlStream()` method. For example, to make an `Activity` output all sound to the "music" audio stream, execute this line: `setVolumeControlStream(AudioManager.STREAM_MUSIC);`

Earcons and prerecorded speech require "adding" before your app can use them. To add, you have to call `addSpeech()` and `addEarcon()`. Both require a textual name to refer to in later calls to `speak()` and `playEarcon()` and a reference to an audio resource or a path to an audio file. The audio format must be a format that Android supports, for example, `.wav` and `.mp3`. Also, all audio resources should be within the res directory, most likely within res/raw.

TRY THIS

The Try Text to Speech screen already has an earcon set. Clicking the earcon but-ton plays a .wav file that sounds like a tone.

While TextToSpeech is playing audio, your app can interrupt or monitor the speaking process. If an app calls stop(), TextToSpeech stops speaking. If your app calls isSpeaking(), it reports if the app is currently speaking.

Another way an app can use TextToSpeech is to synthesize text to a file. Instead of immediately speaking the passed-in text, you can use the TextToSpeech engine to write it as a .wav file via the synthesizeToFile() method.

TextToSpeech has some other parameters that an app might want to set before speaking. These are *speechRate* and *pitch*, outlined in the following list. An app can set these values after TextToSpeech calls onInit().

➤ speechRate: How fast to speak. 1 is the normal value, 2 is twice as fast. 0.5 is half as fast.

➤ pitch: Pitch of the voice. 1.0 is the normal value. Lower values make lower pitches; higher values make higher pitches. The particular TextToSpeech engine determines how much of a change this causes.

There is one last consideration to keep in mind. This consid-eration only applies to devices running versions of Android before 4.0. In those versions, the users are ultimately in control of their TTS settings. They can configure certain TTS settings and if they do, your app cannot override them. Figure 16-7 shows the "Text-to-speech settings" Activity for an Android 2.3 device.

FIGURE 16-7: TTS settings screen for Android devices before 4.0

If the user selects Always use my settings, the settings configured override any changes your app makes. Under these conditions, even if your app calls setSpeechRate() or setLanguage(), the TTS will use the user's settings instead. The only action your app can do is to check if the user has overridden the defaults. If so, TextToSpeech.areDefaultsEnforced() will return true.

TRY THIS

The Try Text to Speech button allows you to experiment with all of the TTS parameters. Here are some specific experiments to try:

See the speaking queue. The Speak, Earcon, and Silence buttons each add something to the queue. To demonstrate the queue, first select some text to speak. Then, click the various three buttons multiple times, and listen to `TextToSpeech` say them one at a time. You can also view when the various clicks were queued by looking at the bottom result output.

➤ **Prerecorded speech:** To hear prerecorded speech, select "android" from the list of Text to speak. When you click Speak, you will hear a prerecorded low voice saying "android" instead of the normal synthesized voice.

➤ **Stop speaking:** Select some long text to speak by selecting (whatisandroid.txt). Then click the Speak button. While it is speaking the Stop Speaking button will be enabled. If you click it, the app will halt speaking before it completes the utterance.

➤ **Change settings:** Change TextToSpeech settings by clicking the Parameters menu option. Test changing volume, pan, speechRate, pitch, and synthesizing to file. If you check Synthesize to file and then click Speak, the app will output a `.wav` file within `\sdcard\Android\data\root.gast.playground\tts`.

Speaking a Script

`TextToSpeechDemo` assembles the various `TextToSpeech` method calls together to speak the following script:

1. Alert user with an earcon.

2. Wait 1000 milliseconds for the user to start listening. Otherwise the information starts too soon without a pause.

3. Speak information.

4. Wait 500 milliseconds.

5. Speak prerecorded speech to personalize the speech with the author's voice.

The code to play this script is shown in Listing 16-10. Any required earcons or prerecorded speech are `.wav` files included within the app's resources.

Available for
download on
Wrox.com

LISTING 16-10: Plays a demo script consisting of earcons, silence, and synthesized and prerecorded speech

```java
private static final String LAST_SPOKEN = "lastSpoken";

private void playScript()
{
    Log.d(TAG, "started script");
    //setup

    //id to send back when saying the last phrase
    //so the app can re-enable the "speak" button
    HashMap<String, String> lastSpokenWord = new HashMap<String, String>();
    lastSpokenWord.put(TextToSpeech.Engine.KEY_PARAM_UTTERANCE_ID, LAST_SPOKEN);

    //add earcon
    final String EARCON_NAME = "[tone]";
    tts.addEarcon(EARCON_NAME, "root.gast.playground", R.raw.tone);
    //add prerecorded speech
    final String CLOSING = "[Thank you]";
    tts.addSpeech(CLOSING, "root.gast.playground", R.raw.enjoytestapplication);

    //pass in null to most of these because we do not want a callback to
    //onDone
    tts.playEarcon(EARCON_NAME, TextToSpeech.QUEUE_ADD, null);
    tts.playSilence(1000, TextToSpeech.QUEUE_ADD, null);
    tts.speak(
            "Attention readers: Use the try button to experiment with" +
            " Text to Speech. Use the diagnostics button to see " +
            "detailed Text to Speech engine information.",
            TextToSpeech.QUEUE_ADD, null);
    tts.playSilence(500, TextToSpeech.QUEUE_ADD, null);
    tts.speak(CLOSING, TextToSpeech.QUEUE_ADD, lastSpokenWord);

}
```

code snippet TextToSpeechDemo.java

First, the `playScript()` method code defines *lastSpokenWord* to hold an utterance ID. The `onDone()` method, shown in Listing 16-11, uses the ID to know when to re-enable the Speak button. For the other utterances, `playScript()` passes null for a parameter. Not specifying an utterance ID causes `TextToSpeech` to not call `onDone()` at the end of those utterances.

Available for
download on
Wrox.com

LISTING 16-11: onDone reenables the view

```java
private void onDone(final String utteranceId)
{
    Log.d(TAG, "utterance completed: " + utteranceId);
    runOnUiThread(new Runnable()
    {
        @Override
```

```
                public void run()
                {
                    if (utteranceId.equals(LAST_SPOKEN))
                    {
                        setViewToDoneSpeaking();
                    }
                }
            });
    }
```

Next, `playScript()` adds a mapping for one earcon and one prerecorded speech instance. The earcon is named "[tone]" and comes from a resource `.wav` file within the raw directory called `tone`. The speech is named "[Thank you]" and references a resource called `enjoytestapplication`.

After adding the earcon and prerecorded speech, the code adds audio to the `TextToSpeech` queue. First it plays the earcon with a call to `playEarcon()` by passing the "[tone]" name. Then, it plays silence for 1000 milliseconds. Next, it calls `speak()` with some text. This causes `TextToSpeech` to convert the text to audio and play it. Following that, the app plays silence again and ends with playing prerecorded speech by passing in "[Thank you]" to `speak()`.

TRY THIS

Click the Text-to-Speech "demo" button and click Speak to hear the script.

Thus far, you've examined two parts of the `TextToSpeech` API: initializing and speaking. You need a few other pieces of code to create an app that can use TTS. Listing 16-12 shows the complete code for `TextToSpeechDemo` that contains the additional code that you need. The code does the following:

➤   Calls `shutdown` in the `onDestroy()` method

➤   Uses various dialogs to inform the user what is happening during initialization

➤   Turns on and off the Speak button based on whether or not the app is speaking

➤   Deactivates the Speak button while `TextToSpeech` is initializing

LISTING 16-12: Demonstrates initializing and using TTS to play a script

Available for
download on
Wrox.com

```
public class TextToSpeechDemo extends Activity implements
        TextToSpeechStartupListener
{
    private static final String TAG = "TextToSpeechDemo";
    private Button speak;
    private Button stopSpeak;

    private static final String LAST_SPOKEN = "lastSpoken";
```

continues

LISTING 16-12 *(continued)*

```java
    private TextToSpeechInitializer ttsInit;
    private TextToSpeech tts;

    @Override
    public void onCreate(Bundle savedInstanceState)
    {
        super.onCreate(savedInstanceState);
        setContentView(R.layout.ttsdemo);
        hookButtons();
        init();
    }

    private void hookButtons()
    {
        speak = (Button) findViewById(R.id.btn_speak);
        speak.setOnClickListener(new View.OnClickListener()
        {
            @Override
            public void onClick(View v)
            {
                setViewToWhileSpeaking();
                playScript();
            }
        });

        stopSpeak = (Button) findViewById(R.id.btn_stop_speak);
        stopSpeak.setOnClickListener(new View.OnClickListener()
        {
            @Override
            public void onClick(View v)
            {
                setViewToDoneSpeaking();
                tts.stop();
            }
        });
    }

    private void init()
    {
        deactivateUi();
        ttsInit = new TextToSpeechInitializer(this, Locale.getDefault(), this);
    }

    @Override
    public void onSuccessfulInit(TextToSpeech tts)
    {
        Log.d(TAG, "successful init");
        this.tts = tts;
        activateUi();
        setTtsListener();
```

```java
    }

    /**
     * set the TTS listener to call {@link #onDone(String)} depending on the
     * Build.Version.SDK_INT
     */
    private void setTtsListener()
    {
        if (Build.VERSION.SDK_INT >= 15)
        {
            int listenerResult =
                    tts.setOnUtteranceProgressListener(new UtteranceProgressListener()
                    {
                        @Override
                        public void onDone(String utteranceId)
                        {
                            TextToSpeechDemo.this.onDone(utteranceId);
                        }

                        @Override
                        public void onError(String utteranceId)
                        {
                            Log.e(TAG, "TTS error");
                        }

                        @Override
                        public void onStart(String utteranceId)
                        {
                            Log.d(TAG, "TTS start");
                        }
                    });
            if (listenerResult != TextToSpeech.SUCCESS)
            {
                Log.e(TAG, "failed to add utterance progress listener");
            }
        }
        else
        {
            int listenerResult =
                    tts.setOnUtteranceCompletedListener(
                            new OnUtteranceCompletedListener()
                    {
                        @Override
                        public void onUtteranceCompleted(String utteranceId)
                        {
                            TextToSpeechDemo.this.onDone(utteranceId);
                        }
                    });
            if (listenerResult != TextToSpeech.SUCCESS)
            {
                Log.e(TAG, "failed to add utterance completed listener");
            }
        }
    }
```

continues

LISTING 16-12 *(continued)*

```java
    private void onDone(final String utteranceId)
    {
        Log.d(TAG, "utterance completed: " + utteranceId);
        runOnUiThread(new Runnable()
        {
            @Override
            public void run()
            {
                if (utteranceId.equals(LAST_SPOKEN))
                {
                    setViewToDoneSpeaking();
                }
            }
        });
    }

    @Override
    public void onFailedToInit()
    {
        DialogInterface.OnClickListener onClickOk = makeOnFailedToInitHandler();
        AlertDialog a =
                new AlertDialog.Builder(this).setTitle("Error")
                        .setMessage("Unable to create text to speech")
                        .setNeutralButton("Ok", onClickOk).create();
        a.show();
    }

    @Override
    public void onRequireLanguageData()
    {
        DialogInterface.OnClickListener onClickOk =
                makeOnClickInstallDialogListener();
        DialogInterface.OnClickListener onClickCancel =
                makeOnFailedToInitHandler();
        AlertDialog a =
                new AlertDialog.Builder(this)
                        .setTitle("Error")
                        .setMessage(
                                "Requires Language data to proceed, " +
                                "would you like to install?")
                        .setPositiveButton("Ok", onClickOk)
                        .setNegativeButton("Cancel", onClickCancel).create();
        a.show();
    }

    @Override
    public void onWaitingForLanguageData()
    {
        // either wait for install
        DialogInterface.OnClickListener onClickWait =
                makeOnFailedToInitHandler();
        DialogInterface.OnClickListener onClickInstall =
                makeOnClickInstallDialogListener();
```

```java
        AlertDialog a =
                new AlertDialog.Builder(this)
                        .setTitle("Info")
                        .setMessage(
                                "Please wait for the language data to finish" +
                                " installing and try again.")
                        .setNegativeButton("Wait", onClickWait)
                        .setPositiveButton("Retry", onClickInstall).create();
        a.show();
    }

    private DialogInterface.OnClickListener makeOnClickInstallDialogListener()
    {
        return new DialogInterface.OnClickListener()
        {
            @Override
            public void onClick(DialogInterface dialog, int which)
            {
                ttsInit.installLanguageData();
            }
        };
    }

    private DialogInterface.OnClickListener makeOnFailedToInitHandler()
    {
        return new DialogInterface.OnClickListener()
        {
            @Override
            public void onClick(DialogInterface dialog, int which)
            {
                finish();
            }
        };
    }

    private void playScript()
    {
        Log.d(TAG, "started script");
        // setup

        // id to send back when saying the last phrase
        // so the app can re-enable the "speak" button
        HashMap<String, String> lastSpokenWord = new HashMap<String, String>();
        lastSpokenWord.put(TextToSpeech.Engine.KEY_PARAM_UTTERANCE_ID,
                LAST_SPOKEN);

        // add earcon
        final String EARCON_NAME = "[tone]";
        tts.addEarcon(EARCON_NAME, "root.gast.playground", R.raw.tone);

        // add prerecorded speech
        final String CLOSING = "[Thank you]";
        tts.addSpeech(CLOSING, "root.gast.playground",
                R.raw.enjoytestapplication);
```

continues

LISTING 16-12 *(continued)*

```
        // pass in null to most of these because we do not want a callback to
        // onDone
        tts.playEarcon(EARCON_NAME, TextToSpeech.QUEUE_ADD, null);
        tts.playSilence(1000, TextToSpeech.QUEUE_ADD, null);
        tts.speak("Attention readers: Use the try button to experiment with"
                + " Text to Speech. Use the diagnostics button to see "
                + "detailed Text to Speech engine information.",
                TextToSpeech.QUEUE_ADD, null);
        tts.playSilence(500, TextToSpeech.QUEUE_ADD, null);
        tts.speak(CLOSING, TextToSpeech.QUEUE_ADD, lastSpokenWord);

    }

    // activate and deactivate the UI based on various states

    private void deactivateUi()
    {
        Log.d(TAG, "deactivate ui");
        // don't enable until the initialization is complete
        speak.setEnabled(false);
    }

    private void activateUi()
    {
        Log.d(TAG, "activate ui");
        speak.setEnabled(true);
    }

    public void setViewToWhileSpeaking()
    {
        stopSpeak.setVisibility(View.VISIBLE);
        speak.setVisibility(View.GONE);
    }

    public void setViewToDoneSpeaking()
    {
        stopSpeak.setVisibility(View.GONE);
        speak.setVisibility(View.VISIBLE);
    }

    @Override
    protected void onDestroy()
    {
        if (tts != null)
        {
            tts.shutdown();
        }
        super.onDestroy();
    }

}
```

code snippet TextToSpeechDemo.java

This section has explained how to initialize and use the TTS API to allow an app to speak. The next section describes how to allow an app to listen using the speech recognition API.

SPEECH RECOGNITION

Using the speech recognition API involves sending an `Intent` with the various actions and extras defined in `RecognizerIntent`. Even though code never instantiates a `RecognizerIntent`, this section still refers to an `Intent` that has constants from it as a `RecognizerIntent`. The `RecognizerIntent` can accomplish many tasks, and this section describes its various use cases.

Also, this section describes a set of six classes that demonstrate and implement common speech recognition methods:

➤   `SpeechRecognizingActivity`: An abstract `Activity` to handle interpreting the `onActivityResult()` response and executing other boilerplate code.

➤   `SpeechRecognizerUtil`: Has common speech recognition methods.

➤   `LanguageDetailsChecker`: `BroadcastReceiver` to receive `RecognizerIntent.ACTION_GET_LANGUAGE_DETAILS` result.

➤   `OnLanguageDetailsListener`: Interface for `LanguageDetailsChecker` to call after receiving language details.

➤   `SpeechRecognitionResultsActivity`: Example of an `Activity` that handles a receiving recognition results in a `PendingIntent`.

➤   `SayMagicWordDemo`: Demo activity that uses speech recognition and TTS.

If your app either extends `SpeechRecognizerActivity` or uses the methods in `SpeechRecognizerUtil`, your app's remaining tasks are to configure the appropriate `RecognizerIntent`, interpret recognition results, and deal with any errors. The subject of interpreting the recognition results and creating complete speech commands is covered in Chapters 17 and 18. Chapter 19 describes different ways to help the user launch the `RecognizerIntent` besides using a button. This chapter gets you started by showing you how to get your app to the point of receiving recognition results.

Initializing

Before an app can use speech recognition it needs to perform two checks. First, it needs to check if the device supports speech recognition. To check, an app must execute the code in Listing 16-13.

LISTING 16-13: Check to determine if a device supports speech recognition

```
public boolean isSpeechAvailable(Context context)
{
    PackageManager pm = context.getPackageManager();
    List<ResolveInfo> activities = pm.queryIntentActivities(
```

```
                            new Intent(RecognizerIntent.ACTION_RECOGNIZE_SPEECH), 0);

            boolean available = true;
            if (activities.size() == 0)
            {
                available = false;
            }
            return available;
        }
```

Second, an app can optionally check if Android supports the desired language. If it does not, there is no way to fix it. Unfortunately, the `RecognizerIntent` makes it easy for an app to set a language, but not to check if Android supports a language. To perform a language check, your app must retrieve the list of supporting languages and then perform string matching between the list and the desired language's `Locale`.

The first part of the language check is to acquire the list of supported languages and the recognizer's preferred language. To do this, your app can send an `Intent` with the `RecognizerIntent.ACTION_GET_LANGUAGE_DETAILS` action. The recognizer uses the preferred language when the app does not specify a language or when it doesn't support the language the app specifies. Figure 16-8 shows the output from the language check on one device.

The language check uses an asynchronous call and a `BroadcastIntent`. `LanguageDetailsChecker` handles the asynchronous nature of the call by calling back to an `OnLanguageDetailsListener` when it receives the language check results.

Listing 16-14 shows `LanguageDetailsChecker`.

FIGURE 16-8: ACTION_GET_ LANGUAGE_DETAILS output

Available for download on Wrox.com

LISTING 16-14: BroadcastReceiver to receive language details result

```
public class LanguageDetailsChecker extends BroadcastReceiver
{
    private static final String TAG = "LanguageDetailsChecker";

    private List<String> supportedLanguages;

    private String languagePreference;

    private OnLanguageDetailsListener doAfterReceive;

    public LanguageDetailsChecker(OnLanguageDetailsListener doAfterReceive)
    {
        supportedLanguages = new ArrayList<String>();
```

```
        this.doAfterReceive = doAfterReceive;
    }

    @Override
    public void onReceive(Context context, Intent intent)
    {
        Bundle results = getResultExtras(true);
        if (results.containsKey(RecognizerIntent.EXTRA_LANGUAGE_PREFERENCE))
        {
            languagePreference =
                    results.getString(RecognizerIntent.EXTRA_LANGUAGE_PREFERENCE);
        }
        if (results.containsKey(RecognizerIntent.EXTRA_SUPPORTED_LANGUAGES))
        {
            supportedLanguages =
                    results.getStringArrayList(
                            RecognizerIntent.EXTRA_SUPPORTED_LANGUAGES);
        }

        if (doAfterReceive != null)
        {
            doAfterReceive.onLanguageDetailsReceived(this);
        }
    }

    public String matchLanguage(Locale toCheck)
    {
        String matchedLanguage = null;
        // modify the returned languages to look like the output from
        // Locale.toString()
        String targetLanguage = toCheck.toString().replace('_', '-');
        for (String supportedLanguage : supportedLanguages)
        {
            // use contains, so that partial matches are possible
            // for example, if the Locale is
            // en-US-POSIX, it will still match en-US
            // and that if the target language is en, it will match something
            Log.d(TAG, targetLanguage + " contains " + supportedLanguage);
            if ((targetLanguage.contains(supportedLanguage))
                    || supportedLanguage.contains(targetLanguage))
            {
                matchedLanguage = supportedLanguage;
            }
        }
        return matchedLanguage;
    }

    /**
     * @return the supportedLanguages
     */
    public List<String> getSupportedLanguages()
    {
        return supportedLanguages;
    }
```

continues

LISTING 16-14 *(continued)*

```
/**
 * @return the languagePreference
 */
public String getLanguagePreference()
{
    return languagePreference;
}

public String toString()
{
    StringBuilder sb = new StringBuilder();
    sb.append("Language Preference: ").append(getLanguagePreference())
            .append("\n");
    sb.append("languages supported: ").append("\n");
    for (String lang : getSupportedLanguages())
    {
        sb.append("  ").append(lang).append("\n");
    }
    return sb.toString();
}
}
```

code snippet LanguageDetailsChecker.java

Listing 16-15 shows the OnLanguageDetailsListener, which receives the result of the language check.

LISTING 16-15: Called by LanguageDetailsChecker with language data

```
public interface OnLanguageDetailsListener
{
    public void onLanguageDetailsReceived(LanguageDetailsChecker data);
}
```

Listing 16-16 shows the SpeechRecognizingActivity.checkForLanguage() method, which checks for language support. It does the following:

➤ Defines OnLanguageDetailsListener that uses the language check result to tell if the device supports a certain Locale. The OnLanguageDetailsListener passes the language check result to the abstract languageCheckResult() method.

➤ Creates a LanguageDetailsChecker to receive the language check results and forward them to the OnLanguageDetailsListener.

➤ Sends a Intent with the RecognizerIntent.ACTION_GET_LANGUAGE_DETAILS action to be received by the LanguageDetailsChecker.

LISTING 16-16: Executes the language check for a given Locale

```
protected void checkForLanguage(final Locale language)
{
    OnLanguageDetailsListener andThen = new OnLanguageDetailsListener()
```

```
    {
        @Override
        public void onLanguageDetailsReceived(LanguageDetailsChecker data)
        {
            // do a best match
            String languageToUse = data.matchLanguage(language);
            languageCheckResult(languageToUse);
        }
    };
    Intent detailsIntent = new Intent(
            RecognizerIntent.ACTION_GET_LANGUAGE_DETAILS);
    LanguageDetailsChecker checker = new LanguageDetailsChecker(andThen);
    sendOrderedBroadcast(detailsIntent, null, checker, null,
            Activity.RESULT_OK, null, null);
    }
}
```

TRY THIS

Click Try Speech, then the Language Details menu option to see the output for your device.

The "languages" returned by the action do not exactly conform to any standard. The API does not specify the format for these "language" strings. As you can see in Figure 16-8, the supported languages in the `RecognizerIntent.GET_LANGUAGE_DETAILS` output have a mixed format. They tend to follow a language-country format, very similar to what `Locale.toString()` provides, but not exactly. For example, the list of languages contains strings such as `cmn-Hans-CN` and `Pig-Latin`, which do not conform to any standard.

This leaves you with a problem. There is no direct way for an app to check if Android supports recognizing the language for a particular `Locale`. Your app can send a `Locale.toString()` as a parameter in the RecognizerIntent to specify a language preference. However, if your app manages to send a `Locale.toString()` to Android that it doesn't support, the recognizer will just use the default. There is no programmatic way to know if Android is using the default or ignoring the `Locale.toString()` your app passed in.

Fortunately, Android supports many languages, so most likely Google will support the language you need. However, it doesn't support all languages, such as Icelandic, whose `Locale` is `is_IS`. Until Android provides additional APIs, your app needs some string matching code, such as the `match-Language()` method in Listing 16-14, if it needs to perform the language check.

TRY THIS

In the Try Speech button, use the Set Language menu option to test different language support. You can change the language to another such as es-US. Then, you can select Vamos a la playa from the list of presets and attempt to speak the phrase.

Also, you can use the Test Locale menu option. It shows all available Locales and passes them to the matchLanguage() method to determine if Android supports it.

Once an app has checked if a device can support speech recognition and optionally checked if Android supports a particular language, it can then use speech recognition. The next section describes how to do so by sending a `RecognizerIntent`.

Using the RecognizerIntent

To use speech recognition, apps must create and send a `RecognizerIntent`. The `RecognizerIntent` class has an entangled list of extras and actions, which work only in certain combinations. The various uses fall into several categories and cover three possible actions, each with its own usage of extras. Table 16-2 describes the three possible actions in `RecognizerIntent`. The previous section covered GET_LANGUAGE_DETAILS and this section focuses on the other two.

TABLE 16-3: The Three Different Actions using in RecognizerIntent

ACTION	SEND WITH	DESCRIPTION
RECOGNIZE_SPEECH	startActivityForResult()	Starts speech recognition.
WEB_SEARCH	startActivityForResult()	Starts speech recognition but allows Android to take an action on the results. Typically, Android decides to perform a web search.
GET_LANGUAGE_DETAILS	sendBroadcast()	Returns some information about the supported and preferred languages.

To perform interactive speech recognition and process the results an app can use ACTION_RECOGNIZE_SPEECH. Table 16-4 shows the relevant extras.

TABLE 16-4: Extras for ACTION_RECOGNIZE_SPEECH

PURPOSE	EXTRA
How to collect	PROMPT SPEECH_INPUT_COMPLETE_SILENCE_LENGTH_MILLIS SPEECH_INPUT_MINIMUM_LENGTH_MILLIS SPEECH_INPUT_POSSIBLY_COMPLETE_SILENCE_LENGTH_MILLIS
What to return	LANGUAGE_MODEL (required) LANGUAGE MAX_RESULTS
Where to send results	RESULTS_PENDINGINTENT RESULTS_PENDINGINTENT_BUNDLE
Results	RESULTS CONFIDENCE_SCORES

To allow Android to take an action based on the speech instead of the app, an app can use ACTION_ WEB_SEARCH. Table 16-5 shows the relevant extras.

TABLE 16-5: Extras for ACTION_WEB_SEARCH

PURPOSE	EXTRA
How to collect	PROMPT
	SPEECH_INPUT_COMPLETE_SILENCE_LENGTH_MILLIS
	SPEECH_INPUT_MINIMUM_LENGTH_MILLIS
	SPEECH_INPUT_POSSIBLY_COMPLETE_SILENCE_LENGTH_ MILLIS
What to return	LANGUAGE_MODEL (required)
	LANGUAGE
	MAX_RESULTS
	PARTIAL_RESULTS
	ORIGIN
Where to send results	WEB_SEARCH_ONLY
Results	RESULTS
	CONFIDENCE_SCORES

To execute the language details check, as described in the previous section, an app can use ACTION_ GET_LANGUAGE_DETAILS. Table 16-6 shows the relevant extras.

TABLE 16-6: Extras for ACTION_GET_LANGUAGE_DETAILS

PURPOSE	EXTRA
How to collect	(none)
What to return	ONLY_RETURN_LANGUAGE_PREFERENCE
Where to send results	(none)
Results	LANGUAGE_PREFERENCE
	SUPPORTED_LANGUAGES

The "how to collect" extras in Tables 16-4 and 16-5 control how Android records speech and what it shows the user while doing so. The "what to return" extras change what values the recognizer returns. The "where to send results" extras determine what receives the results. For ACTION_ RECOGNIZE_SPEECH, the extras enable the developer to specify a PendingIntent to receive the recognition results. In ACTION_WEB_SEARCH, an app can optionally force Android to send the result to the web browser. Finally, an app uses the "results" extras to extract data, such as the speech-to-text conversations, returned from the RecogizerIntent.

The Speech Recording Process

Once an app sends a `RecognizerIntent`, Android proceeds through a process of showing dialogs, recording audio, and waiting for silence in order to record a speech utterance. As mentioned previously, the app can use extras in the `Intent` to control some aspects of how the recognizer executes this process. The speech recording process involves the following steps:

1. App sends a `RecognizerIntent`.

2. User waits up to several seconds.

3. Speech prompt dialog appears with an optional prompt.

4. User starts speaking.

5. App records until a minimum time passes and it hears silence for long enough.

6. Speech prompt dialog changes to "Working" while app communicates with Google servers.

7. If an error occurs, the device plays a beeping sound, vibrates, and displays one of three retry dialogs.

8. Android returns results to the app via `onActivityResult()`.

The extras that affect the speech recording have several categories:

➤ **Prompt:** Adjusts the words the user sees in the first prompt. In Figure 16-9, the prompt to the left shows the prompt "Speak: My android and I went to the store." To set the prompt, set the following extra:

➤ `PROMPT`: Text to put in the Speech prompt dialog.

➤ **Timing:** The recognizer determines when to stop recording based on how much silence it hears and a minimum recording time parameter. The "Working" prompt in Figure 16-9 shows a picture of the waveform the user recorded over time. The horizontal line in the middle is bumpy when user was speaking and flat when there was silence. Normally, an app does not change the timing parameters. If it needs to, an app can set the following extras:

➤ `MINIMUM_LENGTH`: Controls the minimum amount of time the recognizer records no matter how much silence it hears. Box 1 in Figure 16-9 shows the minimum length time.

➤ `COMPLETE_SILENCE_LENGTH`: Amount of silence needed before the recognizer stops recording. In Figure 16-9, during box 2 there was silence, but not enough to stop recording until during box 3.

➤ `POSSIBLY_COMPLETE_SILENCE_LENGTH`: Amount of silence needed before the recognizer considers stopping recording. This extra works in a similar way to `COMPLETE_SILENCE_LENGTH`. If your app specifies both values, the recognizer uses the smaller value as the amount of silence it needs.

➤ **Errors:** Various errors can occur. Figure 16-9 shows the dialogs Android shows when they do. The various errors are "No matches found," "No speech heard," and "Connection problem." These conditions all return a `resultCode` of 0, whereas successful executions return a `resultCode` of RESULT_OK. Android does not return the error codes referenced in the RecognizerIntent documentation.

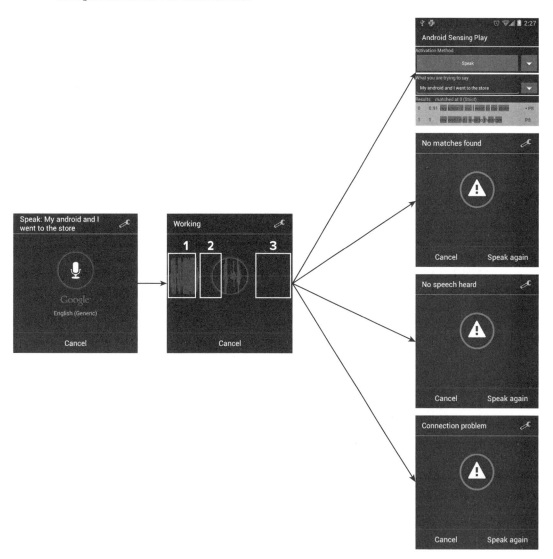

FIGURE 16-9: Figure showing flow of speech dialogs ending in four possible outcomes

Configuring and Processing the Result

Beyond configuring how the recognizer records speech, your app can also specify how the recognizer should interpret the recorded speech and what it should return. The possible extras are:

➤ LANGUAGE_MODEL: A required extra having a value of LANGUAGE_MODEL_FREE_FORM or LANGUAGE_MODEL_WEB_SEARCH. Each value causes the recognizer to use a certain "language model."

  ➤ The results from using either language model are very similar and the recognizer can recognize any speech using either option. However, the results will differ slightly in what possible speech-to-text conversions they return and in what order.

  ➤ Each language model is best suited to recognize the words for a certain manner of speaking. You should select the model that you think most closely corresponds to way your users speak in your app. Android's speech input document advises that free form is for dictation and web search is for shorter, search-like phrases. (http://developer.android.com/resources/articles/speech-input.html)

➤ LANGUAGE: A voice string or a Locale.toString().

➤ MAX_RESULTS: The maximum number of possible speech-to-text conversions to return.

When the user completes a recognition, the recognizer returns some results within an Intent that contains two possible extras:

➤ RESULTS: An ArrayList<String> that contains strings representing possible speech-to-text conversions. It lists the strings in descending order of recognition confidence. For example, if you say "next step" the results could contain the following: "next step, next steps, next stat, next that, next best, nah that, yes that, neck that, nex that." The correct conversion happens to be first and other possibilities follow. Also, if your app sets RESULTS_PENDINGINTENT, and the RESULTS extra is empty, it means that there was a recognition failure.

➤ CONFIDENCE_SCORES: An optional float [] from 0.0 to 1.0 or –1.0 representing recognition confidence. Each value corresponds to a speech-to-text conversion in the RESULTS array in the same array position. A value of 0 means low confidence and 1.0 means high confidence. If the value is –1, it means the confidence value was unavailable. The confidence values are useful in helping the app make decisions about how to respond to a user's utterance when an app does not understand it. For example, if the confidence scores are low and the possible conversions do not match any expected values, it might indicate that the app didn't understand. If the confidence scores are high and the possible conversions do not match, it might indicate that the user said the wrong thing. Both suggest different app responses. Chapter 19 goes into greater detail about how to use the confidence score.

RecognizerIntent Use Cases

You can use the RecognizerIntent in three ways, depending on what your app plans to do with the results. To activate the different use cases, your app uses a combination of an action type and potentially additional extras beyond the common ones already described.

Use case 1 is to return results to the calling Activity's onActivityResult() method.

This is a basic use case in which an Activity sends a RecognizerIntent and receives the result. Listing 16-17 shows code that constructs an Intent with two extras, LANGUAGE_MODEL and PROMPT.

LISTING 16-17: Creates a typical RecognizerIntent

```
public static Intent getSimpleRecognizerIntent(String prompt)
{
    Intent intent = new Intent(RecognizerIntent.ACTION_RECOGNIZE_SPEECH);
    intent.putExtra(RecognizerIntent.EXTRA_LANGUAGE_MODEL,
            RecognizerIntent.LANGUAGE_MODEL_WEB_SEARCH);
    intent.putExtra(RecognizerIntent.EXTRA_PROMPT, prompt);
    return intent;
}
```

Use case 2 is to handle results with a `PendingIntent`.

Normally, the recognizer returns results to the caller of `startActivityForResult()`. However, apps can make the recognizer send results along with a `PendingIntent` instead. To do so, an app sets the following extras:

➤ `RESULTS_PENDINGINTENT`: A `PendingIntent` for the recognizer to send with the recognition results.

➤ `RESULTS_PENDINGINTENT_BUNDLE`: A `Bundle` containing additional extras to pass with the `PendingIntent`. If an app sets this extra, the `Intent`'s receiver receives the recognition result extras as well as the contents of the bundle.

Using the `PendingIntent` could be useful to, for example, handle displaying search query results. In this scenario, your app would start a `RecognizerIntent` with a `PendingIntent` that would launch another `Activity`. The other `Activity` would interpret the recognition results and display a list of matching database entries.

Listings 16-18 and 16-19 show how to use a `PendingIntent` to receive recognition results and display them. The code in Listing 16-18 configures a `RecognizerIntent` called *intentToSend* to send a `PendingIntent` along with data inside an extra named `WHAT_YOU_ARE_TRYING_TO_SAY_INTENT_INPUT`.

LISTING 16-18: Configures a PendingIntent to receive the recognition results along with another extra

```
Intent pendingIntentSource =
        new Intent(this, SpeechRecognitionResultsActivity.class);
PendingIntent pi =
        PendingIntent.getActivity(this, 0, pendingIntentSource, 0);

Bundle extraInfoBundle = new Bundle();
// pass in what you are trying to say so the results activity can
// show it
extraInfoBundle
        .putString(
                SpeechRecognitionResultsActivity.
                    WHAT_YOU_ARE_TRYING_TO_SAY_INTENT_INPUT,
                whatYouAreTryingToSay.getText().toString());
```

continues

LISTING 16-18 *(continued)*

```
// set the variables in the intent this is sending
        intentToSend.putExtra(RecognizerIntent.EXTRA_RESULTS_PENDINGINTENT, pi);
        intentToSend.putExtra(
            RecognizerIntent.EXTRA_RESULTS_PENDINGINTENT_BUNDLE,
            extraInfoBundle);
```

The code in Listing 16-19 is an `Activity` that receives the `Intent`, and displays the recognition results and the `WHAT_YOU_ARE_TRYING_TO_SAY_INTENT_INPUT` value. The `Activity` reports an error dialog if the passed-in `Intent` does not contain `EXTRA_RESULTS`.

Figure 16-10 shows a possible result of running the code.

LISTING 16-19: Activity to receive the PendingIntent and display its contents

Available for download on Wrox.com

```java
public class SpeechRecognitionResultsActivity extends Activity
{
    private static final String TAG = "SpeechRecognitionResultsActivity";

    /**
     * for passing in the input
     */
    public static String WHAT_YOU_ARE_TRYING_TO_SAY_INTENT_INPUT =
        "WHAT_YOU_ARE_TRYING_TO_SAY_INPUT";

    private ListView log;

    private TextView resultsSummary;

    @Override
    protected void onCreate(Bundle savedInstanceState)
    {
        super.onCreate(savedInstanceState);
        setContentView(R.layout.speechrecognition_result);
        Log.d(TAG, "SpeechRecognition Pending intent received");
        hookButtons();
        init();
    }

    private void hookButtons()
    {
        log = (ListView) findViewById(R.id.lv_resultlog);
        resultsSummary = (TextView) findViewById(R.id.tv_speechResultsSummary);
    }

    private void init()
    {
        if (getIntent() != null)
        {
            if (getIntent().hasExtra(WHAT_YOU_ARE_TRYING_TO_SAY_INTENT_INPUT))
            {
                String whatSayFromIntent =
```

```
                        getIntent().getStringExtra(
                            WHAT_YOU_ARE_TRYING_TO_SAY_INTENT_INPUT);
             resultsSummary.setText(whatSayFromIntent);
         }

         String whatSayFromIntent =
                 getIntent().getStringExtra(
                     WHAT_YOU_ARE_TRYING_TO_SAY_INTENT_INPUT);
         resultsSummary.setText(whatSayFromIntent);

         if (getIntent().hasExtra(RecognizerIntent.EXTRA_RESULTS))
         {
             List<String> results =
                     getIntent().getStringArrayListExtra(
                         RecognizerIntent.EXTRA_RESULTS);
             ArrayAdapter<String> adapter =
                     new ArrayAdapter<String>(this,
                         R.layout.speechresultactivity_listitem,
                         R.id.tv_speech_activity_result, results);
             log.setAdapter(adapter);
         }
         else
         {
             // if RESULT_EXTRA is not present, the recognition had an
             // error
             DialogInterface.OnClickListener onClickFinish =
                     new DialogInterface.OnClickListener()
                     {
                         @Override
                         public void onClick(DialogInterface dialog,
                             int which)
                         {
                             finish();
                         }
                     };
             AlertDialog a =
                     new AlertDialog.Builder(this)
                         .setTitle(
                             getResources().getString(
                                 R.string.d_info))
                         .setMessage(
                             getResources()
                                 .getString(
                                 R.string.
                                 speechRecognitionFailed))
                         .setPositiveButton(
                             getResources().getString(R.string.d_ok),
                             onClickFinish).create();
             a.show();
         }
     }
   }
}
```

code snippet SpeechRecognitionResultsActivity.java

Use case 3 is to let the Android device decide what to do with the results. Most likely, it will decide to start a web search.

Your app can tell the Android to initiate an action of its choosing based on recognition results, by using the ACTION_WEB_SEARCH action instead of ACTION_RECOGNIZE_SPEECH. Typically, the recognizer sends the user to the web browser with the recognized speech. However, the Android documentation says that it may "trigger another type of action." Your app can disable other actions and force the user to go to a web browser by including the WEB_SEARCH_ONLY extra.

Android does trigger other actions based on what the user says. For example, if the user says "e-mail programming is fun," Android opens an e-mail prompt with the text "programming is fun." If the user just says "programming is fun," Android sends "programming is fun" to the web browser. Figure 16-11 shows both results.

You can use a few other extras with ACTION_WEB_SEARCH. If you set the ORIGIN field, the recognizer will include the value as the referring URL in the resulting HTML request.

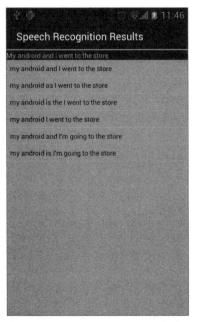

FIGURE 16-10: Displays the recognition results sent in a PendingIntent

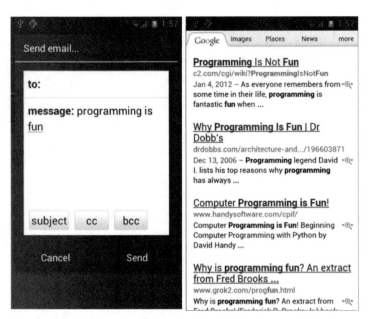

FIGURE 16-11: Two results from executing ACTION_WEB_SEARCH, when speaking "e-mail programming is fun" (left) or "Programming is fun" (right).

You can also set the PARTIAL_RESULTS extra in the hopes of getting partial results while the user speaks. However, it may not work in all cases because as the Android documentation states: "The server may ignore a request for partial results in some or all cases." In my experience, the server does a lot of ignoring.

In summary, by using the three use cases an app can have some control over what happens with the recognition results. Using the typical use case, an Activity sends a RecognizerIntent and then processes the results itself. However, an app can also forward the results to a PendingIntent by specifying one and to Android by using ACTION_WEB_SEARCH. The next section looks at some code that helps you to implement these use cases.

TRY THIS

Use the Try Speech button to adjust the various parameters and observe how closely Android recognizes your speech. Here are some experiments to try:

➤ **Difficult-to-recognize phrases:** Try selecting "Cumin seeds" or "It's not easy to wreck a nice beach" presets, and then trying to speak those words. Observe how closely the results match what you said.

➤ **Timing:** Try setting the three timing parameters, to see how long it allows you to pause your speech and how long the speech recording lasts.

➤ **Web search:** Check off Web Search in the settings. Then speak something.

➤ **PendingIntent:** Check "Pending intent for results." Then speak something and observe how the recognizer launches another Activity to show the results.

Implementation

Executing speech recognition requires a fair amount of boilerplate code. This section describes the reusable code you need within two classes. SpeechRecognizingActivity and SpeechRecognitionUtil combine the pieces described in this section to make a reusable library. Also, SayTheMagicWordDemo demonstrates how to use these new classes.

SpeechRecognitionUtil contains common speech-recognition-related methods such as initialization. SpeechRecognizingActivity is an abstract class that executes the initialization, sends the RecognizerIntent, and extracts data from the recognition results.

The easiest way to use these two classes is to extend SpeechRecognizingActivity. If your app can do so, almost all boilerplate code will be in the abstract class. If it cannot, your app can use SpeechRecognizingActivity as a template.

> **SPEECH RECOGNIZING AND SPEAKING ACTIVITY**
>
> If your app needs to use speech recognition and TTS, it may extend
> `SpeechRecognizingAndSpeakingActivity`, which extends
> `SpeechRecognizingActivity` to include TTS. It also handles prompting the user
> during initialization if required. The source code for this book includes this handy
> class for your use.

Listing 16-20 contains part of `SpeechRecognitionUtil`. It has two methods for initialization, among other convenient methods. `isSpeechAvailable()` determines if the device supports speech. `getLanguageDetails()` sends an `Intent` with the `ACTION_GET_LANGUAGE_DETAILS` action and calls back to an `OnLanguageDetailsListener` implementation with the result.

LISTING 16-20: A utility class that contains some common speech recognition methods

```
public class SpeechRecognitionUtil
{
    /**
     * checks if the device supports speech recognition
     * at all
     */
    public static boolean isSpeechAvailable(Context context)
    {
        PackageManager pm = context.getPackageManager();
        List<ResolveInfo> activities = pm.queryIntentActivities(
                new Intent(RecognizerIntent.ACTION_RECOGNIZE_SPEECH), 0);

        boolean available = true;
        if (activities.size() == 0)
        {
            available = false;
        }
        return available;
    }

    /**
     * collects language details and returns result to andThen
     */
    public static void getLanguageDetails(Context context,
            OnLanguageDetailsListener andThen)
    {
        Intent detailsIntent = new Intent(
                RecognizerIntent.ACTION_GET_LANGUAGE_DETAILS);
        LanguageDetailsChecker checker = new LanguageDetailsChecker(andThen);
        context.sendOrderedBroadcast(detailsIntent, null, checker, null,
                Activity.RESULT_OK, null, null);
    }
}
```

Listing 16-21 contains the abstract SpeechRecognizingActivity class. It has four methods that the extending class must implement to handle various callbacks from initialization and receiving recognition results. It has two methods the extending class may call.

For initialization, SpeechRecognizingActivity executes the speech availability check during onCreate(). If the device doesn't support speech recognition, SpeechRecognizingActivity calls speechNotAvailable(). If the extending Activity requests a language check via the checkForLanguage() method, SpeechRecognizingActivity calls languageCheckResult() with the result.

For executing, SpeechRecognizingActivity provides a recognize() method to send a passed-in RecognizeIntent. Using recognize() ensures that onActivityResult() can properly process the recognition result. When onActivityResult() receives recognition results, it either calls receiveWhatWasHeard() with the results, or recognitionFailure() if there was a recognition problem.

SpeechRecognizingActivity also provides different methods for direct speech recognition using SpeechRecognizer instead of RecognizerIntent. The next section describes how to use those.

Available for download on Wrox.com

LISTING 16-21: Abstract Activity to handle common speech recognition processes

```
public abstract class SpeechRecognizingActivity extends Activity implements
        RecognitionListener
{
    private static final String TAG = "SpeechRecognizingActivity";

    /**
     * code to identify return recognition results
     */
    public static final int VOICE_RECOGNITION_REQUEST_CODE = 1234;

    public static final int UNKNOWN_ERROR = -1;

    private SpeechRecognizer recognizer;

    // private VoiceAction active;

    @Override
    protected void onCreate(Bundle savedInstanceState)
    {
        super.onCreate(savedInstanceState);

        boolean recognizerIntent =
                SpeechRecognitionUtil.isSpeechAvailable(this);
        if (!recognizerIntent)
        {
            speechNotAvailable();
        }
        boolean direct = SpeechRecognizer.isRecognitionAvailable(this);
        if (!direct)
        {
            directSpeechNotAvailable();
        }
    }
```

continues

LISTING 16-21 *(continued)*

```
protected void checkForLanguage(final Locale language)
{
    OnLanguageDetailsListener andThen = new OnLanguageDetailsListener()
    {
        @Override
        public void onLanguageDetailsReceived(LanguageDetailsChecker data)
        {
            // do a best match
            String languageToUse = data.matchLanguage(language);
            languageCheckResult(languageToUse);
        }
    };
    SpeechRecognitionUtil.getLanguageDetails(this, andThen);
}

/**
 * execute the RecognizerIntent, then call
 * {@link #receiveWhatWasHeard(List, List)} when done
 */
public void recognize(Intent recognizerIntent)
{
    startActivityForResult(recognizerIntent,
            VOICE_RECOGNITION_REQUEST_CODE);
}

/**
 * Handle the results from the RecognizerIntent.
 */
@Override
protected void
        onActivityResult(int requestCode, int resultCode, Intent data)
{
    if (requestCode == VOICE_RECOGNITION_REQUEST_CODE)
    {
        if (resultCode == RESULT_OK)
        {
            List<String> heard =
                    data.
                    getStringArrayListExtra
                        (RecognizerIntent.EXTRA_RESULTS);
            float[] scores =
                    data.
                    getFloatArrayExtra
                        (RecognizerIntent.EXTRA_CONFIDENCE_SCORES);
            if (scores == null)
            {
                for (int i = 0; i < heard.size(); i++)
                {
                    Log.d(TAG, i + ": " + heard.get(i));
                }
            }
            else
            {
                for (int i = 0; i < heard.size(); i++)
```

```
                    {
                        Log.d(TAG, i + ": " + heard.get(i) + " score: "
                                + scores[i]);
                    }
                }

                receiveWhatWasHeard(heard, scores);
            }
            else
            {
                Log.d(TAG, "error code: " + resultCode);
                recognitionFailure(UNKNOWN_ERROR);
            }
        }
        super.onActivityResult(requestCode, resultCode, data);
    }

    /**
     * called when speech is not available on this device, and when
     * {@link #recognize(Intent)} will not work
     */
    abstract protected void speechNotAvailable();

    /**
     * called when {@link SpeechRecognizer} cannot be used on this device and
     * {@link #recognizeDirectly(Intent)} will not work
     */
    abstract protected void directSpeechNotAvailable();

    /**
     * call back the result from {@link #checkForLanguage(Locale)}
     *
     * @param languageToUse
     *            the language string to use or null if failure
     */
    abstract protected void languageCheckResult(String languageToUse);

    /**
     * result of speech recognition
     *
     * @param heard
     *            possible speech to text conversions
     * @param confidenceScores
     *            the confidence for the strings in heard
     */
    abstract protected void receiveWhatWasHeard(List<String> heard,
            float[] confidenceScores);

    /**
     * @param code
     *            If using {@link #recognizeDirectly(Intent) it will be
     *            the error code from {@link SpeechRecognizer}
     *            if using {@link #recognize(Intent)}
     *            it will be {@link #UNKNOWN_ERROR}.
     */
    abstract protected void recognitionFailure(int errorCode);
```

continues

LISTING 16-21 *(continued)*

```
//direct speech recognition methods follow

/**
 * Uses {@link SpeechRecognizer} to perform recognition and then calls
 * {@link #receiveWhatWasHeard(List, float[])} with the results <br>
 * check {@link SpeechRecognizer.isRecognitionAvailable(context)} before
 * calling this method otherwise if it isn't available the code will report
 * an error
 */
public void recognizeDirectly(Intent recognizerIntent)
{
    // SpeechRecognizer requires EXTRA_CALLING_PACKAGE, so add if it's not
    // here
    if (!recognizerIntent.hasExtra(RecognizerIntent.EXTRA_CALLING_PACKAGE))
    {
        recognizerIntent.putExtra(RecognizerIntent.EXTRA_CALLING_PACKAGE,
                "com.dummy");
    }
    SpeechRecognizer recognizer = getSpeechRecognizer();
    recognizer.startListening(recognizerIntent);
}

@Override
public void onResults(Bundle results)
{
    Log.d(TAG, "full results");
    receiveResults(results);
}

@Override
public void onPartialResults(Bundle partialResults)
{
    Log.d(TAG, "partial results");
    receiveResults(partialResults);
}

/**
 * common method to process any results bundle from {@link SpeechRecognizer}
 */
private void receiveResults(Bundle results)
{
    if ((results != null)
            && results.containsKey(SpeechRecognizer.RESULTS_RECOGNITION))
    {
        List<String> heard =
                results.getStringArrayList(SpeechRecognizer.RESULTS_RECOGNITION);
        float[] scores =
                results.getFloatArray(SpeechRecognizer.CONFIDENCE_SCORES);
        receiveWhatWasHeard(heard, scores);
    }
}
```

```
    @Override
    public void onError(int errorCode)
    {
        recognitionFailure(errorCode);
    }

    /**
     * stop the speech recognizer
     */
    @Override
    protected void onPause()
    {
        if (getSpeechRecognizer() != null)
        {
            getSpeechRecognizer().stopListening();
            getSpeechRecognizer().cancel();
            getSpeechRecognizer().destroy();
        }
        super.onPause();
    }

    /**
     * lazy initialize the speech recognizer
     */
    private SpeechRecognizer getSpeechRecognizer()
    {
        if (recognizer == null)
        {
            recognizer = SpeechRecognizer.createSpeechRecognizer(this);
            recognizer.setRecognitionListener(this);
        }
        return recognizer;
    }

    // other unused methods from RecognitionListener...
}
```

code snippet SpeechRecognizingActivity.java

Listing 16-22 shows `SayMagicWordDemo`, which uses both TTS and speech recognition. It contains the code similar to `TextToSpeechDemo`, only instead of playing a script the `Activity` records speech and speaks a response back to the user.

The class extends `SpeechRecognizingActivity`. Therefore, most of the speech recognition details are in `SpeechRecognizingActivity`. To execute the speech recognition, the `acquireGuess()` method configures an `Intent` and calls `recognize()` to send it. Then, `SpeechRecognizingActivity` calls `receiveWhatWasHeard()` with the results. `receiveWhat-WasHeard()` processes the recognition result by executing a simple `if` statement.

In `SayMagicWordDemo`, TTS and speech recognition have one simple interaction. By activating and deactivating the Speak button, `SayMagicWordDemo` does not allow speech recognition to start until

TTS finishes speaking. This is an important feature an app needs if it is using both TTS and speech recognition, because it could lead to the app talking to itself.

Available for
download on
Wrox.com

LISTING 16-22: Demonstration Activity using TTS and speech recognition

```java
public class SayMagicWordDemo extends SpeechRecognizingActivity implements
        TextToSpeechStartupListener
{
    private static final String TAG = "SayMagicWordDemo";
    private Button speak;
    private TextToSpeechInitializer ttsInit;
    private TextToSpeech tts;

    @Override
    public void onCreate(Bundle savedInstanceState)
    {
        super.onCreate(savedInstanceState);
        setContentView(R.layout.magicworddemo);
        hookButtons();
        init();
    }

    private void hookButtons()
    {
        speak = (Button) findViewById(R.id.btn_speak);
        speak.setOnClickListener(new View.OnClickListener()
        {
            @Override
            public void onClick(View v)
            {
                acquireGuess();
            }
        });
    }

    private void init()
    {
        deactivateUi();
        ttsInit = new TextToSpeechInitializer(this, Locale.getDefault(), this);
    }

    @Override
    public void onSuccessfulInit(TextToSpeech tts)
    {
        Log.d(TAG, "successful init");
        this.tts = tts;
        activateUi();
        setTtsListener();
    }

    /**
     * set the TTS listener to call {@link #onDone(String)} depending on the
     * Build.Version
```

```
    */
    private void setTtsListener()
    {
        final SayMagicWordDemo callWithResult = this;
        if (Build.VERSION.SDK_INT >= 15)
        {
            int listenerResult =
                    tts.setOnUtteranceProgressListener(
                            new UtteranceProgressListener()
                    {
                        @Override
                        public void onDone(String utteranceId)
                        {
                            callWithResult.onDone(utteranceId);
                        }

                        @Override
                        public void onError(String utteranceId)
                        {
                            Log.e(TAG, "TTS error");
                        }

                        @Override
                        public void onStart(String utteranceId)
                        {
                            Log.d(TAG, "TTS start");
                        }
                    });
            if (listenerResult != TextToSpeech.SUCCESS)
            {
                Log.e(TAG, "failed to add utterance progress listener");
            }
        }
        else
        {
            int listenerResult =
                    tts.setOnUtteranceCompletedListener(
                            new OnUtteranceCompletedListener()
                    {
                        @Override
                        public void onUtteranceCompleted(String utteranceId)
                        {
                            callWithResult.onDone(utteranceId);
                        }
                    });
            if (listenerResult != TextToSpeech.SUCCESS)
            {
                Log.e(TAG, "failed to add utterance completed listener");
            }
        }
    }

    public void onDone(String utteranceId)
    {
```

continues

LISTING 16-22 *(continued)*

```
        Log.d(TAG, "utterance completed: " + utteranceId);
        runOnUiThread(new Runnable()
        {
            @Override
            public void run()
            {
                activateUi();
            }
        });
    }

    @Override
    public void onFailedToInit()
    {
        DialogInterface.OnClickListener onClickOk =
            makeOnFailedToInitHandler();
        AlertDialog a =
                new AlertDialog.Builder(this).setTitle("Error")
                        .setMessage("Unable to create text to speech")
                        .setNeutralButton("Ok", onClickOk).create();
        a.show();
    }

    @Override
    public void onRequireLanguageData()
    {
        DialogInterface.OnClickListener onClickOk =
                makeOnClickInstallDialogListener();
        DialogInterface.OnClickListener onClickCancel =
                makeOnFailedToInitHandler();
        AlertDialog a =
                new AlertDialog.Builder(this)
                        .setTitle("Error")
                        .setMessage(
                                "Requires Language data to proceed," +
                                " would you like to install?")
                        .setPositiveButton("Ok", onClickOk)
                        .setNegativeButton("Cancel", onClickCancel).create();
        a.show();
    }

    @Override
    public void onWaitingForLanguageData()
    {
        // either wait for install
        DialogInterface.OnClickListener onClickWait =
                makeOnFailedToInitHandler();
        DialogInterface.OnClickListener onClickInstall =
                makeOnClickInstallDialogListener();

        AlertDialog a =
                new AlertDialog.Builder(this)
```

```
                          .setTitle("Info")
                          .setMessage(
                                  "Please wait for the language data " +
                                  "to finish installing and try again.")
                          .setNegativeButton("Wait", onClickWait)
                          .setPositiveButton("Retry", onClickInstall).create();
        a.show();
    }

    private DialogInterface.OnClickListener makeOnClickInstallDialogListener()
    {
        return new DialogInterface.OnClickListener()
        {
            @Override
            public void onClick(DialogInterface dialog, int which)
            {
                ttsInit.installLanguageData();
            }
        };
    }

    private DialogInterface.OnClickListener makeOnFailedToInitHandler()
    {
        return new DialogInterface.OnClickListener()
        {
            @Override
            public void onClick(DialogInterface dialog, int which)
            {
                finish();
            }
        };
    }

    private void acquireGuess()
    {
        Intent intent = new Intent(RecognizerIntent.ACTION_RECOGNIZE_SPEECH);
        intent.putExtra(RecognizerIntent.EXTRA_LANGUAGE_MODEL,
                RecognizerIntent.LANGUAGE_MODEL_WEB_SEARCH);
        intent.putExtra(RecognizerIntent.EXTRA_PROMPT,
                "What is the magic word?");

        recognize(intent);
    }

    public void speechNotAvailable()
    {
        DialogInterface.OnClickListener onClickOk =
            makeOnFailedToInitHandler();
        AlertDialog a =
                new AlertDialog.Builder(this)
                        .setTitle("Error")
                        .setMessage(
                                "This device does not support " +
                                "speech recognition. Click ok to quit.")
```

continues

LISTING 16-22 *(continued)*

```java
                            .setPositiveButton("Ok", onClickOk).create();
        a.show();
    }

    @Override
    protected void directSpeechNotAvailable()
    {
        // not using it
    }

    protected void languageCheckResult(String languageToUse)
    {
        // not used
    }

    /**
     * determine if the user said the magic word and speak the result
     */
    protected void receiveWhatWasHeard(List<String> heard,
            float[] confidenceScores)
    {
        String magicWord = "tree";
        String mostLikelyThingHeard = heard.get(0);
        String message = "";
        if (mostLikelyThingHeard.equals(magicWord))
        {
            message =
                    "Correct! You said the magic word: " + mostLikelyThingHeard;
        }
        else
        {
            message = "Wrong! The magic word is not: " + mostLikelyThingHeard;
        }

        AlertDialog a =
                new AlertDialog.Builder(this).setTitle("Result")
                        .setMessage(message).setPositiveButton("Ok", null)
                        .create();
        a.show();

        deactivateUi();
        HashMap<String, String> params = new HashMap<String, String>();
        params.put(TextToSpeech.Engine.KEY_PARAM_UTTERANCE_ID, "anyid");
        tts.speak(message, TextToSpeech.QUEUE_ADD, params);
    }

    protected void recognitionFailure(int errorCode)
    {
        AlertDialog a =
                new AlertDialog.Builder(this)
                        .setTitle("Error")
                        .setMessage(
```

```
                              SpeechRecognitionUtil
                                 .diagnoseErrorCode(errorCode))
                      .setPositiveButton("Ok", null).create();
        a.show();
    }

    // activate and deactivate the UI based on various states

    private void deactivateUi()
    {
        Log.d(TAG, "deactivate ui");
        // don't enable until the initialization is complete
        speak.setEnabled(false);
    }

    private void activateUi()
    {
        Log.d(TAG, "activate ui");
        speak.setEnabled(true);
    }

    @Override
    protected void onDestroy()
    {
        tts.shutdown();
        super.onDestroy();
    }

}
```

code snippet SayMagicWordDemo.java

Thus far, this chapter has covered how to send a `RecognizerIntent` by using the `recognize()` method. There is an alternative method to using speech recognition that uses the `SpeechRecognizer` class instead of `RecognizerIntent`. In addition to supporting `RecognizerIntent`, the code just described in this section also supports the alternative, `SpeechRecognizer` approach via a `recognizeDirectly()` method. The next section describes using it in detail and the code that `SpeechRecognizingActivity` uses to implement the `recognizeDirectly()` method.

Direct Speech Recognition Using SpeechRecognizer

The previous sections discussed how to send a `RecognizerIntent` to execute speech recognition. Sending a `RecognizerIntent` simplifies the code you need to write because it delegates the speech recognition process to a receiving `Activity`. However, this process can be insufficient for some apps.

Alternately, an app can use the `SpeechRecognizer` API to access lower-level information and get tighter control while the device is executing speech recognition. This book calls using the API "direct speech recognition."

In particular, direct speech recognition is useful when:

➤ You want to show a different or no dialog while recording speech.

➤ You want your app to respond while recognition is taking place.

➤ You want your app to run speech recognition in the background while the user is doing something else.

➤ You want to better diagnose errors from the speech recognizer.

➤ You want access to some low-level details of the speech processing.

TRY THIS

In the Try Speech screen you can try `SpeechRecognizer` by switching on the Use `SpeechRecognizer` parameter inside the Speech Parameters menu option. You can see how `SpeechRecognizer` gives the same output as sending a `RecognizerIntent`. One visible difference is that instead of showing a dialog, the app makes a toast to alert the user that speech recognition is occurring.

To use `SpeechRecognizer` an app needs to perform several steps. Listing 16-21, shown in the previous section, shows how `SpeechRecognizingActivity` does it. The necessary steps are as follows.

For setup:

➤ Check if `SpeechRecognizer` is available by calling `SpeechRecognizer.isRecognitionAvailable()`.

➤ Create a `SpeechRecognizer` by calling `SpeechRecognizer.createSpeechRecognizer()`.

➤ Destroy `SpeechRecognizer` when done with it.

➤ Set a `RecognitionListener`.

For execution:

➤ Set a `RecognizerIntent.EXTRA_CALLING_PACKAGE`.

➤ Call `startListening()` with a configured `RecognizerIntent`.

➤ Optionally, alert the user that speech recognition is occurring.

The first part of setting up is to create a `SpeechRecognizer` object using `SpeechRecognizer.createSpeechRecognizer()`. `SpeechRecognizingActivity` creates a `SpeechRecognizer` once and maintains a single instance. It also cleans up the object during `onPause()`.

The second part of setting up is to check whether the device supports using `SpeechRecognizer`. To do this an app needs to call `SpeechRecognizer.isRecognitionAvailable()`. The method checks for whether the app can respond to the `RecognitionService.SERVICE_INTERFACE` action. This action is different from the `ACTION_RECOGNIZE_SPEECH` action that apps need to check before sending the `RecognizerIntent`. Typically, if a device supports `ACTION_RECOGNIZE_SPEECH`, it will also support `RecognitionService.SERVICE_INTERFACE`. Google Voice and other speech recognizers support both. However, it is possible that a user could activate a speech recognizer that does not support one or the other.

`SpeechRecognizingActivity` calls `SpeechRecognizer.isRecognitionAvailable()` when it checks `ACTION_RECOGNIZE_SPEECH` during `onCreate()`. It calls `directSpeechNotAvailable()` if it fails.

To execute `SpeechRecognizer` an app registers a `RecognitionListener` and calls `startListening()` with a configured `RecognizerIntent`. An app can configure the `RecognizerIntent` by setting the various available extras such as `EXTRA_SPEECH_INPUT_MINIMUM_LENGTH_MILLIS` as previously described in this chapter.

As `SpeechRecognizer` collects speech, it calls the `RecognitionListener` with various callbacks. The callbacks give your app access to low-level details such as `onBufferReceived()`, which provides raw sound bytes. The callbacks also have state callbacks such as `onBeginningOfSpeech()` and `onEndOfSpeech()`, and report errors via `onError()`. None of these functions are available when sending the `RecognizerIntent`. The `RecognitionListener` receives results via `onPartialResults()` or `onResults()`. In contrast, when sending the `RecognizerIntent`, an app receives results in the `onActivityResult()` method.

To implement this, `SpeechRecognizingActivity` contains a convenient `recognizeDirectly()` method and implements part of the `RecognitionListener` interface. When executing, `recognizeDirectly()` sets the calling package and starts speech recognition. Then, `SpeechRecognizer` calls back to `SpeechRecognizingActivity` when recognition is complete, partially complete, or when there is an error. `SpeechRecognizingActivity` responds by forwarding results to the abstract `receiveWhatWasHeard()` method in both cases.

SUMMARY

This chapter showed you the mechanics of using the TTS and speech recognition APIs. It covered how to initialize and check for language support and provided you with reusable code to help you use the APIs in various ways. This chapter also contained a complete `Activity` that uses both technologies together.

Knowing how to use the APIs is not enough to implement voice actions, however. An app also has to process the list of recognitions and confidences to arrive at what the user most likely said so that your app can take the appropriate action. It also has to organize the voice action implementation to support multiple commands at a single prompt and to execute a sequence of voice actions if necessary. By using the approaches described in Chapters 17–19, and the mechanics learned in this chapter, you will be able fully implement sophisticated voice actions in your apps.

17

Matching What Was Said

WHAT'S IN THIS CHAPTER?

➤   Matching using word spotting

➤   Matching against command words in persistent storage

➤   Matching single and multi-part commands

The previous chapter showed how to use the speech recognition and TTS APIs. The chapter provided code that extracts speech recognition results from `onActivityResult()` and passes them to the following method:

```
abstract protected void receiveWhatWasHeard(
        List<String> heard, float[] confidenceScores);
```

Your implementation of the abstract `receiveWhatWasHeard()` method has to decide if your app heard any commands. To do this your implementation must iterate over the recognition results and try to match them with command words. You could implement `receiveWhat-WasHeard()` using a `Set<String>` that succeeds if any heard strings are in the `Set`. However, that does not allow you to implement all the types of commands you may want, nor does it allow you to handle all the speech recognition issues that can decrease accuracy.

This chapter reviews the issues involved in reliably matching commands with the user's utterances. Also, this chapter presents a word spotting algorithm for matching and an implementation of it that can match various command types. Word spotting works well for simple commands and the type of information Android returns.

PARTS OF A VOICE COMMAND

Designing commands requires determining what kinds of text the command needs to recognize to activate it and supply information, how many different parts a command has, and whether or not the parts need to come in a particular order. When executing, the app must match the command words to the users' utterances.

Here are the different kinds of command words your command may contain:

➤ **Static:** Words your app knows before deployment. For instance, names of commands like "add" or "delete."

➤ **Dynamic:** Words your app doesn't know before deployment, but still require matching against, such as names of items a user added to a list.

➤ **Free text:** Portion of an utterance the user specifies as input — something like the name of new item.

As stated, you know static words before deployment but do not know dynamic words. If your app allows users to enter items in a list, a possible voice command may be to query for those items. In that case, your voice command could be "find <something in list>," where <something in list> contains dynamic words and find is a static word. In such a command, the app must match <something in list> with any list items the user may have entered and also match the static word find.

Two differences between dynamic and static words influence which type of words to include in your command and how to implement them. First, dynamic words are harder to recognize than static words. With static words, you can carefully choose words that are easier for your app to understand. With dynamic words, you have no such luxury. The words can contain any text, some of which may be hard to recognize.

A second difference is that matching the two types of words may require different storage and query mechanisms. Static words often have few enough words to fit in memory, whereas dynamic commands may have many words and require queries to persistent storage.

Free text could be another part of a voice command. Imagine a voice command where the user speaks "add <something to add>" to add a new item to a list. In this case <something to add> could be any text. To capture the free text, your app has to select any words after "add" as being the new item text. Thus, capturing free text involves bounding a user's utterance by position so your app knows what part is the free text.

Instead of trying to locate the free text within a user's utterance by position, another, more robust way to handle free text is to make the entire command free text. To implement the add command, for instance, you could make a two-step command where the user uses the speech recognition prompt twice. The first time, the user says "add." The second time, the user speaks the free text. The drawback of this approach is that it takes much more time for the user to specify the entire command.

Each of the types of command words just discussed — static words, dynamic words, and free text — can be combined together to create commands that have multiple parts. For example, "add" is a single-part command, but "add <something to add>" is a multi-part command. A command with only one part is easier to recognize because it only has one part to match. In contrast, a multi-part command incurs additional difficulties, such as collisions that increase recognition mistakes.

Multi-part commands can be ordered or unordered based on whether they require one word to come before another. Requiring the user to speak the words in a certain order adds additional requirements on the user's speech and additional processing by your app. The result is a command that is more expressive and can accomplish more, but one that may be harder to understand than single-part or unordered commands.

To address these challenges, an app needs an algorithm that allows it to accurately recognize expressive commands with multiple parts if necessary. The next section describes how to use a word spotting algorithm to do so.

WORD SPOTTING

To recognize static and dynamic command words, apps can use a word-spotting algorithm. A word spotting algorithm scans text for particular whole command words, ignoring all other words. For example, if the command word is "add," a word-spotting algorithm would find it within utterances such as "add" or "I'd uh like to add maybe" but not "I am addicted to Android" even though "addicted" contains "add" as a substring.

Word spotting is a robust way to determine if a user said a particular command. A user's speech may not be grammatically correct, have extra words, or contain words in the wrong order. With word spotting, these abnormalities don't matter as long as the correct word exists in the spoken utterance.

One issue with word spotting is that it cannot comprehend the semantic meaning of what the user said. For example, word spotting algorithms can't understand negation. If the user says "do not add" the word spotting algorithm might spot the "add" word and assume the user wanted to add something when he or she really wanted the opposite.

Another potential issue is that any command words become keywords that can't be used elsewhere in the command. For example, your app might have a two-part command like "add <item>" and another command "remove <item>" where "add" and "remove" are both command words. If the user tries to remove an item named "add," he might say "remove add." However, the word spotting algorithm might detect "add" first and assume the user meant "add" instead of "remove." You can modify the basic word spotting algorithm to handle such errors by handling ordered commands, though doing so complicates processing.

In summary, word spotting is good at scanning for command words within a user's utterance. It is robust against added words, incorrect word order, and grammatically incorrect speech. Word spotting cannot understand any complex semantic meanings, and multi-part commands introduce additional potential for misrecognitions.

The two classes in Listings 17-1 and 17-2 show code that does word spotting by detecting single, static command words using an in-memory `Set` object. `WordMatcher`, shown in Listing 17-1, handles representing the command words in a `Set<String>` and then checking the `Set`.

Available for
download on
Wrox.com

LISTING 17-1: Utility class for matching words to a predefined Set

```
public class WordMatcher
{
    private Set<String> words;

    public WordMatcher(String... wordsIn)
    {
        this(Arrays.asList(wordsIn));
```

continues

LISTING 17-1 *(continued)*

```java
    }

    public WordMatcher(List<String> wordsIn)
    {
        words = new LinkedHashSet<String>(wordsIn);
    }

    public Set<String> getWords()
    {
        return words;
    }

    public boolean isIn(String word)
    {
        return words.contains(word);
    }

    public boolean isIn(String [] wordsIn)
    {
        boolean wordIn = false;
        for (String word : wordsIn)
        {
            if (isIn(word))
            {
                wordIn = true;
                break;
            }
        }
        return wordIn;
    }
}
```

code snippet WordMatcher.java

The code in Listing 17-2 contains a `receiveWhatWasHeard()` method that creates a `WordMatcher` and uses it to check against the possible recognitions in *heard*.

LISTING 17-2: Using WordMatcher to interpret recognition results for an "add" command

```java
    protected void receiveWhatWasHeard(List<String> heard,
            float[] confidenceScores)
    {
        WordMatcher command = new WordMatcher("add");
        for (String said : heard)
        {
            if (command.isIn(said.split("\\s")))
            {
                Log.d(TAG, "heard add");
                break;
            }
        }
    }
```

Indexing to Improve Word Spotting

Word spotting can only work as well as the speech recognizer can successfully understand the user's speech. The recognizer is limited because it cannot understand all words. Also, the recognizer's chance of successful recognition is complicated by the fact that the recognizer is biased toward recognizing certain words more readily than others. The only control your app has over how the recognizer is biased is to select the most appropriate LANGUAGE_MODEL parameter. Usually, the recognizer's bias helps because it makes Android understand what users commonly say. However, sometimes an app needs to understand uncommon words.

The recognizer's bias and accuracy of recognizing words can lead to words that an app cannot recognize at all or has a difficult time recognizing. If the user expects the app to recognize words that the app is incapable of recognizing, the user may enter a never-ending frustrating loop of the app not understanding and the user not knowing why.

You can avoid such hard-to-understand words if you use static command words that you know beforehand. However, you cannot know dynamic commands beforehand and hence your app could eventually encounter a rare word. If you want your app to work in those cases, you need to index the command words so your app can match them regardless.

Unfortunately, the only way to determine which words are hard to understand is trial and error. Android does not publish the necessary information, and what's more, the recognizer's performance is likely to change over time.

Certain types of words are hard to understand:

➤ **Rare words:** Words people use infrequently. For example, Android almost never understands the word "cumin." Figure 17-1 shows an attempt to speak "cumin" and what Android recognized. As you can see in Figure 17-1, the app was unable to match "cumin" exactly, though the ampersand symbol (&) near the sixth result shows that by using indexing, the app was able to match "cumin" with "canon."

➤ **Invented words:** Users may speak invented words or abbreviations and expect the app to understand. The recognizer recognizes many phrases and even appears to reply with phonetic interpretations of words it does not know. Still, sometimes the speech recognizer either does not understand certain words or does not exactly understand in the way you expect. This situation can be easier to encounter than you might expect. For example, the common abbreviation "decaf" is difficult for the recognizer to understand, and when it does it returns "decaff" with an extra f. That slight variation of adding an f would cause WordMatcher from Listing 17-1 to fail. To get a correct match, you need StemmedWordMatcher or SoundsLikeWordMatcher instead, which this chapter describes later.

➤ **Homophones:** Homophones are two words that sound the same although they're spelled differently. Your app may have to do more processing if it is searching for a word that is a homophone and the meaning it requires is rare. Fortunately, Android usually returns all versions of a homophone. For example, when speaking "thyme" the recognizer returns "time, timer, times, thyme." As you can see, the correct word appears in the returned values. However, the correct word is used less frequently so it is at the end of the list.

Android doesn't always return all homophones, however. For example, if you speak "feint" the recognizer returns "faint" and never returns "feint." The same is true for "raze."

➤ **Poorly recorded words:** The user could speak poorly or introduce some other audio interference. In such cases, the recognized words may resemble the command words, but will not be exactly alike.

As described earlier, some kinds of words and conditions prevent the recognizer from understanding what the user is saying. In some cases, the problems can be overcome if the user tries again. In other cases, no matter how many times the user tries, the recognizer simply will not work. Additionally, you may prefer that your app make a best guess at what users said, rather than cause them to retry.

The only way to recognize the unrecognizable or to make a best guess is to reduce the command words to more general forms by indexing them. Indexing can cause two slightly different words to map to the same general form. The result is that words that don't have the exactly same string can still match. For example, a simple indexing scheme might be to reduce all words to their first letter. Such a scheme would index "apple, apples, and appeal" as "a," which would allow an app to consider them the same.

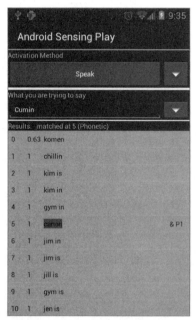

Using indexing involves considering the following trade-off: Allowing matches on indexed forms of words decreases recognition failure, but potentially increases recognizing the wrong commands. Users may be tolerant of or annoyed by the app responding incorrectly sometimes. The response you get from users is dependent on the voice command's task. For

FIGURE 17-1: Recognition and phonetic matching results from speaking "cumin"

example, if the result of the command is to change something that is hard to undo, users will not want to tolerate failure and indexing may not be appropriate. However, if the result of the command is just speaking a short phrase, it is possible users can easily ignore the spoken text and not get annoyed by any incorrect responses.

You could use many kinds of string manipulation to index. Two particularly useful methods are *stemming* and *phonetic indexing*.

Stemming

Stemming is a language-dependent type of language processing that reduces words to their roots by removing suffixes. For example, a stemmer reduces all these words to the same root: "walk, walks, walked, walking." Although the recognizer sometimes includes word variations, such as "walk and walks," in its recognition results, it may not provide the variations your app needs.

Fortunately, stemmer code is freely available for a variety of languages. Many implementations provide the standard Porter stemmer, but some provide better-performing stemmers. Third-party libraries like Lucene's analyzers project (`http://lucene.apache.org/core/old_versioned_docs/versions/3_5_0/api/contrib-analyzers/`) have stemmers for many languages, and SQLite has a stemmer option for its Full Text Search (FTS) mechanism. Listing 17-3 shows code that utilizes Lucene's `org.tartarus.snowball.ext.EnglishStemmer` to implement a `WordMatcher`.

WHICH LUCENE STEMMER TO USE

`org.tartarus.snowball.ext.EnglishStemmer` is available as a small jar in the Lucene snowball contrib project. You can download it from `http://archive.apache.org/dist/lucene/java/3.0.3/`. In later versions of Lucene the same class is available as part of the Lucene analyzers contrib project. The drawback of using analyzers is that it is larger in size than the snowball jar from 3.0.3. However, using later versions of Lucene allows you to use different stemmer implementations, such as `KStemmer`, and other text indexing methods such as `EnglishPossessiveFilter`. Therefore, it may be worth it to include the larger analyzer jar in your app.

Available for download on Wrox.com

LISTING 17-3: Compares words by their stems

```
//Note: org.tartarus is part of the lucene snowball contrib project in 3.0.3 and
//analyzers contrib project in versions 3.1.0 and greater
import org.tartarus.snowball.ext.EnglishStemmer;

public class StemmedWordMatcher extends WordMatcher
{
    public StemmedWordMatcher(String... wordsIn)
    {
        this(Arrays.asList(wordsIn));
    }

    public StemmedWordMatcher(List<String> wordsIn)
    {
        super(encode(wordsIn));
    }

    private static List<String> encode(List<String> input)
    {
        List<String> encoded = new ArrayList<String>();
        for (String in : input)
        {
            encoded.add(stem(in));
        }
        return encoded;
    }

    @Override
    public boolean isIn(String word)
    {
        return super.isIn(stem(word));
```

continues

LISTING 17-3 *(continued)*

```java
    }

    /**
     * run the stemmer from Lucene
     */
    private static String stem(String word)
    {
        EnglishStemmer stemmer = new EnglishStemmer();
        stemmer.setCurrent(word);
        boolean result = stemmer.stem();
        if (!result)
        {
            return word;
        }
        return stemmer.getCurrent();
    }
}
```

code snippet StemmedWordMatcher.java

Stemming helps an app match words even when the recognizer makes a mistake and recognizes a different form of the desired words. For example, if the recognizer recognizes a singular verb, using a stemmer allows an app to match the recognized singular form with the plural form. Another kind of mistake the recognizer can make is to recognize a word that sounds like the word the user said instead of the actual word. To match words in such cases, an app needs to use phonetic indexing.

Phonetic Indexing

Phonetic indexing allows your app to determine word similarity based on how the words sound instead of what characters they have. Phonetic indexing is particularly applicable to processing recognizer results because when the recognizer fails to precisely understand what the user says, it often returns words that sound like the word the user said instead. For example, if the user tries to say "apple," but the recognizer makes a mistake and recognizes "appeal" instead, phonetic indexing would allow your app to still match "apple" with "appeal."

There is a suite of algorithms that perform phonetic indexing in various ways. You can find implementations at `http://commons.apache.org/codec/` and `www.tangentum.biz/en/products/phonetix/index/html`. Apache's implementation has the following phonetic matching algorithms: Soundex, RefinedSoundex, Metaphone, DoubleMetaphone, and Caverphone. Phonetix has alternate implementations. The implementations are somewhat language dependent, and all are rule-based.

Soundex is the simplest phonetic indexing algorithm. Other algorithms are more complicated and came after Soundex was developed. This section explains Soundex to give you a sense for how these algorithms work.

Soundex was designed to help compare names for the U.S. census, but it can also help to compare any two strings. The algorithm reduces any string to a four-character code consisting of a letter followed by three numerical digits. You can find more details here: `www.archives.gov/research/census/soundex.html`.

Soundex executes the following rules to compute a code:

1. The first letter is the first letter of the string.

2. Replace the remaining letters with the letter-to-number mapping shown here, ignoring a, e, h, i, o, u, w, and y:

   ➤ 1: B, F, P, V

   ➤ 2: C, G, J, K, Q, S, X, Z

   ➤ 3: D, T

   ➤ 4: L

   ➤ 5: M, N

   ➤ 6: R

3. Treat double letters as one letter. For example, "ss" would be 2.

4. Include only one code if two side-by-side letters have the same code.

5. Use the code for the first consonant if two consonants with the same code are separated by "H" or "W."

6. Use the code for the second consonant if two consonants with the same code are separated a vowel.

7. Stop when there is one letter and three numbers. If the final code has fewer than three numbers, add additional 0s until there are three numbers.

You can tweak the Soundex algorithm to increase the number of matches in exchange for increased false matches. For example, you may decide to report a match if the Soundex code only partially overlaps by one or more characters. Another possibility is to compute the variable-length Soundex codes by not stopping after computing a four-character code.

For example, tweaking helps match the word "cumin" with "human." The Soundex code for cumin is C550 and the Soundex code for human is H550. If code drops the first letter of the Soundex code, it can match the two words.

Listing 17-4 shows a modified `SoundListWordMatcher` to utilize Apache Commons Codec to compare based on Soundex codes.

LISTING 17-4: WordMatcher variation that uses Soundex comparisons

```
import org.apache.commons.codec.language.Soundex;
public class SoundsLikeWordMatcher extends WordMatcher
{
    protected static Soundex soundex;

    static
    {
        soundex = new Soundex();
    }
```

continues

LISTING 17-4 *(continued)*

```java
    public SoundsLikeWordMatcher(String... wordsIn)
    {
        this(Arrays.asList(wordsIn));
    }

    public SoundsLikeWordMatcher(List<String> wordsIn)
    {
        super(encode(wordsIn));
    }

    @Override
    public boolean isIn(String word)
    {
        return super.isIn(encode(word));
    }

    protected static List<String> encode(List<String> input)
    {
        List<String> encoded = new ArrayList<String>();
        for (String in : input)
        {
            encoded.add(encode(in));
        }
        return encoded;
    }

    private static String encode(String in)
    {
        return soundex.encode(in);
    }
}
```

Listing 17-5 shows code that tests `SoundsLikeWordMatcher`. The tests show that Soundex allows the code to determine that the homophones for beat, faint, and thyme sound the same.

LISTING 17-5: Test code for SoundsLikeMatcher

```java
public class TestSoundsLikeWordMatcher extends TestCase
{
    public void testSoundsLikeMatcher()
    {
        SoundsLikeWordMatcher wd =
                new SoundsLikeWordMatcher("beat", "faint", "thyme");
        assertTrue(wd.isIn("beat"));
        assertTrue(wd.isIn("faint"));
        assertTrue(wd.isIn("thyme"));
        assertTrue(wd.isIn("beet"));
        assertTrue(wd.isIn("feint"));
        assertTrue(wd.isIn("time"));
        assertFalse(wd.isIn("thy"));
```

```
            assertFalse(wd.isIn("trine"));
        }
    }
```

Listing 17-6 shows an extension that allows for partial matches needed to more easily recognize "cumin" using Soundex.

LISTING 17-6: Allows for partial matches if two words sound alike

```java
public class SoundsLikeThresholdWordMatcher extends SoundsLikeWordMatcher
{
    private int minimumCharactersSame;

    public SoundsLikeThresholdWordMatcher(int minimumCharactersSame,
            String... wordsIn)
    {
        super(wordsIn);
        this.minimumCharactersSame = minimumCharactersSame;
    }

    @Override
    public boolean isIn(String wordCheck)
    {
        boolean in = false;
        String compareTo = soundex.encode(wordCheck);
        for (String word : getWords())
        {
            if (sameEncodedString(word, compareTo))
            {
                in = true;
                break;
            }
        }
        return in;
    }

    private boolean sameEncodedString(String s1, String s2)
    {
        int numSame = 0;
        for (int i = 0; i < s1.length(); i++)
        {
            char c1 = s1.charAt(i);
            char c2 = s2.charAt(i);
            if (c1 == c2)
            {
                numSame++;
            }
        }
        return (numSame >= minimumCharactersSame);
    }
}
```

TRY THIS

The Try Speech button provides a playground where you can experiment with speech recognition. Select or type in some words, click Speak, and view the recognition results. The app marks any successful matches in the right column.

Can you succeed in getting the recognizer to recognize "cumin" or "cumin seeds"?

You can also change various parameters by clicking "speech parameters" within the menu. Change the Matching Method to Phonetic or Stem, and retry speaking. Does this improve the matches?

The menu also contains a Compute Index option that allows you to view the Soundex code and stem for any word.

MATCHING COMMAND WORDS IN PERSISTENT STORAGE

Sometimes voice commands contain dynamic words stored in persistent storage. If the list of words in the command is small enough to fit in memory, you can use an in-memory approach, such as a `WordMatcher`. Otherwise, your app must query the persistent storage and rely on it to index and match the words.

This section explores using two persistent storage mechanisms: Android's SQLite database, and Lucene, a text search engine. Using the SQLite database is convenient for Android because it is a part of the Android operating system and an app may have its data stored in it for other purposes. By using the Full Text Search (FTS) option, you can add a search capability that you can use for matching.

Lucene is a search engine that has slightly different features than FTS, and accomplishes the same goal. If your app can handle the complexity of maintaining a Lucene index of the command words, it may be a better option. Lucene has more configuration options and also allows you to scale across multiple languages.

SQLite Full Text Search

FTS allows your app to search all the text within its SQLite database. You can use FTS to find the best match between a user's utterance and one or more columns in your database. This section shows you how to create an FTS index and then how to best query it for matching users' utterances.

Android's SQLite database supports FTS, but to use it you need to first create a VIRTUAL TABLE. Listing 17-7 shows how to create such a table. The code creates a table with two fields: a text field for a food name indexed by a Porter stemmer and a numerical calorie field.

LISTING 17-7: Creating a virtual FTS table

```
private static final String TABLE_FOOD = "foodlist";
public static final String COLUMN_FOOD = "food";
public static final String COLUMN_CALORIE = "calorie";

public void createTables(SQLiteDatabase db)
{
    db.execSQL("CREATE VIRTUAL TABLE " +
            TABLE_FOOD +
            " USING fts3(tokenize=porter," +
            COLUMN_FOOD + " TEXT, " +
            COLUMN_CALORIE + " REAL);");
}
```

Once your app has created the database, it can utilize the various FTS commands in addition to the normal SQLite queries. The examples in this discussion assume there is a food database with the following data:

➤ Red Concord Grapes

➤ red grape

➤ grape leaves

➤ orangegrapefruit juice

➤ Grapes

➤ Grape

➤ Grapefruit

➤ Red Grapefruit

Using the LIKE Operator

Before explaining how FTS works, it is useful to understand the alternative, using normal SQLite and its LIKE operator. In SQLite you can use LIKE to make pattern-matching comparisons between strings and a pattern. The pattern consists of text and two possible operators. If you include the percent symbol (%), SQLite matches text plus zero or more characters in the string. If you include an underscore (_), it matches any single character in the string.

For example, query Q1 matches any item that starts with "grape," namely grape leaves, Grapes, Grape, and Grapefruit:

```
Q1: SELECT * from Food WHERE food LIKE 'grape%'
```

Query Q2 matches all the data because grape is part of all the strings:

```
Q2: SELECT * from Food WHERE food LIKE '%grape%'
```

The problem with the LIKE operator is that it performs a string comparison between the pattern and the whole text within each database field instead of comparing the pattern with each whole word. This can result in matching strings within words such as matching the grape pattern with Grapefruit. Such matches are not helpful for matching with users' utterances. Another weakness of the LIKE operator is that it returns results in no particular order.

Using the FTS MATCH Operator

FTS executes a text search query to find matching rows in the database. It matches on individual, whole search terms. Additionally, FTS has other functions that return information you can use to rank results from a search query.

Query Q1 could be written in FTS as the prefix query Q3 with slightly different results:

```
Q3: SELECT * from Food WHERE food MATCH 'grape*'
```

Instead of LIKE, FTS uses MATCH. Query Q3 matches everything except orangegrapefruit juice because all other rows contain a word that starts with grape. You can make several variations to your MATCH expression to change how strict it is at matching. Some possible variations are as follows:

➤ **Term query:** Without adding any additional syntax, a query might look like Q4:

```
Q4: SELECT * from Food WHERE food MATCH 'red grape'
```

Q4 searches for text fields that have the words "red" and "grape" in it. Therefore, it matches red grape and Red Concord Grapes, but not Red Grapefruit.

➤ **Phrase query:** Phrase queries allow the query to match multiple words in a row with no words in between. To specify a phrase query you surround the phrase you want to match with quotes.

Phrase queries are stricter than term queries. If the user happens to add a word within a command like "red uh grape," FTS will be unable to match with "red grape."

Q5 matches red grape, but not Red Grapefruit nor Red Concord Grapes:

```
Q5: SELECT * from Food WHERE food MATCH "red grape"
```

➤ **Prefix query:** Prefix queries match strings with variable endings. If you add an asterisk (*) at the end of your pattern, FTS matches any token that has the initial characters before the *. For example, query Q6 matches red grape, Red Grapefruit, and Red Concord Grapes. It matches Red Grapefruit because the grape* pattern indicates that as long as the string starts with grape, match it. It doesn't match grape leaves because it doesn't contain a word that starts with red:

```
Q6: SELECT * from Food WHERE food MATCH 'red* grape*'
```

➤ **Restrict column:** Instead of searching all columns, you can search for specific columns in your database by specifying "column:" before each of the search terms. For example, Q7 searches only the food column:

```
Q7: SELECT * from Food WHERE food MATCH 'food:grape'
```

➤ **OR operator:** Normally match uses the AND operator between tokens. If you use OR instead the query can return partial matches. Partial matches could be useful for making a best guess at what the user said. Query Q8 returns Red Concord Grapes, red grape, grape leaves, Grapes, Grape, and Red Grapefruit. It doesn't match orangegrapefruit juice because the matches must contain red or grape. It matches the other words because they contain either red or grape.

```
Q8: SELECT * from Food WHERE food MATCH 'red OR grape'
```

Additionally, as the queries this section describes show, FTS queries are case-insensitive. The only way to change this is to change the tokenizer that FTS uses. However, the tokenizers available by default in Android's SQLite are both case-insensitive. Therefore, to create a case-sensitive FTS tokenizer you either need to somehow modify the default Android SQLite to add a new tokenizer, written in C, or use your own SQLite version.

Implementing FTS

To implement FTS for speech recognition, your app needs two pieces of code. First, it needs code to query the main SQLite database. Second, it needs code to match query results with a user's utterances.

Listing 17-8 shows the `FtsIndexedFoodDatabase` class. It has all the code to create, access, and query the database. For querying, the class contains the following `retrieveBestMatch()` method:

```
public List<Food> retrieveBestMatch(String input,
            boolean prefix, boolean or,
            boolean phrase)
```

`retrieveBestMatch()` allows an app to specify the different types of queries described earlier. The method creates a query with input text. Then, the method modifies the query in various ways to add query operators according to the method parameters. For example, if you set the *or* parameter to true, the method turns the query from an AND query into an OR query by adding add the OR operator between each input word.

In addition to allowing an app to specify a query, `retrieveBestMatch()` also ranks the query results so that the best match appears first. To do this, the method requests a special FTS return value called offsets for each query. The information in offsets allows the code to determine which terms in the query were matched. `retrieveBestMatch()` uses the number of matched terms to rank the results.

Available for
download on
Wrox.com

LISTING 17-8: Queries an FTS indexed food database.

```
public class FtsIndexedFoodDatabase
{
    private static final String TAG = "FtsIndexedFoodDatabase";
    private static final int DATABASE_VERSION = 1;
    private static final String DATABASE_NAME = "FoodDatabaseFts";
    private static final String TABLE_FOOD = "foodlist";

    public static final String COLUMN_FOOD = "food";
    public static final String COLUMN_CALORIE = "calorie";

    private static FtsIndexedFoodDatabase instance;

    private DatabaseHelper databaseHelper;
    private SQLiteDatabase database;
```

continues

LISTING 17-8 *(continued)*

```java
private FtsIndexedFoodDatabase(Context context)
{
    databaseHelper = new DatabaseHelper(context.getApplicationContext());
    database = databaseHelper.getWritableDatabase();
}

public static synchronized FtsIndexedFoodDatabase getInstance(
        Context context)
{
    if (instance == null)
    {
        instance =
                new FtsIndexedFoodDatabase(context.getApplicationContext());
    }

    return instance;
}

public List<MatchedFood> retrieveBestMatch(String input)
{
    return retrieveBestMatch(input, false, false, false);
}

/**
 * return a list of best matching Foods ordered by best match
 */
public List<MatchedFood> retrieveBestMatch(String input, boolean prefix,
        boolean or, boolean phrase)
{
    final String[] columns =
            { COLUMN_FOOD, COLUMN_CALORIE, "offsets(foodlist) as offsets" };

    // sort the food by a score
    TreeMap<Integer, List<MatchedFood>> scoredMatches =
            new TreeMap<Integer, List<MatchedFood>>();

    input = input.trim();
    // handle different types
    if (prefix)
    {
        // add start at end of the input words
        input = input.replaceAll("\\s", "* ");
        input = input + "*";
    }
    if (or)
    {
        input = input.replaceAll("\\s", " OR ");
    }
    if (phrase)
    {
        input = "\"" + input + "\"";
    }
    Log.d(TAG, "query: " + input);
```

```java
String query = COLUMN_FOOD + " MATCH ?";
Cursor cursor =
        database.query(TABLE_FOOD, columns, query,
                new String[] { input }, null, null, null);
try
{
    if (cursor.getCount() > 0)
    {
        cursor.moveToFirst();
        while (cursor.isAfterLast() == false)
        {
            String food =
                    cursor.getString(cursor.getColumnIndex(COLUMN_FOOD));
            float cal =
                    cursor.getFloat(cursor
                            .getColumnIndex(COLUMN_CALORIE));
            String offsets =
                    cursor.getString(cursor.getColumnIndex("offsets"));
            // each matching term consists of 4 integers separated by
            // spaces
            // offsetTokens[0]: db column number, unused
            // offsetTokens[1]: term number of matching term
            // offsetTokens[2,3]: byte values, unused
            // for more info, see: http://sqlite.org/fts3.html#offsets

            // add 1 because the last integer has no space after it
            // divide by 2 because each integer takes up two characters
            // divide by 4 because each matching term has 4 integers
            int numMatches = ((offsets.length() + 1) / 2) / 4;
            // find which tokens matched
            String[] offsetTokens = offsets.split("\\s");
            int firstMatchTerm = Integer.valueOf(offsetTokens[1]);
            int lastMatchTerm =
                    Integer.valueOf(offsetTokens[offsetTokens.length - 3]);
            Log.d(TAG, "food found: " + food + " num matches: "
                    + numMatches + " offsets: " + offsets);
            MatchedFood found =
                    new MatchedFood(firstMatchTerm, lastMatchTerm,
                            new Food(food, cal));
            List<MatchedFood> foodsAt;
            if (!scoredMatches.containsKey(numMatches))
            {
                foodsAt = new ArrayList<MatchedFood>();
                scoredMatches.put(numMatches, foodsAt);
            }
            else
            {
                foodsAt = scoredMatches.get(numMatches);
            }
            foodsAt.add(found);

            cursor.moveToNext();
        }
    }
} finally
```

continues

LISTING 17-8 *(continued)*

```
        {
            cursor.close();
        }

        List<MatchedFood> match = new ArrayList<MatchedFood>();
        for (List<MatchedFood> foodLists : scoredMatches.descendingMap()
                .values())
        {
            match.addAll(foodLists);
        }
        Log.d(TAG, match.size() + " matches.");
        for (MatchedFood matchedFood : match)
        {
            Log.d(TAG, matchedFood.getFood().toString());
        }
        return match;
    }

    public boolean isEmpty()
    {
        Cursor cursor = database.rawQuery("SELECT * FROM " + TABLE_FOOD, null);
        boolean isEmpty = (cursor.getCount() == 0);
        cursor.close();
        return isEmpty;
    }

    public void loadFrom(InputStream csvFile) throws IOException
    {
        BufferedReader is =
                new BufferedReader(new InputStreamReader(csvFile, "UTF8"));
        String line;

        line = is.readLine();
        while (line != null)
        {
            String[] parts = line.split(",");
            String food = parts[0];
            float cals = Float.valueOf(parts[1]);
            insertFood(food, cals);
            Log.d(TAG, "inserted: " + food + " " + cals);
            line = is.readLine();
        }
    }

    public long insertFood(String food, float calorie)
    {
        ContentValues contentValues = new ContentValues();
        contentValues.put(COLUMN_FOOD, food);
        contentValues.put(COLUMN_CALORIE, calorie);
        return database.insert(TABLE_FOOD, null, contentValues);
```

```
    }

    public int removeFood(String food)
    {
        return database.delete(TABLE_FOOD, COLUMN_FOOD + " = ?",
                new String[] { food });
    }

    public void close()
    {
        synchronized (FtsIndexedFoodDatabase.class)
        {
            databaseHelper.close();
            instance = null;
            database = null;
        }
    }

    public Cursor getAllFood()
    {
        Cursor cursor = database.rawQuery("SELECT * FROM " + TABLE_FOOD, null);
        return cursor;
    }

    public void clean(Context context)
    {
        databaseHelper.dropTables(database);
        databaseHelper.createTables(database);
        instance = new FtsIndexedFoodDatabase(context.getApplicationContext());
    }

    private static final class DatabaseHelper extends SQLiteOpenHelper
    {
        public DatabaseHelper(Context context)
        {
            super(context, DATABASE_NAME, null, DATABASE_VERSION);
        }

        @Override
        public void onCreate(SQLiteDatabase db)
        {
            createTables(db);
        }

        @Override
        public void
                onUpgrade(SQLiteDatabase db, int oldVersion, int newVersion)
        {
            dropTables(db);
            createTables(db);
        }
```

continues

LISTING 17-8 *(continued)*

```java
        public void dropTables(SQLiteDatabase db)
        {
            db.execSQL("DROP TABLE IF EXISTS " + TABLE_FOOD + ";");
        }

        public void createTables(SQLiteDatabase db)
        {
            db.execSQL("CREATE VIRTUAL TABLE " + TABLE_FOOD
                    + " USING fts3(tokenize=porter," + BaseColumns._ID
                    + " INTEGER PRIMARY KEY AUTOINCREMENT, " + COLUMN_FOOD
                    + " TEXT, " + COLUMN_CALORIE + " REAL);");
        }
    }
}
```

code snippet FtsIndexedFoodDatabase.java

To execute `FtsIndexedFoodDatabase`, an app needs to implement a `receiveWhatWasHeard()` method that queries the database with each potential recognition until it finds a match or fails. Listing 17-9 shows the necessary code.

LISTING 17-9: Use FTS to match a food query

```java
    protected void receiveWhatWasHeard(List<String> heard,
            float[] confidenceScores)
    {
        FtsIndexedFoodDatabase food = FtsIndexedFoodDatabase.getInstance(this);

        for (String said : heard)
        {
            if (food.retrieveBestMatch(said).size() > 0)
            {
                Log.d(TAG, "heard a food");
                break;
            }
        }
    }
```

As this section showed, FTS is a useful tool for matching speech recognition results. It has a stemmer and different query options that allow it to flexibly match possible user utterances with values within a SQLite database. However, it is not the only persistent storage mechanism available. The next section describes Lucene, a search engine library that was built specifically for searching and ranking text, and is of particular use for matching.

Word Searching with Lucene

FTS provides a search capability for a SQLite database, but it is somewhat limited in its indexing and searching capabilities. In contrast, Lucene is a search engine library that was specifically designed for searching text. Because of this, Lucene provides a variety of options for matching textual user utterances with parts of a voice command.

Lucene is expandable, offers a wider array of indexing and query types than FTS, and has built-in search result ranking methods. Lucene has text `Filters` that perform indexing functions such as converting query text to lowercase, stemming, and removing certain irrelevant characters and words. The source code from this book contains a Lucene `Filter` that converts a query to its phonetic representation.

Lucene also has some additional query operators than FTS. For example, FTS allows an app to perform prefix queries via a `*` operator. Lucene also supports prefix queries, however queries can also treat the operator as a wildcard and place it anywhere within a search string, not just at the end. Queries can also use the `?` operator to require only one wildcard character instead of multiple characters. Other types of queries are possible from the Lucene library and third parties.

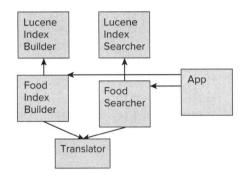

FIGURE 17-2: Utility and domain classes needed to create and search an index for the food dialogue. The arrows represent dependencies between classes.

To use Lucene your app needs to create an index and then search it. The index can be an in-memory index or can reside on the SD card. Figure 17-2 shows a block diagram of the needed classes to implement a food dialogue.

Listing 17-10 shows code that creates an index and then executes some searchers within a unit test. Listings 17-11 and 17-12 show the food-related classes.

LISTING 17-10: Creates an index and executes some queries

```
public void testRunLuceneQuery()
    {
        boolean overwrite = false;
        String outputDir = "testDir";
        boolean phonetic = true;
        boolean doStem = true;
        FoodIndexBuilder builder =
                new FoodIndexBuilder(getContext()
                        .getExternalFilesDir(outputDir).getAbsolutePath(),
                        overwrite, phonetic, doStem);
        builder.addFood("Apple", 100.0f);
        FoodSearcher searcher = null;
        try
        {
            searcher = builder.get();
        } catch (IOException e)
        {
            Log.e(TAG, "error", e);
```

continues

LISTING 17-10 *(continued)*

```
        }
        assertTrue(searcher.findMatching("Apple").size() > 0);
        assertTrue("stem", searcher.findMatching("Apples").size() > 0);
        assertTrue("sounds like", searcher.findMatching("Appeal").size() > 0);
        assertFalse("not close enough",
                searcher.findMatching("peel").size() > 0);
    }
```

First, the test code creates a `FoodIndexBuilder`. `FoodIndexBuilder` allows for several options. You change the path to store the index on disk. If you pass a value of true for the *overwrite* parameter, the class overwrites the existing index; otherwise, if the index already exists, `FoodIndexBuilder` does nothing. If you pass null, `FoodIndexBuilder` uses an in-memory index.

Once created, the code adds some `Food` objects to the index. Behind the scenes, `FoodIndexBuilder` uses `FoodDocumentTranslator` to translate the `Food` objects to Lucene `Documents`. `FoodIndexBuilder` uses a class called `RecognitionIndexer` to preprocess any text and optionally performs the two indexing strategies discussed earlier, stemming and phonetic indexing. When complete, the test calls `get` to commit all changes and create a `FoodIndexSearcher`.

`FoodIndexSearcher` contains methods to search the index for `Food` objects. To initialize, `FoodIndexSearcher` uses methods in `LuceneSearcher` to load the previously built indexes from whichever Lucene `Directory` `FoodIndexBuilder` used. From there, the test can execute some searches.

LISTING 17-11: Builds a Food index

```
public class FoodIndexBuilder
{
    private static final String TAG = "FoodIndexBuilder";

    private LuceneIndexBuilder builder;

    private Analyzer analyzer;

    public FoodIndexBuilder(boolean phonetic, boolean doStem)
    {
        analyzer = new RecognitionIndexer(phonetic, doStem);
        builder =
                new LuceneIndexBuilder(new RecognitionIndexer(phonetic, doStem));
    }

    public FoodIndexBuilder(String outputDir, boolean overwrite,
            boolean phonetic, boolean doStem)
    {
        analyzer = new RecognitionIndexer(phonetic, doStem);
        builder =
                new LuceneIndexBuilder(outputDir, overwrite,
                        new RecognitionIndexer(phonetic, doStem));
    }
```

```
    public void addFood(String name, float calories)
    {
        Document doc =
                FoodDocumentTranslator.toDocument(new Food(name, calories));
        builder.addDocument(doc);
        Log.d(TAG, "added: " + doc);
    }

    public FoodSearcher get() throws IOException
    {
        builder.doneWriting();
        return new FoodSearcher(builder.getDirectory(), analyzer);
    }
}
```

Available for
download on
Wrox.com

LISTING 17-12: Searches a previously built Food index

```
public class FoodSearcher
{
    private static final String TAG = "FoodSearcher";

    private static final int MAX_NUM_RESULTS = 10000;

    private LuceneIndexSearcher searcher;

    private Analyzer analyzer;

    public FoodSearcher(Directory dir, Analyzer analyzer) throws IOException
    {
        // load the index
        searcher = new LuceneIndexSearcher(dir);
        this.analyzer = analyzer;
    }

    /**
     * if any documents match return true
     */
    public boolean matches(String target)
    {
        return findMatching(target).size() > 0;
    }

    public List<Food> findMatching(String target)
    {
        try
        {
            //Note: this creates a query using the Lucene query syntax
            //by default it OR's all terms in the query
            QueryParser parser =
                    new QueryParser(LuceneParameters.VERSION,
                            FoodDocumentTranslator.FOOD_NAME, analyzer);
            Query query = parser.parse(target);
```

continues

LISTING 17-12 *(continued)*

```
            return executeQuery(query);
        } catch (ParseException e)
        {
            Log.e(TAG, "error", e);
            return new ArrayList<Food>();
        }
    }

    private List<Food> executeQuery(Query query)
    {
        Log.d(TAG, "searching...");

        List<Food> result = new ArrayList<Food>();

        TopDocs rs = null;
        try
        {
            Log.d(TAG, "query: " + query);
            rs = searcher.getSearcher().search(query, null, MAX_NUM_RESULTS);
            Log.d(TAG, "found this many documents: " + rs.totalHits);
        } catch (IOException e)
        {
            Log.e(TAG, "failed to search", e);
            return result;
        }

        // retrieve search docs
        List<Document> docs = searcher.getDocs(rs, searcher.getSearcher());

        // convert to food objects
        for (Document document : docs)
        {
            result.add(FoodDocumentTranslator.getFood(document));
        }

        return result;
    }
}
```

code snippet FoodSearcher.java

Once an app has created a Lucene index, it needs to use it to match a user's utterances. Listing 17-13 shows the necessary code to implement a food lookup query using Lucene.

LISTING 17-13: Uses Lucene index to match a food query

```
    protected void receiveWhatWasHeardLuceneFood(List<String> heard,
            float[] confidenceScores)
    {
        // create the food index only once
        if (luceneSearcher == null)
```

```
    {
        // don't overwrite, but do stemming
        FoodIndexBuilder builder =
                new FoodIndexBuilder(getExternalFilesDir("foodindex")
                        .getAbsolutePath(), false, false, true);
        try
        {
            // read the foods file and add foods to the builder
            loadLuceneIndex(builder);
        } catch (IOException e)
        {
            Log.e(TAG, "unable to load index", e);
        }

        try
        {
            luceneSearcher = builder.get();
        } catch (IOException e)
        {
            Log.e(TAG, "error", e);
        }
    }

    for (String said : heard)
    {
        if (luceneSearcher.findMatching(said).size() > 0)
        {
            Log.d(TAG, "heard a food");
            break;
        }
    }
}
```

TRY THIS

This section shows how the matching techniques perform on test cases. However, it's interesting to see how the techniques perform in response to actual speech. Try the Food Dialogue Matcher Playground button to test out the persistent matching. Use the Matching Preferences menu option to change various settings. When you click the Lookup button, you can say a fruit or vegetable it knows about and the app will report its number of calories.

MULTI-PART COMMANDS

The techniques described thus far assume there is only one command word within a user's utterance to match. Although it complicates things, sometimes it is necessary to for an app accept a multiple command words create more expressive commands. Each command word makes up a part of a multi-part command.

This section discusses the issues involved in making code that matches multiple command words within a single possible utterance and presents some possible solutions. It considers two approaches:

ignoring collisions and considering ordering. To illustrate implementing multi-part commands, this section discusses how to implement several example multi-part commands shown in Table 17-1. The example commands contain free text, static, and dynamic words to match.

TABLE 17-1: Multi-part Commands

VOICE COMMAND	FORM	DESCRIPTION
Add	Add <new food name>	User speaks "add" and then some free text for the name of the new food to add.
Remove	Remove <food name>	User speaks "remove" and then a known food name.
Compare	<food name 1> <food name 2>	User speaks two foods and the system reports which food has more calories.

Ignoring Potential Collisions

Collisions occur when a word in the user's utterance matches more than one command word. If such collisions are rare for your particular voice command, it is safe to ignore them. For example, if you have a command that requires two parts, "add" and "list," it is unlikely that the word-spotting algorithm would confuse the two so it is fine for your code to scan the input twice, once for each command word. However, for dynamic words, it is easy to see how a user's utterance could match more than one. For example, if a user utters "green" he or she might be referring to either "green onion" or "green bean."

Listing 17-14 shows the implementation for matching "remove." First the code uses a `WordMatcher` to match "remove," then the code uses `FtsIndexedFoodDatabase` to look up any food. This code assumes that "remove" is not likely to be part of a food word, and thus, will not disrupt the food name lookup.

LISTING 17-14: Matches remove

```
public Food removeExistingFood(String toMatch)
{
    Food removed = null;
    WordMatcher dc = new WordMatcher("remove");
    String[] tokens = toMatch.split("\\s");
    if (dc.isIn(tokens) && tokens.length > 1)
    {
        FtsIndexedFoodDatabase food =
                FtsIndexedFoodDatabase.getInstance(null);
        List<MatchedFood> match =
                food.retrieveBestMatch(toMatch, false, true, false);
        if (match.size() > 0)
        {
            Food toRemove = match.get(0).getFood();
            Log.d(TAG, "matched remove " + toRemove);
```

```
                        removed = toRemove;
                }
        }

        return removed;
}
```

Listing 17-15 shows an implementation of "compare." It executes `FtsIndexedFoodDatabase` and then selects the top two matches. It assumes the food names are not easily confused with each other and don't usually have overlapping words.

LISTING 17-15: Matches compare

```
public String compareCalories(String toMatch)
{
    String comparison = null;
    FtsIndexedFoodDatabase food = FtsIndexedFoodDatabase.getInstance(null);
    //do or match
    List<MatchedFood> match = food.retrieveBestMatch(toMatch, false, true, false);
    if (match.size() > 1)
    {
        Food firstMatch = match.get(0).getFood();
        Food secondMatch = match.get(1).getFood();
        Log.d(TAG, "matched compare: " + firstMatch + " with " + secondMatch);
        comparison = makeComparisonResultString(firstMatch, secondMatch);
    }
    return comparison;
}
```

Finally, Listing 17-16 shows the code for "add." First, the code uses a `WordMatcher` to match "add"; if it matches, the code takes all the text after the first string to be the free text. It then uses the free text as the name of the food to add. The code makes an assumption that "add" will always be the first word in the user's utterance.

LISTING 17-16: Matches add

```
public Food addFreeText(String toMatch)
{
    Food toAdd = null;
    WordMatcher dc = new WordMatcher("add");
    String [] tokens = toMatch.split("\\s");
    if (dc.isIn(tokens) && tokens.length > 1)
    {
        //after the first space
        String freeText = toMatch.substring(toMatch.indexOf(" "));
        Log.d(TAG, "matched add " + freeText);
        toAdd = new Food(freeText);
    }
    return toAdd;
}
```

Although the assumptions made by these implementations may make them seem less than optimal, they perform robustly on real speech inputs. The implementations have the benefits of word spotting in that it is resistant to inserted words and the order in which they come. These benefits could mean easy input for the user.

Considering Ordering

The previous section showed implementations of multi-part commands that did not require the app to consider order. The approach ignores the potential for collisions and makes assumptions that could lead to some failed recognitions. This section explores several approaches for considering order. The approaches require some processing and more constraint on user input.

Matching multi-part commands considering ordering requires your app to introduce a new object, `WordList`. The source for `WordList` is in Listing 17-17. `WordList` splits the string into tokens and then `getStringAfter()` allows the matching methods to retrieve strings after a certain index in the source string. `getStringWithout()` allows code to retrieve versions of the string without certain words.

LISTING 17-17: Extracts parts of an utterance by position

```
public class WordList
{
    private String [] words;

    private String source;

    public WordList(String source)
    {
        this.source = source;
        words = source.split("\\s");
    }

    public String getStringAfter(int wordIndex)
    {
        int startAt = wordIndex + 1;
        if (startAt >= words.length)
        {
            return "";
        }

        StringBuilder sb = new StringBuilder();
        for (int i = startAt; i < words.length; i++)
        {
            sb.append(words[i]).append(" ");
        }
        return sb.toString();
    }

    public String getStringWithout(int indexToRemove)
    {
        if (indexToRemove >= words.length)
        {
            return "";
```

```
        }

        StringBuilder sb = new StringBuilder();
        for (int i = 0; i < words.length; i++)
        {
            if (i != indexToRemove)
            {
                sb.append(words[i]).append(" ");
            }
        }
        return sb.toString();
    }
}
```

You also need some additional methods inside of WordMatcher to help identify the position
of any matches. Listing 17-18 shows the necessary methods and Listing 17-1 shows the rest of
WordMatcher.

LISTING 17-18: Additional methods in WordMatcher to identify the location of matches

```
public int isInAt(String [] wordsIn)
{
    int which = NOT_IN;
    for (String word : wordsIn)
    {
        which = isInAt(word);
        if (which != NOT_IN)
        {
            break;
        }
    }
    return which;
}

public int isInAt(String wordCheck)
{
    int which = NOT_IN;
    int ct = 0;
    for (String word : words)
    {
        if (word.equals(wordCheck))
        {
            which = ct;
            break;
        }
        ct++;
    }
    return which;
}
```

Using these two utilities you can implement position-aware matching. Listing 17-19 shows "add,"
Listing 17-20 shows "remove," and Listing 17-21 shows "compare calories."

Matching "remove" and "add" requires the same first step. First the code recognizes "add" or "remove." Then the code processes the remaining text after "add" or "remove" word. For "add," the code collects all the remaining string as free text and uses that as the new food name. For "remove," the code matches the remaining string with the food database and identifies the best matching as the food to remove. For example, while processing a user utterance of "remove red grapes" the code would recognize "remove" and then pass the remaining "red grapes" string to the food database.

Selecting the text after the command word allows the code to ignore any words the user may have added before the static command word. For example, the user might say something like, "apple remove grapes." This could happen if the speech prompt appeared while the user was saying something else. The non-ordered approach could potentially have a problem and remove apple instead of grapes because apple appears just as many times as grapes and it appears first. In contrast, using the ordered approach, the code can ignore any words before the command word and hence correctly ignore apple and consider only grapes.

For comparing foods, the code needs to identify two foods within the same search string. Without ordering, incorrect matches could result. For example, if the user executed a compare command by saying "apple avocado," it is possible that the FTS query could return two kinds of apple instead of apple and avocado. To handle this, the code in Listing 17-21 executes the query twice. The code removes the first matched word before the second query. For the input "apple avocado," removing the first match, apple, allows the code to recognize apple during the first query and avocado during the second.

LISTING 17-19: Creates a new Food to add using the free text after the command "add" as the food name

```
public Food addFreeText(String toMatch)
{
    Food toAdd = null;
    WordList wordList = new WordList(toMatch);
    WordMatcher dc = new WordMatcher("add");
    int matchIndex = dc.isInAt(wordList.getWords());
    if (matchIndex >= 0)
    {
        String freeText = wordList.getStringAfter(matchIndex);
        if (freeText.length() > 0)
        {
            Log.d(TAG, "matched add " + freeText);
            toAdd = new Food(freeText);
        }
    }
    return toAdd;
}
```

LISTING 17-20: Selects a food to remove as the one mentioned after the command "remove"

```
public Food removeExistingFood(String toMatch)
{
    Food removed = null;
    WordList wordList = new WordList(toMatch);
```

```
WordMatcher dc = new WordMatcher("remove");
int matchIndex = dc.isInAt(wordList.getWords());
if (matchIndex >= 0)
{
    String freeText = wordList.getStringAfter(matchIndex);
    FtsIndexedFoodDatabase food =
            FtsIndexedFoodDatabase.getInstance(null);
    List<MatchedFood> match =
            food.retrieveBestMatch(freeText, false, true, false);
    if (match.size() > 0)
    {
        Food toRemove = match.get(0).getFood();
        Log.d(TAG, "matched remove " + toRemove);
        removed = toRemove;
    }
}
return removed;
}
```

LISTING 17-21: Compares two foods by running two queries

```
public String compareCalories(String toMatch)
{
    String comparison = null;
    FtsIndexedFoodDatabase food = FtsIndexedFoodDatabase.getInstance(null);
    List<MatchedFood> match =
            food.retrieveBestMatch(toMatch, false, true, false);
    if (match.size() > 0)
    {
        MatchedFood matchedFood = match.get(0);
        Food firstMatch = matchedFood.getFood();

        // remove the first term of the matched string so
        // that the food won't be matched again
        WordList wordList = new WordList(toMatch);
        String withoutFirstMatch =
                wordList.getStringWithout(matchedFood
                        .getFirstMatchTermIndex());
        List<MatchedFood> matchSecond =
                food.retrieveBestMatch(withoutFirstMatch, false, true,
                        false);
        if (matchSecond.size() > 0)
        {
            Food secondMatch = matchSecond.get(0).getFood();
            Log.d(TAG, "matched compare: " + firstMatch + " with "
                    + secondMatch);
            comparison =
                    makeComparisonResultString(firstMatch, secondMatch);
        }
    }
    return comparison;
}
```

TRY THIS

Select the Food Dialogue Matcher Playground button. You can say any of the three commands described in this section after you click the Edit and Compare button. You can use the Matching Preferences menu option to experiment with using ordered and unordered matching.

USING A GRAMMAR

Word spotting is not the only matching algorithm. One alternative you might consider is to use a grammar instead. Grammars are useful for scenarios beyond the ones this chapter describes. This section briefly describes how you might use a grammar and provides links for additional information.

One type of grammar you might use is JSGF (Java Speech Grammar Format) (`http://java.sun.com/products/java-media/speech/forDevelopers/JSGF/`). A project like Sphinx (`http://cmusphinx.sourceforge.net/2011/05/building-pocketsphinx-on-android/`) contains code to work with JSGF grammars.

Using a JSGF grammar, you could define an add command with the following rule:

```
<addcommand> = <add> <apple | pear | grape>
```

The preceding grammar specifies a rule named "addcommand" that matches the word "add" followed by "apple," "pear," or "grape." Using a grammar with the rule allows an app to match when the user wanted to add one of the three specified foods.

The JSGF grammar is very flexible. You can expand it further using wildcard operators to allow it to handle words inserted between expected command words. You can create a set of composable, reusable rules. You can weight certain words as being more important than others. You can tag certain rules to help code identify results.

The advantage of a using a grammar is that it can handle complex speech patterns. If you are trying to implement a multi-part command that has many parts and many variants, or want to have many voice commands available from one prompt, a grammar may be a better approach than word spotting. For simple commands, like the ones this chapter has discussed, restricting the user to follow the grammar's specifications and the processing overhead of using a grammar may not be worth it.

SUMMARY

After executing speech recognition, Android returns a list of strings representing what the user might have said. This chapter described various ways to determine if those strings match desired command words. To implement this matching, your app may need to use in-memory matching, query persistent storage, match multiple command parts, or determine in what order the parts appeared.

To handle in-memory matching, this chapter described using an in-memory class that used a `Set` to represent static keywords. To handle querying persistent storage, this chapter described how to use Android's built-in FTS search or Lucene. To handle ordered and unordered, multi-part commands, this chapter showed you some possible implementation approaches. To capture free text and to handle multi-part commands with increased accuracy, this chapter showed you how to match command words according to the order in which the words appeared in a user's utterance. Also, this chapter described how to make it easier to match by using two indexing strategies: stemming and phonetic indexing.

The techniques in this chapter described how to match recognition results to create voice commands. These voice commands represent single functions a user can activate. The next chapter describes techniques to combine these commands together to create voice actions that can have multiple functions and span multiple turns. In addition, it describes the software components you need to execute voice actions in a user-friendly, modular way.

18

Executing Voice Actions

WHAT'S IN THIS CHAPTER?

➤ Software components for defining and executing voice actions

➤ AlertDialog for voice actions

➤ Multi-turn voice actions

➤ A best guess to minimize recognition failure

➤ Diagnosing recognition failure

Chapter 17 described matching in detail. Android's speech recognizer rarely returns a single result. Instead it returns a list of possible strings that represent what the user might have said. Matching involves comparing those strings with the desired command words your voice user interface (VUI) expects.

If your VUI is simple enough, you can implement matching in the way that Chapter 17 does directly within the `receiveWhatWasHeard()` method. However, to include features that improve usability and to organize multi-turn voice actions, you can benefit from some additional code that this chapter describes.

The code in this chapter helps organize your VUI into `VoiceAction` objects and execute them. The code also provides some methods for improving the usability of your VUI by showing how your app can make a best guess and respond when recognition fails. To illustrate these concepts, the code in this chapter creates an improved version of the food dialogue example that Chapter 17 introduced.

FOOD DIALOGUE VUI DESIGN

The food VUI design, implemented in Chapter 17, had several flaws:

➤ It did not use any indexing, so the app failed to understand commands failed more often than necessary.

➤ It didn't have any multi-turn voice actions, so users could never add calories for any new food, nor could they cancel a remove operation.

➤ The app never spoke any replies after any command, so, for example, users would have no way of knowing if they successfully added or removed a food.

➤ If recognition failed the code simply reported "I don't understand" instead of attempting to diagnose why or make a best guess.

To address these shortcomings, the refined food VUI design consists of two voice actions: Food Lookup and Food Edit. Users activate either by a button press. Table 18-1 describes the turns for the commands within the voice actions.

TABLE 18-1: VUI Design for Multi-turn Food Dialogue

VOICE ACTION	COMMAND	TURNS
Food Lookup	`FoodLookup`	Turn 1: User says "<foodname>." App replies "<foodname> has X calories."
Food Edit	`AddFood`	Turn 1: User says "add <new food name>." Turn 2: App says "How many calories for <new food name>?" User says a number or "cancel." App replies: "Added <new food name> with <calories>" or "cancelled" if the user said "cancel."
Food Edit	`RemoveFood`	Turn 1: User says "remove <foodname>." Turn 2: App says "Are you sure you want to remove <food-name>?" User says "Yes" or "No" or "Cancel." App replies "removed <foodname> or "canceled" if the user said "cancel."

In addition, the VUI adds several features needed for a more user-friendly conversation:

➤ **Uses implicit prompting:** To make users aware of the result of their voice action, the design uses implicit prompting in the remove and add commands to report what food was removed or added.

➤ **Provides feedback if recognition fails:** If the app can't match what the user said with any expected inputs, it makes a best guess. If it cannot guess, it tries to diagnose why recognition failed and provides feedback to the user.

➤ **Allows for cancel:** At any speech prompt, it allows the user to say "cancel" to end the dialog.

The remaining sections in this chapter show you how to implement this VUI design.

TRY THIS

Use the Multi-turn Food Dialogue button to explore how the VUI works.

DEFINING AND EXECUTING VOICE ACTIONS

In a GUI, apps have various APIs to help them create `Dialog`s with buttons, show them, and respond when the user clicks. With VUIs, none of that exists. Additionally, `Dialog`s run on the UI thread, which keeps them from interfering with each other. Similarly, VUIs must make sure that voice actions do not interfere with each other's audio input and output. The app must make sure not to be listening and speaking at the same time, or else it may talk to itself. This section describes the missing code you need to define and execute voice action.

Executing a voice action refers to the five-step process shown in Figure 18-1.

FIGURE 18-1: Flow through the various steps in executing a voice action.

The five steps involved in executing a voice action are:

1. Activate: User starts the voice action. A simple way the user can do this is by pressing a button, but Chapter 19 describes other options.

2. Speak Prompt: Optionally speak something.

3. Listen: Start speech recognition.

4. Speak Response: Optionally say something in response.

5. Action: Do something, then possibly begin another speak prompt or listen step.

Executing voice actions requires several classes. Figure 18-2 shows how they relate. A `VoiceActionExecutor` controls speaking prompts, listening, and activating one active `VoiceAction` at a time. A `VoiceAction` uses one or more `VoiceActionCommand`s to interpret recognition results. If the `VoiceActionCommand`s match the recognition results, they may take any necessary actions or speak any responses. An app activates `VoiceActionExecutor` in an app specific way, such as by presenting the user with a "push to talk" button.

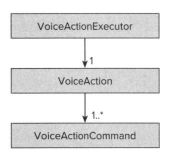

FIGURE 18-2: Relationship between voice action-related classes

A `VoiceAction` is analogous to a GUI `Dialog` and a `VoiceActionCommand` is analogous to a `Button` in a GUI `Dialog`. `VoiceActionExecutor` has the equivalent of a `Dialog`'s `show()` method for `VoiceActions`. Listing 18-1 shows the `VoiceAction` and `VoiceActionCommand` interfaces and Listing 18-2 shows the implementation of `VoiceActionExecutor`.

All of these components are required to implement a VUI. For example, implementing the Food Edit voice action involves configuring a `VoiceAction` and executing it using a `VoiceActionExecutor`. The configured `VoiceAction` uses one implementation of a `VoiceActionCommand` for each possible command the user may say: add food, remove food, or cancel. If any of the three `VoiceActionCommands` match the recognition results, they take appropriate action. Next, this section describes the `VoiceActionExecutor` implementation. Later sections in this chapter explore how to implement `VoiceAction` and `VoiceActionCommands`.

`VoiceActionExecutor` controls executing speech recognition and speaking for a single active `VoiceAction` with several methods. To make `VoiceActionExecutor` work, the code using `VoiceActionExecutor` must pass it results from `receiveWhatWasHeard()`. The `execute()` and `reExecute()` methods allow apps to start and restart `VoiceActions`. If a `VoiceActionCommand` needs to speak something, it can conveniently call `speak()`. While speaking a prompt, `VoiceActionExecutor` ensures that the app is not listening and speaking at the same time. To implement this it passes *EXECUTE_AFTER_SPEAK* as the *utteranceId* to its TTS using the following code:

```
tts.speak(voiceAction.getSpokenPrompt(), TextToSpeech.QUEUE_FLUSH,
          TextToSpeechUtils.makeParamsWith(EXECUTE_AFTER_SPEAK));
```

TTS calls the `onDone()` method after it is done speaking and `VoiceActionExecutor` forwards it to `onDoneSpeaking()`. When `onDoneSpeaking()` receives an *utteranceId* equal to *EXECUTE_AFTER_SPEAK*, it can start speech recognition again because it knows that the app has completed speaking the speech prompt.

LISTING 18-1: Interfaces for VoiceAction and VoiceActionCommand

```
public interface VoiceAction
{
    /**
     * match String in heard, optionally take action and
     * call OnNotUnderstoodListener if cannot match.
     * @param heard recognition results
     * @param confidenceScores score for each String in heard
     */
    boolean interpret(List<String> heard, float[] confidenceScores);

    /**
     * return the text to show as a prompt when executing <br>
     * if there is no prompt, then return null or an empty string
     */
    public String getPrompt();

    public void setPrompt(String prompt);

    /**
     * the prompt to speak before presenting the recognition dialog
     */
```

```java
        public String getSpokenPrompt();

        public void setSpokenPrompt(String prompt);

        public boolean hasSpokenPrompt();

        /**
         * to call when interpret cannot understand
         */
        public void setNotUnderstood(OnNotUnderstoodListener notUnderstood);

        public OnNotUnderstoodListener getNotUnderstood();

        /**
         * ignore any responses below this minimum confidence
         */
        public float getMinConfidenceRequired();

        /**
         * confidence greater than this means
         * {@link OnNotUnderstoodListener#REASON_NOT_A_COMMAND}
         */
        public float getNotACommandConfidenceThreshold();

        public void setNotACommandConfidenceThreshold(
                float notACommandConfidenceThreshold);

        /**
         * confidence less than this means
         * {@link OnNotUnderstoodListener#REASON_INACCURATE_RECOGNITION}
         */
        public float getInaccurateConfidenceThreshold();

        public void setInaccurateConfidenceThreshold(
                float inaccurateConfidenceThreshold);
}
public interface VoiceActionCommand
{
    boolean interpret(WordList heard, float [] confidenceScores);
}
```

LISTING 18-2: Executes VoiceActions

Available for
download on
Wrox.com

```java
public class VoiceActionExecutor
{
    private static final String TAG = "VoiceActionExecutor";

    private VoiceAction active;

    private SpeechRecognizingActivity speech;

    /**
     * parameter for TTS to identify utterance
     */
    private final String EXECUTE_AFTER_SPEAK = "EXECUTE_AFTER_SPEAK";

    private TextToSpeech tts;

    public VoiceActionExecutor(SpeechRecognizingActivity speech)
```

continues

LISTING 18-2 *(continued)*

```java
    {
        this.speech = speech;
        active = null;
    }

    /**
     * set the tts when it is ready to complete initialization
     */
    public void setTts(TextToSpeech tts)
    {
        this.tts = tts;
        if (Build.VERSION.SDK_INT >= 15)
        {
            tts.setOnUtteranceProgressListener(new UtteranceProgressListener()
            {
                @Override
                public void onDone(String utteranceId)
                {
                    onDoneSpeaking(utteranceId);
                }

                @Override
                public void onError(String utteranceId)
                {
                }

                @Override
                public void onStart(String utteranceId)
                {
                }
            });
        }
        else
        {
            tts.setOnUtteranceCompletedListener(new OnUtteranceCompletedListener()
            {
                @Override
                public void onUtteranceCompleted(String utteranceId)
                {
                    onDoneSpeaking(utteranceId);
                }
            });
        }
    }

    /**
     * external handleReceiveWhatWasHeard must call this
     */
    public void handleReceiveWhatWasHeard(List<String> heard,
            float[] confidenceScores)
    {
        active.interpret(heard, confidenceScores);
```

```java
    }

    private void onDoneSpeaking(String utteranceId)
    {
        if (utteranceId.equals(EXECUTE_AFTER_SPEAK))
        {
            doRecognitionOnActive();
        }
    }

    /**
     * convenient way to just reply with something spoken
     */
    public void speak(String toSay)
    {
        tts.speak(toSay, TextToSpeech.QUEUE_FLUSH,
                TextToSpeechUtils.EMPTY_PARAMS);
    }

    /**
     * execute the current active {@link VoiceAction} again speaking
     * extraPrompt before
     */
    public void reExecute(String extraPrompt)
    {
        if ((extraPrompt != null) && (extraPrompt.length() > 0))
        {
            tts.speak(extraPrompt, TextToSpeech.QUEUE_FLUSH,
                    TextToSpeechUtils.makeParamsWith(EXECUTE_AFTER_SPEAK));
        }
        else
        {
            execute(getActive());
        }
    }

    /**
     * change the current voice action to this and then execute it, optionally
     * saying a prompt first
     */
    public void execute(VoiceAction voiceAction)
    {
        if (tts == null)
        {
            throw new RuntimeException("Text to speech not initialized");
        }

        setActive(voiceAction);

        if (voiceAction.hasSpokenPrompt())
        {
            tts.speak(voiceAction.getSpokenPrompt(), TextToSpeech.QUEUE_FLUSH,
                    TextToSpeechUtils.makeParamsWith(EXECUTE_AFTER_SPEAK));
        }
        else
```

continues

LISTING 18-2 *(continued)*

```
        {
            doRecognitionOnActive();
        }
    }

    private void doRecognitionOnActive()
    {
        Intent recognizerIntent =
                new Intent(RecognizerIntent.ACTION_RECOGNIZE_SPEECH);
        recognizerIntent.putExtra(RecognizerIntent.EXTRA_LANGUAGE_MODEL,
                RecognizerIntent.LANGUAGE_MODEL_WEB_SEARCH);
        recognizerIntent.putExtra(RecognizerIntent.EXTRA_PROMPT, getActive()
                .getPrompt());
        speech.recognize(recognizerIntent);
    }

    private VoiceAction getActive()
    {
        return active;
    }

    private void setActive(VoiceAction active)
    {
        this.active = active;
    }
}
```

code snippet VoiceActionExecutor.java

This section described how you could define a VUI in terms of `VoiceActions` and `VoiceActionCommands`. It also described `VoiceActionExecutor` and how it executes `VoiceActions` with it. Now that you've seen how to run `VoiceActions`, the next two sections describe ways to implement them.

EXECUTING VOICEACTIONCOMMANDS

A `VoiceAction` is responsible for matching the recognition results. If it cannot match the results it calls back to an `OnNotUnderstoodListener`, described later in listing 18-12.

You can use `MultiCommandVoiceAction` to implement a `VoiceAction`. Listing 18-3 shows its implementation. The implementation uses `AbstractVoiceAction`, which contains simple getter and setter implementations that the `VoiceAction` interface requires. `MultiCommandVoiceAction` has to perform several functions.

First, `MultiCommandVoiceAction` uses a given `List` of `VoiceActionCommands` to match the recognition results. It iterates over each one for each possible recognition result until one matches. When multiple `VoiceActionCommands` can match a particular utterance, the `VoiceAction` enforces a policy, that the first one that matches takes effect.

Second, `MultiCommandVoiceAction` must handle when no `VoiceActionCommands` match, by calling back to an `OnNotUnderstoodListener`. Later sections in this chapter explain different ways to minimize how many times this occurs and how to handle it when it does.

Third, repeated tokenizing of the recognition results to split the single string into individual words can be inefficient. Therefore, MultiCommandVoiceAction uses a helper class, WordList, to perform the tokenizing once. The previous chapter presented WordList in Listing 17-17.

Available for
download on
Wrox.com

LISTING 18-3: Executes one or more VoiceActionCommands

```java
public class MultiCommandVoiceAction extends AbstractVoiceAction
{
    private static final String TAG = "MultiCommandVoiceAction";

    private List<VoiceActionCommand> commands;

    public MultiCommandVoiceAction(List<VoiceActionCommand> commands)
    {
        this.commands = commands;
    }

    @Override
    public boolean interpret(List<String> heard, float[] confidenceScores)
    {
        boolean understood = false;

        //Android version 4.0 and less devices will have null
        boolean hasConfidenceScores = (confidenceScores != null);

        // halt after understood something
        for (int i = 0; i < heard.size() && !understood; i++)
        {
            String said = heard.get(i);

            //only check confidence if the app supports it
            boolean exceedsMinConfidence = true;
            if (hasConfidenceScores)
            {
                exceedsMinConfidence =
                    (confidenceScores[i] > getMinConfidenceRequired());
            }

            if (exceedsMinConfidence)
            {
                WordList saidWords = new WordList(said);
                for (VoiceActionCommand command : commands)
                {
                    understood = command.interpret(
                        saidWords, confidenceScores);
                    if (understood)
                    {
                        Log.d(TAG, "Command successful: "
                            + command.getClass().getSimpleName());
                        break;
                    }
                }
            }
```

continues

LISTING 18-3 *(continued)*

```
        }
    }

    if (!understood)
    {
        if (hasConfidenceScores)
        {
            Log.d(TAG, "VoiceAction unsuccessful: " + getPrompt());
            // interpret confidence so as to provide a reason to
            // notUnderstood

            // check only the highest confidence score, which should be the
            // first
            float highestConfidenceScore = confidenceScores[0];
            if (highestConfidenceScore < 0.0)
            {
                getNotUnderstood().notUnderstood(heard,
                    OnNotUnderstoodListener.REASON_UNKNOWN);
            }
            else
            {
                if (highestConfidenceScore <
                            getInaccurateConfidenceThreshold())
                {
                    getNotUnderstood()
                                .notUnderstood(
                                    heard,
                                    OnNotUnderstoodListener.
                                        REASON_INACCURATE_RECOGNITION);
                }
                else if (highestConfidenceScore > =
                    getNotACommandConfidenceThreshold())
                {
                    getNotUnderstood().notUnderstood(heard,
                        OnNotUnderstoodListener.REASON_NOT_A_COMMAND);
                }
                else
                {
                    getNotUnderstood().notUnderstood(heard,
                        OnNotUnderstoodListener.REASON_UNKNOWN);
                }
            }
        }
        else
        {
            getNotUnderstood().notUnderstood(heard,
                OnNotUnderstoodListener.REASON_UNKNOWN);
        }
    }

    return understood;
```

```
    }

    protected void add(VoiceActionCommand command)
    {
        commands.add(command);
    }
}
```

code snippet MultiCommandVoiceAction.java

`MultiCommandVoiceAction` allows you to execute a given set of `VoiceActionCommand`s that you develop. However, some kinds of `VoiceActions` are useful across multiple applications. It is helpful to have a utility class that helps implement those.

While developing GUI `Dialog`s, a developer does not always create new views, with new buttons in it, for every `Dialog` he or she wants to show. Instead there is an `AlertDialog` class that helps create common `Dialog`s. The next section describes how to extend `MultiCommandVoiceAction` to implement a class that is similar to an `AlertDialog`, but designed for voice actions. The class helps you implement common voice actions.

IMPLEMENTING AN ALERTDIALOG FOR VOICE ACTIONS

`AlertDialog`s are a useful class in GUIs because they make it easy to create many kinds of `Dialog`s you need in your app. It is also useful to have the same kind of class with `VoiceActions`. For this purpose, you can use `VoiceAlertDialog`, which extends `MultiCommandVoiceAction`, along with the `MatcherCommand` helper class and `OnUnderstoodListener`.

Instead of the buttons that an `AlertDialog` has, `VoiceAlertDialog` has spoken command words. Instead of indicating results with an `OnClickListener`, it uses an `OnUnderstoodListener`.

To use a `VoiceAlertDialog` an app specifies `OnUnderstoodListeners` for positive, negative, or neutral words. Also, an app may modify the following parameters:

➤ Change the positive, negative, and neutral command words.

➤ Use "relaxed" matching that uses indexing such as stemmers and phonetic matching to make it easier to match what the user said. Chapter 17 explains how these work in more detail.

➤ Add new commands beyond positive, negative, and neutral.

Using these classes you might create a voice command using the following code, taken from the `RemoveFood VoiceActionCommand`:

```
final VoiceAlertDialog confirmDialog = new VoiceAlertDialog();
// positive, try all possible ways to find it
confirmDialog.addRelaxedPositive(new OnUnderstoodListener()
{
    @Override
    public void understood()
```

```
                        {
                            Log.d(TAG, "REMOVE!: " + foodToRemove);
                            FtsIndexedFoodDatabase.getInstance(context).removeFood(
                                    foodToRemove.getName());
                            String toSayRemoved =
                                    String.format(
                                            context.getResources().getString(
                                                    R.string.food_remove_complete),
                                            foodToRemove.getName());
                            executor.speak(toSayRemoved);
                        }
                });
                String toSay =
                        String.format(
                                context.getResources().getString(
                                        R.string.food_remove_confirm_prompt),
                                foodToRemove.getName());
                confirmDialog.setPrompt(toSay);
                confirmDialog.setSpokenPrompt(toSay);
```

The code creates a voice-controlled confirmation dialog that responds when the user responds posi-
tively, by saying "yes" or "ok." It also changes what would be the "title" field in a `Dialog` by using
the `setPrompt()` and `setSpokenPrompt()` methods.

Listing 18-4 shows the implementation of `VoiceAlertDialog`. Listing 18-5 shows the implementation of `MatcherCommand` and `OnUnderstoodListener`.

Available for
download on
Wrox.com

LISTING 18-4: Implements a yes/no/cancel VoiceAction

```java
public class VoiceAlertDialog extends MultiCommandVoiceAction
{
    // use match levels to indicate when you want less
    // to allow less strict matches
    public static final int MATCH_LEVEL_STRICT = 0;
    public static final int MATCH_LEVEL_STEM = 1;
    public static final int MATCH_LEVEL_PHONETIC = 2;
    public static final int MATCH_LEVEL_PHONETIC_LESS_STRICT = 3;

    private String[] yesWords = new String[] { "yes", "ok" };
    private String[] noWords = new String[] { "no" };
    private String[] neutralWords = new String[] { "cancel", "done" };

    public VoiceAlertDialog()
    {
        super(new ArrayList<VoiceActionCommand>());
    }

    /**
     * get the command words from resources
     */
```

```java
public VoiceAlertDialog(Context context)
{
    super(new ArrayList<VoiceActionCommand>());
    yesWords =
            context.getResources().getStringArray(
                    R.array.voiceaction_yeswords);
    noWords =
            context.getResources().getStringArray(
                    R.array.voiceaction_nowords);
    neutralWords =
            context.getResources().getStringArray(
                    R.array.voiceaction_neutralwords);
}

/**
 * add your own command to the dialog here if it consists of words
 */
public void add(OnUnderstoodListener listener, String... words)
{
    add(new MatcherCommand(new WordMatcher(words), listener));
}

public void addPositive(OnUnderstoodListener listener)
{
    add(listener, yesWords);
}

public void addNegative(OnUnderstoodListener listener)
{
    add(listener, noWords);
}

public void addNeutral(OnUnderstoodListener listener)
{
    add(listener, neutralWords);
}

public void addRelaxedPositive(OnUnderstoodListener listener)
{
    addRelaxedAll(listener, yesWords);
}

public void addRelaxedNegative(OnUnderstoodListener listener)
{
    addRelaxedAll(listener, noWords);
}

public void addRelaxedNeutral(OnUnderstoodListener listener)
{
    addRelaxedAll(listener, neutralWords);
```

continues

LISTING 18-4 *(continued)*

```java
    }

    /**
     * add some command words, but allow for less strict matching
     */
    public void addRelaxedAll(OnUnderstoodListener listener, String... words)
    {
        add(listener, MATCH_LEVEL_STRICT, words);
        add(listener, MATCH_LEVEL_STEM, words);
        add(listener, MATCH_LEVEL_PHONETIC, words);
        add(listener, MATCH_LEVEL_PHONETIC_LESS_STRICT, words);
    }

    /**
     * allow matching at different levels of confidence
     */
    private void add(OnUnderstoodListener listener, int matchType,
            String... words)
    {
        WordMatcher matcher;
        switch (matchType)
        {
            case MATCH_LEVEL_STEM:
                matcher = new StemmedWordMatcher(words);
                break;
            case MATCH_LEVEL_PHONETIC:
                matcher = new SoundsLikeWordMatcher(words);
                break;
            case MATCH_LEVEL_PHONETIC_LESS_STRICT:
                matcher = new SoundsLikeThresholdWordMatcher(3, words);
                break;
            case MATCH_LEVEL_STRICT:
            default:
                matcher = new WordMatcher(words);
                break;
        }
        add(new MatcherCommand(matcher, listener));
    }
}
```

code snippet VoiceAlertDialog.java

LISTING 18-5: Helper class and interface needed to implement VoiceAlertDialog

```java
public class MatcherCommand implements VoiceActionCommand
{
    private WordMatcher matcher;

    private OnUnderstoodListener onUnderstood;

    public MatcherCommand(WordMatcher matcher,
```

```
                OnUnderstoodListener onUnderstood)
    {
        this.matcher = matcher;
        this.onUnderstood = onUnderstood;
    }

    @Override
    public boolean interpret(WordList heard, float[] confidence)
    {
        boolean understood = false;
        if (matcher.isIn(heard.getWords()))
        {
            understood = true;
            if (onUnderstood != null)
            {
                onUnderstood.understood();
            }
        }
        return understood;
    }

    public OnUnderstoodListener getOnUnderstood()
    {
        return onUnderstood;
    }
}

public interface OnUnderstoodListener
{
    public void understood();
}
```

The `VoiceAlertDialog` class is a convenient way to implement many voice actions. You can use it or the `MultiCommandVoiceAction` class, described previously, to construct single turn dialogues. The next section discusses combining voice actions together to produce multiple turn dialogues.

IMPLEMENTING MULTI-TURN VOICE ACTIONS

Some voice actions require multiple turns. For example, a voice action may require a second turn to allow the user to confirm before proceeding. Beyond soliciting confirmation some voice actions require multiple turns in order for the users to input all the information they need.

This section examines how to implement such multi-turn voice actions for food dialogue's Edit Food voice action. In the dialogue's first turn, users activate either the `AddFood` or `RemoveFood` `VoiceActionCommands` and specify part of the input each command needs. The `VoiceActionCommands` then start a second turn to gather the remaining needed input by executing a `VoiceAction`.

Implementing Multi-Turn AddFood

Adding food requires two pieces of information: a name and a number of calories. The user uses two turns to specify the information one piece at a time. `AddFood`, shown in Listing 18-6, implements the first turn.

Available for
download on
Wrox.com

LISTING 18-6: Matches add command words then starts a new turn to ask for a number of calories.

```java
public class AddFood implements VoiceActionCommand
{
    private static final String TAG = "AddFood";

    private WordMatcher match;
    private VoiceActionExecutor executor;

    private FtsIndexedFoodDatabase foodFts;
    private Context context;

    public AddFood(Context context, VoiceActionExecutor executor,
            FtsIndexedFoodDatabase foodFts, boolean relaxed)
    {
        String[] commandWords =
                context.getResources().getStringArray(R.array.food_add_command);
        Log.d(TAG, "add with words: " + Arrays.toString(commandWords));

        if (relaxed)
        {
            // match "add" if 3 of the 4 soundex characters match
            // allows it to match add (code: A300) with bad (code: B300)
            match = new SoundsLikeThresholdWordMatcher(3, commandWords);
        }
        else
        {
            // match only if the use says "add" exactly
            match = new WordMatcher(commandWords);
        }
        this.context = context;
        this.executor = executor;
        this.foodFts = foodFts;
    }

    @Override
    public boolean interpret(WordList heard, float[] confidenceScores)
    {
        boolean understood = false;

        //match first part: "add"
        int matchIndex = match.isInAt(heard.getWords());
        if (matchIndex >= 0)
        {
            //match second part: the food name
            String freeText = heard.getStringAfter(matchIndex);
            if (freeText.length() > 0)
            {
                String foodToAdd = freeText;

                // first command
```

```
            VoiceActionCommand askForCalories =
                    new AskForCalories(context, executor, foodFts,
                            foodToAdd);
            String calPromptFormat =
                    context.getString(R.string.food_add_calories_prompt);
            String calPrompt = String.format(calPromptFormat, foodToAdd);

            // second command
            CancelCommand cancel = new CancelCommand(context, executor);

            // match either command, cancel first
            MultiCommandVoiceAction responseAction =
                    new MultiCommandVoiceAction(Arrays.asList(cancel,
                            askForCalories));

            // speak and display the same prompt when executing
            responseAction.setPrompt(calPrompt);
            responseAction.setSpokenPrompt(calPrompt);

            // retry if did not understood
            responseAction.setNotUnderstood(new WhyNotUnderstoodListener(
                    context, executor, true));

            understood = true;
            executor.execute(responseAction);
        }
    }

    return understood;
}
}
```

code snippet AddFood.java

The first turn involves the user activating the command by saying "add" and specifying part of the required information by saying a food name. If AddFood's interpret() method can't find either, it returns false and fails. Otherwise, it starts a a second turn with a MultiCommandVoiceAction that has two VoiceActionCommands. One is a CancelCommand to allow the user to stop the turn and the other is an AskForCalories to query the user a number of calories.

This VoiceAction has two features that help improve usability. First, it speaks the prompt: "How many calories for <foodname>?" The prompt accomplishes two things: it lets the user know what to say next, and it implicitly confirms that the app understood which food the user wanted to add.

Second, if users do not recognize the name of the food used in the calorie prompt, they can cancel because they know that the voice recognition failed.

Listing 18-7 shows the code for AskForCalories. AskForCalories matches any numbers in the recognition result, completes adding food to the database, and speaks a prompt to notify the user when it is done.

LISTING 18-7: Matches the number of calories and adds the new Food

```java
public class AskForCalories implements VoiceActionCommand
{
    private String foodToAdd;
    private FtsIndexedFoodDatabase foodFts;
    private VoiceActionExecutor executor;
    private Context context;

    public AskForCalories(Context context, VoiceActionExecutor executor,
            FtsIndexedFoodDatabase foodFts, String foodToAdd)
    {
        this.context = context;
        this.executor = executor;
        this.foodFts = foodFts;
        this.foodToAdd = foodToAdd;
    }

    @Override
    public boolean interpret(WordList heard, float[] confidenceScores)
    {
        boolean understood = false;
        // look for a number within "heard"
        for (String word : heard.getWords())
        {
            if (isNumber(word))
            {
                String responseFormat =
                        context.getResources().getString(
                                R.string.food_add_result);
                String response =
                        String.format(responseFormat, foodToAdd, word);
                // insert food
                foodFts.insertFood(foodToAdd, Float.parseFloat(word));
                executor.speak(response);
                understood = true;
            }
        }
        return understood;
    }

    private boolean isNumber(String word)
    {
        boolean isNumber = false;
        try
        {
            Integer.parseInt(word);
            isNumber = true;
        } catch (NumberFormatException e)
        {
            isNumber = false;
        }
        return isNumber;
    }
}
```

Implementing Multi-Turn RemoveFood

Users remove a food by saying "remove" and the name of a food. RemoveFood recognizes this by matching the "remove" command word and using the database to match the spoken food name. Because the user cannot undo removing a food, RemoveFood starts a VoiceAlertDialog so the user can confirm before deleting.

Listing 18-8 shows the RemoveFood implementation.

Available for
download on
Wrox.com

LISTING 18-8: Matches remove command words and confirms before taking action

```java
public class RemoveFood implements VoiceActionCommand
{
    private static final String TAG = "RemoveFood";

    private WordMatcher match;

    private Context context;
    private VoiceActionExecutor executor;
    private FtsIndexedFoodDatabase foodFts;
    private boolean relaxed;

    public RemoveFood(Context context, VoiceActionExecutor executor,
            FtsIndexedFoodDatabase foodFts, boolean relaxed)
    {
        String[] commandWords =
                context.getResources().getStringArray(
                        R.array.food_remove_command);
        if (relaxed)
        {
            // match "remove" if 3 of the 4 soundex characters match
            match = new SoundsLikeThresholdWordMatcher(3, commandWords);
        }
        else
        {
            //exact match
            match = new WordMatcher(commandWords);
        }
        this.context = context;
        this.executor = executor;
        this.foodFts = foodFts;
        this.relaxed = relaxed;
    }

    public boolean interpret(WordList heard, float[] confidence)
    {
        Food toRemove = null;

        //match "remove"
        int matchIndex = match.isInAt(heard.getWords());

        //match the food to remove
        if (matchIndex >= 0)
        {
```

continues

LISTING 18-8 *(continued)*

```
        String freeText = heard.getStringAfter(matchIndex);
        List<MatchedFood> match;
        if (relaxed)
        {
            // for relaxed add prefix matching
            match = foodFts.retrieveBestMatch(freeText, true, true, false);
        }
        else
        {
            match = foodFts.retrieveBestMatch(freeText, false, true, false);
        }
        if (match.size() > 0)
        {
            toRemove = match.get(0).getFood();
        }
    }

    //start another VoiceAction
    //to confirm before removing
    if (toRemove != null)
    {
        final Food foodToRemove = toRemove;
        final VoiceAlertDialog confirmDialog = new VoiceAlertDialog();
        // add listener for positive response
        // use relaxed matching to increase chance of understanding user
        confirmDialog.addRelaxedPositive(new OnUnderstoodListener()
        {
            @Override
            public void understood()
            {
                Log.d(TAG, "REMOVE!: " + foodToRemove);
                FtsIndexedFoodDatabase.getInstance(context).removeFood(
                        foodToRemove.getName());
                String toSayRemoved =
                        String.format(
                                context.getResources().getString(
                                        R.string.food_remove_complete),
                                foodToRemove.getName());
                executor.speak(toSayRemoved);
            }
        });

        //prompt for the confirm VoiceAction
        String toSay =
                String.format(
                        context.getResources().getString(
                                R.string.food_remove_confirm_prompt),
                        foodToRemove.getName());
        confirmDialog.setPrompt(toSay);
        confirmDialog.setSpokenPrompt(toSay);

        // if the user says anything else besides the yes words cancel
        confirmDialog.setNotUnderstood(new OnNotUnderstoodListener()
        {
```

```
            @Override
            public void notUnderstood(List<String> heard, int reason)
            {
                String toSayCancelled = context.getResources().getString(
                        R.string.voiceaction_cancelled_response);
                executor.speak(toSayCancelled);
            }
        });
        executor.execute(confirmDialog);
    }
    return (toRemove != null);
}
}
```

 Use Android resources to define all prompts and command words. Also, use the `String.format` *syntax to construct any prompts. By doing so you can utilize Android's resources mechanism to support multiple languages, even if they have different grammatical structure.*

`AddFood` and `RemoveFood` are two `VoiceActionCommand`s that implement the Food Edit voice action. When successfully used, the commands allow the user to manipulate the food database. However, this chapter has not yet described what the app can do to help the user succeed. The next two sections show how to reduce the chances of failure and how to respond if failure occurs so that it does not occur repeatedly.

MAKING A BEST GUESS

If an app cannot match what the user said exactly, perhaps it could make a best guess. When the guess is correct, the app will appear to work as normal. When incorrect, the user will have to wait as the app incorrectly responds. As long as the app guesses correct more times than not and incorrect responses don't annoy the user too much, continuing to make a best guess is a good idea. An app can make a best guess by relaxing match strictness or by using domain knowledge to make an educated guess.

Relaxing Match Strictness

To highlight how relaxing match strictness works consider the `FoodLookup` `VoiceActionCommand`. `FoodLookup` is an example of a `VoiceActionCommand` that is likely to have trouble understanding what the user said. It needs to match dynamic command words, which consist of any foods in the food database. There could be a large number of foods in the database and some could be hard to understand. Therefore, `FoodLookup` must do extra work to find a match. If it relies on matching that is too strict, the user will have to retry often due to `FoodLookup` not understanding.

To improve the chances of a match, `FoodLookup` performs multiple database searches, each with more relaxed search criteria. The more relaxed the criteria, the more the correct result relies on the database's ranking mechanism. Additionally, the database indexes use FTS's stemmer for all food names. Chapter 17 describes using the FTS database and stemmers. Both these strategies allow FoodLookup to make a best guess and increase the number of times that it understands the user. Listing 18-9 shows the code.

Available for download on Wrox.com

LISTING 18-9: Searches for a match with relaxed criteria if necessary

```java
public class FoodLookup implements VoiceActionCommand
{
    private static final String TAG = "FoodLookup";

    private VoiceActionExecutor executor;
    private FtsIndexedFoodDatabase foodFts;
    private Context context;

    public FoodLookup(Context context, VoiceActionExecutor executor,
            FtsIndexedFoodDatabase foodFts)
    {
        this.context = context;
        this.executor = executor;
        this.foodFts = foodFts;
    }

    public boolean interpret(WordList heard, float[] confidence)
    {
        boolean success = false;

        boolean or = false;
        boolean prefix = false;
        boolean phrase = true;

        String said = heard.getSource();
        List<MatchedFood> foods =
                foodFts.retrieveBestMatch(said, prefix, or, phrase);

        // phrase query
        if (foods.size() == 0)
        {
            or = false;
            prefix = false;
            phrase = true;
            foods = foodFts.retrieveBestMatch(said, prefix, or, phrase);
        }

        // word query
        if (foods.size() == 0)
        {
            or = false;
            prefix = false;
            phrase = false;
            foods = foodFts.retrieveBestMatch(said, prefix, or, phrase);
        }

        // word or query
        if (foods.size() == 0)
        {
            or = true;
            prefix = false;
```

```
                phrase = false;
                foods = foodFts.retrieveBestMatch(said, prefix, or, phrase);
            }

        // word, prefix, or query
        if (foods.size() == 0)
        {
            or = true;
            prefix = true;
            phrase = false;
            foods = foodFts.retrieveBestMatch(said, prefix, or, phrase);
        }

        if (foods.size() > 0)
        {
            Food heardFood = foods.get(0).getFood();
            String resultFormat =
                    context.getResources().getString(
                            R.string.food_lookup_result);
            String toSay =
                    String.format(resultFormat, heardFood.getName(),
                            heardFood.getFormattedCalories());
            Log.d(TAG, "heard a food " + heardFood);
            success = true;
            executor.speak(toSay);
        }
        return success;
    }
}
```

code snippet FoodLookup.java

`FoodLookup` performs a series of queries in the following order:

1. Phrase query: Matches the entire recognition phrase with the foods in the database.

2. Word query: Relaxes the phrase requirement, but all words must still match.

3. Word or query: Turns the query from an AND to an OR query.

4. Word, prefix, or query: Adds prefix matching.

Beyond these relaxations, the code could use the same queries on phonetic forms of the words. This would require creating and populating a new database field or using Lucene's indexing mechanism.

The result of these multiple database searches is a `VoiceActionCommand` that makes a best guess at what the user says using functions available from the database.

Relaxing Strictness Between Commands

`FoodLookup` shows an example of a single command that relaxes its search criteria. When an app has a `VoiceAction` with multiple commands, you may prefer that it try all possible commands with strict criteria and then try again with more relaxed criteria only if necessary. That way, each command has an equal chance to match before resorting to relaxed matching. To implement this, your app can create multiple versions of a `VoiceCommandAction`, each with different levels of relaxed matching, and call them in order.

Listing 18-10 shows code that creates the Food Edit voice action. It includes two instances of *addCommand* and *removeCommand* with different values of *relaxed*. The commands that have *relaxed* set to true use less strict matching criteria. Including both in the list of `VoiceActionCommands` causes the *voiceAction* to match strict add and remove first. If it cannot match the strict versions, it then tries the relaxed versions.

LISTING 18-10: Creates a VoiceAction that uses two levels of matching strictness

```
private VoiceAction makeFoodEdit()
    {
        FtsIndexedFoodDatabase foodDb =
                FtsIndexedFoodDatabase
                    .getInstance(MultiTurnFoodDialogActivity.this);

        // match it with two levels of strictness
        boolean relaxed = false;

        VoiceActionCommand cancelCommand = new CancelCommand(this, executor);
        VoiceActionCommand removeCommand =
                new RemoveFood(this, executor, foodDb, relaxed);
        VoiceActionCommand addCommand =
                new AddFood(this, executor, foodDb, relaxed);

        relaxed = true;
        VoiceActionCommand removeCommandRelaxed =
                new RemoveFood(this, executor, foodDb, relaxed);
        VoiceActionCommand addCommandRelaxed =
                new AddFood(this, executor, foodDb, relaxed);

        VoiceAction voiceAction =
                new MultiCommandVoiceAction(Arrays.asList(cancelCommand,
                        addCommand, removeCommand, addCommandRelaxed,
                        removeCommandRelaxed));
        // don't retry
        voiceAction.setNotUnderstood(new WhyNotUnderstoodListener(this,
                executor, false));
        final String EDIT_PROMPT =
                getResources().getString(R.string.food_edit_prompt);
        // no spoken prompt
        voiceAction.setPrompt(EDIT_PROMPT);

        return voiceAction;
    }
```

Making an Educated Guess

Beyond relaxing matching criteria, your app may be able to make an intelligent guess if it takes into account the other information it knows. For example, a calendar app might guess what the user meant based on the current date. How you use such information is dependent on your app. However, it may allow your app to make an educated guess at what the user said when your app has no other way of guessing.

For example, in Digital Recipe Sidekick's voice-controlled recipe reader I utilized knowledge of the user's current progress in the recipe to determine how to respond in ambiguous situations. One example of this is what I call the "green beans problem."

The "green beans problem" occurs when the app does not know what kind of beans the user is referring to in a recipe that has multiple bean types. For example, minestrone soup has three kinds of beans: kidney beans, white beans, and green beans. If a user says "beans," to which bean does it refer?

The app could report three answers — one for each bean type — but it could do better because the app knows which step in the recipe the user is most likely on. For example, if the app thinks the user is cooking a step that contains green beans, it can guess that the user meant "green beans" and not the other two.

In the food dialogue example you might use knowledge of what foods a user dislikes to make an educated guess during a food lookup. For example, if the recognizer only recognized "green," the food database would return "Green Beans," "Green Cabbage," and "Green Onion" and FoodLookup would pick the first to speak to the user. If the app knows that the user does not like beans or onions, it can guess that the user meant cabbage. You could use code such as the code below to filter food lookup results if there are more than one. The code returns the first food, unless it is part of the foods that the user dislikes or if the user dislikes all the recognized foods.

```
private static final Set<String> foodsDislike;

static
{
    foodsDislike = new HashSet<String>();
    foodsDislike.add("Green Onion");
    foodsDislike.add("Green Beans");
}

public static Food pickMostLikelyFood(List<Food> possibleFoods)
{
    if (possibleFoods.size() == 0)
    {
        return null;
    }

    Food mostLikely = possibleFoods.get(0);
    for (Food food : possibleFoods)
    {
        if (!foodsDislike.contains(food.getName()))
        {
            mostLikely = food;
            break;
        }
    }
    return mostLikely;
}
```

A best guess can be a way to disambiguate when there are multiple possible matches and to respond when matching is difficult. However, there are scenarios when a best guess is not possible such as when recognition failure occurs because of external factors. The next section describes how to diagnose and respond in those situations.

RESPONDING WHEN RECOGNITION FAILS

If an active voice action cannot match any of the recognition results, it fails. In such cases, your app should report failure to the user while providing feedback, if possible, about why it thinks it could not understand. The feedback can help the user be more successful in the future. Without it, a user may continue to make the same mistakes repeatedly and become frustrated.

It is important that an app be conservative when diagnosing why recognition failed. It should send feedback only if it is sure the app will be correct. The trouble is that if an app continually reports feedback to users, they will eventually ignore it, or even worse, become annoyed and uninstall your app.

An app might make several responses when recognition failure occurs:

➤ **"That is not a command":** The user said something accurate, but it wasn't a command.

➤ **"I didn't hear you well":** The user spoke, but the recognizer was not able to clearly recognize what the user said.

➤ **"I don't understand, please try again":** The app cannot determine reliably why it did not understand what the user said. Optionally, the app can show the speech prompt again immediately without requiring the user to reactivate speech recognition.

To handle recognition failure, `MultiCommandVoiceAction` diagnoses why and `WhyNotUnderstoodListener` reports feedback to the user. `MultiCommandVoiceAction` diagnoses the cause of the failure by examining the highest confidence score from the `EXTRA_CONFIDENCE_SCORES` recognizer output and using the thresholds shown in Table 18-2. You saw `MultiCommandVoiceAction` in Listing 18-3. Listing 18-11 shows `WhyNotUnderstoodListener`. Listing 18-12 shows the `OnNotUnderstoodListener` interface.

TABLE 18-2: Which Confidence Scores Result in which Diagnosis and Feedback

DIAGNOSIS	CONFIDENCE RANGE	FEEDBACK
Inaccurate recognition	0.0 to 0.3	I did not understand because I did not hear you well.
Don't understand	0.3 to 0.9	I did not understand.
Not a command	0.9 to 1.0	<most likely recognition> is not a command.

LISTING 18-11: Determines how to reply if recognition failed

```java
public class WhyNotUnderstoodListener implements OnNotUnderstoodListener
{
    private Context context;
    private boolean retry;
    private VoiceActionExecutor executor;

    public WhyNotUnderstoodListener(Context context,
            VoiceActionExecutor executor, boolean retry)
    {
        this.context = context;
        this.executor = executor;
        this.retry = retry;
    }

    @Override
    public void notUnderstood(List<String> heard, int reason)
    {
        String prompt;
        switch (reason)
        {
            case OnNotUnderstoodListener.REASON_INACCURATE_RECOGNITION:
                prompt =
                        context.getResources().getString(
                                R.string.voiceaction_inaccurate);
                break;
            case OnNotUnderstoodListener.REASON_NOT_A_COMMAND:
                String firstMatchingWord = heard.get(0);
                String promptFormat =
                        context.getResources().getString(
                                R.string.voiceaction_not_command);
                prompt = String.format(promptFormat, firstMatchingWord);
                break;
            case OnNotUnderstoodListener.REASON_UNKNOWN:
            default:
                prompt =
                        context.getResources().getString(
                                R.string.voiceaction_unknown);
                break;
        }

        if (retry)
        {
            String retryPrompt =
                    context.getResources().getString(
                            R.string.voiceaction_retry);
            prompt = prompt + retryPrompt;
            executor.reExecute(prompt);
```

continues

LISTING 18-11 *(continued)*

```
        } else
        {
            executor.speak(prompt);
        }
    }
}
```

LISTING 18-12: Called when a VoiceAction fails to match

```java
public interface OnNotUnderstoodListener
{
    /**
     * no explanation
     */
    public static final int REASON_UNKNOWN = 0;
    /**
     * Recognition was inaccurate, perhaps because of poor audio quality
     */
    public static final int REASON_INACCURATE_RECOGNITION = 1;
    /**
     * Recognition was accurate, but no match was found
     */
    public static final int REASON_NOT_A_COMMAND = 2;

    /**
     * didn't understand the user's utterance for a particular reason
     * and provide some contextual information to construct useful feedback
     */
    public void notUnderstood(List<String> heard, int reason);
}
```

The following sections describe each diagnosis in greater detail.

Determining Not a Command

If users say something that has high recognition confidence, they may be saying something that is not a command. The high confidence means they are likely speaking clearly enough for the recognizer to understand. This means that if the voice action didn't match what the user said, the cause is not likely due to inaccurate recognition. Instead it is likely because the user is saying the wrong words.

Also, because the user is speaking clearly, the recognizer will likely return similar results when the user retries. This can lead to a frustrating situation where the user repeats the same command over and over with the speech recognizer recognizing it each time. Because the user is speaking something that is not a real command, the app will never recognize it.

To avoid this trouble, your app should tell users that they are saying something that is not a command. Two possible ways to provide feedback are:

➤ **Correct the user:** An app could tell users what they said is not a command. To do so, it must pick one of the possible recognitions as the text of what the user meant to say, and then proceed to say that the recognized text is not a command. The problem is that, often, the first recognition result is not what the user was trying to say. In such cases, the feedback will not contain the words that the user said.

➤ **Instruct the user:** An app could tell the user what the possible commands are. This avoids the problem with correcting the user, but could lead to a long lecture that users will find annoying.

Using either of these two feedback approaches, if the recognizer recognizes "broccoli" as "brooklyn, rocklin, or rockledge" in that order, the app can either respond "Brooklyn is not a command" or "Please say a food name."

To determine if a user spoke a word that is not a command, `MultiCommandVoiceAction` checks if the highest confidence the recognizer returned is greater than 0.9. If it is, `WhyNotUnderstoodListener` tells the user that the first possible recognition is not a command.

Determining Inaccurate Recognition

Inaccurate recognition could occur for several reasons. Inaccurate recognition could result if the app received poor-quality audio. It also could occur because the user did not use proper speech hygiene — by yelling or over-pronouncing, for example. Another reason could be that the user is in a noisy environment and the interference from the environment reduced the recognizer's accuracy. Whatever the reason, telling the user that inaccurate recognition was the cause of failure may improve success in subsequent tries because if the user speaks more correctly the next time, recognition accuracy will improve.

To check for inaccurate recognition, `MultiCommandVoiceAction` checks if the highest confidence the recognizer returned is below a threshold of 0.3.

Not Understanding

If the confidence scores are in between the thresholds for the inaccurate recognition and not a command diagnoses, the app cannot determine why the recognition failed and must report failure for an unknown reason. One way to potentially help users recover is to restart the voice action. Trying again automatically can be useful when it takes considerable time to activate speech. Also, if users are in the middle of a multi-turn voice action, restarting the current turn is useful because they might get frustrated if failure causes them to have to start all over. On the other hand, a speech recognition prompt that refuses to stop asking can make users upset. To avoid this situation, you should include a way for users to cancel the voice action.

SUMMARY

This chapter armed you with all the code you need to utilize the matching techniques you learned in Chapter 17 to create a modular, user-friendly VUI. Using the techniques this chapter describes, your app can define and execute multi-turn voice action. To improve usability when the speech recognizer recognizes poorly, this chapter showed you how an app can make a best guess and give useful feedback about why recognition failed. This chapter also highlighted how you can further improve usability by adding other features to your VUI such as allowing the user to cancel.

In designing a VUI, one usability issue remains to be addressed by this part: how to activate speech recognition. Using a button to start a voice action can be limiting for some tasks. To use Android's TTS and speech recognition capabilities in a wider variety of scenarios, it is sometimes useful to not require the user to touch a button to activate it. Fortunately, there are many other ways an app can activate speech, beyond just a button press. Chapter 19 describes several techniques you can use to create hands-free and eyes-free VUIs.

19

Implementing Speech Activation

WHAT'S IN THIS CHAPTER?

➤ Activating speech using Android's sensors and continuous speech recognition

➤ Persistently running speech activation using a Service

The first thing a user must do to use speech recognition is to tell the app to start recognizing. One way the user could do it, which the previous chapters relied on, is to press a button. However, pressing a button assumes the user is looking at the screen and can touch it. This is not always the case. For certain tasks, like sending e-mail while driving, users need to activate speech recognition hands-free and eyes-free. In such cases, an app needs different speech activation techniques beyond just a button. Fortunately, Android's sensors provide you with a wide variety of ways to implement speech activation.

In addition to deciding how your app implements speech activation, you must decide when the user can activate it. Your users may need to activate speech only while using the app, or they may need to activate speech at any time, even if the app is not running.

This chapter presents four speech activation implementations, summarized in Table 19-1, that use the sensor techniques discussed in other chapters of this book. It also describes how to run speech activation persistently using a `Service`.

TABLE 19-1: Four Different Ways to Use Android Sensors for Speech Activation

NAME	TECH	HOW
Movement	Physical Sensors	Move phone with sufficient acceleration
Clap	Microphone	Make a single clap or loud noise
Speak Hello	Direct Speech Recognition	Say "hello"
NFC Scan	NFC	Scan an NFC with a certain MIME type

TRY THIS

You can try different speech activation approaches by using the Try Speech button and changing the activation method to other options. You can also use the Write Speech Activation Tag menu option to write an NFC that activates speech when you scan it.

IMPLEMENTING SPEECH ACTIVATION

To implement speech activation, an app needs to listen and then start speech recognition if it detects an activation. This section describes the issues involved in starting speech recognition in response to a detected activation. It describes four speech activator implementations that use the Android sensors and concepts from previous chapters. This section also describes how to use these implementations within an `Activity`.

The speech activators described in this chapter enable the user to activate speech in various ways. Each requires a slightly different implementation. Most of the speech activators use the callback mechanism specified by the `SpeechActivator` interface, and some use a sensor-specific callback such as `MovementDetectionListener`. Listing 19-1 shows the `SpeechActivator` interface. The behavior of `SpeechActivator` is:

➤ External code calls `detectActivation()`.

➤ `SpeechActivator` starts listening for a single speech activation.

➤ If external code calls `stop()`, the `SpeechActivator` stops listening and calls `SpeechActivationListener.activated(false)`.

➤ If the `SpeechActivator` detects an activation, it calls `SpeechActivationListener.activated(true)` and stops.

➤ If `SpeechActivator` has an error or otherwise stops it calls `SpeechActivationListener.activated(false)`.

LISTING 19-1: Interface for a class that listens for speech activation

```
public interface SpeechActivator
{
    /**
     * listen for speech activation, when heard, call a {@link SpeechActivationListener}
     * and stop listening
     */
    public void detectActivation();

    /**
     * stop waiting for activation.
     */
    public void stop();
}
```

Starting Speech Recognition

After a `SpeechActivator` detects an activation, the app must begin the speech recognition process. However, not all users will be able to see the screen when this occurs. This presents a difficulty: the app must make users aware that their speech activation was successful and that the app is now recording speech. This difficulty is complicated by two time delays that occur between when the user activates speech and when the app starts recording. Additionally, the time delays have different lengths depending on the device and its current workload.

The first time delay occurs after the user successfully activates speech and before the app speaks a prompt. The prompt is useful to tell users that their speech activation was successful and that the app is about to start speech recognition, but it is not required. Until users hear the prompt, they do not have any way to know that their activation was successful. This could result in users activating speech multiple times while waiting to hear the prompt. To avoid multiple activations, code that calls the `SpeechActivator` implementations must respond to only one activation at a time.

The second time delay occurs after the app decides to start the speech recognizer. It occurs after the app finishes speaking the prompt and before recognition starts. The delay can result in the user speaking before the app is listening. Unfortunately, it is not easy to address this problem. Here are two ways an app might do it:

➤ Train the user to wait a short amount of time after the prompt completes before speaking.

➤ Make your voice commands long enough so that if the user happens to speak only part of the command, your app can still recognize it.

Delays inserted within voice commands are periods of awkward inactivity that are not intuitive for the user because they do not occur in normal speech. For example, a person might greet someone else by saying, "Hi, how are you?" When interacting with an app, a user might say, "Hi, send an e-mail" where "Hi" activates the speech recognition and "send an e-mail" is the voice command. However, when interacting with an Android device, the user has to say "Hi, (one second pause) send an e-mail" to give the app enough time to detect a speech activation and start speech recognition. This dialogue between the user and the app can be even slower if there is a prompt. Using a prompt, the dialogue would be:

> User: Hi
>
> (one second pause)
>
> App: Say a command
>
> (one second pause)
>
> User: Send an e-mail

The dialogue is awkward because if the user were interacting with another person, neither of the two pauses would exist. Prompts are usually necessary to help remind users what they can say, so most likely your app must have both of these pauses and the awkward speech pattern it causes.

Your code has to bring users through the process of activating speech, waiting through the app's delays, and finally, recording speech for recognition. Apps could handle this in various ways. `SpeechActivationLauncher`, shown in Listing 19-2, is an example of one way to do it.

SpeechActivator implementations can use it to trigger speech recognition from an Intent. SpeechActivationLauncher relies on a prompt to tell the user that speech recognition is about to occur and shows recognition results by forwarding them to SpeechRecognitionResultsActivity. The implementation uses the abstract SpeechRecognizingAndSpeakingActivity to handle using speech recognition and TextToSpeech.

SpeechRecognitionLauncher processes an incoming Intent with several steps:

1. Wait for TextToSpeech initialization.

2. Say a prompt.

3. When the prompt completes, TextToSpeech calls onDone(). onDone() starts speech recognition.

4. When Android finishes recognizing speech it calls onActivityResult(), which forwards the recognition results to SpeechRecognitionResultsActivity for display.

5. onActivityResult() calls finish() to remove the SpeechActivationLauncher Activity from the user's view.

Available for download on Wrox.com

LISTING 19-2: Speaks a prompt and then sends results to SpeechRecognitionResultsActivity for display

```
public class SpeechRecognitionLauncher extends
        SpeechRecognizingAndSpeakingActivity
{
    private static final String TAG = "SpeechRecognitionLauncher";

    private static final String ON_DONE_PROMPT_TTS_PARAM = "ON_DONE_PROMPT";

    @Override
    protected void onCreate(Bundle savedInstanceState)
    {
        super.onCreate(savedInstanceState);
    }

    @Override
    public void onSuccessfulInit(TextToSpeech tts)
    {
        super.onSuccessfulInit(tts);
        prompt();
    }

    private void prompt()
    {
        Log.d(TAG, "Speak prompt");
        getTts().speak(getString(R.string.speech_launcher_prompt),
                TextToSpeech.QUEUE_FLUSH,
                TextToSpeechUtils.makeParamsWith(ON_DONE_PROMPT_TTS_PARAM));
    }

    /**
```

```
     * super class handles registering the UtteranceProgressListener
     * and calling this
     */
    @Override
    public void onDone(String utteranceId)
    {
        if (utteranceId.equals(ON_DONE_PROMPT_TTS_PARAM))
        {
            Intent recognizerIntent =
                    new Intent(RecognizerIntent.ACTION_RECOGNIZE_SPEECH);
            recognizerIntent.putExtra(RecognizerIntent.EXTRA_LANGUAGE_MODEL,
                    RecognizerIntent.LANGUAGE_MODEL_WEB_SEARCH);
            recognizerIntent.putExtra(RecognizerIntent.EXTRA_PROMPT,
                    getString(R.string.speech_launcher_prompt));
            recognize(recognizerIntent);
        }
    }

    @Override
    protected void
            onActivityResult(int requestCode, int resultCode, Intent data)
    {
        super.onActivityResult(requestCode, resultCode, data);

        if (requestCode == VOICE_RECOGNITION_REQUEST_CODE)
        {
            if (resultCode == RESULT_OK)
            {
                Intent showResults = new Intent(data);
                showResults.setClass(this,
                        SpeechRecognitionResultsActivity.class);
                startActivity(showResults);
            }
        }

        finish();
    }

    @Override
    protected void receiveWhatWasHeard(List<String> heard,
            float[] confidenceScores)
    {
        // satisfy abstract class, this class handles the results directly
        // instead of using this method
    }
}
```

code snippet SpeechRecognitionLauncher.java

Implementing Speech Activation within an Activity

Using a SpeechActivator in an Activity requires several features to make it work in the way users expect. The Activity has to run SpeechActivator asynchronously so the user can perform other tasks and it must not allow the user to accidently activate speech recognition twice.

Additionally, the `Activity` has to manage lifecycle events to handle when the user switches away from the `Activity` while it is running a `SpeechActivator`. If this occurs, the `Activity` needs to stop the `SpeechActivator` while the user is away and restart it when he or she returns. The `SpeechActivatorStartStop` class, shown in Listing 19-3, implements the required code.

First, `SpeechActivatorStartStop` ensures the user cannot accidently activate speech recognition twice by allowing only one `SpeechActivator` to run at a time. It also makes sure that it does not execute its complete `activated()` method multiple times for a single intended activation. `SpeechActivatorStartStop` accomplishes these by using the *isListeningForActivation* state variable. The code checks it before starting a `SpeechActivator` in the `startActivator()` method and before responding to an activation in the `activated()` method. `SpeechActivatorStartStop` needs the check within `activated()` to make it more robust to errors that could occur due to the asynchronous nature of running the `SpeechActivator`. The check ensures that if a `SpeechActivator` happens to call `activated()` twice before it stops itself, `SpeechActivatorStartStop` will still respond only once. Also, the check handles the race condition that can occur when the `SpeechActivator` is in the process of calling `activated()` while the app has intended to stop it. This could occur, for example, when a user hits the Home button and pressing the Home button makes enough sound to trigger a sound based `SpeechActivator`. In this example, the `SpeechActivator` may call `activated()` while the `SpeechActivatorStartStop` is in the middle of shutting down.

Second, `SpeechActivatorStartStop` starts and stops an active `SpeechActivator` according to the appropriate `Activity` lifecycle events. It does this by remembering whether or not the `SpeechActivator` was running when it was paused or destroyed. The `onPause()` method stores this state within the `wasListeningForActivation` variable. `onResume()` restarts the `SpeechActivator` depending on the value of `wasListeningForActivation`. If Android destroys `SpeechActivatorStartStop`, the `onSaveInstanceState()` and `onRestoreInstanceState()` methods work to save and restore the `wasListeningForActivation` value so that `onResume()` can sufficiently restart the `SpeechActivator` if necessary.

LISTING 19-3: Activity to execute a SpeechActivator

```
public class SpeechActivatorStartStop extends Activity implements
        SpeechActivationListener
{
    private static final String TAG = "SpeechActivatorStartStop";

    /**
     * store if currently listening
     */
    private boolean isListeningForActivation;

    /**
     * if paused, store what was happening so that onResume can restart it
     */
    private boolean wasListeningForActivation;

    private SpeechActivator speechActivator;
```

```java
/**
 * for saving {@link #wasListeningForActivation}
 * in the saved instance state
 */
private static final String WAS_LISTENING_STATE = "WAS_LISTENING";

@Override
protected void onCreate(Bundle savedInstanceState)
{
    super.onCreate(savedInstanceState);
    setContentView(R.layout.speechactivationstart_stop);

    isListeningForActivation = false;
    speechActivator = new MovementActivator(this, this);

    // start and stop buttons
    Button start = (Button) findViewById(R.id.btn_start);
    start.setOnClickListener(new View.OnClickListener()
    {
        @Override
        public void onClick(View v)
        {
            startActivator();
        }
    });

    Button stop = (Button) findViewById(R.id.btn_stop);
    stop.setOnClickListener(new View.OnClickListener()
    {
        @Override
        public void onClick(View v)
        {
            stopActivator();
        }
    });
}

private void startActivator()
{
    if (isListeningForActivation)
    {
        Toast.makeText(this, "Not started: already started",
                Toast.LENGTH_SHORT).show();
        Log.d(TAG, "not started, already started");
        // only activate once
        return;
    }

    if (speechActivator != null)
    {
        isListeningForActivation = true;
        Toast.makeText(this, "Started movement activator",
                Toast.LENGTH_SHORT).show();
        Log.d(TAG, "started");
```

continues

LISTING 19-3 *(continued)*

```java
                speechActivator.detectActivation();
        }
    }

    private void stopActivator()
    {
        if (speechActivator != null)
        {
            Toast.makeText(this, "Stopped", Toast.LENGTH_SHORT).show();
            Log.d(TAG, "stopped");
            speechActivator.stop();
        }
        isListeningForActivation = false;
    }

    @Override
    public void activated(boolean success)
    {
        Log.d(TAG, "activated...");

        //don't allow multiple activations
        if (!isListeningForActivation)
        {
            Toast.makeText(this, "Not activated because stopped",
                    Toast.LENGTH_SHORT).show();
            return;
        }

        if (success)
        {
            Toast.makeText(this, "Activated, no longer listening",
                    Toast.LENGTH_SHORT).show();
            //start speech recognition here
        }
        else
        {
            Toast.makeText(this, "activation failed, no longer listening",
                    Toast.LENGTH_SHORT).show();
        }

        isListeningForActivation = false;
    }

    @Override
    protected void onPause()
    {
        super.onPause();
        Log.d(TAG, "ON PAUSE stop");
        // save before stopping
        wasListeningForActivation = isListeningForActivation;
        stopActivator();
    }
```

```java
@Override
protected void onResume()
{
    super.onResume();
    Log.d(TAG, "ON RESUME was listening: " + wasListeningForActivation);
    if (wasListeningForActivation)
    {
        startActivator();
    }
}

// Note: onDestroy not needed since the activator was
// stopped during onPause()

// if the activity was destroyed these two methods are needed
// to restore wasListening
@Override
protected void onSaveInstanceState(Bundle outState)
{
    outState.putBoolean(WAS_LISTENING_STATE, isListeningForActivation);
    Log.d(TAG, "saved state: " + isListeningForActivation);
    super.onSaveInstanceState(outState);
}

@Override
protected void onRestoreInstanceState(Bundle savedInstanceState)
{
    wasListeningForActivation =
            savedInstanceState.getBoolean(WAS_LISTENING_STATE);
    Log.d(TAG, "restored state: " + wasListeningForActivation);
    super.onRestoreInstanceState(savedInstanceState);
}
}
```

SpeechActivatorStartStop shows how to run a SpeechActivator within an Activity. The next several sections discuss how to implement various SpeechActivators.

Activating Speech Recognition with Movement Detection

To activate speech recognition using movement, users move their device with sufficient acceleration. Movement requires hands to operate, but users do not have to touch the screen. Therefore, speech activation using movement can be faster than activating using a button because it does not require a user's eyes to find the button on the screen. The user can just pick up the device and move it.

To implement movement detection, you need several classes:

➤ MovementActivator (Listing 19-4): Implements SpeechActivator.

➤ MovementDetectionListener (Listing 19-5): Callback from AccelerationEventListener.

➤ MovementDetector (see Chapter 8): Starts and stops the sensors just as in DetermineMovementActivity from Chapter 8.

➤ AccelerationEventListener (see Chapter 8): Processes the sensor data to determine if movement occurred.

Executing these classes requires several steps:

1. External code calls `MovementActivator.detectActivation()`.

2. `MovementActivator` starts `MovementDetector`.

3. `MovementDetector` starts an `AccelerationEventListener`.

4. When `AccelerationEventListener` detects movement, it calls back to `MovementActivator` via its `MovementDetectionListener` interface.

5. `MovementActivator` stops detecting movement and calls back to its `SpeechActivationListener`.

LISTING 19-4: Detects speech activation based on movement

```
public class MovementActivator implements SpeechActivator,
        MovementDetectionListener
{
    private MovementDetector detector;

    private SpeechActivationListener resultListener;

    public MovementActivator(Context context,
            SpeechActivationListener resultListener)
    {
        detector = new MovementDetector(context);
        this.resultListener = resultListener;
    }

    @Override
    public void detectActivation()
    {
        detector.startReadingAccelerationData(this);
    }

    @Override
    public void stop()
    {
        detector.stopReadingAccelerationData();
    }

    @Override
    public void movementDetected(boolean success)
    {
        stop();
        resultListener.activated(success);
    }
}
```

LISTING 19-5: Callback for when AccelerationEventListener detects movement

```
public interface MovementDetectionListener
{
    public void movementDetected(boolean success);
}
```

Activating Speech Recognition with the Microphone

To activate speech recognition using the microphone, an app can use the clapper (described in Chapter 14) to detect when the user makes a single clap or makes another loud noise. The clapper is a reliable way to activate speech because it is easy for the user to activate. However, it can be vulnerable to false triggering because other unintended loud noises may trigger it.

The clapper must run asynchronously to continuously check the MediaRecorder to see if any loud sounds occurred. Therefore, you need two classes: ClapperActivator to implement the SpeechActivator interface, and ClapperSpeechActivationTask to execute the clapper asynchronously using an AsyncTask. When the task completes, it calls the SpeechActivationListener callback. Listings 19-6 and 19-7 show both implementations.

LISTING 19-6: Detects speech activation by starting a ClapperSpeechActivationTask

```
public class ClapperActivator implements SpeechActivator
{
    private static final String TAG = "ClapperActivator";

    private ClapperSpeechActivationTask activeTask;
    private SpeechActivationListener listener;
    private Context context;

    public ClapperActivator(Context context, SpeechActivationListener listener)
    {
        this.context = context;
        this.listener = listener;
    }

    @Override
    public void detectActivation()
    {
        Log.d(TAG, "started clapper activation");
        activeTask = new ClapperSpeechActivationTask(context, listener);
        activeTask.execute();
    }

    @Override
    public void stop()
    if (activeTask != null)
    {
        activeTask.cancel(true);
    }
    }
}
```

Available for download on Wrox.com

LISTING 19-7: Reports speech activation when it hears a single clap

```
public class ClapperSpeechActivationTask extends AsyncTask<Void, Void, Boolean>
{
    private static final String TAG = "ClapperSpeechActivationTask";
```

continues

LISTING 19-7 *(continued)*

```java
    private SpeechActivationListener listener;

    private Context context;

    private MaxAmplitudeRecorder recorder;

    private static final String TEMP_AUDIO_DIRECTORY = "tempaudio";

    /**
     * time between amplitude checks
     */
    private static final int CLIP_TIME = 1000;

    public ClapperSpeechActivationTask(Context context,
            SpeechActivationListener listener)
    {
        this.context = context;
        this.listener = listener;
    }

    @Override
    protected void onPreExecute()
    {
        super.onPreExecute();
    }

    @Override
    protected Boolean doInBackground(Void... params)
    {
        boolean heard = detectClap();
        return heard;
    }

    /**
     * start detecting a clap, return when done
     */
    private boolean detectClap()
    {
        SingleClapDetector clapper =
                new SingleClapDetector(SingleClapDetector.AMPLITUDE_DIFF_MED);
        Log.d(TAG, "recording amplitude");
        String audioStorageDirectory =
                context.getExternalFilesDir(TEMP_AUDIO_DIRECTORY)
                        + File.separator + "audio.3gp";

        // pass in this so recording can stop if this task is canceled
        MaxAmplitudeRecorder recorder =
                new MaxAmplitudeRecorder(CLIP_TIME, audioStorageDirectory,
                        clapper, this);
```

```java
        // start recording
        boolean heard = false;
        try
        {
            heard = recorder.startRecording();
        } catch (IOException io)
        {
            Log.e(TAG, "failed to record", io);
            heard = false;
        } catch (IllegalStateException se)
        {
            Log.e(TAG, "failed to record, recorder not setup properly", se);
            heard = false;
        } catch (RuntimeException se)
        {
            Log.e(TAG, "failed to record, recorder already being used", se);
            heard = false;
        }
        return heard;
    }

    @Override
    protected void onPostExecute(Boolean result)
    {
        listener.activated(result);
        super.onPostExecute(result);
    }

    @Override
    protected void onCancelled()
    {
        Log.d(TAG, "cancelled");
        super.onCancelled();
    }
}
```

code snippet ClapperSpeechActivationTask.java

Activating Speech Recognition with Continuous Speech Recognition

To activate speech recognition using continuous speech recognition, the app continuously listens for the user to speak a certain target word, such as "hello." Continuous speech recognition is valuable because saying a certain word is a very specific sound. All other sounds and noise will not cause false triggers. However, it may be hard for users to trigger because they must speak the target words such that the app hears it clearly. If users are using the app eyes-free or hands-free, they may be far from the device or the device may be in their pocket. If so, the audio recording quality might be poor and the speech recognizer could have a hard time recognizing target words.

Implementation requires using direct speech recognition to record speech without showing the speech recognizer dialog. Chapter 16 provides more details about implementing direct speech recognition using `SpeechRecognizer`. However, to use direct speech recognition for speech activation, an app needs to extend the example from Chapter 16 further so that the recognition occurs continuously until the app hears a certain word rather than stopping after one recording.

Listing 19-8 shows the code for `WordActivator`, which implements speech activation using continuous speech recognition. The code has several features to help match recognized speech with target words and to keep it running:

➤ **Uses indexed matching:** `SoundsLikeWordMatcher` matches any recognition result that sounds like the target word.

➤ **Keeps restarting:** The `receiveWhatWasHeard()` method restarts the speech recognizer if no matches occur. Because the recognizer runs only for a fixed amount of time before stopping and returning results, `receiveWhatWasHeard()` needs to restart recognition in order to make it run continuously.

➤ **Restarts on certain errors:** `WordActivator` cannot recover from some `SpeechRecognizer` errors, but when others occur the speech recognizer can continue. These errors may happen when the user does not speak well or does not speak at all. Therefore, the `onError()` method restarts speech recognition when the recognizer finds no matches or when the recognizer times out.

Available for
download on
Wrox.com

LISTING 19-8: Detects speech activation by continuously listening for target words

```
public class WordActivator implements SpeechActivator, RecognitionListener
{
    private static final String TAG = "WordActivator";

    private Context context;
    private SpeechRecognizer recognizer;
    private SoundsLikeWordMatcher matcher;

    private SpeechActivationListener resultListener;

    public WordActivator(Context context,
            SpeechActivationListener resultListener, String... targetWords)
    {
        this.context = context;
        this.matcher = new SoundsLikeWordMatcher(targetWords);
        this.resultListener = resultListener;
    }

    @Override
    public void detectActivation()
    {
        recognizeSpeechDirectly();
    }

    private void recognizeSpeechDirectly()
```

```
{
    Intent recognizerIntent =
            new Intent(RecognizerIntent.ACTION_RECOGNIZE_SPEECH);
    recognizerIntent.putExtra(RecognizerIntent.EXTRA_LANGUAGE_MODEL,
            RecognizerIntent.LANGUAGE_MODEL_WEB_SEARCH);
    // accept partial results if they come
    recognizerIntent.putExtra(RecognizerIntent.EXTRA_PARTIAL_RESULTS, true);
    SpeechRecognitionUtil.recognizeSpeechDirectly(context,
            recognizerIntent, this, getSpeechRecognizer());
}

public void stop()
{
    if (getSpeechRecognizer() != null)
    {
        getSpeechRecognizer().stopListening();
        getSpeechRecognizer().cancel();
        getSpeechRecognizer().destroy();
    }
}

@Override
public void onResults(Bundle results)
{
    Log.d(TAG, "full results");
    receiveResults(results);
}

@Override
public void onPartialResults(Bundle partialResults)
{
    Log.d(TAG, "partial results");
    receiveResults(partialResults);
}

/**
 * common method to process any results bundle from {@link SpeechRecognizer}
 */
private void receiveResults(Bundle results)
{
    if ((results != null)
            && results.containsKey(SpeechRecognizer.RESULTS_RECOGNITION))
    {
        List<String> heard =
                results.getStringArrayList(SpeechRecognizer.RESULTS_RECOGNITION);
        float[] scores =
                results.getFloatArray(SpeechRecognizer.CONFIDENCE_SCORES);
        receiveWhatWasHeard(heard, scores);
    }
    else
    {
        Log.d(TAG, "no results");
    }
}
```

continues

LISTING 19-8 *(continued)*

```java
    private void receiveWhatWasHeard(List<String> heard, float[] scores)
    {
        boolean heardTargetWord = false;
        // find the target word
        for (String possible : heard)
        {
            WordList wordList = new WordList(possible);
            if (matcher.isIn(wordList.getWords()))
            {
                Log.d(TAG, "HEARD IT!");
                heardTargetWord = true;
                break;
            }
        }

        if (heardTargetWord)
        {
            stop();
            resultListener.activated(true);
        }
        else
        {
            // keep going
            recognizeSpeechDirectly();
        }
    }

    @Override
    public void onError(int errorCode)
    {
        if ((errorCode == SpeechRecognizer.ERROR_NO_MATCH)
                || (errorCode == SpeechRecognizer.ERROR_SPEECH_TIMEOUT))
        {
            Log.d(TAG, "didn't recognize anything");
            // keep going
            recognizeSpeechDirectly();
        }
        else
        {
            Log.d(TAG,
                    "FAILED "
                        + SpeechRecognitionUtil
                            .diagnoseErrorCode(errorCode));
        }
    }

    /**
     * lazy initialize the speech recognizer
     */
    private SpeechRecognizer getSpeechRecognizer()
```

```
    {
        if (recognizer == null)
        {
            recognizer = SpeechRecognizer.createSpeechRecognizer(context);
        }
        return recognizer;
    }

    // other unused methods from RecognitionListener...
}
```

code snippet WordActivator.java

Activating Speech Recognition with NFC

The user can scan a custom NFC tag to trigger speech recognition from within the app and from outside the app. Scanning an NFC tag is a fast way to activate speech recognition because the user does not have to start the app to trigger the speech recognition prompt.

Unlike the other speech activation techniques in this section, using an NFC tag does not require a `SpeechActivator` implementation. Instead, an app writes and reads tags that have `application/root.gast.speech.activation` as a MIME type.

To use the custom MIME type for speech activation, an app needs a manifest entry to define the MIME type, a receiving `Activity`, an `Activity` that helps the user write a tag with the MIME type in it, and an `Activity` that can activate speech when the user scans the tag.

The manifest requires one entry to define an `Activity` that receives any NFCs that have the custom MIME type. Listing 19-9 shows how to specify `SpeechActivationNfcTagReceiver` as the receiving `Activity` for any tags with an `application/root.gast.speech.activation` MIME type.

LISTING 19-9: Manifest entry to define new MIME type and to specify an Activity to receive the speech activation tag

```
<activity android:name=
    "root.gast.playground.speech.activation.SpeechActivationNfcTagReceiver">
 <intent-filter>
  <action android:name="android.nfc.action.NDEF_DISCOVERED" />
  <category android:name="android.intent.category.DEFAULT" />
  <data android:mimeType="application/root.gast.speech.activation"/>
 </intent-filter>
</activity>
```

Android starts `SpeechActivationNfcTagReceiver`, shown in Listing 19-10, when the user scans an NFC tag with the right MIME type. One started, it activates speech recognition by starting `SpeechRecognitionLauncher`.

LISTING 19-10: Receives the speech activation NFC tag and starts SpeechRecognitionLauncher

```
public class SpeechActivationNfcTagReceiver extends Activity
{
    private static final String TAG = "SpeechActivationNfcTagReceiver";

    @Override
    protected void onCreate(Bundle savedInstanceState)
    {
        super.onCreate(savedInstanceState);

        // manifest filters the intent to make sure it is the
        // correct type so it is safe to launch
        launchSpeech();
    }

    private void launchSpeech()
    {
        Log.d(TAG, "Launching speech activation");
        Intent i = new Intent(this, SpeechRecognitionLauncher.class);
        i.setFlags(Intent.FLAG_ACTIVITY_NEW_TASK);
        this.startActivity(i);
    }
}
```

To help users create the NFC tag, an app can use a modified version of the inventory `Activity` from Chapter 11. The `Activity` enables users to write a tag when they click a button. To reuse the implementation, you need to modify the code to write a tag with custom MIME type and no other data using the following method:

```
private NdefMessage createNdefFromJson()
{
    String mimeType = "application/root.gast.speech.activation";
    byte[] mimeBytes = mimeType.getBytes(Charset.forName("UTF-8"));
    byte[] id = new byte[0];
    byte[] data = new byte[0];
    NdefRecord record =
            new NdefRecord(NdefRecord.TNF_MIME_MEDIA, mimeBytes, id, data);
    NdefMessage m = new NdefMessage(new NdefRecord[] { record });

    return m;
}
```

Thus far, this chapter has covered how to implement various kinds of `SpeechActivators` and run them within an `Activity`. Running within an `Activity` may not always be convenient. The next section discusses how to use the same `SpeechActivator` implementations to execute speech activation in a more persistent way that outlives any particular `Activity`.

IMPLEMENTING PERSISTENT SPEECH ACTIVATION

The previous section described how to use the `SpeechActivator` implementations to implement speech activation asynchronously within a single `Activity`. However, in some cases, it is useful for an app to listen for speech activation while it is not running or while the user switches `Activities` within the same app. To implement this, an app can use a `Service`.

Using a Service for Persistent Speech Activation

A speech activation `Service` needs to perform two functions. First, it must start and stop speech activation and communicate the resulting activation to the app. Second, it needs to make the user aware when it is active or not.

`SpeechActivationService`, shown in Listing 19-11, implements a speech activation `Service`. External code uses `Intents` to start and stop the service and receives results using a `BroadcastReceiver`, such as the one in Listing 19-12. While `SpeechActivationService` is actively listening for activation, it displays a notification. If the user clicks the notification, it stops the service.

`SpeechActivationService` has the following features:

➤ **It keeps the service running:** Android may stop a `Service` at any time. If Android stops the `SpeechActivationService`, it could cause the user to try to activate speech when the app is not listening. This could be especially confusing if the user is not looking at the device and is unaware that the app stopped listening. `SpeechActivationService` has two features that help reduce potential confusion. First, to make it less likely that Android stops the service, `SpeechActivationService` uses `startForeground()` to give it the same priority as an active `Activity`. Second, to make the service automatically restart if it is stopped without user intervention, the service returns the `START_REDELIVER_INTENT` setting from `onStartCommand()`.

➤ **It allows only one activation at a time:** It is possible that external code may start the service multiple times, but only one `SpeechActivator` should run at a time. To prevent multiple `SpeechActivators` from running, `SpeechActivationService` uses *isStarted* to know if a `SpeechActivator` is currently running. Also, if `SpeechActivationService` receives an `Intent` to start a `SpeechActivator` type it is currently running, it ignores the `Intent`. If the `Intent` indicates a different `SpeechActivator` type than the one that is currently running, `SpeechActivationService` stops the current `SpeechActivator` before starting the new one.

➤ **It allows users to stop the service:** By clicking on the notification, the users can stop the service. To implement this feature, `SpeechActivationService` needs to receive a special `Intent` extra. The `makeServiceStopIntent()` method creates the necessary `Intent` to stop the service. The `Notification` sends it when clicked.

Available for download on Wrox.com

LISTING 19-11: Persistently listens for speech activation

```
public class SpeechActivationService extends Service implements
        SpeechActivationListener
{
    private static final String TAG = "SpeechActivationService";
    public static final String ACTIVATION_TYPE_INTENT_KEY =
            "ACTIVATION_TYPE_INTENT_KEY";
    public static final String ACTIVATION_RESULT_INTENT_KEY =
            "ACTIVATION_RESULT_INTENT_KEY";
    public static final String ACTIVATION_RESULT_BROADCAST_NAME =
```

continues

LISTING 19-11 *(continued)*

```java
            "root.gast.playground.speech.ACTIVATION";

    /**
     * send this when external code wants the Service to stop
     */
    public static final String ACTIVATION_STOP_INTENT_KEY =
            "ACTIVATION_STOP_INTENT_KEY";

    public static final int NOTIFICATION_ID = 10298;

    private boolean isStarted;

    private SpeechActivator activator;

    @Override
    public void onCreate()
    {
        super.onCreate();
        isStarted = false;
    }

    public static Intent makeStartServiceIntent(Context context,
            String activationType)
    {
        Intent i = new Intent(context, SpeechActivationService.class);
        i.putExtra(ACTIVATION_TYPE_INTENT_KEY, activationType);
        return i;
    }

    public static Intent makeServiceStopIntent(Context context)
    {
        Intent i = new Intent(context, SpeechActivationService.class);
        i.putExtra(ACTIVATION_STOP_INTENT_KEY, true);
        return i;
    }

    /**
     * stop or start an activator based on the activator type and if an
     * activator is currently running
     */
    @Override
    public int onStartCommand(Intent intent, int flags, int startId)
    {
        if (intent != null)
        {
            if (intent.hasExtra(ACTIVATION_STOP_INTENT_KEY))
            {
                Log.d(TAG, "stop service intent");
                activated(false);
            }
            else
            {
```

```
            if (isStarted)
            {
                // the activator is currently started
                // if the intent is requesting a new activator
                // stop the current activator and start
                // the new one
                if (isDifferentType(intent))
                {
                    Log.d(TAG, "is differnet type");
                    stopActivator();
                    startDetecting(intent);
                }
                else
                {
                    Log.d(TAG, "already started this type");
                }
            }
            else
            {
                // activator not started, start it
                startDetecting(intent);
            }
        }
    }

    // restart in case the Service gets canceled
    return START_REDELIVER_INTENT;
}

private void startDetecting(Intent intent)
{
    activator = getRequestedActivator(intent);
    Log.d(TAG, "started: " + activator.getClass().getSimpleName());
    isStarted = true;
    activator.detectActivation();
    startForeground(NOTIFICATION_ID, getNotification());
}

private SpeechActivator getRequestedActivator(Intent intent)
{
    String type = intent.getStringExtra(ACTIVATION_TYPE_INTENT_KEY);
    // create based on a type name
    SpeechActivator speechActivator =
            SpeechActivatorFactory.createSpeechActivator(this, this, type);
    return speechActivator;
}

/**
 * determine if the intent contains an activator type
 * that is different than the currently running type
 */
private boolean isDifferentType(Intent intent)
{
    boolean different = false;
```

continues

LISTING 19-11 *(continued)*

```java
        if (activator == null)
        {
            return true;
        }
        else
        {
            SpeechActivator possibleOther = getRequestedActivator(intent);
            different = !(possibleOther.getClass().getName().
                    equals(activator.getClass().getName()));
        }
        return different;
    }

    @Override
    public void activated(boolean success)
    {
        // make sure the activator is stopped before doing anything else
        stopActivator();

        // broadcast result
        Intent intent = new Intent(ACTIVATION_RESULT_BROADCAST_NAME);
        intent.putExtra(ACTIVATION_RESULT_INTENT_KEY, success);
        sendBroadcast(intent);

        // always stop after receive an activation
        stopSelf();
    }

    @Override
    public void onDestroy()
    {
        Log.d(TAG, "On destroy");
        super.onDestroy();
        stopActivator();
        stopForeground(true);
    }

    private void stopActivator()
    {
        if (activator != null)
        {
            Log.d(TAG, "stopped: " + activator.getClass().getSimpleName());
            activator.stop();
            isStarted = false;
        }
    }

    private Notification getNotification()
    {
        // determine label based on the class
        String name = SpeechActivatorFactory.getLabel(this, activator);
        String message =
```

```
                    getString(R.string.speech_activation_notification_listening)
                        + " " + name;
        String title = getString(R.string.speech_activation_notification_title);

        PendingIntent pi =
                PendingIntent.getService(this, 0, makeServiceStopIntent(this),
                    0);

        Notification notification;
        if (Build.VERSION.SDK_INT >= Build.VERSION_CODES.HONEYCOMB)
        {
            Notification.Builder builder = new Notification.Builder(this);
            builder.setSmallIcon(R.drawable.icon)
                    .setWhen(System.currentTimeMillis()).setTicker(message)
                    .setContentTitle(title).setContentText(message)
                    .setContentIntent(pi);
            notification = builder.getNotification();
        }
        else
        {
            notification =
                    new Notification(R.drawable.icon, message,
                            System.currentTimeMillis());
            notification.setLatestEventInfo(this, title, message, pi);
        }

        return notification;
    }

    @Override
    public IBinder onBind(Intent intent)
    {
        return null;
    }
}
```

code snippet SpeechActivationService.java

LISTING 19-12: Receives activation broadcast and if it was successful starts the
SpeechRecognitionLauncher

```
public class ShowResultsSpeechActivationBroadcastReceiver extends
        BroadcastReceiver
{
    private static final String TAG =
            "ShowResultsSpeechActivationBroadcastReceiver";

    @Override
    public void onReceive(Context context, Intent intent)
    {
        if (intent.getAction().equals(
                SpeechActivationService.ACTIVATION_RESULT_BROADCAST_NAME))
```

continues

LISTING 19-12 *(continued)*

```
        {
            if (intent
                    .getBooleanExtra(
                            SpeechActivationService.ACTIVATION_RESULT_INTENT_KEY,
                            false))
            {
                Log.d(TAG,
                        "ShowResultsSpeechActivationBroadcastReceiver taking action");
                // launch something that prompts the user...
                Intent i = new Intent(context, SpeechRecognitionLauncher.class);
                i.setFlags(Intent.FLAG_ACTIVITY_NEW_TASK);
                context.startActivity(i);
            }
        }
    }
}
```

TRY THIS

You can turn the service on and off for different activation methods using the
Activation Service Control button.

SUMMARY

Speech activation begins the speech recognition process. To implement it, an app needs to allow the
user to start a `SpeechActivator`, detect when a speech activation occurs, and start the speech recognizer when it does.

An app can allow the user to activate speech only within an `Activity` or allow the user to activate it
at any time using a `Service`. This chapter described how to implement both scenarios.

An app can detect speech activation in many ways. To implement certain voice actions, especially ones
that operate hands-free or eyes-free, an app has to allow the user to activate speech using other means
than a button. This chapter described four alternative techniques that use the device's sensors instead.

Besides implementation details, starting speech recognition also involves intelligently handling the
time delays that occur between when the app detects speech activation and when the app starts
recording speech. The delays can make speech activation awkward to use. Prompts and user training
are possible ways to help the user be successful despite the delays.

The discussion of speech activation in this chapter concludes the part of this book that describes
how to use speech recognition and Text-To-Speech to implement Voice User Interfaces (VUI).
The chapters in this part showed that implementing VUIs involves much more than starting a
`RecognizerIntent`. It requires proper design to create usable VUIs, matching techniques to reliably
interpret the recognizer's responses, and supporting code to organize voice action execution and
handle speech activation. This part described the strategies and code libraries you need to wisely
and quickly implement VUIs in your app. Use them to let your users enjoy the benefits of speaking
to their Android.

INDEX

N

Try Safari Books Online FREE
for 15 days + 15% off for up to 12 Months*

Read this book for free online—along with thousands of others—with this 15-day trial offer.

With Safari Books Online, you can experience searchable, unlimited access to thousands of technology, digital media and professional development books and videos from dozens of leading publishers. With one low monthly or yearly subscription price, you get:

- Access to hundreds of expert-led instructional videos on today's hottest topics.

- Sample code to help accelerate a wide variety of software projects

- Robust organizing features including favorites, highlights, tags, notes, mash-ups and more

- Mobile access using any device with a browser

- Rough Cuts pre-published manuscripts

START YOUR FREE TRIAL TODAY!
Visit www.**safaribooksonline.com/wrox46** to get started.

*Available to new subscribers only. Discount applies to the Safari Library and is valid for first 12 consecutive monthly billing cycles. Safari Library is not available in all countries.

An Imprint of ⊛WILEY
Now you know.